The Audubon Society Field Guide to North American Fishes, Whales, and Dolphins

A Chanticleer Press Edition

The Audubon Society Field Guide to North American Fishes, Whales, and Dolphins

Atlantic and Gulf Coast Fishes — Herbert T. Boschung, Jr.
Professor of Zoology, University of Alabama

Freshwater Fishes — James D. Williams
Research Associate, National Museum of Natural History

Pacific Coast Fishes — Daniel W. Gotshall
Senior Marine Biologist, California Department of Fish and Game

Whales and Dolphins — David K. Caldwell
Research Scientist, University of Florida

Melba C. Caldwell
Associate Research Scientist, University of Florida

Visual Key by
Carol Nehring and Jordan Verner

Alfred A. Knopf, New York

This is a Borzoi Book
Published by Alfred A. Knopf, Inc.

All rights reserved. Copyright under
the International Union for the
protection of literary and artistic works
(Berne). Published in the United States
by Alfred A. Knopf, Inc., New York,
and simultaneously in Canada by
Random House of Canada Limited,
Toronto. Distributed by Random
House, Inc., New York.

Prepared and produced by Chanticleer
Press, Inc., New York.

Printed and bound by Dai Nippon,
Tokyo, Japan.
Type set in Garamond by Dix Type,
Inc., Syracuse, New York.

First Printing

Library of Congress Catalog Number:
83-47962
ISBN 0-394-53405-0

Trademark "Audubon Society" used by
publisher under license from the
National Audubon Society, Inc.

19 Oaks Pond, Maine

20 Duck Lake, Atchafalaya Basin, Louisiana

21 Lake Superior, Minnesota

16   Colorado River, Utah

17   Beaverhead River, Montana

18   Boundary Waters Canoe Area, Minnesota

Fresh and salt water habitats

13 Suwannee River, Florida

14 Buffalo River, Arkansas

15 Salmon River, Idaho

10   Mangrove swamp, Sanibel Island, Florida

11   Coastal dunes, Padre Island, Texas

12   Coastal bog, Cape Disappointment, Washington

7 Salt marsh estuary, Brigantine, New Jersey

8 Tideland marsh, Chincoteague, Virginia

9 Inland channel, Bodre Island, North Carolina

4   Olympic National Park, Washington

5   Cape Kiwanda, Oregon

6   Northern California

Fresh and salt water habitats

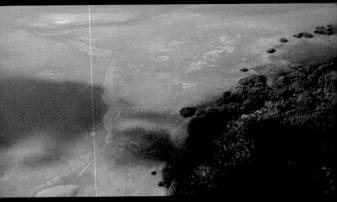

1 Florida Keys

 H

2 Florida Everglades

3 Acadia, Maine

Fresh and salt water habitats

Many fishes can only survive in a specific habitat. Some live in large bodies of water, but numerous fishes can only function in small streams. Certain species live solely in flat areas; others are found in mountains and hills. Some need little or no vegetation, while others must have an abundance. This section illustrates some of the enormous range of North American water habitats. It represents various types of salt, brackish, and fresh water, ranging from tropical to cold temperatures and from sandy bottoms to mud and rocks. Additionally, the water is shown acting in many different ways—stagnant, still, trickling slowly, rushing fast, or flowing in a whirl of foam. Recognizing a habitat will enable you to identify fishes by ruling out species that do not occur in your surroundings. In the following section, the letter "H" is used on the thumb tab to indicate fresh and salt water habitats.

Part I
Color Plates

conical or cardiform teeth

villiform teeth

canine teeth

molarlike teeth

incisor teeth

head, superior if the lower jaw projects beyond the upper, and subterminal when the upper jaw projects beyond the lower.

Fishes absorb oxygen from water, which is taken in through the mouth, flows over the gills located in the gill chambers, and then passes out through the gill openings. In lampreys, hagfishes, sharks, skates, rays, and related fishes, the gills lie behind pores or slits, but in bony fishes the gills are protected by a cover, called the opercle. Fishes can have teeth in the jaws, mouth, and pharynx. There are 5 basic kinds. Conical teeth are short, pointed, and fine and are usually arranged in rows. Villiform teeth are somewhat conical, but they are arranged in masses. Canine teeth are long, conical or lancelike, and sharp. Molarlike teeth are flattened for grinding and crushing. Incisors are sharp cutting teeth.

Body: The area just behind the opercle is called the pectoral or chest region. The humeral area, or shoulder, lies above the base of the pectoral fin, while the belly extends from the pectoral fins to the anus.

Tail: The tail is that part of a fish posterior to the anus. The slender section between the base of the tail fin and the anal or dorsal fin, depending on which is longer, is called the caudal peduncle.

Fins: Fins are used for swimming. In bony fishes, they are membranous and supported by stiff, pointed, unbranched spines, or by flexible, jointed, and often branched soft rays. The fins of sharks, rays, and eel-like fishes are not membranous but fleshy. There are paired pectoral and pelvic fins, one of each on either side of the body. The pectoral fins may be located behind the opercle, in the chest area, or on the side of the body behind the head. The pelvic or ventral fins may be positioned anywhere between the throat and the abdomen.

Parts of a Fish

Mouths and Snouts

superior mouth

inferior mouth

disc-like mouth

pointed snout

Bodies

ovate

fusiform

eel-like

depressed

Caudal Fins

heterocercal caudal fin

forked caudal fin

truncate caudal fin

rounded caudal fin

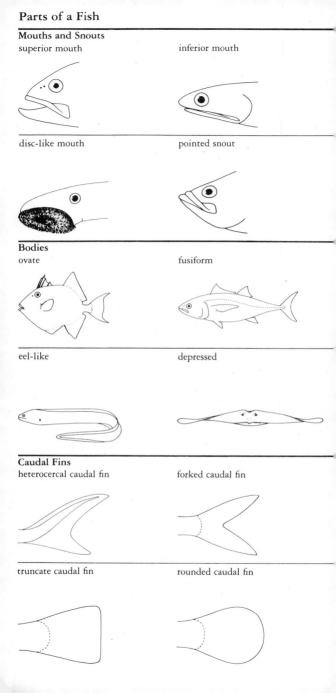

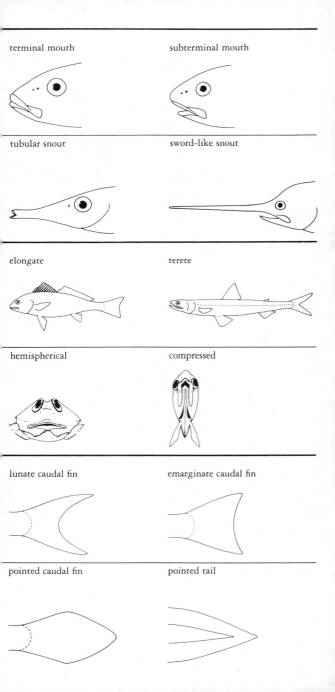

terminal mouth

subterminal mouth

tubular snout

sword-like snout

elongate

terete

hemispherical

compressed

lunate caudal fin

emarginate caudal fin

pointed caudal fin

pointed tail

There are 3 unpaired fins, collectively known as the median fins. The dorsal fin is located on the midline of the back. It may be divided into 2 (or occasionally 3) sections, which, for clarity in this book, are referred to as the first and second (or third) dorsal fins. Some fishes, such as trouts, have an additional small adipose fin on the midline of the back behind the dorsal fin. The anal fin is on the underside just behind the anus. The caudal fin is attached to the end of the caudal peduncle.

Scales and Lateral Line: In most fishes the body is covered with scales. Some primitive fishes have interlocking ganoid scales that do not overlap. However, most bony fishes have overlapping disc-like scales; these may either be smooth (cycloid scales) or have a spiny margin (ctenoid scales). Some fishes may have modified scales, such as the axillary process. Specialized pores or pored scales are present in a series along the side of the body and usually extend from just behind the opercle to the base of the caudal fin. These scales may form a visible lateral line. Each pore leads into a canal that contains sensory nerve endings. The sensory structures record vibrations, helping the fish avoid obstacles and locate prey. The number of scales on the lateral line is important in identifying species of bony fishes.

ganoid scales

cycloid scales

ctenoid scales

axillary process

How to Count Fin Rays: The number and kind of fin rays in a species is often an identification feature. To count rays, first determine whether they are soft rays or spines.

Dorsal and Anal Fins: In soft-rayed fishes, start counting from front to back with the first well-developed (principal) unbranched ray; do not count more than 1 unbranched ray anteriorly. Count the last 2 ray elements as 1. In spiny-rayed fishes, count all spines and all soft rays, but count the last 2 as 1.

Pectoral, Pelvic,   For the pectoral and pelvic fins, count
and Caudal Fins: all rays regardless of size or whether
they are branched or unbranched. In
both soft-rayed and spiny-rayed fishes,
count all branched rays in the caudal
fin and then add 2.

How to Count   After you have captured a fish and
Fish Scales: noted its obvious characteristics, such
as size and color, it may be necessary to
count the number of scales in the
lateral line. To find the lateral line,
look for a dark line or ridge running
from the shoulder just above the
opercle to the caudal fin. Each pore will
appear as a little hole, or you may be
able to see or feel a ridge, indicating
the canal underneath. It may be helpful
to lift each scale as you count, using a
needle or a thin-bladed knife. On some
fishes the scales may be difficult to see
and may require a magnifying glass.
Begin by counting the first scale
behind the opercle and continue to the
last vertebra, located at the crease made
by flexing the caudal fin. Some fishes
do not have a visible lateral line, so you
will need to determine the number of
scales in the lateral series by counting
oblique (diagonal) rows of scales,
beginning at the junction of the upper
side of the opercle and the head,
counting along a line to the base of the
caudal fin.
Some additional scale counts may be
necessary for identification. To find the
number of scales above the lateral line,
start at the front of the first dorsal fin
and count the number of scales in an
oblique row downward and backward
to the lateral line. For the number of
scales below the lateral line, begin at
the front of the anal fin and count
scales in an oblique row upward and
forward to the lateral line.
To find the number of predorsal scales
on the midline in front of the dorsal fin,
count the scales from the back of the
head to the dorsal fin origin.

Parts of a Fish

Parts of a Head
Lateral View

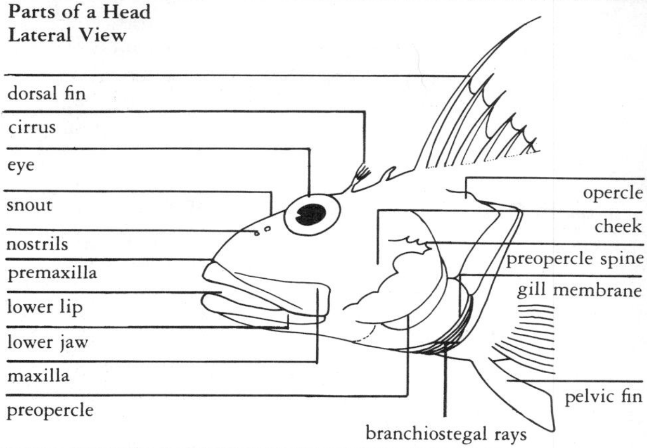

dorsal fin
cirrus
eye
snout
nostrils
premaxilla
lower lip
lower jaw
maxilla
preopercle

opercle
cheek
preopercle spine
gill membrane
pelvic fin

branchiostegal rays

Parts of a Bony Fish

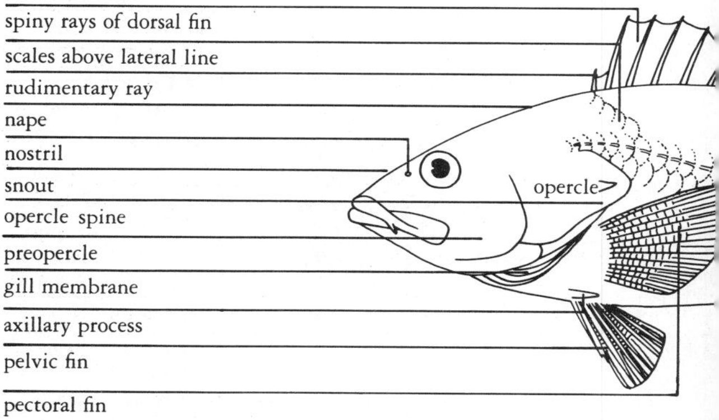

spiny rays of dorsal fin
scales above lateral line
rudimentary ray
nape
nostril
snout
opercle spine
preopercle
gill membrane
axillary process
pelvic fin
pectoral fin

opercle

Parts of a Ray
Dorsal View

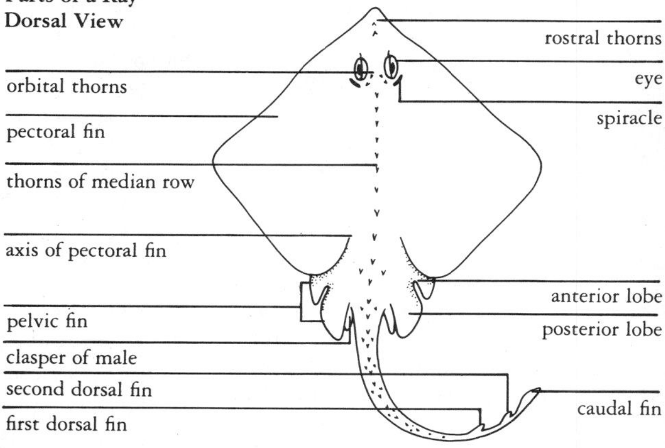

rostral thorns
eye
spiracle

orbital thorns
pectoral fin
thorns of median row
axis of pectoral fin
pelvic fin
clasper of male
second dorsal fin
first dorsal fin

anterior lobe
posterior lobe

caudal fin

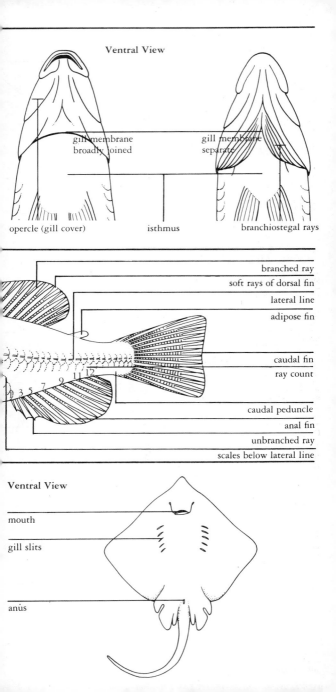

Ventral View

gill membrane broadly joined

gill membrane separate

opercle (gill cover)

isthmus

branchiostegal rays

branched ray
soft rays of dorsal fin
lateral line
adipose fin

caudal fin
ray count

caudal peduncle
anal fin
unbranched ray
scales below lateral line

Ventral View

mouth

gill slits

anus

Parts of a Shark

first dorsal fin

fin spine

spiracle

eye with nictitating lower eyelid

snout

nostril

mouth

gill openings

pectoral fin

How to Measure a Fish

1 total length
2 standard length
3 head length
4 snout length
5 eye length
6 first dorsal fin base
7 second dorsal fin base
8 length of caudal peduncle
9 upper jaw length
10 pelvic fin length
11 pectoral fin length
12 anal fin base
13 body depth

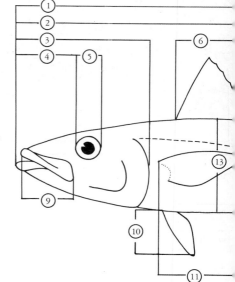

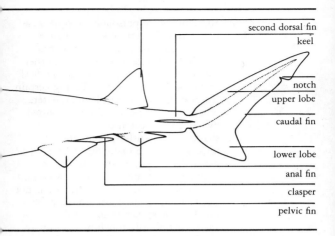

second dorsal fin
keel
notch
upper lobe
caudal fin
lower lobe
anal fin
clasper
pelvic fin

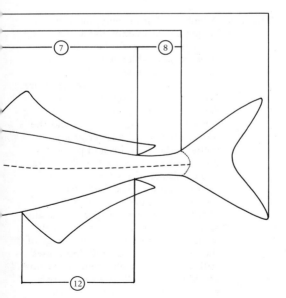

⑦ ⑧

⑫

Dangerous Fishes: Some fishes are poisonous or otherwise dangerous. In certain species spines may produce puncture wounds into which toxins can be injected. In other fishes the skin may be toxic or the flesh or roe poisonous if eaten. Eating certain tropical fishes may result in ciguatera poisoning, a type of poisoning caused by toxic algae eaten by fishes. All sharks are potentially dangerous if provoked, as are many other large fishes. These large fishes are not the only ones that may bite. Even a salmon can inflict a painful wound if care is not taken when removing it from a hook. Finally, the spines in some fishes are so sharp that simply touching them may result in a wound. All species that are known to be poisonous or otherwise dangerous are indicated in this book by the symbol ⚠.

What is a Cetacean? Whales, dolphins, and porpoises belong to the mammalian order Cetacea. Like most other mammals, they are warm-blooded, have hair on their body at some stage in their life, maintain a constant body temperature, and bear their young alive. Scientists divide cetaceans into 2 suborders, the baleen whales and the toothed whales; the latter group also includes the dolphins and porpoises. Baleen whales have paired blowholes and comblike plates through which food is strained. Toothed whales, dolphins, and porpoises have a single blowhole and teeth. Experts generally agree on the use of the term "whale" for the largest cetaceans, but usage of the terms "dolphins" and "porpoises" is still somewhat inconsistent. Dolphins are generally small cetaceans with a sickle-shaped dorsal fin, an obvious snout, and conical teeth; porpoises, which are also relatively small, generally have a triangular dorsal fin, a rounded forehead, and laterally flattened, spadelike teeth.

Parts of a Cetacean: Like a fish a cetacean has 3 major parts: the head, body, and tail. Similarly they have 2 pectoral fins, and most species also possess a dorsal fin.

Head: The head bears the eyes, mouth, teeth or baleen plates, and 1 or 2 blowholes on the top of the head. The long section in front of the eyes above the mouth is called the snout, or rostrum. Some whales also have a median ridge running from the tip of the snout to the blowholes.

Toothed whales, dolphins, and porpoises have from 1 to more than 250 teeth; sometimes teeth are concealed under the gums. Instead of teeth, baleen whales have up to several hundred plates suspended from the upper jaw.

Body: The body bears a pair of pectoral fins called flippers, 1 on each side. Almost all species also have a dorsal fin on the back.

Tail: Unlike the vertical caudal fins of fishes, the cetacean tail is horizontal. A distinct notch usually separates the tail into 2 sections called flukes. The long, thin section that connects the tail and body is called the tail stock.

How to Identify Fishes and Cetaceans: Because fishes are so varied and abundant, their identification may at first seem difficult. In this guide you can easily find the fish you are looking for because the photographs are arranged by shape and color.

Whales, dolphins, and porpoises may also be difficult to identify at first. These large mammals typically reveal only a part of their body for a short time before they submerge again in the water. For these animals we have not only provided color photographs of how they appear in the field, but have also provided color paintings illustrating the entire body.

After you have located the picture of the species most like the one you have

Parts of Whales

Baleen Whale

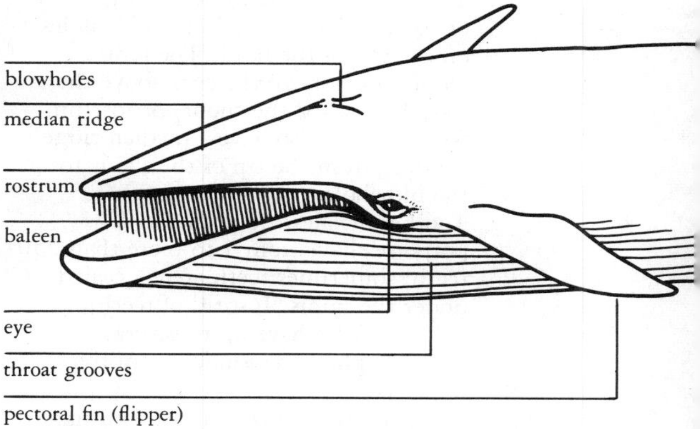

blowholes
median ridge
rostrum
baleen
eye
throat grooves
pectoral fin (flipper)

Toothed Whale

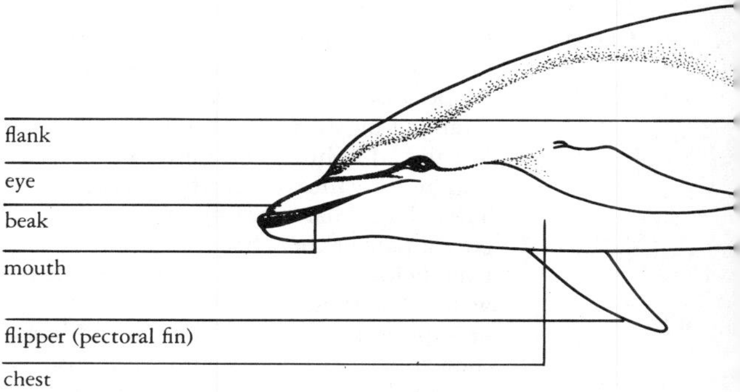

flank
eye
beak
mouth
flipper (pectoral fin)
chest

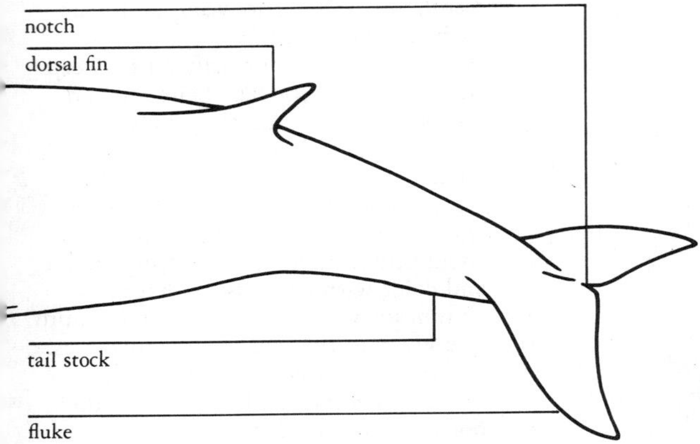

notch

dorsal fin

tail stock

fluke

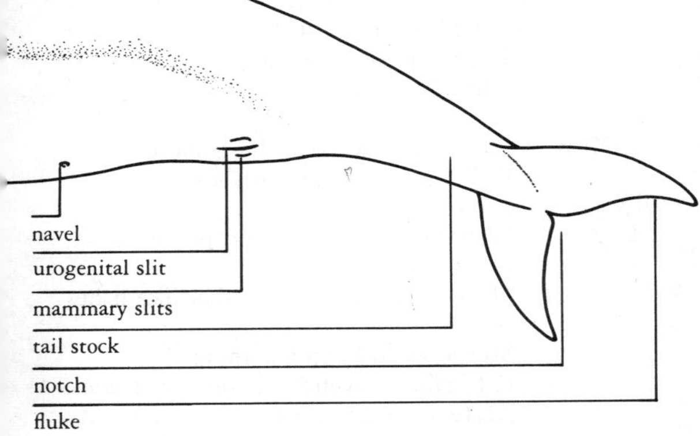

dorsal fin

navel

urogenital slit

mammary slits

tail stock

notch

fluke

seen, turn to the text description.
Examine your fish or cetacean in detail,
comparing its features to those given in
the text. Check the Related Species and
Similar Species sections and eliminate
each, item by item.

As you attempt to identify a fish, keep
in mind that color can change in and
out of the water, and that it also
changes under different lighting
conditions. As a result, some of the
photographs of the fishes included in
this guide may reflect these variables.
In addition, many species change shape
and color with age. Fishes that are
significantly smaller than the maximum
size given in the text may be juveniles.
Finally, fishes may occasionally be
found in habitats and ranges they do
not normally frequent.

Organization of the Color Plates: The photographs are divided into 2
habitat sections: fresh water and salt
water. Those species that live in both
types of water or move between them
appear in both the freshwater and
saltwater sections. To find your species,
select the water type of your location.
Within each section the color plates are
arranged according to the features you
see in the field—shape and color.
Thus, the freshwater group called
"Killifishes, cavefishes, and
sticklebacks" also contains the
Mosquitofish, which somewhat
resembles the others.
The color plates are arranged in the
following order:

Fresh Water: Elongate fishes with long snouts
Eel-like fishes and catfishes
Trouts and salmons
Flatfishes, sunfishes, and perchlike
fishes
Minnows, suckers, and shadlike fishes
over 7″
Minnows and shiners under 7″
Killifishes, cavefishes, and sticklebacks
Darters and sculpins

Salt Water: Skates and ray-like fishes
Flatfishes
Puffers, boxfishes, and fishes with lures
Angelfishes and disc-like fishes
Killifishes, livebearers, and sticklebacks
Parrotfishes and wrasses
Fishes with spiny rays or tapering bodies
Long, slender fishes and seahorses
Eel-like fishes and long dorsal-finned fishes
Drumlike fishes, cods, trouts, and catfishes
Basslike fishes, grunts, and snappers
Spindle-shaped fishes and large, robust fishes
Sharklike fishes
Whales, dolphins, and porpoises

Thumb Tab Guide: The organization of the color plates is explained in a table preceding them. A silhouette of a typical member of each group appears on the left. Silhouettes of fishes, whales, or dolphins in the group are shown on the right. For example, the silhouette of a gar represents the freshwater group "Elongate fishes with long snouts." These representative silhouettes are also found on thumb tabs at the left edge of each double page of color plates devoted to the group. Thumb tabs for the freshwater section are blue; for the saltwater section they are white.

Key to Fish Families: The chart preceding the text entries will help you determine the family to which a fish belongs. Here, drawings of the fish families included in this guide are arranged in groups according to their most distinctive features—body shape and fin type. Choose the drawing resembling your fish, then turn to the page number indicated for the family description to learn the diagnostic characteristics of that family.

Captions: The caption under each photograph gives the plate number, common name

of the fish, whale, or dolphin, its maximum size, and the page number of the text description. The sex or age— male (♂), female (♀), or juvenile (juv.) —are indicated if the male and female or adult and juvenile of a species differ greatly. If the fish or whale should be approached or handled with caution, the danger symbol ⚠ precedes the caption. The measurement given is total length, but for rays and skates, the width is given. The color plate number is repeated in front of each text description.

Organization of the Text:
This guide covers all 3 classes of fishes and the order of whales, dolphins, and porpoises of the class Mammalia. All of these belong to the large phylum Chordata, animals having a spinal cord, and to the subphylum Vertebrata, along with amphibians, reptiles, birds, and land-dwelling mammals.
Each class in this book is introduced by a discussion of its distinctive features. For the fish species, in each class the orders and families are arranged in the sequence adopted by the American Fisheries Society in 1980. For the cetaceans, the orders and families are arranged in taxonomical order. The arrangement of genera and species within each family is alphabetical by scientific name.

Plate Numbers:
Each species account begins with the number of the color plate or plates.

Common and Scientific Names:
The common and scientific names of fishes used in this guide are those given in *A List of Common and Scientific Names of Fishes from the United States and Canada,* published by the American Fisheries Society in 1980. The common and scientific names of whales, dolphins, and porpoises given here reflect prevailing usage. Widely used alternate common names are noted in the comments.
Scientific names for genera and species

are always italicized; those for classes, orders, and families are not. Each scientific name consists of 2 words usually based on Latin or Greek forms. The first, always capitalized, is the name of the genus; the second, in lower case, is the species epithet. For example, the scientific name of the Rainbow Trout is *Salmo gairdneri*. It is the only member of the genus *Salmo* that bears the species name *gairdneri*.

Description: Every description begins with measurements in feet and inches and in the metric equivalent. The measurement given is the verified maximum total length of the adult, from the tip of the head to the tip of the caudal fin. Width, rather than length, is given for rays and skates. For game fishes, the maximum recorded weight in pounds and kilograms is also provided. The weight measurement does not always correspond to the maximum length, and these weights are not necessarily North American records. Next, the adult is described, indicating its body shape, color, distinguishing marks, and, where pertinent, the number of fins, rays, spines, or scales. If they vary greatly, the coloration and body shape of males, females, and juveniles may be described separately. Some whales, dolphins, and porpoises are rare and have been little studied. Their appearance is variable, and therefore interpretation and definition of the coloration is controversial. The most commonly observed coloration is described here. Diagnostic features that will help you identify species appear in italics. Drawings in the margin illustrate features that are not visible in the color photographs. Wherever possible, nontechnical terms are used; technical terms are defined in the glossary or illustrated with labeled drawings in the introduction. In some cases, where no outstanding photograph was available,

a line drawing appears in the margin of the text description.

Habitat: Many fishes can only survive in certain kinds of environments. Their habitats are therefore described as specifically as possible. However, whales, dolphins, and porpoises often travel considerable distances far out at sea; their habitat is described in terms of the distance from the shore and the water depth.

Range: The geographical range of each species is given from north to south and from east to west. It is the verified range on this continent, extending south into South America if applicable.

Range Maps: For species found in fresh water, range maps are provided in the margins. These maps show natural ranges; areas where the species is introduced are only included if the species is well established there.

Related Species: Species in the same family or genus sometimes resemble one another closely but can be distinguished by certain key differences. This section describes related species, providing identifying features, habitats, and ranges.

Similar Species: To help you distinguish between species that appear similar, the differences between these look-alikes, which may or may not be related, are discussed here. The habitat and range are given if the species is not discussed elsewhere in the book.

Comments: Each species account concludes with comments on behavior, reproduction, food preferences, and alternate common names. Comments also indicate whether the species is good for sportfishing or desirable for eating.

⚠: Remarks on any species that should be handled with caution are indicated in the Comments by the danger symbol.

HOW TO USE THIS GUIDE

Example 1
Fish in a lake in eastern Alabama

You hook an olive-colored fish with a deep, laterally compressed body. It is speckled and has a reddish belly. On its shoulder there is an earlike flap edged in white; the fish also has a single dorsal fin, spiny in front and soft behind, and a slightly forked tail.

1. Turn to the fresh water section of the Thumb Tab Guide. Look for the silhouette that most resembles your fish. From the group called flatfishes, sunfishes, and perchlike fishes, you choose the silhouette for sunfishes, cichlids, and basses, which refers you to color plates 73–87 and 90–92.

2. Check the color plates. Both the Longear Sunfish and the Redbreast Sunfish, color plates 74 and 75, are speckled and have a reddish belly. The captions refer you to text pages 556 and 553, respectively.

3. Reading the text you find that both species are in your range, but only the Longear Sunfish has a flap edged in white. Under Related Species, you note that the Dollar Sunfish has 4 scale rows on its cheeks while your fish has 6; it is the Longear Sunfish.

Example 2
Fish in an estuary in North Carolina

You catch a silvery, spindle-shaped fish with a yellowish belly. It has very small scales, a single, short-based dorsal fin, and a deeply forked tail.

1. In the salt water section of the Thumb Tab Guide you find 2 silhouettes that resemble your catch: one representing anchovies, herrings, and the Rainbow Smelt, plates 571–577, and the other for tarpons and the Bonefish, plates 578–581.

2. Turning to the color plates, you narrow your choice to the Bonefish, the Machete, the Ladyfish, and the Tarpon, plates 578–581; text pages 372–375.

3. Checking each fish's range, you learn that the Machete is not in your area. Reading the descriptions of the remaining 3 fishes, you note that, unlike your fish, the Bonefish has an upper jaw that overhangs the lower jaw. The Tarpon has extremely large scales and a threadlike fin ray, while the Ladyfish has very small scales and its last dorsal fin ray is not threadlike. Examining your fish, you conclude that it is a Ladyfish.

Example 3
Whale in the
Pacific Ocean off
southern
California

From a ship, you spot a whale that is black with slight mottling. It blows a V-shaped spout, then lifts its head revealing comblike baleen plates and light yellowish bumps on its head. The whale does not have a dorsal fin.

1. From the group whales, dolphins, and porpoises, you select the silhouette of a whale, color plates 610–627, 659–671, and 674–684.

2. Turning to the color plates, you narrow your choice to the Right Whale, the Gray Whale, and the Bowhead Whale, plates 619–621, 624, and 676–678; text pages 777, 778, and 780.

3. Reading the text, you eliminate the Gray Whale because it is too mottled, and its back has a low hump and a serrated ridge. The Bowhead is not found in your area. The text for the Right Whale states that it has yellowish bumps and a V-shaped blow, confirming that you have spotted a Right Whale.

Geographical Scope:
This is the first one-volume field guide to cover North America's most common freshwater and saltwater fishes as well as the 45 species of whales, dolphins, and porpoises known to occur in North American waters north of Mexico. Whales, dolphins, and porpoises are included in this guide not only because these sea-going mammals have a fishlike shape, but also to provide coverage of both marine fishes and marine mammals in a single, convenient guide. The geographic scope includes the coastal waters of the United States and Canada as far off shore as the continental shelf as well as all freshwater habitats. In the East, it ranges from Hudson Bay to the tip of Florida, and in the West from Alaska to Baja California.

What Is a Fish?
A fish is a cold-blooded vertebrate that lives in water, breathes with gills, and has fins rather than legs. There are 3 classes of living fishes: the jawless fishes (lampreys and hagfishes), the cartilaginous fishes (sharks, skates, rays, and related fishes), and the bony fishes. There are about 20,000 known species worldwide, 97 percent of them bony fishes. More than 2,200 species can be found in North American waters.

Parts of a Fish:
Fishes vary tremendously in shape but always have 3 major parts: the head, the body, and the tail.

Head:
The head bears the eyes, nostrils, mouth, and gills. The area in front of the eyes above the mouth is called the snout. Except for lampreys and hagfishes, fishes have 2 jaws: the upper jaw, consisting of the premaxillary and maxillary (maxilla) bones, and the lower jaw. The position of the mouth varies among species. It is described as terminal if it is at the very tip of the head, inferior if it is underneath the

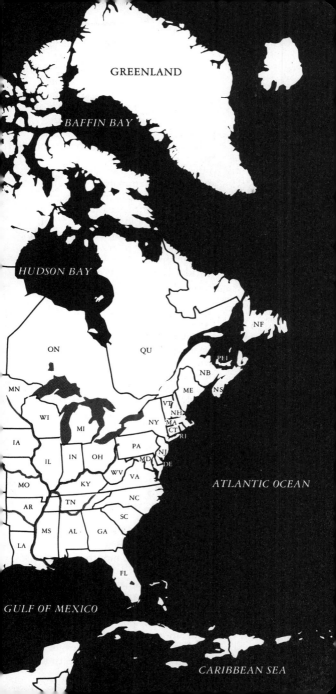

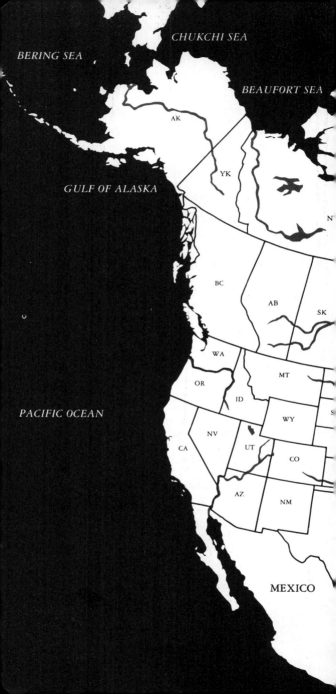

INTRODUCTION

The importance of fishes in our history and culture has been reflected throughout the ages in paintings, sculpture, and tapestries. Fishes abound in the rock carvings left by North American Indians and in frescoes made by the ancient Minoans, dating from the second millennium B.C.

Fishes are also an important food. Almost every known culture, ancient and modern, has made use of them, and today they have become a major source of protein for the ever-increasing human population. Whales, dolphins, and porpoises have also long inspired artists. The hunt for whales has been immortalized in the classic, *Moby-Dick*. Long feared by the superstitious as enormous, strange fishes, some of these splendid mammals are now among the world's most endangered species.

Fascination with fishes, whales, dolphins, and porpoises has always led people to pursue, watch, and study them. While the sports-minded turn to game-fishing for relaxation, others seek whale-watching for adventure. This guide is designed for all those who want to identify the aquatic animals they see—whether strolling along a beach, fishing in a stream, sailing on the open sea, or diving over a reef.

Randall and *Fishes of the Bahamas and Adjacent Tropical Waters* (Wynnewood, Pennsylvania, 1968) by James E. Böhlke and Charles C. G. Chaplin. Dr. Williams wishes to thank Dr. Boschung, who stimulated his interest in ichthyology and guided him through his graduate career, and is grateful for the support and patience of his family—Donna, David, Rob, and Dana. Mr. Gotshall expresses his appreciation of Robert N. Lea and the late John E. Fitch, who provided up-to-date information on several Pacific Coast species. Dr. and Mrs. Caldwell acknowledge their use of information from their previous publications.

We are grateful for permission from the International Game Fish Association to use the maximum weights of fishes from the all-tackle records in the *1983 World Record Game Fishes*.

Our special thanks go to Paul Steiner and the staff of Chanticleer Press. Gudrun Buettner provided support and encouragement, Susan Costello helped resolve various problems, and John Farrand was always on hand to advise as our scientific consultant. Particular thanks are due to Jordan Verner who, with the help of Jill Hamilton and Constance Mersel, patiently edited the text. Jane Opper, Mary Beth Brewer, Michael Goldman, Lenore Malen, and Ann Whitman gave many valuable suggestions. Thanks also go to Helga Lose and Amy Roche, who saw the book through production; to Carol Nehring, who supervised the art and layout; and to Ayn Svoboda and Karen Wollman, her assistants. Finally, we wish to express our appreciation to Anjali Gallup and the members of Chanticleer Press for their editorial assistance.

ACKNOWLEDGMENTS

Many people helped in the preparation of this book. We are particularly grateful to the following consultants who reviewed text and photographs: Dr. Reeve M. Bailey (Freshwater Fishes), Emeritus Curator of Fishes, Museum of Zoology, University of Michigan, who read the entire manuscript on fishes; Dr. Carter R. Gilbert (Atlantic and Gulf Coast Fishes), Associate Curator in Fishes, Florida State Museum, University of Florida; Dr. William N. Eschmeyer (Pacific Coast Fishes), Senior Curator, Department of Ichthyology, California Academy of Sciences; Dr. James G. Mead (Whales and Dolphins), Curator of Marine Mammals, National Museum of Natural History, Smithsonian Institution.

In addition, Dr. Gareth Nelson, Curator, The American Museum of Natural History, advised us in our initial selection of fish species and photographs.

We wish to acknowledge some of the many icthyologists and cetologists whose works provided the background literature for this guide. Unfortunately, not all can be mentioned here.

In particular, Dr. Boschung would like to acknowledge *Caribbean Reef Fishes* (Hong Kong, 1968), by John E.

CONTENTS

22 Lake Mead, Arizona

23 Green River Lake, Wyoming

24 St. Mary's Lake, Glacier Park, Montana

Key to the Color Plates

The color plates on the following pages are divided into 22 groups, arranged according to their fresh or salt water habitats. Because some species live in both types of water, they are pictured in both the fresh water and salt water sections. You can find your species by selecting the water type that matches your location.

Fresh Water:
Elongate fishes with long snouts
Eel-like fishes and catfishes
Trouts and salmons
Flatfishes, sunfishes, and perchlike fishes
Minnows, suckers, and shadlike fishes over 7″
Minnows and shiners under 7″
Killifishes, cavefishes, and sticklebacks
Darters and sculpins

Salt Water:
Skates and raylike fishes
Flatfishes
Puffers, boxfishes, and fishes with lures
Angelfishes and disc-like fishes
Killifishes, livebearers, and sticklebacks
Parrotfishes and wrasses
Fishes with spiny rays or tapering bodies
Long, slender fishes and seahorses
Eel-like fishes and long dorsal-finned fishes
Drumlike fishes, cods, trouts, and catfishes
Basslike fishes, grunts, and snappers
Spindle-shaped fishes and large, robust fishes
Sharklike fishes
Whales, dolphins, and porpoises

Thumb Tab Guide: To help you find the correct group, a table of silhouettes precedes the color plates. Each group is represented by a silhouette of a typical member of that group on the left side of the table. On the right, you will find the silhouettes of fishes, whales, or dolphins found within that group.

The representative silhouette for each group is repeated as a thumb tab at the left edge of each double page of color plates, providing a quick and convenient index to the color section.

Thumb tabs for fishes in the fresh water section are blue. Thumb tabs for species in the salt water section are white.

Thumb Tab	Group	Plate Numbers
	Elongate fishes with long snouts	25–36
	Eel-like fishes and catfishes	37–57
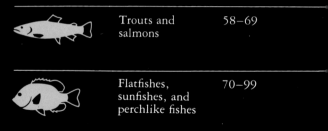	Trouts and salmons	58–69
	Flatfishes, sunfishes, and perchlike fishes	70–99

Typical Shapes		Plate Numbers
	gars	25–28
	Paddlefish	29
	sturgeons	30–33
	pikes	34–36
	lampreys	37, 38, 40–42
	American Eel	39
	Burbot, Bowfin	43, 44
	catfishes	45–57
	trouts, salmons	58–69
	flounders, Hogchoker	70–72

Thumb Tab	Group	Plate Numbers
	Flatfishes, sunfishes, and perchlike fishes (continued)	70–99
	Minnows, suckers, and shadlike fishes over 7″	100–141
	Minnows and shiners under 7″	142–192
	Killifishes, cavefishes, and sticklebacks	193–219

Typical Shapes		Plate Numbers
	sunfishes, cichlids, basses	73–87, 90–92
	Fat Sleeper	88
	perches, basses, Freshwater Drum	89, 93–99
	suckers	100–111
	chubs, carps, minnows	112–121, 125–136, 138, 139, 141
	herrings, Goldeye	122–124, 140
	Rainbow Smelt	137
	daces, chubs, shiners, minnows	142–179, 181–192
	Brook Silverside	180
	livebearers, mudminnows, killifishes, topminnows	193–214

Typical Shapes		Plate Numbers
	cavefishes	215, 216
	Pirate Perch	217
	sticklebacks	218, 219
	darters	220–243, 247–255
	sculpins	244–246

Thumb Tab	Group	Plate Numbers
	Skates and ray-like fishes	256–273
	Flatfishes	274–291
	Puffers, boxfishes, and fishes with lures	292–318

Typical Shapes		Plate Numbers
	eagle rays, mantas, stingrays, skates	256–268
	electric rays, Thornback	269, 270, 272, 273
	Pacific Angel Shark	271
	flounders, soles	274–291
	batfishes, Goosefish, Skilletfish	292–294, 300
	frogfishes, Lumpfish	295–299
	puffers, porcupinefishes	301–308, 310, 311
	Ocean Sunfish	309
	boxfishes	312–315
	filefishes	316–318

Thumb Tab	Group	Plate Numbers
	Angelfishes and disc-like fishes	319–345
	Killifishes, livebearers, and sticklebacks	346–354
	Parrotfishes and wrasses	355–381

Typical Shapes		Plate Numbers
	damselfishes, Opaleye, Sergeant Major	319, 320, 322–324, 326, 327, 342
	angelfishes, Atlantic Spadefish	321, 331–336, 344
	leatherjackets	325, 330
	surgeonfishes	328, 329, 337
	butterflyfishes	338–341
	Jackknife-Fish	343
	African Pompano	345
	killifishes, livebearers	346–353
	Threespine Stickleback	354
	parrotfishes	355, 356, 358–362, 364, 365, 375, 376, 379

Typical Shapes		Plate Numbers
	wrasses	357, 363, 366–374, 377, 380, 381
	Flamefish	378
	squirrelfishes, bigeyes	382–387
	rockfishes and other scorpionfishes	388–394, 396–399, 401–410, 422
	Sheepshead	395
	greenlings	400, 411, 428
	scorpionfishes, sculpins, Red Goatfish	412–421
	searobins	423–426
	lizardfishes, Sturgeon Poacher	427, 429, 430
	Fat Sleeper	431

Thumb Tab	Group	Plate Numbers
	Fishes with spiny rays or tapering bodies (continued)	382–432
	Long, slender fishes and seahorses	433–441
	Eel-like fishes and long dorsal-finned fishes	442–474

Typical Shapes		Plate Numbers
	Sablefish	432
	Atlantic Cutlassfish	433
	Halfbeak	434
	pipefishes, Atlantic Needlefish, Red Cornetfish, Tube-Snout, Trumpetfish	435–440
	Lined Seahorse	441
	lampreys, cusk-eels, Pacific Hagfish, American Eel, Shrimp Eel, Penpoint Gunnel	442–450
	morays	451–453
	wolffishes, Ocean Pout, Monkeyface Prickleback, Oyster Toadfish, Plainfin Midshipman	454–457, 460, 463

Thumb Tab	Group	Plate Numbers
	Eel-like fishes and long dorsal-finned fishes (continued)	442–474
	Drumlike fishes, cods, trouts, and catfishes	475–501
	Basslike fishes, grunts, and snappers	502–543
	Spindle-shaped fishes and large, robust fishes	544–588

Typical Shapes		Plate Numbers
	clinids, blennies, gobies	458, 459, 461, 462, 464–470
	hakes, Sand Tilefish, Giant Kelpfish	471–474
	drums, Striped Mullet, Snook	475–486
	cods	487–492
	trouts, salmons	493–499
	sea catfishes	500, 501
	temperate basses, sea basses, Greater Soapfish, Tripletail	502–517, 521, 524
	mojarras, surfperches, sea chubs	518–520, 525–531, 541–543
	snappers, grunts, Mozambique Tilapia, Pinfish	522, 523, 532–540
	jacks, Harvestfish	544–546, 549, 550

Spindle-shaped
fishes and large,
robust fishes
(continued)

544–588

Typical Shapes		Plate Numbers
	porgies	547, 548
	jacks, Ocean Whitefish, Bluefish	551–560
	tunas, mackerels, and other scombrids	561–567
	silversides	568–570
	anchovies, herrings, Rainbow Smelt	571–577
	tarpons, Bonefish	578–581
	Dolphin	582
	Great Barracuda	583, 584
	Sailfish	585
	Cobia, Sharksucker	586, 587

Thumb Tab	Group	Plate Numbers
	Spindle-shaped fishes and large, robust fishes (continued)	544–588
	Sharklike fishes	589–609
	Whales, dolphins, and porpoises	610–684

Typical Shapes		Plate Numbers
	White Sturgeon	588
	sharks, Smalltooth Sawfish	589–608
	Spotted Ratfish	609
	whales	610–627, 659–671, 674–684
	ocean dolphins, porpoises	628–658, 672, 673

The color plates on the following pages are numbered to correspond with the numbers preceding the text descriptions. The caption under each photograph gives the plate number, common name of the fish, whale, or dolphin, its maximum size, and the page number of the text description. The sex or age—male (♂), female (♀), or juvenile (juv.)—are indicated when the male and female or adult and juvenile of a species differ greatly. If the fish or whale should be approached or handled with caution, the danger symbol ⚠ precedes the caption.

Fresh water

The fishes in this section can be found in fresh water. Because some species also live in salt water or move between fresh and salt water, they appear again in the salt water section.

Elongate fishes with long snouts

 This group includes gars, sturgeons, and pikes, as well as the Paddlefish, the only species in North America that has a long, paddle-like snout. All are easily recognized by their distinctive elongate shape. Some of these large fishes are prized for sport. Sturgeons are also noted as excellent food.

Elongate fishes with long snouts

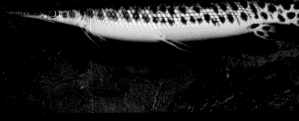

△25   Longnose Gar, 6', *p. 369*

26   Spotted Gar, 3', *p. 368*

27   Alligator Gar, 10', *p. 370*

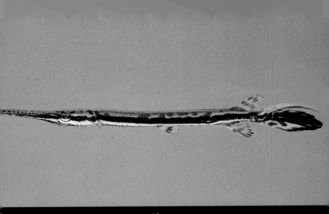

28　Longnose Gar, juv., 6′, *p.* 369

29　Paddlefish, 7′1″, *p.* 367

31   Lake Sturgeon, 8', *p. 364*

32   Shovelnose Sturgeon, 32", *p. 366*

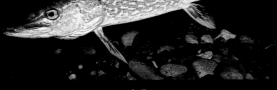

34   Muskellunge, 6', *p. 403*

35   Northern Pike, 4'4", *p. 402*

36   Chain Pickerel, 31", *p. 404*

Eel-like fishes and catfishes

The eel-like fishes shown here include eels and lampreys. Eels can be distinguished from lampreys by the presence of pectoral fins. In addition, lampreys have a round, jawless mouth. This group also contains the Burbot and the Bowfin, both of which have a long, continuous dorsal fin. All North American catfishes have 4 pairs of whisker-like barbels near the mouth and a small, fleshy fin, known as the adipose fin, on the back behind the dorsal fin. Some catfishes can inflict a painful sting with the venomous pectoral fin spine.

37 Least Brook Lamprey, 6", *p. 327*

38 Sea Lamprey on carp, 33", *p. 328*

40 Southern Brook Lamprey, 7″, *p. 326*

41 Chestnut Lamprey, 15″, *p. 325*

43 Burbot, 3'2", *p. 493*

44 Bowfin, 34", *p. 371*

46   Slender Madtom, 5″, *p. 471*

47   Flathead Catfish, 4′5″, *p. 475*

48   Brindled Madtom, 5″, *p. 474*

49   Stonecat, 12″, *p. 472*

50   Freckled Madtom, 4″, *p. 475*

51   Tadpole Madtom, 4½″, *p. 473*

52   Speckled Madtom, 3½", *p. 473*

53   Black Bullhead, 17", *p. 468*

55 Channel Catfish, 3'11", *p. 470*

56 Brown Bullhead, 19", *p. 470*

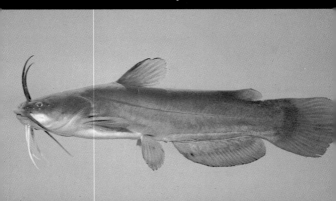

Trouts and salmons

Frequently seen as they move to or from their spawning grounds, trouts and salmons are heavy bodied fishes with a small, fleshy fin, known as the adipose fin, on the back behind the dorsal fin. Many species exhibit sexual differences in coloring and shape while spawning. Widely distributed in cold waters, some inhabit fresh water, others salt water, and still others migrate between the 2 types. Many trouts and salmons are valued commercially and as game fishes.

58   Atlantic Salmon, 4′5″, *p. 395*

59   Apache Trout, 18″, *p. 392*

60   Cutthroat Trout, 30″, *p. 393*

61   Rainbow Trout, 3'9", *p. 394*

62   Brown Trout, 3'4", *p. 396*

63   Chinook Salmon ♂, 4'10", *p. 391*

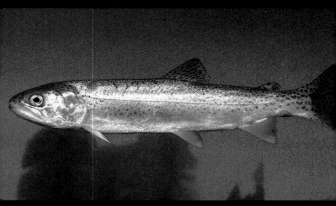

64   Cutthroat Trout, 30″, *p. 393*

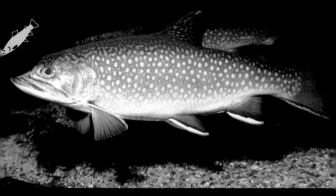

65   Brook Trout, 21″, *p. 396*

66   Lake Trout, 4′2″, *p. 397*

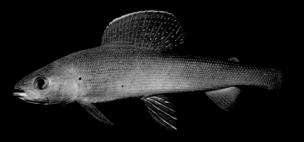

67   Arctic Grayling, 30″, *p. 398*

68   Round Whitefish, 22″, *p. 392*

69   Lake Whitefish, 24″, *p. 388*

Flatfishes, sunfishes, and perchlike fishes

This large, diverse group includes members of several different families. Flatfishes are extremely flattened from side to side and have both eyes on the same side of the body. In contrast, sunfishes and perchlike fishes have deep bodies. The largest members of the sunfish family, along with the temperate basses and perches, are probably the most renowned game fishes in North America. The cichlids, which somewhat resemble the sunfishes, and the Fat Sleeper are also in this group. Many of these fishes, in addition to living in fresh water, can be found in salt and brackish water, and are pictured again in the salt water section.

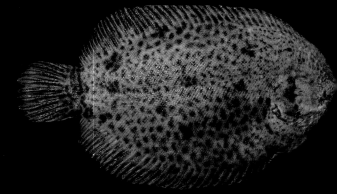

70 Hogchoker, 6″, *p. 750*

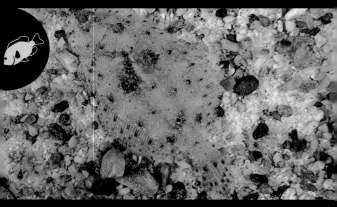

71 Gulf Flounder, 15″, *p. 741*

72 Starry Flounder, 3′, *p. 747*

73 Pumpkinseed, 10", *p. 554*

74 Longear Sunfish, 9", *p. 556*

76 Green Sunfish, 10″, *p. 553*

77 Mozambique Tilapia, 15″, *p. 636*

79 Rio Grande Cichlid, 12", *p. 635*

80 Bluespotted Sunfish, 4", *p. 552*

81 Black Crappie, 16", *p. 560*

82 Rock Bass, 13″, *p. 549*

83 Flier, 6″, *p. 551*

85   Bluegill, 12", *p. 555*

86   Warmouth, 10", *p. 555*

88 Fat Sleeper, 10", *p. 676*

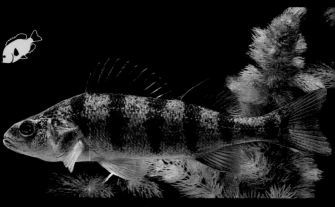

89 Yellow Perch, 15", *p. 578*

91   Spotted Bass, 24", *p.* 558

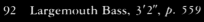

92   Largemouth Bass, 3'2", *p.* 559

94   Striped Bass, 6', *p. 535*

95   White Bass, 18", *p. 534*

97 White Perch, 19″, *p. 533*

98 Walleye, 3′5″, *p. 585*

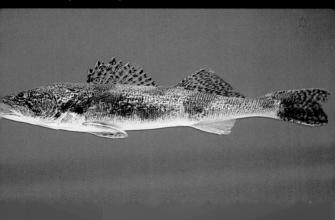

Minnows, suckers, and shadlike fishes over 7″

Many of these fishes are members of the large family of carps and minnows that measure more than 7″ in length. These include minnows, carps, shiners, daces, and chubs. The bigger species shown here make good eating and are sought by anglers. Suckers, which belong to another family, somewhat resemble minnows except that suckers, as their name implies, have a ventral sucker-type mouth. The shadlike fishes include herrings and the Goldeye, which may be confused with them. The American Shad and the Rainbow Smelt, which move into fresh water only to spawn, are also pictured here. All of these shadlike fishes are commercially valuable.

100 Blue Sucker, 3'4", *p. 459*

101 Smallmouth Buffalo, 3', *p. 462*

illback, 24", *p*

103   Spotted Sucker, 20″, *p. 462*

104   Creek Chubsucker, 11″, *p. 460*

105   Razorback Sucker, 3′, *p. 466*

106 White Sucker, 24", *p. 459*

107 River Redhorse, 30", *p. 463*

108 Golden Redhorse ♂, 24", *p. 464*

109   Northern Hog Sucker, 24″, *p. 461*

110   Striped Jumprock, 10″, *p. 465*

111   Blacktail Redhorse, 18″, *p. 465*

112 Hornyhead Chub ♀ front, 10", *p. 428*

113 River Chub ♂, 10", *p. 430*

114 River Chub ♀, 10", *p. 430*

115   Central Stoneroller, 9″, *p. 409*

116   Bluehead Chub, 8″, *p. 429*

117   Grass Carp, 3′3″, *p. 412*

118 Common Carp, 30", *p. 412*

119 Common Carp, 30", *p. 412*

120 Goldfish, wild, 16", *p. 410*

121 Goldfish, domestic, 16″, *p. 410*

122 Gizzard Shad, 16″, *p. 383*

123 American Shad, 30″, *p. 381*

124   Goldeye, 20", *p.* 387

125   Hitch, 13", *p.* 425

126   Flathead Chub, 12½", *p.* 422

127 Tui Chub, 16″, *p. 415*

128 Chiselmouth, 12″, *p. 408*

129 Roundtail Chub, 17″, *p. 416*

130 Bonytail ♀, 24", p. 416

131 Golden Shiner ♀, 12", p. 431

132 Sacramento Blackfish, 18", p. 416

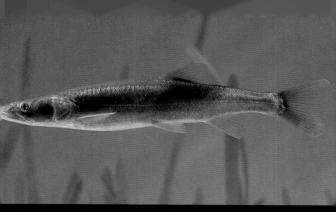

133   Colorado Squawfish, 5′, *p. 453*

134   Sacramento Squawfish, 3′, *p. 452*

135   Silver Chub, 9″, *p. 424*

136   Hardhead, 18″, *p. 428*

137   Rainbow Smelt, 13″, *p. 400*

139   Creek Chub, 12″, *p. 456*

140   Alewife, 15″, *p. 381*

141   Golden Shiner, 12″, *p. 431*

Minnows and shiners under 7"

Fishes in this group have a maximum recorded length of less than 7". All are members of the family of carps and minnows, characterized by both the lack of teeth in the jaws and the absence of a small, fleshy fin, known as the adipose fin, on the back behind the dorsal fin. Breeding males have small swellings, called tubercles, on the head and frequently are more brightly colored than non-breeding males and females. This family has the most extensive freshwater distribution in North America.

142 Longfin Dace ♂, 3½″, *p. 409*

143 Bigeye Chub, 3″, *p. 420*

144 Woundfin, 3″, *p. 451*

145   Mimic Shiner, 3″, *p. 444*

146   Spottail Shiner, 6″, *p. 438*

147   Mississippi Silvery Minnow, 7″, p. 419

148   Bigeye Shiner, 3", *p. 433*

149   Spotfin Shiner, 4½", *p. 441*

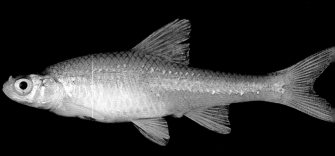

151 Satinfin Shiner, 3½″, *p. 432*

152 Whitetail Shiner, 5″, *p. 437*

153 Redfin Shiner, ♂, 3½″, *p. 443*

154 Fathead Minnow, 4", *p. 450*

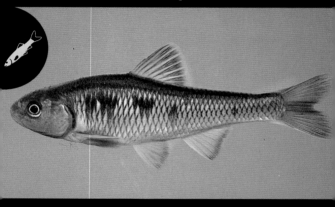

155 Common Shiner, 6", *p. 436*

156 Speckled Dace, 4", *p. 455*

157 Loach Minnow ♂, 2½″, *p. 457*

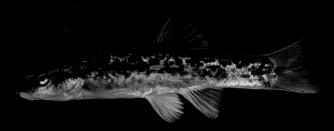

158 Blacknose Dace, 3½″, *p. 453*

160 Little Colorado Spinedace, *4″, p. 425*

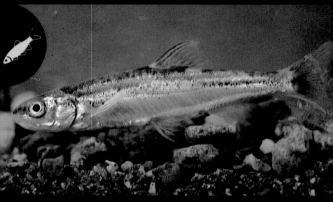

161 Spikedace, *3″, p. 426*

163 Roundnose Minnow, 2½", *p. 413*

164 Streamline Chub, 4½", *p. 421*

166   Lake Chub, 7", *p. 411*

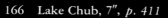

167   Brassy Minnow, 4", *p. 418*

169 Suckermouth Minnow, 4", *p. 446*

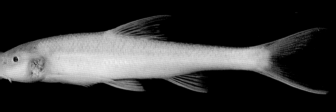

170 Sicklefin Chub, 4", *p. 422*

172 Silverjaw Minnow, 3½″, *p. 414*

173 Pugnose Minnow ♀, 2½″, *p. 436*

175 Blacktail Shiner, 7″, *p. 444*

176 Moapa Dace, 3″, *p. 427*

177 Sailfin Shiner, 2½″, *p. 438*

178   Bluntnose Minnow, *4″, p. 449*

179   Taillight Shiner, *3″, p. 439*

181 Redside Shiner, 7", *p. 455*

182 Ozark Minnow, 3", *p. 440*

183 Bleeding Shiner, 4½", *p. 445*

184 Southern Redbelly Dace, 3″, p. 448

185 Mountain Redbelly Dace, 2½″, p. 449

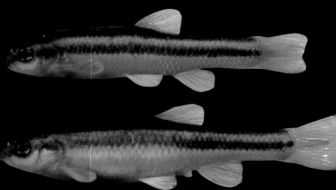

186 Flame Chub ♂ above ♀, 3″, p. 417

187   Least Chub, 2½″, *p. 424*

188   Rosyface Shiner, 3½″, *p. 441*

189   Warpaint Shiner, 5″, *p. 435*

190   Red Shiner, 3½″, *p. 439*

191   Striped Shiner, 7″, *p. 434*

192   Rosyside Dace, 4″, *p. 411*

Killifishes, cavefishes, and sticklebacks

This group contains killifishes, their close relations the livebearers, and the similar looking mudminnows, as well as cavefishes and sticklebacks. Killifishes and livebearers are found in fresh water, but since some also occur in brackish and salt water, they appear again in the salt water section. Livebearers are especially unusual because they give birth to their young. Cavefishes can be recognized by their eyes, which are either reduced, modified, or entirely absent. Sticklebacks have isolated dorsal spines and often bony plates along their sides. The Pirate Perch, also included here, has a single dorsal fin with spines and rays.

193   Sailfin Molly, 5″, *p. 518*

194   Alaska Blackfish, 7″, *p. 401*

195   Central Mudminnow, 5″, *p. 401*

196 Flagfish ♀, 2½″, *p. 514*

197 Sheepshead Minnow, 3″, *p. 507*

199 Pygmy Killifish, 1¼″, *p. 515*

200 Bayou Killifish ♂, 3″, *p. 511*

202   Starhead Topminnow, 3″, *p. 510*

203   Blackspotted Topminnow, 4″, *p. 510*

204   Gila Topminnow, 2″, *p. 518*

205 White River Springfish, 3″, *p. 505*

206 Bayou Killifish ♀, 3″, *p. 511*

208 Mosquitofish, 2½", *p. 516*

209 Desert Pupfish ♂, 2½", *p. 506*

210 Gulf Killifish, 6", *p. 509*

211   Golden Topminnow, 3″, *p. 508*

212   Northern Studfish, 5″, *p. 507*

214 Seminole Killifish ♀, 6", *p. 512*

215 Spring Cavefish, 3", *p. 480*

216 Southern Cavefish, 2", *p. 481*

217 Pirate Perch, 4½″, *p. 481*

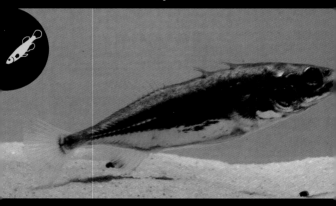

218 Threespine Stickleback, 4″, *p. 527*

219 Brook Stickleback, 2″, *p. 526*

Darters and sculpins

Darters are small, colorful fishes; the males are usually brighter than the females and are sometimes even thought to be different species. Despite their bright coloring, they are difficult to see without close observation, since they bury themselves in the bottom among debris. They are found east of the Continental Divide. Sculpins have spines on the head and are more drably colored. Occurring further west, they are often used as live bait and serve as food for many fishes, particularly trouts.

220 Stippled Darter, 3½″, *p.* 571

221 Slackwater Darter, 2½″, *p.* 565

222 Redline Darter, 3½″, *p.* 572

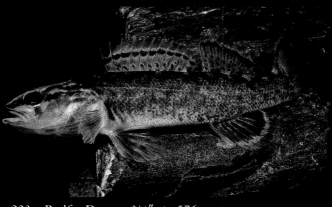

223   Redfin Darter, 3½″, *p. 576*

224   Gulf Darter, 2½″, *p. 574*

225   Striped Darter, 3″, *p. 575*

226 Slenderhead Darter, 4", *p. 583*

227 Iowa Darter, 3", *p. 566*

228 Gilt Darter, 3", *p. 580*

229 Speckled Darter, 2½", *p. 573*

230 Rainbow Darter, 3", *p. 566*

231 Orangethroat Darter, 2¼", *p. 572*

232 Spotted Darter, 3″, *p. 569*

233 Tennessee Snubnose Darter, 3″, *p. 572*

235 Bluestripe Darter, 4″, *p.* 579

236 Bluestripe Darter, 4″, *p.* 579

237 Shield Darter, 3″, *p.* 582

238   Fantail Darter, 3″, *p. 567*

239   Logperch, 7″, *p. 578*

240   Banded Darter, 3″, *p. 577*

241 Snail Darter, 3″, *p. 583*

242 Blackside Darter, 4″, *p. 580*

243 Sp___ish D___r, ___″, *p. 56___*

244 Slimy Sculpin, 4", *p. 728*

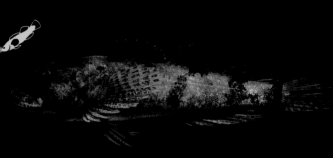

245 Banded Sculpin, 5", *p. 727*

246 Mottled Sculpin, 4", *p. 728*

247   Tessellated Darter, 3½″, *p. 570*

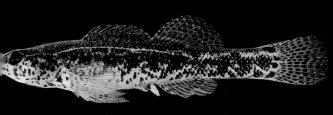

248   Swamp Darter, 2″, *p. 568*

249   Johnny Darter, 2½″, *p. 569*

250 Glassy Darter, 2½″, *p. 576*

251 Crystal Darter, 5″, *p. 561*

252 Scaly Sand Darter, 3″, *p. 564*

253   Eastern Sand Darter, 2½", *p. 563*

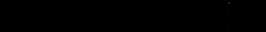

254   Western Sand Darter, 2¾", *p. 563*

255   Naked Sand Darter, 2½", *p. 562*

Salt water

All of these species are found in salt
water. They include fishes and whales,
dolphins, and porpoises. Because some
fishes also live in fresh water or move
between fresh and salt water, they
appear again in the fresh water section.

Skates and ray-like fishes

Easily recognized by their shape, all of these fishes are greatly flattened from top to bottom so that their body forms a disc with the expanded pectoral fins. They are widely distributed in a variety of salt water habitats throughout North America. Most tend to live on the bottom over mud or sand. Some of these fishes, such as the electric rays, stingrays, and batrays, can produce a painful electric charge or are capable of giving a piercing sting. Also included here is the Pacific Angel Shark, which has a flattened, disc-like body, but unlike skates and rays, its large pectoral fins are separated from its head.

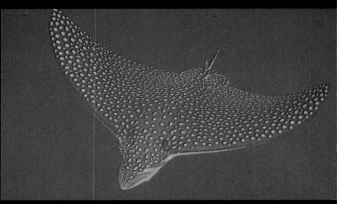

256   Spotted Eagle Ray, 9′, *p. 359*

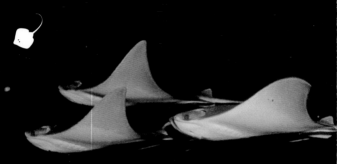

⬙257   Cownose Ray, 3′, *p. 360*

⬙258   Bat Ray, 6′, *p. 359*

259 Atlantic Manta, 22′, *p. 361*

260 Atlantic Manta, 22′, *p. 361*

△261 Cownose Ray, 3′, *p. 360*

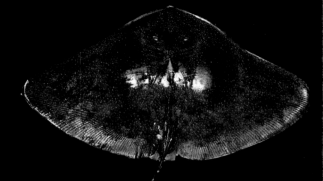

262   Smooth Butterfly Ray, 3', *p. 357*

263   Clearnose Skate, 3'1", *p. 354*

264   Roundel Skate, 24", *p. 355*

265   Big Skate, juv., 8′, *p.* 353

266   Little Skate, 21″, *p.* 355

⚠267   Southern Stingray, 5′, *p.* 356

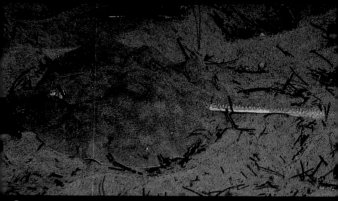

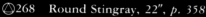

△268   Round Stingray, 22″, *p. 358*

269   Thornback, 3′, *p. 350*

△270   Pacific Electric Ray, 4′6″, *p. 352*

271   Pacific Angel Shark, 5′, *p. 348*

272   Lesser Electric Ray, 18″, *p. 351*

273   Atlantic Torpedo, 6′, *p. 352*

Flatfishes

This group includes lefteye flounders, righteye flounders, and soles. All are known as flatfishes because they are extremely flattened from side to side. They have both eyes on the same side of the body, and generally only this side is pigmented; the blind side is usually whitish. Flatfishes live on mud or sandy bottoms with the eyed side uppermost. They can rapidly nestle down so that they blend with their surroundings. Since some of these species may also be found in brackish and fresh water they are also pictured in the fresh water section.

274   C-O Sole, 14″, *p. 747*

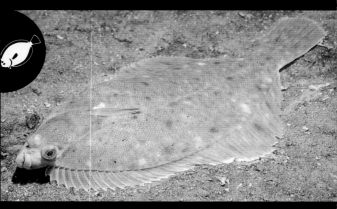

275   Winter Flounder, 23″, *p. 748*

276   English Sole, 22″, *p. 746*

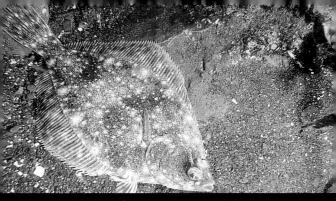

277   Rock Sole, 24″, *p. 745*

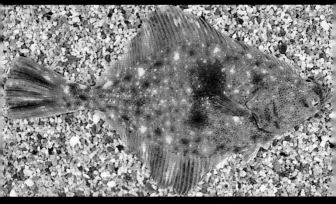

278   Starry Flounder, 3′, *p. 747*

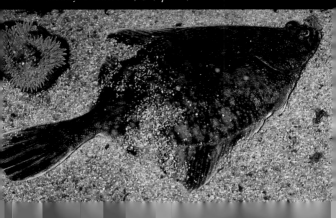

280   Pacific Halibut, 8'9", *p. 744*

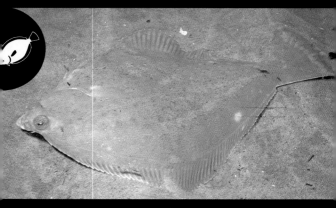

281   Diamond Turbot, 18", *p. 745*

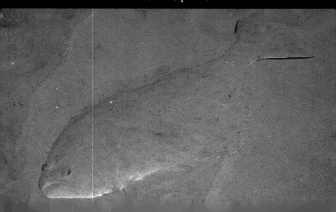

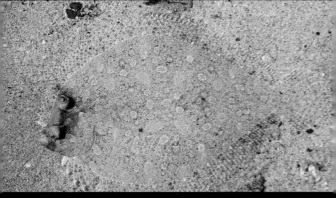

283 Eyed Flounder, 7", *p. 738*

284 Pacific Sanddab, 16", *p. 740*

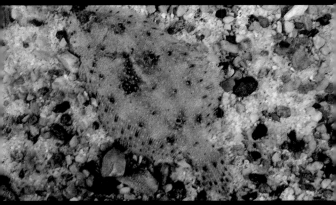

285 Gulf Flounder, 15", *p. 741*

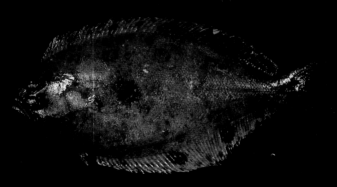

286 Spotfin Flounder, 15″, *p. 740*

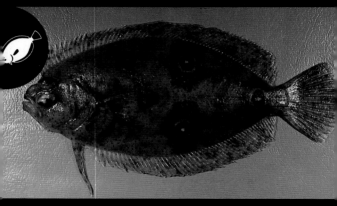

287 Three-eye Flounder, 7″, *p. 737*

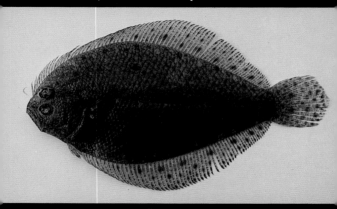

288 Spotted Whiff, 6″, *p. 739*

289   Windowpane, 18″, *p. 743*

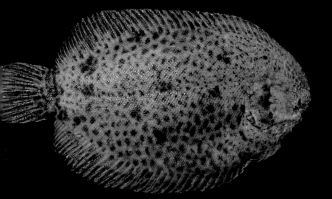

290   Hogchoker, 6″, *p. 750*

Puffers, boxfishes, and fishes with lures

This group contains unusually shaped fishes: Some are globe-shaped, others have lures on their bodies, and still others appear lumpy or craggy. Puffers are slender, elongate fishes that swell into a globe when threatened; some species also have spines that become erect. Boxfishes, such as the cowfishes and trunkfishes, have a unique, hard shell that covers most of their body. These and the similarly shaped leatherjackets have distinctive markings. Other fishes called the lophiiform fishes have lures on their heads, which they use as bait to attract prey. Some lophiiform fishes, such as the frogfishes, appear lumpy and can change color. Similarly, the ridged and craggy Lumpfish changes hues. This section also includes the oval Ocean Sunfish and the Clingfish, which has a ventral sucker.

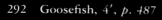

292   Goosefish, 4′, *p. 487*

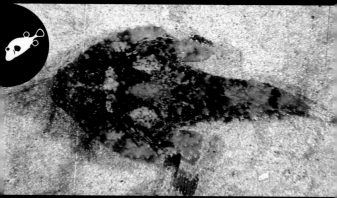

293   Roughback Batfish, 3¼″, *p. 491*

294   Pancake Batfish, 4″, *p. 490*

295   Sargassumfish, 6″, *p. 489*

296   Longlure Frogfish, 6″, *p. 488*

297   Lumpfish, 23″, *p. 736*

298   Longlure Frogfish, 6″, *p. 488*

299   Lumpfish, guarding eggs, 23″, *p. 736*

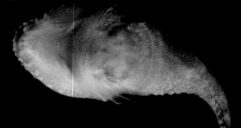

300   Skilletfish, 2¾″, *p. 486*

301 Sharpnose Puffer, 3¾", *p.* 760

302 Porcupinefish, inflated, 3', *p.* 765

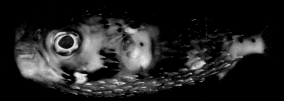

303 Porcupinefish, 3', *p.* 765

△304　Balloonfish, 18″, *p. 764*

△305　Bandtail Puffer, 6½″, *p. 762*

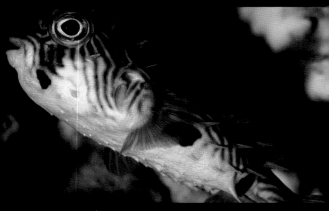

306　Striped Burrfish, 10″, *p. 763*

307   Smooth Puffer, 3′3″, *p. 760*

308   Smooth Puffer, inflated, 3′3″, *p. 760*

309   Ocean Sunfish, 13′, *p. 766*

310 Northern Puffer, 10″, *p. 761*

311 Checkered Puffer, 15″, *p. 762*

312 Smooth Trunkfish, 11″, *p. 758*

313   Trunkfish, 21″, *p. 758*

314   Spotted Trunkfish, 21″, *p. 757*

315   Scrawled Cowfish, 19″, *p. 757*

316   Scrawled Filefish, 3′, *p.* 753

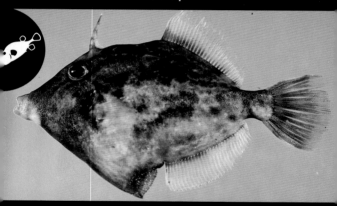

317   Planehead Filefish, 9″, *p.* 755

318   Orange Filefish, 24″, *p.* 753

Angelfishes and disc-like fishes

Spectacular fishes with bright and elaborate markings, angelfishes and the other disc-like fishes included here often show differences in coloring between adults and juveniles and males and females. Most are restricted to tropical waters and are found around reefs. All have a deep, disc-like body, highly flattened from side to side, which allows them easy movement through nooks and crannies. Also pictured are the atypical Jackknife-fish and the African Pompano, the most flattened member of the Jack family.

319   Garibaldi, 14″, *p. 645*

320   Garibaldi, juv., 14″, *p. 645*

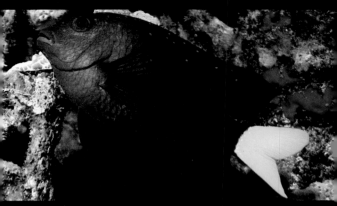

322   Yellowtail Damselfish, 7½″, *p. 646*

323   Beaugregory, 4″, *p. 646*

324   Cocoa Damselfish, 4¼″, *p. 647*

325 Black Durgon, 20″, *p.* 755

326 Blacksmith, 12″, *p.* 644

327 Opaleye, 26″, *p.* 626

328   Blue Tang, 14″, *p. 680*

329   Ocean Surgeon, 14″, *p. 680*

330   Queen Triggerfish, 20″, *p. 754*

331   Queen Angelfish, juv., 18″, *p. 632*

332   French Angelfish, juv., 14″, *p. 634*

333   Rock Beauty, 14″, *p. 633*

334 Gray Angelfish, 24", *p. 634*

335 French Angelfish, 14", *p. 634*

336 Queen Angelfish, 18", *p. 632*

337   Blue Tang, juv., 14″, *p. 680*

338   Spotfin Butterflyfish, 8″, *p. 630*

339   Foureye Butterflyfish, 6″, *p. 629*

340   Reef Butterflyfish, 6″, *p. 630*

341   Banded Butterflyfish, 6″, *p. 631*

342   Sergeant Major, 7″, *p. 644*

343 Jackknife-Fish, 9″, *p. 620*

344 Atlantic Spadefish, 3′, *p. 628*

ican Pompano

Killifishes, livebearers, and sticklebacks

These small fishes are widely distributed throughout North America. Most male killifishes display striking colors, making them popular aquarium fishes. Killifishes and the closely related livebearers are similar looking except that male killifishes do not have external genitals and the females lay eggs. Sticklebacks, named for their isolated dorsal spines, may also have bony plates along their sides. Many killifishes, livebearers, and sticklebacks can tolerate a wide range of salinities. In addition to occurring in salt water, they can be found in brackish and fresh water and are pictured again in the fresh water section.

346 Diamond Killifish, 2″, *p. 505*

347 Longnose Killifish, 6″, *p. 513*

349   Sheepshead Minnow, 3″, *p. 507*

350   Sailfin Molly ♂, 5″, *p. 518*

351   Mosquitofish ♀, 2½″, *p. 516*

352 Rainwater Killifish, 2", *p. 515*

353 Gulf Killifish ♂, 6", *p. 509*

Parrotfishes and wrasses

Living mostly on or near coral reefs in tropical waters, these fishes are well known to divers. As their name implies, many parrotfishes have striking bright hues. Both these fishes and wrasses often show color differences between males and females and juveniles and adults. Many of these fishes have an extremely unusual sexual development: They change appearance and sex as they age. The Flamefish, although in another family, is included here because of its distinctive hues. It is also found around tropical coral reefs.

355   Redband Parrotfish, 11″, *p. 657*

356   Bucktooth Parrotfish, 8″, *p. 658*

357   Cunner, 10″, *p. 654*

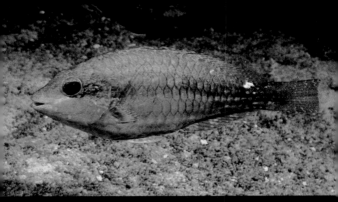

358   Redband Parrotfish, 11″, *p. 657*

359   Redband Parrotfish, 11″, *p. 657*

360   Princess Parrotfish ♂, 13″, *p. 656*

361 Stoplight Parrotfish ♂, 24″, *p. 659*

362 Queen Parrotfish ♂, 24″, *p. 657*

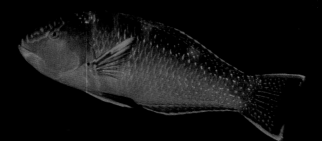

363 Puddingwife, 20″, *p. 651*

364   Redfin Parrotfish, 18″, *p. 659*

365   Blue Parrotfish, 4′, *p. 655*

366   Creole Wrasse, 12″, *p. 649*

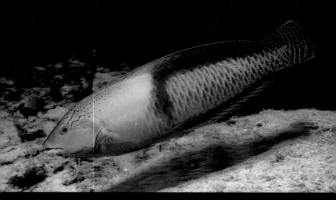

367 Yellowhead Wrasse ♂, 7½″, *p. 650*

368 Bluehead ♂, 6″, *p. 654*

370 Bluehead ♀, 6″, *p. 654*

371 Señorita, 10″, *p. 652*

372 Yellowhead Wrasse, juv., 7½″, *p. 650*

373   Puddingwife, juv., 20″, *p. 651*

374   Slippery Dick, 9″, *p. 649*

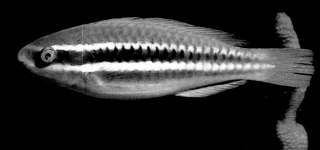

376   Bucktooth Parrotfish, 8″, *p. 658*

377   California Sheephead, juv., 3′, *p. 652*

378   Flamefish, 4″, *p. 600*

379   Stoplight Parrotfish, 24", *p. 659*

380   California Sheephead ♂, 3', *p. 652*

Fishes with spiny rays or tapering bodies

This large, diverse group includes such robust, brightly colored, spiny fishes as the bigeyes, squirrelfishes, scorpionfishes, greenlings, and the Sheepshead. Many of these fishes can be recognized by their distinctive markings. The rockfishes, part of the scorpionfish family, are the largest group found on the Pacific Coast. Many can be difficult to distinguish from one another. They should be handled with care, since their venomous spines can give a nasty sting. Also pictured here are some fishes with spiny fins and tapering bodies, such as the sculpins, searobins, Red Goatfish, Sturgeon Poacher, and Sablefish. The lizardfishes have tapering bodies but lack spiny fins. These fishes occur in a variety of habitats, but most live on the bottom among debris, rocks, sand, or mud. Some are noted for their behavior: Searobins use the fingerlike pectoral fin rays to walk along the bottom, and lizardfishes wait to dart after prey. Sculpins are common in intertidal areas, and, since some may be found in both fresh and salt water, they are pictured in both sections. The Fat Sleeper, included here, also appears in the fresh water section.

△382   Squirrelfish, 14″, *p. 523*

△383   Longspine Squirrelfish, 12″, *p. 523*

384   Blackbar Soldierfish, 8½″, *p. 524*

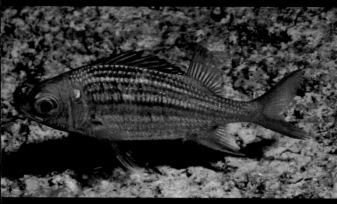

⚠385   Dusky Squirrelfish, 6″, *p. 524*

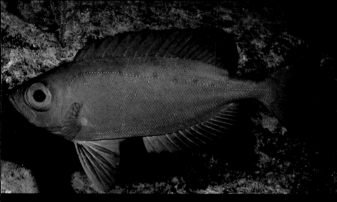

386   Bigeye, 16″, *p. 586*

387   Short Bigeye, 10″, *p. 587*

△388　Vermilion Rockfish, 30″, *p. 710*

△389　Canary Rockfish, 30″, *p. 714*

△390　Yelloweye Rockfish, 3′, *p. 715*

391 **Tiger Rockfish**, 24″, *p. 712*

392 **Flag Rockfish**, 25″, *p. 716*

393 **Copper Rockfish**, 22″, *p. 704*

△394　Treefish, 16″, *p. 718*

395　Sheepshead, 30″, *p. 613*

△396　Quillback Rockfish, 24″, *p. 708*

△397　China Rockfish, 17″, *p. 711*

△398　Black-and-yellow Rockfish, 15″, *p. 705*

△399　Gopher Rockfish, 15″, *p. 704*

400 Kelp Greenling ♂, 21″, p. 725

401 Yellowtail Rockfish, 26″, p. 707

402 Honeycomb Rockfish, 10¼″, p. 718

403   Olive Rockfish, 24", *p.* 717

404   Rosy Rockfish, 14", *p.* 715

405   Bocaccio, juv., 3', *p.* 713

△406   Kelp Rockfish, 17″, *p. 702*

Brown Rockfish, 21½″, *p. 703*

△408   Widow Rockfish, 21″, *p. 706*

409   Black Rockfish, 24″, *p. 709*

410   Blue Rockfish, 21″, *p. 711*

411   Kelp Greenling ♀ 21″ *p. 725*

△412 Shortspine Thornyhead, juv., 30″, *p. 719*

413 Red Irish Lord, 20″, *p. 730*

415 Red Goatfish, 8″, *p. 625*

416 Lavender Sculpin, 10″, *p. 730*

417 California Scorpionfish, 17″, *p. 760*

418 Grunt Sculpin, 3¼", *p. 733*

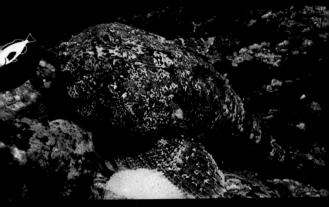

419 Buffalo Sculpin, 15", *p. 729*

421   Spotted Scorpionfish, 17″, *p. 700*

422   Barbfish, 8″, *p. 699*

423   Bighead Searobin, 14″, *p. 722*

424 Bandtail Searobin, 7", *p. 721*

425 Leopard Searobin, 8", *p. 722*

426 Northern Searobin, 17", *p. 723*

427 Sturgeon Poacher, 12″, *p. 735*

428 Lingcod, 5′, *p. 725*

429 Sand Diver, 18″, *p. 406*

430   Inshore Lizardfish, 16", *p. 405*

431   Fat Sleeper, 10", *p. 676*

432   Sablefish, 3'4", *p. 723*

Long, slender fishes and seahorses

The extremely unusual long, slender shape of these fishes is reflected in their names: pipefishes, Atlantic Needlefish, Red Cornetfish, Tube-Snout, and Trumpetfish. Some of these fishes camouflage themselves by hanging vertically in the water among plants and corals. Pipefishes and seahorses, both in the same family, have a unique feature—males have a breeding pouch in which the young are reared. Also included in this group is the ribbon-like Atlantic Cutlassfish and the Halfbeak, a member of the Flyingfishes family. Like needlefishes, the Halfbeak is a surface dweller. Both may be seen skittering across the water.

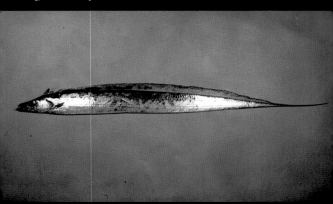

433 Atlantic Cutlassfish, 5′, *p. 681*

434 Halfbeak, 10½″, *p. 502*

435 Atlantic Needlefish, 25″, *p. 504*

436   Red Cornetfish, 6', *p. 529*

437   Tube-Snout, 7", *p. 526*

438   Trumpetfish, 30", *p. 528*

439 Bay Pipefish, 14″, *p. 531*

440 Gulf Pipefish, 6″, *p. 531*

441 Lined Seahorse, 5″, *p. 530*

Eel-like fishes and long dorsal-finned fishes

All of the fishes pictured here are either distinctly eel-like in shape or have long-based dorsal and anal fins. Most of these eel-like fishes can be distinguished by the presence or absence of pectoral, pelvic, dorsal, or anal fins. They are found in a wide range of habitats and some can live in both salt and fresh water, although the American Eel only enters salt water when migrating and spawning. Moray eels, snake eels, and wolffishes are all capable of causing painful wounds, and should be approached and handled with caution. The fishes with long-based dorsal and anal fins include the clinids, blennies, gobies, hakes, and the Sand Tilefish.

442   Pacific Lamprey, 30″, *p. 327*

443   Sea Lamprey, on carp, 33″, *p. 328*

444   Pacific Hagfish, 25″, *p. 324*

Salt water

445   American Eel, 4′11″, *p.* 376

⊘446   Shrimp Eel, 30″, *p.* 379

447   Penpoint Gunnel, 18″, *p.* 672

448 Bank Cusk-Eel, 8″, *p. 500*

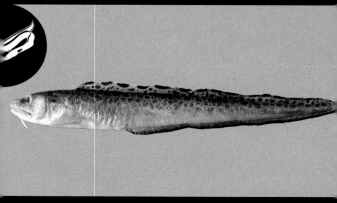

449 Mottled Cusk-Eel, 8″, *p. 500*

450 Spotted Cusk-Eel, 14½″, *p. 499*

451　California Moray, 5', *p.* 377

452　Blackedge Moray, 24", *p.* 378

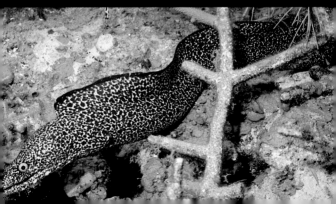

454   Ocean Pout, 3'6", *p. 501*

455   Wolf-Eel, 6'8", *p. 674*

456   Monkeyface Prickleback, 30", *p. 671*

△457   Atlantic Wolffish, 5′, *p. 673*

458   Hairy Blenny, 8¹₂″, *p. 666*

459   Striped Blenny, 3″, *p. 667*

△460   Oyster Toadfish, 15″, *p. 484*

461   Feather Blenny, 4″, *p. 669*

462   Barred Blenny, 3½″, *p. 668*

463 Plainfin Midshipman, 15″, *p. 485*

464 Molly Miller, 4½″, *p. 670*

465 Onespot Fri... che... *p. 9″*

466 Sailfin Blenny, juv., 2″, *p. 664*

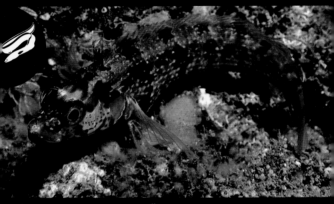

467 Island Kelpfish, 4″, *p. 663*

469   Blackeye Goby, 6″, *p.* 677

470   Sharptail Goby, 8″, *p.* 678

471   Sand Tilefish, 24″, *p.* 580

472   Giant Kelpfish, 24″, *p. 665*

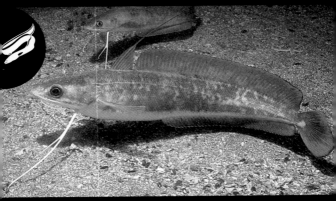

473   Red Hake, 30″, *p. 498*

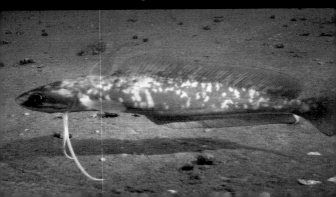

Drumlike fishes, cods, trouts, and catfishes

Almost all of these fishes are valued for sport or commercially as food. Drums are elongate fishes with distinctly notched dorsal fins; some have been known to weigh over 100 lbs. They can be caught in the surf, over shallow sand flats, and in coastal and deeper waters. The drumlike Striped Mullet swims in schools, sometimes entering estuaries and rivers, while the similarly shaped Snook, another highly esteemed sport fish, is found mainly in tropical waters off the coast as well as in estuaries. The Snook should be handled with caution, since its sharp gill covers can cause deep cuts.

Most members of the codfishes family are harvested commercially. They have an elongate, tapering body and long dorsal and anal fins. Some trouts and salmons pictured here are repeated in the fresh water section "Trouts and salmons," since they inhabit both salt and fresh water or migrate between the 2 types. Popular with anglers, these heavy-bodied fishes have a small, fleshy fin, known as the adipose fin, on the back behind the dorsal fin. The distinctive sea catfishes have long, ribbonlike whiskers, known as barbels, on the head; their sharp dorsal and pectoral spines can cause painful wounds.

475 Black Drum, 3'3", *p. 622*

476 Spotted Seatrout, 28", *p. 618*

478 Red Drum, 5′, *p. 623*

479 Atlantic Croaker, 24″, *p. 621*

480 Yellowfin Croaker, 18″, *p. 624*

481 Southern Kingfish, 20", *p. 620*

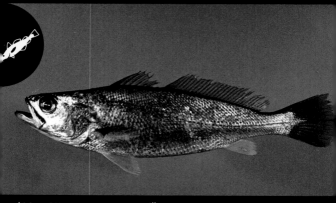

482 Silver Seatrout, 14", *p. 618*

484   Striped Mullet, 18″, *p. 660*

485·   Striped Mullet, 18″, *p. 660*

△486   Snook, 4′7″, *p. 532*

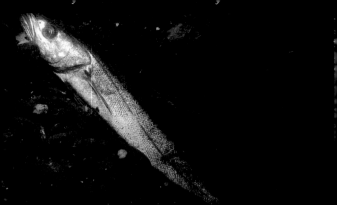

487 Pacific Hake, 3', *p. 495*

488 Silver Hake, 30", *p. 494*

489 Pollock, 3'6", *p. 497*

490   Pacific Tomcod, 12″, *p. 496*

491   Haddock, 3′8″, *p. 494*

492   Atlantic Cod, 6′, *p. 493*

493   Rainbow Trout, 3'9", *p. 394*

494   Atlantic Salmon, 4'5", *p. 395*

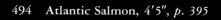

495   Cutthroat Trout, 30", *p. 393*

496   Brown Trout, 3′4″, *p. 396*

497   Chinook Salmon ♂, 4′10″, *p. 391*

498   Brook Trout, 17″, *p. 396*

499   Sockeye Salmon, 33″, *p. 390*

△500   Hardhead Catfish, 24″, *p. 477*

△501   Gafftopsail Catfish, 3′3″, *p. 478*

Basslike fishes, grunts, and snappers

Most of these oblong, slightly flattened fishes are sought for sport and food. The Striped Bass is important throughout its range and is frequently caught by surf fishing. Although it lives in salt water, it spawns in fresh, and is also pictured in the fresh water section. Popular game fishes, many species of sea basses change markings as they become adults. Among basslike fishes are the soapfishes, so named because they secrete a slimy, irritating mucus when handled, and the Tripletail, distinguished by its long, soft dorsal and anal fins, which, along with the caudal fin, give the impression of 3 tails.

Additional oblong fishes include the mojarras, whose protractile, downward-pointing jaws enable them to feed on bottom-dwelling invertebrates; the surfperches, which eat parasites gleaned from the skin of other fishes; and the sea chubs, which are known for their habit of following ships. Grunts, named for the grunting noises they produce, also somewhat resemble basses. Most snappers are caught by anglers and are important commercially. The Mozambique Tilapia, shown here, appears again in the fresh water section.

502   Red Hind, 24", *p. 540*

503   Speckled Hind, 18", *p. 540*

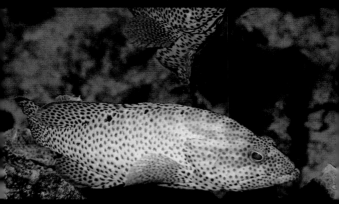

505   Rock Hind, 24″, *p. 539*

506   Greater Soapfish, 13″, *p. 548*

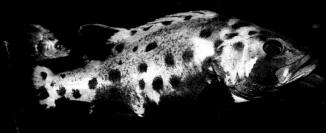

507   Giant Sea Bass, 7′5″, *p. 536*

508   Jewfish, 7′10″, *p. 541*

509   Réd Grouper, 28″, *p. 542*

510   Striped Bass, 6′, *p. 535*

511 Black Grouper, 4', *p. 544*

512 Kelp Bass, 28", *p. 545*

514   Belted Sandfish, 4½″, *p.* 547

515   Black Sea Bass, 24″, *p.* 537

516   Nassau Grouper, 4′, *p.* 543

517 Tripletail, 3'4", *p. 608*

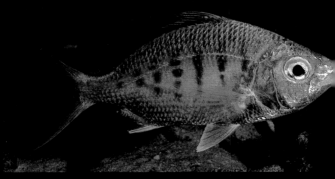

518 Yellowfin Mojarra, 16", *p. 610*

519 Black Perch, 15½", *p. 639*

520 Rainbow Seaperch, 12", *p. 641*

521 Tattler, 8", *p. 546*

522 Red Snapper, 31", *p. 695*

523 Mozambique Tilapia, 15″, *p. 636*

524 White Perch, 19″, *p. 533*

525 Walleye Surfperch, 12″, *p. 641*

526   Bermuda Chub, 20″, *p. 626*

527   Sharpnose Seaperch, 12″, *p. 642*

528   Redtail Surfperch, 16″, *p. 637*

529　Rubberlip Seaperch, 18″, *p. 643*

530　Kelp Perch, 8½″, *p. 638*

532 White Grunt, 16″, *p. 612*

533 Pinfish, 15″, *p. 615*

535   Tomtate, 10″, *p. 611*

536   Yellow Snapper, 24″, *p. 607*

537   Porkfish, 14″, *p. 611*

538 Schoolmaster, 24″, *p. 604*

539 Gray Snapper, 3′, *p. 605*

540 Dog Snapper, 29″, *p. 606*

541   Halfmoon, 19″, *p. 627*

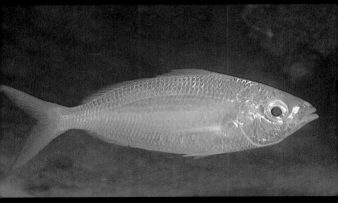

542   Spotfin Mojarra, 8″, *p. 609*

543   Shiner Perch, 8″, *p. 639*

Spindle-shaped fishes and large, robust fishes

Many of these species are fast-swimming schooling fishes, whose spindle-shaped bodies are designed for speed. Most are popular with anglers, since their strength and lightning pace make them exciting sport. Within this group, the progression of shapes moves from the deep-bodied jacks to the more slender jacks and the Bluefish, to the torpedo-shaped tunas and mackerels. Also shown are some slender, elongate fishes, such as the anchovies and herrings. Among the large, robust fishes, popular for sport, are the tarpons, the Great Barracuda, and the Sailfish. Various other large, unusually shaped fishes, such as the Dolphin, Cobia, and White Sturgeon, also appear here.

544 Atlantic Moonfish, 15", *p. 598*

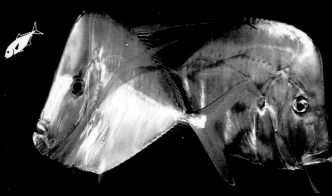

545 Lookdown, 16", *p. 598*

546 Harvestfish, 12", *p. 698*

547   Jolthead Porgy, 27″, *p. 614*

548   Saucereye Porgy, 16″, *p. 614*

549   Palometa, 13″, *p. 601*

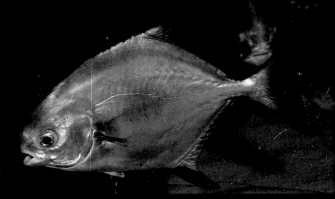

550   Florida Pompano, 17″, *p. 600*

551   Crevalle Jack, 3′4″, *p. 594*

552   Horse-eye Jack, 25″, *p. 594*

553   Ocean Whitefish, 3′4″, *p. 589*

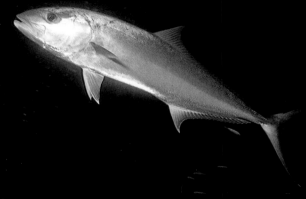

△554   Greater Amberjack, 5′, *p. 599*

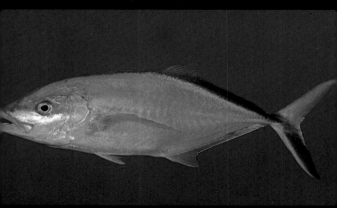

555   Bar Jack, 22″, *p. 595*

△556 Bluefish, 3′7″, *p.* 590

557 Yellowtail, 5′, *p.* 599

558 Rainbow Runner, 4′, *p.* 596

559　Bigeye Scad, 11″, *p. 597*

560　Jack Mackerel, 32″, *p. 602*

561　Yellowfin Tuna, 6′, *p. 690*

562   Cero, 32″, *p. 689*

563   Spanish Mackerel, 3′, *p. 688*

564   Chub Mackerel, 25″, *p. 686*

565 Atlantic Mackerel, 22″, *p. 686*

566 Little Tunny, 4′, *p. 684*

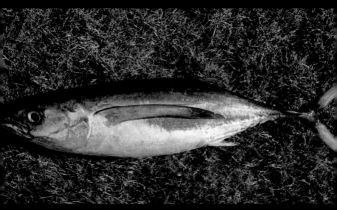

567 Albacore, 5′, *p. 689*

568   Inland Silverside, 6″, *p. 521*

569   California Grunion ♀ with ♂s, 7½″, *p. 521*

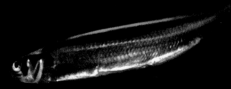

570   Topsmelt, 14½″, *p. 519*

571   Northern Anchovy, 9″, *p. 385*

572   Striped Anchovy, 6″, *p. 385*

573   Rainbow Smelt ♀ above ♂, 13″, *p. 400*

574   Pacific Herring, 18″, *p. 383*

575   Alewife, 15″, *p. 381*

576   Atlantic Menhaden, 18″, *p. 382*

577 American Shad, 30", *p. 381*

578 Bonefish, 3', *p. 375*

579 Machete, 3', *p. 372*

580 Ladyfish, 3'3", *p.* 373

581 Tarpon, 8', *p.* 374

582 Dolphin, 6'6", *p.* 603

583 Great Barracuda, 6', *p. 662*

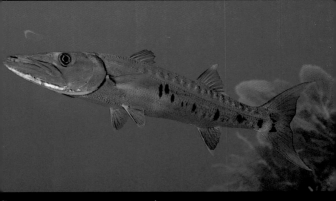

584 Great Barracuda, 6', *p. 662*

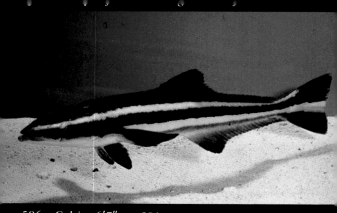

586   Cobia, 6'7", *p. 591*

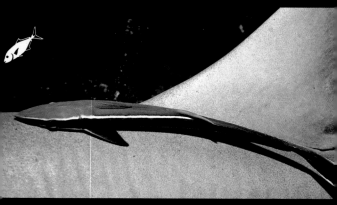

587   Sharksucker, 32", *p. 592*

Sharklike fishes

Powerful fishes, some sharks are prized for sport and a few are eaten. They vary greatly in size and type; some species are comparatively small, most measure about 10' (3 m), and the Whale Shark, the largest fish in the world, reaches a length of 60' (18.3 m). While certain sharks are sluggish and peaceable, several are extremely dangerous and have caused deaths. All sharks, unless bottom-dwelling, must swim continually, since they lack a swim bladder and would sink if they kept still. Also included here are the Spotted Ratfish, which should be handled with caution because it has venomous spines, and the sharklike Smalltooth Sawfish.

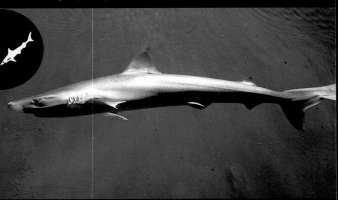

589 Spiny Dogfish, 5′, *p. 347*

590 Soupfin Shark, 6′, *p. 343*

591 Sevengill Shark, 9′, *p. 330*

592   Bonnethead, 4′6″, *p. 346*

593   Blue Shark, 12′7″, *p. 344*

594   Blacktip Shark, 8′, *p. 341*

595   Sandbar Shark, 8′, *p. 342*

⚠596   Bull Shark, 11′, *p. 340*

⚠597   White Shark, 21′, *p. 336*

598 Sandbar Shark, 8′, *p. 342*

599 Leopard Shark, 7′, *p. 344*

600 Whale Shark, 60′, *p. 333*

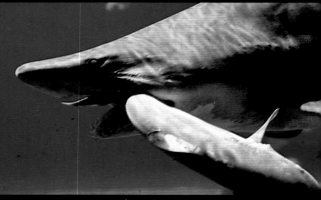

⚠601 **Sand Tiger**, 10′, *p. 334*

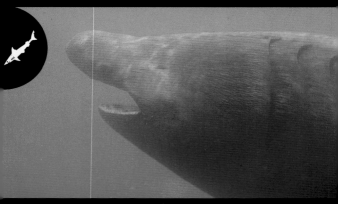

602 **Basking Shark**, 45′, *p. 337*

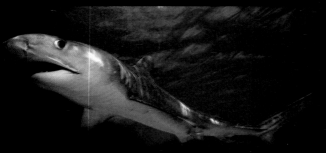

⚠603 **Tiger Shark**, 18′, *p. 342*

604 Nurse Shark, 14″, *p. 332*

⚠605 Swell Shark, 3′4″, *p. 339*

606 Horn Shark, 4′, *p. 331*

△607   Scalloped Hammerhead, 13′9″, *p. 345*

608   Smalltooth Sawfish, 18′, *p. 349*

Whales, dolphins, and porpoises

These warm-blooded animals are found
in salt waters throughout North
America. They vary greatly in size and
shape: The Blue Whale, the largest
animal to exist, has been known to
reach a length of 98′ (29.9 m), while
certain dolphins may be only a few feet
long. Some of these animals can be seen
relatively easily and frequently as they
swim on the surface of the ocean,
migrating from their summer to their
winter grounds. Others are believed to
be rare or are observed only with
difficulty, since they are deep divers.
Most whales should be approached with
caution due to their enormous size.
Moreover, the Killer Whale can be
dangerous.
Species commonly seen are shown in
photographs. To help identification,
these pictures are supplemented by
diagnostic color paintings of all known
North American whales, dolphins, and
porpoises.

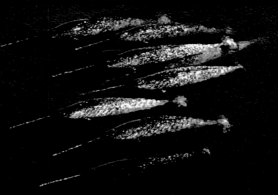

610   Narwhal, 16′, *p.* 793

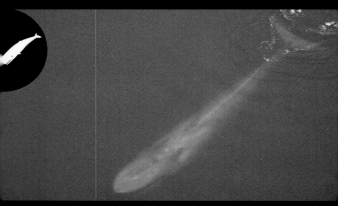

611   Blue Whale, 98′, *p.* 774

612   White Whale, 16′, *p.* 793

613 Fin Whale, 79′, *p.* 775

614 Bryde's Whale, 46′, *p.* 773

616　Humpback Whale, 53′, *p.* 776

617　White Whale, 16′, *p.* 793

619   Right Whale, 53′, *p.* 778

620   Gray Whale, 46′, *p.* 780

621   Right Whale, feeding, 53′, *p.* 778

622   Blue Whale, 98′, *p.* 774

623   Humpback Whale, 53′, *p.* 776

624   Gray Whale, 46′, *p.* 780

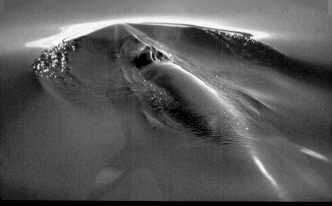

625 Minke Whale, 33′, *p.* 771

626 Fin Whale, 79′, *p.* 775

627 Blainville's Beaked Whale, 17′, *p.* 784

△628 Killer Whale, 31′, *p. 802*

△629 Killer Whale, 31′, *p. 802*

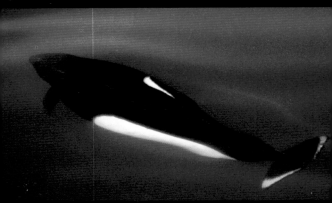

631   Atlantic White-sided Dolphin, 9′, *p.* 799

632   Pacific White-sided Dolphin, 7′6″, *p.* 800

634   Rough-toothed Dolphin, 8′, *p. 809*

635   Pilot Whale, 23′, *pp. 796 , 797*

636   Risso's Dolphin, 13′, *p. 798*

637   False Killer Whale, 19'6", *p. 803*

638   Spinner Dolphin, 7', *p. 807*

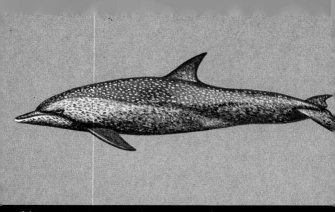

640 Atlantic Spotted Dolphin, 8', *p. 808*

641 Bridled Dolphin, 7', *p. 806*

lenosed Dolp   2', *p. 809*

643 Rough-toothed Dolphin, 8', *p. 809*

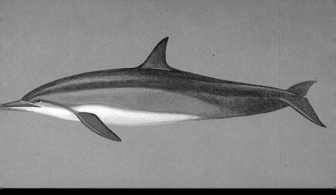

644 Spinner Dolphin, 7', *p. 807*

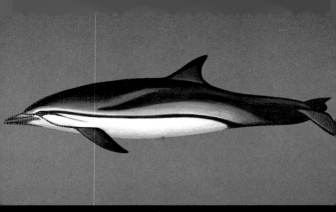

646 Striped Dolphin, 9', *p. 805*

647 Pacific White-sided Dolphin, 7'6", *p. 800*

649　Atlantic White-sided Dolphin, 9′, *p. 799*

650　White-beaked Dolphin, 10′, *p. 800*

652 Dall's Porpoise, 7′, *p. 812*

653 Harbor Porpoise, 6′, *p. 811*

655 False Killer Whale, 19'6", *p. 803*

656 Pygmy Killer Whale, 9', *p. 796*

658   Short-finned Pilot Whale, 23', *p. 796*

659   Dwarf Sperm Whale, 9', *p. 790*

661 True's Beaked Whale, 17′, *p.* 787

662 Baird's Beaked Whale, 42′, *p.* 781

h Sea Beaked   e, 16′6″, *p.* 7

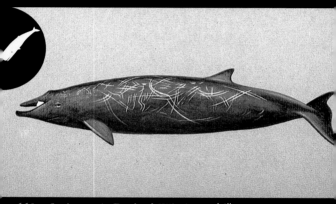

664   Hector's Beaked Whale, 14′6″, *p. 786*

665   Stejneger's Beaked Whale, 17′6″, *p. 788*

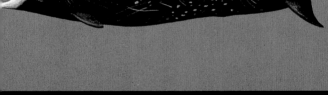

667 Antillean Beaked Whale, 15'5", *p. 785*

668 Hubb's Beaked Whale, 17'6", *p. 784*

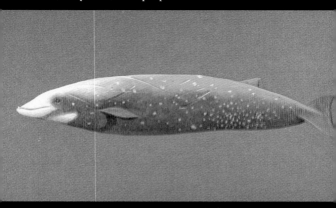

670 Cuvier's Beaked Whale, 24′ 9″, *p.* 788

671 Northern Bottlenosed Whale, 32′, *p.* 782

672 White Whale, 16′, *p.* 792

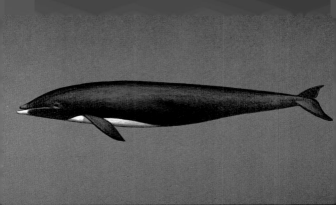

673 Northern Right Whale Dolphin, 10', *p. 801*

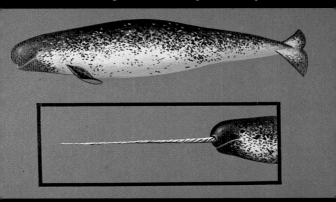

674 Narwhal, 16', *p. 793*

n Whale, 69',

676　Bowhead Whale, 65', *p.* 777

677　Right Whale, 53', *p.* 778

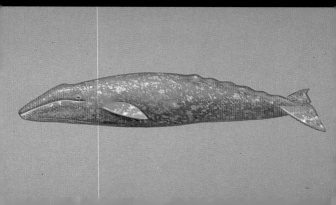

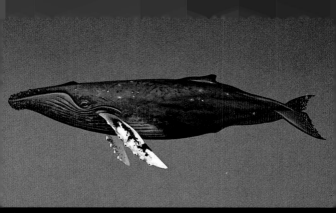

679 Humpback Whale, 53', *p. 776*

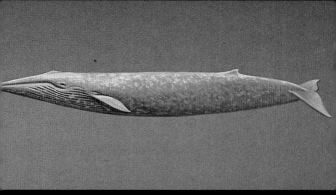

680 Blue Whale, 98', *p. 774*

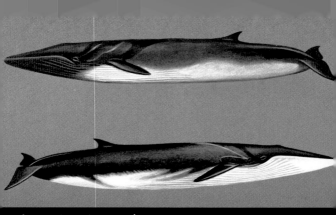

682   Fin Whale, 79′, *p.* 775

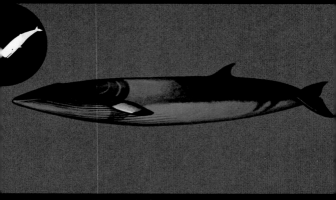

683   Minke Whale, 33′, *p.* 771

Part II
Text

Key to Families of Fishes

This key will help you pinpoint the family to which a fish belongs, based on its body shape as well as such obvious characteristics as the number of fins, their size, shape, and placement. For each family a typical fish is shown; its shape is repeated next to the family description in the text. Remember that young fishes may differ significantly from older ones, and that in each family some species may be atypical. Thus, although most species in a family may have 2 or more separated dorsal fins, a few species may have only 1 dorsal fin. Similarly, body shape may vary.

Using the Key: First, turn to the appropriate section— either fresh water or salt water. Those fishes that have very distinctive shapes are grouped by body shape, and they are further divided by characteristics such as fin shape. Other families that are not distinctively shaped are grouped by the number and shape of their fins. Primary identification characteristics are indicated in bold face type; secondary features follow.

The name of each family is given next to the representative shape, along with the page number for the family account. Turn to that page and read the family description, which will make it easy for you to determine if you successfully identified the family to which your fish belongs.

Fresh water

Flat body

Righteye Flounders, *p. 743*

Soles, *p. 749*

Elongate body with elongate snout

Pikes, *p. 402*

Gars, *p. 368*

Eel-like body

Freshwater Eels, *p. 375*

Lampreys, *p. 325*

1 long dorsal fin

Labyrinth Catfishes, *p. 476*

Bowfins, *p. 371*

1 small, rounded dorsal fin, square-to-round tail

Killifishes, *p. 504*

Pirate Perches, *p. 481*

Mudminnows, *p. 400*

Livebearers, *p. 516*

1 high, pointed dorsal fin, forked tail

Carps and Minnows, *p. 408*

Suckers, *p. 457*

1 angular dorsal fin, forked tail

Carps and Minnows, *p. 408*

Suckers, *p. 457*

1 dorsal fin, spiny and soft portions joined

Cichlids, *p. 635*

Sunfishes, *p. 548*

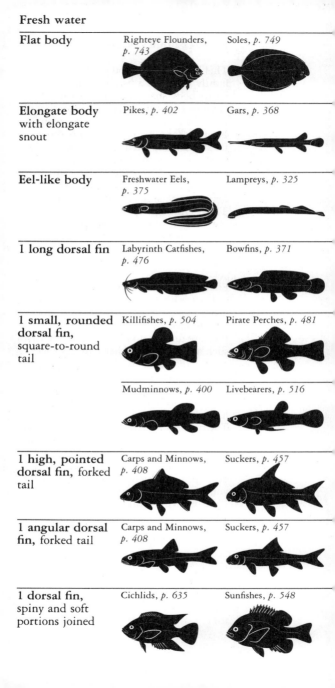

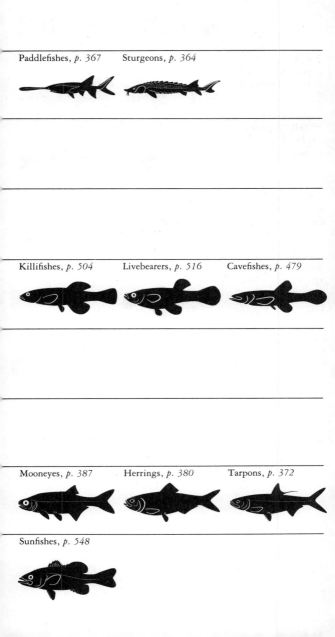

Paddlefishes, *p. 367*   Sturgeons, *p. 364*

Killifishes, *p. 504*   Livebearers, *p. 516*   Cavefishes, *p. 479*

Mooneyes, *p. 387*   Herrings, *p. 380*   Tarpons, *p. 372*

Sunfishes, *p. 548*

Fresh water

2 or more separated dorsal fins	Perches, *p. 560*	Temperate Basses, *p. 533*

2 widely separated dorsal fins, forked tail	Mullets, *p. 660*	Silversides, *p. 519*

Small, fleshy fin on back behind dorsal fin Trouts, *p. 388* Smelts, *p. 398*

2 widely separated dorsal fins, rounded tail Sleepers, *p. 675*

3–11 separated spines on back Sticklebacks, *p. 525*

Perches, *p. 560*

Sculpins, *p. 726*

Codfishes, *p. 492*

Bullhead Catfishes, *p. 467*

Characins, *p. 407*

Trout-Perches, *p. 482*

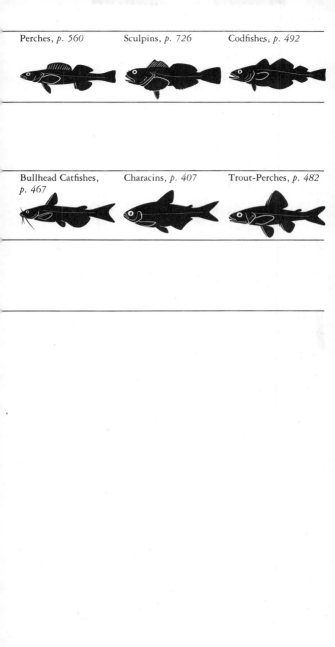

Salt water

Seahorse
Pipefishes, *p. 530*

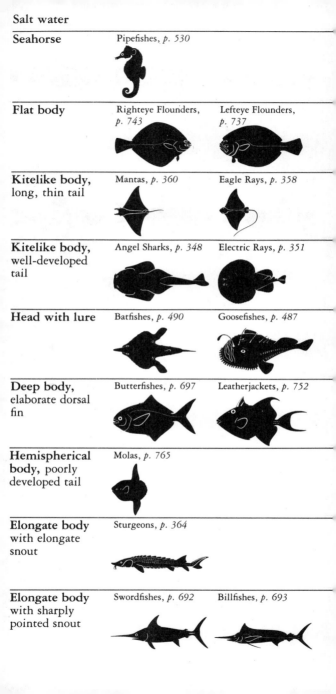

Flat body
Righteye Flounders, *p. 743* Lefteye Flounders, *p. 737*

Kitelike body, long, thin tail
Mantas, *p. 360* Eagle Rays, *p. 358*

Kitelike body, well-developed tail
Angel Sharks, *p. 348* Electric Rays, *p. 351*

Head with lure
Batfishes, *p. 490* Goosefishes, *p. 487*

Deep body, elaborate dorsal fin
Butterfishes, *p. 697* Leatherjackets, *p. 752*

Hemispherical body, poorly developed tail
Molas, *p. 765*

Elongate body with elongate snout
Sturgeons, *p. 364*

Elongate body with sharply pointed snout
Swordfishes, *p. 692* Billfishes, *p. 693*

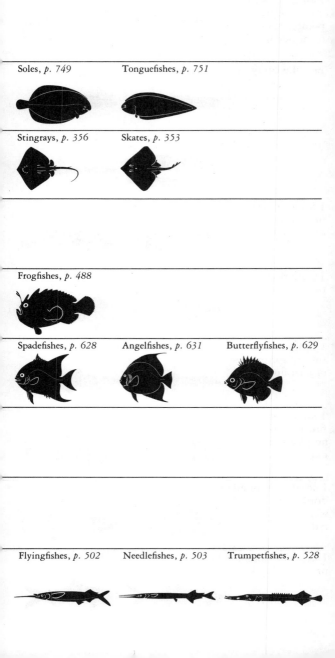

Soles, *p. 749*

Tonguefishes, *p. 751*

Stingrays, *p. 356*

Skates, *p. 353*

Frogfishes, *p. 488*

Spadefishes, *p. 628*

Angelfishes, *p. 631*

Butterflyfishes, *p. 629*

Flyingfishes, *p. 502*

Needlefishes, *p. 503*

Trumpetfishes, *p. 528*

Elongate body with sharply pointed snout (continued)

Pipefishes, *p. 530*

Cornetfishes, *p. 529*

Eel-like body

Cusk-Eels, *p. 499*

Eelpouts, *p. 501*

Cutlassfishes, *p. 681*

Hagfishes, *p. 324*

1 long dorsal fin, square-to-round tail

Toadfishes, *p. 483*

Clingfishes, *p. 486*

1 long dorsal fin, forked tail

Tilefishes, *p. 588*

Dolphins, *p. 602*

1 long dorsal fin, mirror image of anal fin

Remoras, *p. 592*

Cobias, *p. 591*

1 small dorsal fin, it and anal fin placed near tail

Porcupinefishes, *p. 763*

Puffers, *p. 759*

1 small, rounded dorsal fin, square-to-round tail

Killifishes, *p. 504*

Killifishes, *p. 504*

1 angular dorsal fin, forked tail

Anchovies, *p. 384*

Herrings, *p. 380*

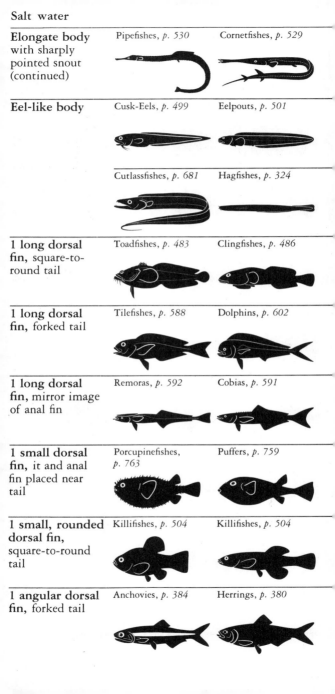

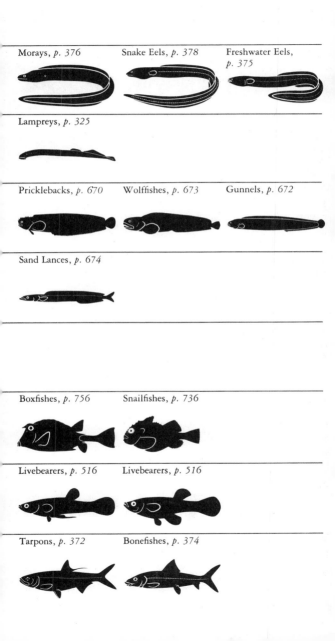

Morays, *p. 376*

Snake Eels, *p. 378*

Freshwater Eels, *p. 375*

Lampreys, *p. 325*

Pricklebacks, *p. 670*

Wolffishes, *p. 673*

Gunnels, *p. 672*

Sand Lances, *p. 674*

Boxfishes, *p. 756*

Snailfishes, *p. 736*

Livebearers, *p. 516*

Livebearers, *p. 516*

Tarpons, *p. 372*

Bonefishes, *p. 374*

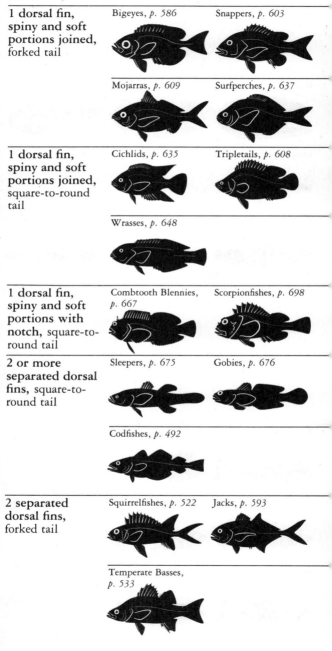

Salt water

1 dorsal fin, spiny and soft portions joined, forked tail

Bigeyes, *p. 586*

Snappers, *p. 603*

Mojarras, *p. 609*

Surfperches, *p. 637*

1 dorsal fin, spiny and soft portions joined, square-to-round tail

Cichlids, *p. 635*

Tripletails, *p. 608*

Wrasses, *p. 648*

1 dorsal fin, spiny and soft portions with notch, square-to-round tail

Combtooth Blennies, *p. 667*

Scorpionfishes, *p. 698*

2 or more separated dorsal fins, square-to-round tail

Sleepers, *p. 675*

Gobies, *p. 676*

Codfishes, *p. 492*

2 separated dorsal fins, forked tail

Squirrelfishes, *p. 522*

Jacks, *p. 593*

Temperate Basses, *p. 533*

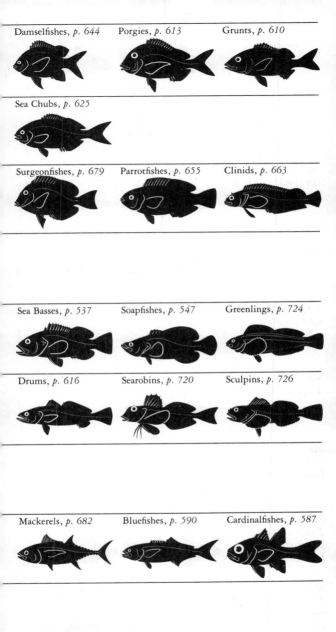

Damselfishes, *p. 644*

Porgies, *p. 613*

Grunts, *p. 610*

Sea Chubs, *p. 625*

Surgeonfishes, *p. 679*

Parrotfishes, *p. 655*

Clinids, *p. 663*

Sea Basses, *p. 537*

Soapfishes, *p. 547*

Greenlings, *p. 724*

Drums, *p. 616*

Searobins, *p. 720*

Sculpins, *p. 726*

Mackerels, *p. 682*

Bluefishes, *p. 590*

Cardinalfishes, *p. 587*

Salt water

2 well-separated dorsal fins, forked tail

Snooks, *p. 532*

Goatfishes, *p. 624*

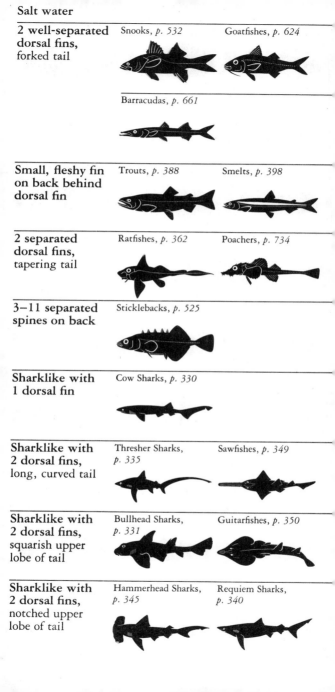

Barracudas, *p. 661*

Small, fleshy fin on back behind dorsal fin

Trouts, *p. 388*

Smelts, *p. 398*

2 separated dorsal fins, tapering tail

Ratfishes, *p. 362*

Poachers, *p. 734*

3–11 separated spines on back

Sticklebacks, *p. 525*

Sharklike with 1 dorsal fin

Cow Sharks, *p. 330*

Sharklike with 2 dorsal fins, long, curved tail

Thresher Sharks, *p. 335*

Sawfishes, *p. 349*

Sharklike with 2 dorsal fins, squarish upper lobe of tail

Bullhead Sharks, *p. 331*

Guitarfishes, *p. 350*

Sharklike with 2 dorsal fins, notched upper lobe of tail

Hammerhead Sharks, *p. 345*

Requiem Sharks, *p. 340*

Mullets, *p. 660* Sablefishes, *p. 723* Silversides, *p. 519*

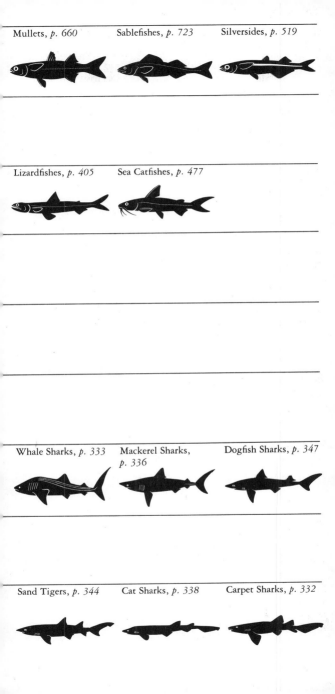

Lizardfishes, *p. 405* Sea Catfishes, *p. 477*

Whale Sharks, *p. 333* Mackerel Sharks, *p. 336* Dogfish Sharks, *p. 347*

Sand Tigers, *p. 344* Cat Sharks, *p. 338* Carpet Sharks, *p. 332*

The numbers preceding the species descriptions in the following pages correspond to the plate numbers in the color section. If the description has no plate number, it is illustrated by a drawing that accompanies the text.

JAWLESS FISHES
(Class Agnatha)

This class contains 2 orders, Myxiniformes, the hagfishes, and Petromyzontiformes, the lampreys. The most primitive living vertebrates, they are elongate and resemble eels. Some species reach a length of 3' (91 cm). Members of this class are easily recognized by their round, suctorial mouth without jaws. Agnathans do not have bones; the skeleton is formed of cartilage. They lack both scales and paired fins, and the primitive gill openings are in the form of paired gill slits or pores.

Hagfishes are found only in a marine environment. They are scavengers and often attack dying fishes caught in commercial nets.

Lampreys occur in freshwater and marine habitats, but spawn only in fresh water. The adults may be parasitic, but all larvae are filter-feeders. As the larvae mature into adults, they undergo a dramatic metamorphosis during which they may lose the filter-feeding apparatus, the mouth becomes round, and the fins grow larger.

Agnathans first appeared during the Ordovician Period, about 450 million years ago. Fossil agnathans differed from present forms in having the body covered with bony plates. There are approximately 65 living species.

Order Myxiniformes

These fishes have an eel-like body with a circular, suckerlike mouth that lacks jaws. Myxiniformes are primitive, cartilaginous fishes without scales, denticles, spines, or paired fins. There is a single family of these animals.

HAGFISHES
(Family Myxinidae)

These blind, primitive fishes have a wormlike body with a slightly rounded tail. They have 2 rows of broad-based, triangular teeth made of a horny material. All 3 species of hagfishes in North America occur in temperate oceans. Hagfishes locate their food by their sense of smell.

444 Pacific Hagfish
(*Eptatretus stouti*)

Description: To 25" (64 cm). Eel-like, elongate and cylindrical; dark brown, tan, gray, or brown, occasionally with patches of white on belly. *Eyes not visible;* 8 barbels; *10–14 gill pores on each side;* from tip of snout to first gill pore about one-quarter of length. Lacks paired fins; no rays or spines; caudal fin broad, rounded, composed of skin fold.

Habitat: Over mud from 10 to 520 fathoms.

Range: From SE. Alaska to Baja California.

Related Species: Black Hagfish (*E. deani*) has first gill pore closer to head; occurs in similar habitat from SE. Alaska to Isla Cedros, Baja California. Atlantic Hagfish (*Myxine glutinosa*) has single exterior connection to gill pouches; occurs in deep water in Atlantic from W. Greenland to North Carolina.

Similar Species: Pacific Lamprey (*Lampetra tridentata*) has only 7 gill pores; eyes visible.

Comments: The Pacific Hagfish enters the mouth or anus of larger fishes and feeds on the insides, leaving only the skin and bones. Each hagfish egg is enclosed in a horny capsule.

Order Petromyzontiformes

Members of this order are found in temperate and boreal marine and freshwater habitats. There is a single family in North America. Adults are characterized by an eel-like body without scales or paired fins, and a round suctorial mouth without jaws.

LAMPREYS
(Family Petromyzontidae)

The 17 species of lampreys in North America are characterized by having a cartilaginous skeleton, a single nostril between the eyes, and 7 pairs of gill pouches, each with a porelike outside opening. In adults, the round suctorial mouth has varying numbers of horny teeth. The larvae, or ammocoetes, are blind and lack teeth, but have a filter-feeding screen in the mouth.

41 Chestnut Lamprey
(*Ichthyomyzon castaneus*)

mouth

Description: To 15″ (38 cm). Eel-like; yellowish-olive above; sides, belly, and fins lighter. Eyes small; mouth without jaws, fringed, and when expanded, wider than head; numerous strong, slender teeth; innermost row usually has 4 lateral bicuspid teeth on each side; innermost tooth plate behind mouth opening curved, with 6–11 sharp cusps; tooth plate in front of mouth narrow with 2–3 cusps. No paired fins; *dorsal fin long with shallow notch. 49–56 muscle segments* between last gill opening and anus.

Habitat: Large rivers and reservoirs, ascending small rivers to large creeks to spawn.

Range: Lake Winnipeg, Red River, S. Manitoba; Lake Michigan; Wisconsin, Minnesota, south to E. Tennessee, NW. Georgia west to E. Texas.

Related Species: Silver Lamprey (*I. unicuspis*) has row of teeth with single cusp surrounding mouth; occurs in upper Mississippi River system and Great Lakes. Ohio Lamprey (*I. bdellium*) has mouth narrower than head; 52–62 muscle segments; lives in Ohio River basin.

Comments: A parasite, the adult Chestnut Lamprey attaches itself to the side of a fish with its sucker mouth, and uses its teeth to rasp a small wound through which it obtains body fluids.

40 Southern Brook Lamprey
(*Ichthyomyzon gagei*)

Description: To 7″ (18 cm). Eel-like, cylindrical; dark olive to brown above, lighter below; belly olive-yellow; fins yellowish. Mouth without jaws, narrower than head when expanded; row of teeth, *each with 2 cusps,* surrounding mouth. No paired fins; *dorsal fin long, with shallow notch; 50–56 muscle segments* between last gill opening and anus.

Habitat: Clear streams with moderate current; pools with riffles over sand and gravel.

Range: SE. Tennessee, W. Georgia, and W. Florida, west to Missouri and E. Texas.

Related Species: Northern Brook Lamprey (*I. fossor*) has row of teeth with single cusp around mouth; occurs in St. Lawrence River drainage west to Lake Winnipeg, south to S. Missouri, Kentucky.

Comments: The nonparasitic Southern Brook Lamprey feeds on microscopic plants.

37 Least Brook Lamprey
(Lampetra aepyptera)

mouth

Description: To 6″ (15 cm). Eel-like; back dark yellowish-brown, often with dark blotches, sides light tan, belly and fins yellowish. Eyes of moderate size; mouth without jaws, usually narrower than head when expanded; teeth poorly developed. No paired fins; *dorsal fin deeply notched, separated into 2 distinct parts. 54–62 muscle segments* between last gill opening and anus.

Habitat: Clear creeks with moderate current, and over sand in pools with organic debris and gravel riffles.

Range: Atlantic coastal plain from extreme SE. Pennsylvania to central North Carolina. SW. Pennsylvania, S. Ohio, and West Virginia west to SE. Missouri, south to Alabama and SE. Mississippi.

Related Species: American Brook Lamprey (*L. appendix*) grows to 12″ (30 cm), has 63–73 muscle segments between last gill opening and anus, and occurs over sand and gravel in clear streams in St. Lawrence River, Great Lakes, south to N. Alabama and NE. Arkansas; Atlantic Coast streams, S. New Hampshire south to S. Virginia.

Comments: Both of these lampreys are nonparasitic. The larval stage lasts for 2 to 3 years.

42, 442 Pacific Lamprey
(Lampetra tridentata)

Description: To 30″ (76 cm). Eel-like; marine coloration: adults steel-blue above, silvery below; freshwater coloration: brownish-red above, lighter below; larvae yellowish. Eyes large; mouth without jaws, broad tooth plate above mouth with 3 cusps, *4 pairs of lateral teeth*. No paired fins; *dorsal fin deeply notched, divided into 2 parts. 64–74 muscle segments* between last gill opening and anus.

Habitat: Close to shore; large inland streams.

Range: From Alaska south to S. California.

Related Species: River Lamprey (*L. ayresi*) grows to 12″ (30 cm); tooth plate above mouth opening with 2 cusps, 3 pairs of lateral teeth; occurs in similar habitat from S. Alaska to central California.

Similar Species: Pacific Hagfish (*Eptatretus stouti*) has 10–14 gill pores; eyes not visible.

Comments: The Pacific Lamprey is parasitic on various ocean fishes for 1 to 2 years. After maturing it ascends streams in the late spring and early summer, and spawns over a gravel nest, up to 2′ (61 cm) in diameter, in shallow water. Adults die soon after spawning. The larvae live in streams for 5 to 6 years before entering the ocean to become parasitic. They appear to have little impact on marine fish populations and do not feed when they move into streams to spawn.

38, 443 Sea Lamprey
(*Petromyzon marinus*)

Description: To 33″ (84 cm). Eel-like; olive-brown above, usually mottled yellowish-brown on sides, pale below; some have shades of red, blue, and green on sides, others blackish. Mouth without jaws, *with numerous rasplike teeth;* eyes small; 7 pairs of gill openings. Dorsal fins separated, distinct from caudal fin; no paired or anal fins. *67–74 muscle segments* between last gill opening and anus.

Habitat: At sea to 500 fathoms or more; along coasts, in estuaries and fresh water.

Range: From Gulf of St. Lawrence south to N. Florida and associated streams; Great Lakes.

Comments: The adult Sea Lamprey is parasitic. The larvae live on the bottom in silt and mud for up to 5 years.

CARTILAGINOUS FISHES
(Class Chondrichthyes)

These fishes have cartilaginous skeletons. They possess well-developed jaws, 5 to 7 pairs of gill openings, and paired fins supported by pectoral and pelvic girdles. Each pelvic fin on the male has a clasper, that is, a fingerlike appendage that facilitates internal fertilization. The pulp cavity of the toothlike scales is surrounded by dentine that is covered by enamel. Cartilaginous fishes include 3 groups: ratfishes, sharks, and the sawfishes, skates, and rays collectively known as batoids. There are 2 simple ways to distinguish sharks from batoids: (1) the gill openings of sharks are at least partly lateral and can be viewed from the side, while the gill openings of batoids are entirely ventral; (2) the pectoral fins of sharks are not attached to the gill openings, while the pectoral fins of batoids are fused to the side of the head and usually form some kind of disc-shaped body. Ratfishes are the only cartilaginous fishes that have a single gill opening on each side.

Cartilaginous fishes, unlike most bony fishes, lack a swim bladder, and must move constantly or sink to the bottom. They have a short intestine, but the surface area for the absorption of digested food is increased by internal spirals.

There are 627 species in this class in the world, 115 in North America, and they are predominantly marine.

Order Hexanchiformes

These sharks possess a single dorsal and a single anal fin. No spines are associated with the dorsal fin, which is located posteriorly. There are 6 or 7 pairs of gill slits and a spiracle. The eye lacks a nictitating membrane. There are 2 families in North America.

COW SHARKS
(Family Hexanchidae)

Members of this family have 6 or 7 gill slits, which are never continuous across the throat. The upper lobe of the caudal fin is elongate. There are 2 species in North America. Cow sharks are ovoviviparous, and the young provide for themselves from birth.

591 Sevengill Shark
(*Notorynchus maculatus*)

Description: To 9′ (2.7 m); 328 lbs (149 kg). Elongate, rounded in cross section; sandy-gray to reddish-brown with black spots. Head depressed, moderately pointed; mouth inferior; 7 *gill slits;* small spiracle present. Single dorsal fin near caudal fin; upper lobe of caudal fin long, about one-third of total length.

Habitat: Over soft bottoms, in bays, and off open coast to 25 fathoms.

Range: From N. British Columbia to Chile.

Related Species: Sixgill Shark (*Hexanchus griseus*) has only 6 gill slits; occurs in similar habitat in Atlantic from Cape Hatteras, North Carolina, to Cuba; in Pacific from N. British Columbia to Bahía de Todos Santos, Baja California.

Comments: A large female Sevengill Shark may bear up to 85 young at one time. These big sharks are considered prime game fishes by many anglers because of their fighting ability, and are sometimes harvested commercially.

Order Heterodontiformes

These sharks have 2 dorsal fins, each preceded by a spine, and an anal fin. They have 5 pairs of gill slits and a spiracle. The eye lacks a nictitating membrane. There is a single family in North America.

BULLHEAD SHARKS
(Family Heterodontidae)

These bottom-dwelling sharks occur in tropical and semitropical waters. They have elongate bodies and large, blunt heads. There is a single species in North America.

606 Horn Shark
(*Heterodontus francisci*)

Description: To 4′ (1.2 m). Elongate, tapering; brown to gray with *numerous dark spots*. Head large, blunt; front teeth small, pointed; rear teeth large, flat-surfaced. No nictitating membrane; mouth and nostrils connected by groove; 5 gill slits; spiracle present. *Each dorsal fin preceded by spine;* first dorsal located above middle of pectoral fins, second dorsal between pelvic fins and anal fin; upper lobe of caudal fin has square posterior profile.

Habitat: Shallow reefs and sandy bottoms to 82 fathoms.

Range: From Monterey Bay, California, to N. Gulf of California; not recorded from S. Gulf.

Similar Species: Spiny Dogfish (*Squalus acanthias*) lacks anal fin.

Comments: Horn Sharks deposit their eggs in grenade-shaped horny cases. These sharks are not desirable sport fishes. Divers off southern California find them easy to approach and thus good photographic subjects.

Order Squaliformes

These sharks, with 10 families on North American coasts, have 2 dorsal fins and 5 pairs of gill openings. Either dorsal spines or an anal fin may be present, but not on the same shark.

CARPET SHARKS
(Family Orectolobidae)

In these sharks, the 2 dorsal fins are of nearly equal size and lack spines; an anal fin is present; and the caudal fin is not lunate. The nostrils are connected to the mouth by a deep groove, and well-developed barbels are present. There is a single North American species, found on both coasts.

604 Nurse Shark
(Ginglymostoma cirratum)

Description: To 14′ (4.3 m). Elongate; grayish-brown or yellowish, darker above than below. Snout short, mouth under its tip; *well-developed barbel attached to front of each nostril.* 2 dorsal fins without spines, first not much larger than second; caudal fin low in profile. Skin appears exceptionally rough due to relatively large, closely spaced dermal denticles.

Habitat: Inshore, often on shallow sand flats, channels, and coral reefs.

Range: In Atlantic from Rhode Island south to

Gulf of Mexico and Brazil. In Pacific
from Gulf of California to Ecuador.

Comments: In North American waters, the Nurse
Shark is most abundant off the coasts
of southern Florida. Small fishes, sea
urchins, and a variety of crustaceans
make up its diet. This shark, thought
harmless to people, is too sluggish to
be actively pursued by anglers.

WHALE SHARKS
(Family Rhincodontidae)

These enormous filter-feeding sharks
are usually seen on the surface far
offshore. The checkered color pattern,
humpback, and large, lunate tail
distinguish the Whale Shark from all
other sharks. There is a single North
American species.

600 Whale Shark
(*Rhincodon typus*)

Description: To 60′ (18.3 m). Very large, elongate,
with 3 ridges on each side from head to
caudal peduncle; dark gray to brown on
back and sides, lower parts much
lighter, fading to yellow or white;
yellow or white spots between narrow
lines of same color result in *checkerboard-
like pattern*. Mouth broad and near end
of short snout; *gill openings very long and
wide*. Pectoral fins large, other fins
relatively small; 2 dorsal fins without
spines, first much larger; *caudal fin
large, lunate*.
Habitat: Open sea.
Range: In Atlantic from New York south to
Brazil, including Gulf of Mexico. In
Pacific from S. California south to Gulf
of California.
Similar Species: Basking Shark (*Cetorhinus maximus*)
lacks distinctive color pattern.
Comments: The Whale Shark, the largest fish in

the world, feeds on small crustaceans
and fishes that it gulps in mouthfuls
and strains with its branchial sieve.

SAND TIGERS
(Family Odontaspididae)

These sharks have 5 pairs of gill slits of
medium length, an anal fin, and 2
dorsal fins that are about equal in size.
The caudal fin is scarcely elevated.
These characteristics, coupled with the
long, tricuspid teeth, distinguish sand
tigers from all other sharks. There are 2
North American species.

601   Sand Tiger
(Odontaspis taurus)

Description: To 10′ (3 m). Elongate; light gray-
brown above, becoming paler on belly;
darker spots behind pectoral fins on
trunk and fins. *Teeth tricuspid, middle
cusp very long and pointed.* Pectoral fins
entirely behind fifth gill opening; 2

lower tooth

dorsal fins without spines, *about equal in
size,* first anterior to pelvic fins; anal fin
present; caudal fin low in profile.

Habitat: On or near the bottom in shallow
inshore waters.

Range: From Gulf of Maine to S. Brazil and
from W. Florida to Texas. Common
north of Cape Hatteras, but relatively
rare in Gulf of Mexico.

Related Species: Ragged-tooth Shark (*O. ferox*) has teeth
with 2 small cusps on each side of large
central cusp; occurs near surface of open
seas in Pacific off S. California.

Comments: The Sand Tiger has been known to
attack people. It is especially
interesting as an example of prebirth
cannibalism. A single embryo develops
in each uterus using nutrients it
obtains by consuming yolks and fellow
embryos.

THRESHER SHARKS
(Family Alopiidae)

These distinctive sharks have extremely long tails, measuring almost half of the total body length. A large dorsal fin is located about mid-body; the second dorsal fin is much smaller. Thresher Sharks have 5 pairs of gill openings, with the third to fifth openings located over the insertion of the pectoral fins. There are 2 species in North America.

Thresher Shark
(*Alopias vulpinus*)

Description: To 25′ (7.6 m). Elongate, greatest depth at pectoral fin; brown, gray, or black above and on undersurfaces of snout and pectoral fins; white below. *Eye diameter about half of snout length.* Pectorals long, sabrelike; first dorsal fin at mid-body, in front of pelvic fin insertion. *Long upper lobe of caudal fin about half total length of body.*

Habitat: Open sea.

Range: In Atlantic from Gulf of Maine to Florida and Gulf of Mexico; in Pacific from British Columbia to S. California.

Related Species: Bigeye Thresher (*A. superciliosus*) has eye diameter more than half of snout length; rear of first dorsal fin over pelvic fin insertion; occurs in similar habitat in Gulf of Mexico and on Pacific Coast south from San Clemente, California, to Gulf of California.

Comments: These sharks are viviparous; a brood consists of 2 to 4 young. Thresher Sharks feed on schooling fishes such as anchovies and herrings, and can use their tail to stun prey. Their flesh is considered by some people to rival swordfish in taste, and they are the target of a gill-net fishery established off southern California.

MACKEREL SHARKS
(Family Lamnidae)

These sharks have torpedo-shaped bodies and large teeth that are used to capture such prey as fishes, squids, and marine mammals. This family occurs worldwide, with 6 species in North America. It includes the White Shark, the most voracious of all the sharks, as well as the Basking Shark, one of the most benign species. The spiracle may be absent. The gill slits are long, and the fifth gill slit is located in front of the insertion of the pectoral fin. There is a distinct keel on the caudal peduncle, and the caudal fin lobes are almost equal in size.

597 White Shark
(*Carcharodon carcharias*)

upper tooth

lower tooth

Description: To 21' (6.4 m); 2,664 lbs (1208.3 kg). Elongate, fusiform; gray or brown above, dirty white below. Snout bluntly pointed; *teeth triangular and serrate. Origin of first dorsal fin above rear of pectorals;* anal fin beneath or behind second dorsal fin. Caudal peduncle has keel; caudal fin lunate, upper and lower lobes almost equal.

Habitat: Coastal surface waters.

Range: On Atlantic Coast south from S. Newfoundland to Brazil, including Gulf of Mexico; on Pacific Coast from Alaska south to Gulf of California.

Comments: White Sharks are ovoviviparous and the young are about 5' (1.5 m) long at birth. These savage predators feed on fishes, sea otters, seals, sea lions, and even crabs. This species is the most dangerous shark that occurs in North America and has attacked and killed humans on both the Atlantic and Pacific coasts. It is occasionally caught by commercial fishermen, and the flesh is reportedly quite palatable.

602 Basking Shark
(*Cetorhinus maximus*)

Description: To 45' (13.7 m). Fusiform; gray-brown
to totally gray or black, occasionally
lighter below. Snout short, nearly
conical, tip rounded; teeth very small,
conical. *Gill slits very long, nearly
meeting under throat;* gill rakers long,
horny, united at their bases, sometimes
absent. First dorsal fin located between
insertions of pectoral and pelvic fins;
caudal fin lunate, upper lobe slightly
larger than lower.

Habitat: Surface of open seas.

Range: In Atlantic from central Newfoundland
south to Florida during winter; in
Pacific from Gulf of Alaska to Gulf of
California.

Similar Species: Whale Shark (*Rhincodon typus*) has
distinctive checkerboard-like color
pattern and shorter gill slits.

Comments: Only the Whale Shark is larger than
this huge fish. Basking Sharks feed on
plankton using their large combs of
horny gill rakers. They have been
harvested by harpoon for their oil.

Shortfin Mako
(*Isurus oxyrinchus*)

Description: To 12'6" (3.8 m); 1,080 lbs (490 kg).
Slender, fusiform; snout sharply
pointed; back grayish-blue to deep
blue; belly white. *Teeth large, relatively
few, long, slender, smooth-edged, pointed
backward, with single cusp.* First dorsal
fin much larger than second, origin
behind inner corner of pectoral fin.

upper tooth

lower tooth

Origin of anal fin behind origin of
second dorsal. Caudal peduncle
depressed, with prominent keel on each
side extending onto caudal fin.

Habitat: Surface of open seas; often near shore.

Range: In Atlantic from Cape Cod to
Argentina, including Gulf of Mexico
and Caribbean; in Pacific from

Columbia River to Chile, including Gulf of California.

Comments: Shortfin Makos feed primarily on schooling fishes such as mackerels and herrings. Active and strong swimmers, they are famous for leaping out of the water when hooked or in pursuit of prey. They are potentially dangerous.

Porbeagle
(*Lamna nasus*)

upper tooth
lower tooth

Description: To 10′ (3 m); 465 lbs (211 kg). Fusiform but stout, tapering to strongly flattened caudal peduncle. Dark bluish-gray above, white on lower sides and below. *Snout conical, acutely pointed;* no spiracle. Teeth alike in both jaws, *each with 3 cusps, middle one long, slender, smooth-edged.* Second dorsal and anal fins small, opposite each other. Each side of anterior part of caudal fin with secondary keel below primary keel.

Habitat: Continental waters, from surface to 80 fathoms or more.

Range: From Gulf of St. Lawrence to New Jersey. Most common off Nova Scotia and in Gulf of Maine.

Related Species: Salmon Shark (*L. ditropis*) has shorter snout; dark blotches on lower sides in adults; occurs in similar habitat in Pacific from Bering Sea to San Diego, California.

Comments: The Porbeagle is also known as the Mackerel Shark because of the shape of its tail. Although a powerful swimmer, it does not put up much of a fight when hooked and is therefore of little interest to the angler.

CAT SHARKS
(Family Scyliorhinidae)

There are 5 species of these small bottom-dwelling sharks in North

America. They occur worldwide, but are most abundant in the western Pacific Ocean. They are among the most spectacularly marked sharks, with blotches, spotting, and vermiculations on their bodies. The fifth gill opening is located over the insertion of the pectoral fin. In most species the dorsal fins are far back on the body. The upper lobe of the caudal fin is longer than the lower.

605 Swell Shark
(*Cephaloscyllium ventriosum*)

Description: To 3'4" (1 m). Elongate, head wider than deep; *brown with dark spots and mottling.* Teeth very small, with multiple cusps. *First dorsal just behind pelvic fin insertion,* second directly above anal fin, dorsal and anal fin tips rounded; caudal fin upper lobe longer than lower.

Habitat: Shallow reefs and kelp beds in caves and crevices to depths of 250 fathoms.

Range: From Monterey Bay, California, to Gulf of California.

Related Species: Brown Cat Shark (*Apristurus brunneus*) brown body, black fin margins; occurs in deep water from SE. Alaska to N. Baja California. Filetail Cat Shark (*Parmaturus xaniurus*) grows to 24" (61 cm); lacks spots; has enlarged scales on anterior edge of caudal fin; occurs in deep water from Bodega Bay, California, to Gulf of California.

Comments: Swell Sharks are nocturnal foragers and eat decaying fishes and living organisms. They are oviparous, depositing each egg in a distinctive purse-shaped case, which is then attached to various objects by curling tendrils. These sharks swell up with water when disturbed in their crevices, making it difficult to remove them. They will bite if provoked, but their teeth are very small.

REQUIEM SHARKS
(Family Carcharhinidae)

Because they resemble each other so closely, many requiem sharks are difficult to identify. They have 2 dorsal fins, the first larger than the second, neither with spines. The upper lobe of the caudal fin is elongate and pointed upward. The teeth are bladelike cusps, and the cutting edges may be smooth or serrate. It is unusual for more than a single row of teeth to be functional at once. This is the largest family of sharks, containing 26 species that occur in North America. Most species are pelagic, although some occur close to shore. While some of the large species are dangerous, many others are harmless to people.

---

596 Bull Shark
(*Carcharhinus leucas*)

Description: To 11' (3.5 m). Fusiform, relatively robust; back grayish, belly white, tips of fins dusky in young. *Snout short, rounded, length less than width of mouth; teeth strongly serrate, those in upper jaw broadly triangular, in lower jaw slender.* No spiracle; no ridge between dorsal fins or keel on caudal peduncle. Pectoral fins large, broad, with pointed tips; first dorsal fin much larger than second, first dorsal fin origin in front of axil of pectoral fins.

upper tooth

lower tooth

Habitat: Inshore, never far from land. Ascends rivers for considerable distances.

Range: In Atlantic from New York to Rio de Janeiro, Brazil, including Bermuda, Gulf of Mexico, and Antilles; in Pacific from S. Baja California to Peru.

Comments: Bull Sharks are often caught on hook and line but do not rise to the surface and leap as do some of the other members of the family. Several attacks on humans have been reported.

594 Blacktip Shark
(*Carcharhinus limbatus*)

Description: To 8' (2.4 m). Moderately slender, fusiform; back gray, belly white; *tips of pelvic fins black,* other fin tips black, but color fades with age. Snout relatively long, pointed; no spiracle; *front teeth erect, sharp-pointed, serrate.* Gill openings moderately long. Pectoral fins falcate; dorsal fins without spines, first much larger than second; anal fin present.

Habitat: Coastal waters and offshore.

Range: In Atlantic from New England to S. Brazil, including Caribbean and Gulf of Mexico; in Pacific from Baja California and Gulf of California to Peru, including offshore islands.

Related Species: Spinner Shark (*C. brevipinna*) has sharper snout and smooth lower teeth; in similar habitat from North Carolina to Florida and E. Gulf of Mexico.

Comments: Both of these sharks are noted for their leaping and spinning antics. In pursuit of food or when hooked, they leap high and rotate on their long axis. They often swim in packs of 6 to 12.

Dusky Shark
(*Carcharhinus obscurus*)

Description: To 12' (3.6 m). Moderately slender, fusiform; blue-gray or lead-gray above, white below; pectoral fin grayish, darker at tips; pelvic and anal fins grayish-white. Snout short, length less than width of mouth, but greater than distance between inner corners of nostrils. Upper teeth broadly triangular, lower with narrow cusps, both serrate. *First dorsal fin relatively small, origin over inner corner of pectoral fin;* origin of second dorsal over or anterior to origin of anal fin. *Dermal ridge between dorsal fins.*

upper tooth
lower tooth

Habitat: Inshore and outer continental shelf.

Range: In Atlantic from Massachusetts to

Brazil, including Gulf of Mexico; in
Pacific from Redondo Beach,
California, to Gulf of California.

Comments: Potentially dangerous, Dusky Sharks
feed primarily on bottom-dwelling
fishes and smaller sharks.

595, 598   Sandbar Shark
(*Carcharhinus plumbeus*)

Description: To 8' (2.4 m). More robust than most
requiem sharks; brown to grayish-
brown above, lighter on sides, whitish
below; no conspicuous markings on
body or fins. Snout relatively short,
broadly rounded; teeth weakly serrate,
upper teeth broadly triangular, erect
but becoming increasingly oblique
toward corners of mouth; lower teeth
erect, slender, symmetrical. *First dorsal
fin large,* origin over axil of pectoral
fins; origins of second dorsal and anal
fins opposite each other. *Dermal ridge
on midline of back between dorsal fins.*

Habitat: Bottom-dwelling in shallow bays,
estuaries, and inshore.

Range: From Massachusetts to Brazil; more
common north of Cape Hatteras; less
frequent in Gulf of Mexico.

Comments: The Sandbar Shark feeds on a variety of
mollusks, crustaceans, and fishes, and,
due to its relatively small size, is not
known to be a threat to people.

---

603   Tiger Shark
(*Galeocerdo cuvieri*)

Description: To 18' (5.5 m); 1,780 lbs (807 kg).
Fusiform; gray or grayish-brown,
darker above than on sides; specimens
less than 6' long prominently marked
on back *with dark spots forming bars.*

upper tooth

lower tooth

Snout short, bluntly rounded, length
much shorter than width of mouth;
teeth alike in both jaws, deeply

notched and strongly serrate. *Small spiracle behind eye.* Dermal ridge on midline of back between dorsal fins, first dorsal much larger than second. *Caudal peduncle with dermal ridge on each side;* caudal fin falcate.

Habitat: Near surface in coastal and offshore waters.

Range: In Atlantic from Gulf of Maine to N. Argentina, including Gulf of Mexico, West Indies, and Caribbean. Most common in S. Florida and Cuba. In Pacific from S. California to Peru.

Comments: Tiger Sharks are voracious and omnivorous. The stomachs of captured specimens have been found to contain other sharks, fishes, porpoises, turtles, beef bones, dogs, tin cans, and garbage. They are dangerous to people, especially in the West Indies and Caribbean.

---

590 Soupfin Shark
(*Galeorhinus zyopterus*)

Description: To 6′ (1.8 m). Fusiform; dark bluish or dusky gray above, paler below, *anterior edges of dorsal fins black in adults.* Snout long, pointed, flattened; *spiracle present;* teeth notched, cusps directed toward corners of mouth. Origin of first dorsal behind rear of pectoral fin; second dorsal smaller, directly above anal fin. Upper lobe of caudal fin enlarged.

upper tooth
lower tooth

Habitat: In surface waters over soft bottoms.

Range: From N. British Columbia to Bahía de San Juanico, Baja California.

Similar Species: Blue Shark (*Prionace glauca*) has teeth long, pointed, without cusps; pectoral fin very long, narrow; first dorsal fin located well behind rear of pectoral fin.

Comments: These sharks may travel 35 miles a day and tend to move northward in the summer. Soupfin Sharks have been fished commercially for some years, with most of the catch going to fresh fish markets.

593   Blue Shark
(*Prionace glauca*)

Description: To 12'7" (3.8 m); 437 lbs (198 kg).
Very slender, fusiform; dark blue
above, bright blue on sides, white
below; tips of pectoral, dorsal, and
anal fins dusky. Snout long, narrowly
rounded, length longer than width of
mouth. Teeth serrate, triangular and
curved in upper jaw, narrower in lower
jaw. *Pectoral fins very long, narrow, and
somewhat falcate.* Dorsal fins relatively
small, no dermal ridge. Keel on caudal
peduncle weak; caudal fin falcate.

Habitat: In shallow coastal waters over sand or
mud, and far out at sea.

Range: In Atlantic from Nova Scotia to Gulf of
Maine, rarely to Chesapeake Bay,
disjunctly to Brazil. In Pacific from
S. Alaska to Chile.

Similar Species: Soupfin Shark (*Galeorhinus zyopterus*) has
notched teeth; anterior edges of dorsal
fins black in adults.

Comments: Blue Sharks are common and well
known to commercial fishers and
whalers. Ordinarily they feed on small
schooling fishes; however, they are
known to follow vessels for days feeding
on offal. They are not considered
dangerous to people.

599   Leopard Shark
(*Triakis semifasciata*)

Description: To 6'6" (2 m). Elongate, fusiform; *gray
with black spots and bars which may stretch
across back.* Snout moderately long,
pointed; fourth and fifth gill slits over
pectoral fin. First dorsal fin origin
above rear of pectoral fin; second dorsal
fin origin in front of anal fin.

Habitat: Over sand and mud in shallow bays to
depths of 50 fathoms.

Range: From Oregon to Mazatlán, Mexico,
including Gulf of California.

Related Species: Gray Smoothhound (*Mustelus*

californicus) lacks black spots; midpoint of first dorsal fin closer to insertion of pelvics than of pectorals; occurs in similar habitat from Cape Mendocino, California, to Mazatlán, Mexico. Smooth Dogfish (*M. canis*) with slate-gray or brown above, lacks markings; occurs on continental shelf in Atlantic from Cape Cod to Texas and Brazil, including Bermuda. Brown Smoothhound (*M. henlei*) lacks black spots and scales on posterior fifth of dorsal fins, red-brown to bronze above, silvery below; occurs in similar habitat from Coos Bay, Oregon, to Peru.

Comments: Leopard Sharks feed on fishes and crustaceans such as crabs and shrimps. These nomadic sharks are quite tasty, are very popular sport fishes, and form part of the commercial shark fishery.

HAMMERHEAD SHARKS
(Family Sphyrnidae)

The hammerheads are unique in having a greatly depressed and laterally expanded head. The position of the eyes, on the lateral expansion, gives the shark vision in all directions as well as better depth perception. The juvenile and young inhabit coastal waters, while adults of the larger species are primarily oceanic. They are voracious predators, and the biggest species are dangerous to people. There are 4 species in North America.

607 **Scalloped Hammerhead**
(*Sphyrna lewini*)

Description: To 13'9" (4.2 m). Elongate, compressed; head greatly expanded laterally, with eyes at each end of lateral expansion; gray above, white below. *Anterior margin of head with*

head

median indentation; corners of mouth in front of line drawn between rear corners of head. *Eye large, separated from nostril by distance equal to diameter of eye;* front of mouth on or near line drawn between eyes.

Habitat: In oceans near surface, sometimes in estuaries.

Range: From New Jersey south to S. Brazil, including Gulf of Mexico and Caribbean.

Related Species: Smooth Hammerhead (*S. zygaena*) lacks median indentation on head; eye and nostril closer together; occurs in similar habitat from Nova Scotia south to Florida, and off S. California.

Comments: Hammerhead sharks are usually found near the surface where they feed on fishes and squids. They are known to attack their own kind as well as people.

592 Bonnethead
(*Sphyrna tiburo*)

Description: To 4'6" (1.4 m). Elongate; gray or grayish-brown above, paler below. Head depressed, expanded laterally, with eyes at end of lateral expansions; *anterior margin rounded or bonnetlike, without indentations;* slightly concave opposite nostrils. Teeth smooth, cusps slanted in upper jaw, erect in lower jaw, becoming flattened in corners of both jaws.

head

Habitat: Shallow inshore waters, bays, and estuaries, usually over sand.

Range: In Atlantic from New England to N. Argentina, including Gulf of Mexico and Caribbean; in Pacific from S. California to Peru.

Comments: The Bonnethead, harmless to people, feeds on a variety of crustaceans, mollusks, and fishes. It is often caught on hook and line, and sometimes eaten.

DOGFISH SHARKS
(Family Squalidae)

Dogfish sharks lack an anal fin. Some species have a spine in front of each of the 2 almost equal-sized dorsal fins. All 5 gill openings are located in front of the pectoral fin insertion. There are no keels or precaudal pits on the caudal peduncle. The family contains 10 species in North America.

589 Spiny Dogfish
(*Squalus acanthias*)

Description: To 5' (1.5 m). Elongate, slender; gray or brown above, dirty white below; young have light spots on back. Snout long, pointed. *Spine in front of each dorsal fin;* origin of first dorsal fin slightly posterior to rear of pectorals; origin of second dorsal fin posterior to rear of pelvics. *Lacks anal fin;* upper lobe of caudal fin larger than lower, tip rounded.

Habitat: In temperate waters over soft bottoms, off coast to 200 fathoms.

Range: On Atlantic Coast from Newfoundland to North Carolina; a few stray to Cuba; on Pacific Coast from Bering Sea to central Baja California.

Related Species: Pacific Sleeper Shark (*Somniosus pacificus*) lacks spine in front of dorsal fins; first dorsal fin closer to insertion of pelvic fins; occurs in deep water from Bering Sea to Baja California.

Similar Species: Horn Shark (*Heterodontus francisci*) with brown-gray body and numerous dark spots; anal fin present.

Comments: The fully developed young are born in broods of 2 to 20 and average 8" to 12" (20 to 30 cm) long at birth. Tagging studies off California suggest that Spiny Dogfishes are migratory. Though they are an important food fish in Europe, these abundant sharks are considered pests in North America.

ANGEL SHARKS
(Family Squatinidae)

These bottom-dwelling sharks have disc-like bodies, with the large pectoral fins separated from the head by a deep groove. The 5 gill slits are in the groove and are not usually visible from above. Angel sharks have a large spiracle, an almost terminal mouth, and barbels. They possess 2 dorsal fins located near the caudal fin and a row of tubercles down the center of the back, but lack an anal fin. There are 2 species that occur in the temperate and tropical waters of either the Atlantic or Pacific oceans.

271 Pacific Angel Shark
(*Squatina californica*)

Description: To 5' (1.5 m). *Flattened, disc-like, but head, and pectoral and pelvic fins separate;* usually gray-brown above, with dark spots on back; underside white. Mouth terminal; barbels and spiracle present; 5 gills on sides in notch behind head. Dorsal fins behind rear of pelvic fins; caudal fin lobes about equal in size.

Habitat: Over sand and mud near reefs, from shallow water to 100 fathoms.

Range: From Washington to Gulf of California; occasional straggler to SE. Alaska.

Related Species: Atlantic Angel Shark (*S. dumerili*) has few reddish spots on underside; occurs over sand and mud from New England to S. Florida and N. Gulf of Mexico.

Comments: Pacific Angel Sharks usually lie partially buried in sand waiting for prey such as Queenfishes and California Halibuts. They are occasionally caught by anglers, but are not highly prized. A small commercial gill-net fishery has recently been developed to supply fish markets.

Order Rajiformes

All of these fishes have an easily recognizable shape. In skates and rays the trunk or body sector is greatly depressed, with the pectoral fins expanded to form a disc. Sawfishes and guitarfishes have a more robust, sharklike body. The tail is usually distinct from the body. A pair of spiracles and 5 pairs of gill openings are always present. None of these fishes have an anal fin. There are 7 families in North America.

SAWFISHES
(Family Pristidae)

These sharklike fishes have 2 well-developed dorsal fins. The most conspicuous feature is the saw, which is an extremely elongate, bladelike snout that is armed on both sides with large teeth. Sawfishes live close to shore, chiefly over sand or mud and seldom in water deeper than 30′ (9.1 m). They are known to ascend rivers. There are 2 species in North America.

608 Smalltooth Sawfish
(*Pristis pectinata*)

Description: To 18′ (5.5 m). Moderately depressed and shark-shaped, tail sector large and not distinct from body; color nearly uniform mousy-gray to blackish above, paler on sides, whitish below. Snout large, bladelike, *with 24 or more teeth on each side.* Pectoral fins not greatly expanded; *origin of first dorsal fin over pelvic fin insertion.* 2 dorsal fins about same size and shape. Caudal fin large and sharklike.

Habitat: Estuaries, lower parts of large rivers, and shallow coastal waters.

Range: From Chesapeake Bay to Brazil; Gulf of
Mexico; rarely north to New York.
Similar Species: Largetooth Sawfish (*P. perotteti*) has only
19 teeth on each side of snout; first
dorsal fin origin well ahead of pelvic fin
insertion; in shallower water from
Florida and Gulf of Mexico to Brazil.
Comments: Used to obtain food, the saw is slashed
from side to side among schooling
fishes, stunning or killing them.

GUITARFISHES
(Family Rhinobatidae)

The skate-like body of guitarfishes
retains some of the characteristics of
sharks. The body behind the pectoral
fins is robust, not depressed as in skates
and rays. The gill slits are on the
underside of the body. There are 2
dorsal fins and a large caudal fin. At
least 1 row of spines is usually found on
the midline of the back. There are 4
species in North America.

269 Thornback
(*Platyrhinoidis triseriata*)

Description: To 3' (91 cm). Skate-like, *disc wider
than long;* brown above, white below.
Front of head rounded; gills on
underside of disc. 3 rows of spines on
back of adults; 2 small dorsal fins
present; caudal fin squarish.
Habitat: Over sand and mud to 25 fathoms.
Range: From San Francisco, California, to
Thurloe Head, Baja California.
Related Species: Shovelnose Guitarfish (*Rhinobatos
productus*) has disc longer than wide;
median row of spines on back; occurs
from San Francisco, California, to Gulf
of California. Banded Guitarfish
(*Zapteryx exasperata*) has disc about as
wide as long; back with dark transverse
bands; occurs from Newport Beach,

California, to Panama. Both occur in similar habitat.

Similar Species: Round Stingray (*Urolophus halleri*) lacks dorsal fins and rows of spines on back.

Comments: Thornbacks eat sand-dwelling worms, snails, clams, crabs, and shrimps. They are ovoviviparous.

ELECTRIC RAYS
(Family Torpedinidae)

These rays stun their prey and protect themselves with 2 groups of specialized muscles located near the head that produce a powerful electric charge and can deliver over 200 volts. Members of this family have a disc-shaped body that is almost circular, and a well-developed caudal fin. Electric rays occur in all oceans from shallow bays to great depths; there are 3 species in North America.

272 Lesser Electric Ray
(*Narcine brasiliensis*)

Description: To 18″ (46 cm). Disc circular, depressed, thick, fleshy; grayish or brownish above, with scattered dark blotches, or rings of dark dots around blotches, especially in young; white below. *Anterior profile rounded;* outline of kidney-shaped electric organ visible beneath sides of head. Tail section thick, broad at base; 2 dorsal fins about equal size and shape; caudal fin well developed, rounded posteriorly. Skin naked.

Habitat: Inshore over bottom in surf zone to about 20 fathoms.

Range: From North Carolina to N. Argentina; Gulf of Mexico and Caribbean.

Comments: This species is reported to deliver 37 volts, but it is unlikely that the electric organs are used as an offensive weapon.

270 Pacific Electric Ray
(*Torpedo californica*)

Description: To 4'6" (1.4 m). Depressed, disc round, fused with head and pectoral fins; dark blue or gray-brown, often with black spots above, dirty white below. *First dorsal fin above pelvic fins,* second dorsal fin between caudal fin and rear of pelvic fins. Caudal fin large, rear profile nearly straight. Skin naked.

Habitat: Over mud and sand in shallow waters, and in kelp beds to 150 fathoms.

Range: From N. British Columbia to Bahía San Sebastián Vizcaino, Baja California.

Similar Species: Round Stingray (*Urolophus halleri*) lacks dorsal fins and has single long spine in front of caudal fin.

Comments: The Pacific Electric Ray feeds on fishes, such as halibuts and herrings, capturing its prey by stunning it with a powerful electric charge. These rays have shown aggressive behavior towards divers off California and may be dangerous.

273 Atlantic Torpedo
(*Torpedo nobiliana*)

Description: To 6' (1.8 m). Disc circular, *little wider than long, truncate in front,* depressed, thick, fleshy; brown, purplish, slate-gray to almost black above, white below. Electric organs visible as large kidney-shaped patches on sides of head. Tail sector thick, broad at base with 2 dorsal fins, *first dorsal fin partly posterior to pelvic fin,* larger than second; caudal fin well developed, truncate. Skin naked.

Habitat: On mud or sand to 60 fathoms.

Range: From Nova Scotia to Florida and N. Gulf of Mexico.

Comments: Owing to its large size, the Atlantic Torpedo can produce 220 volts of electricity, but has not been known to seriously injure humans.

SKATES
(Family Rajidae)

These fish have a flattened, disc-like body formed by the large wings that are shaped by the pectoral fins and attached to the head and body. The wings are used for propulsion. The dorsal, anal, and caudal fins are much reduced in size or absent. There are large thorns on the midline of the back, and males possess long, prominent claspers used in mating. Skates spend their time on the bottom partially buried in the mud or sand. There are 21 species in North America.

265 Big Skate
(*Raja binoculata*)

Description: To 8′ (2.4 m). Depressed, almost rhomboid; *front of disc concave;* olive-brown or gray above, whitish below; *ocellus on each side of disc.* Moderate thorns between eyes; 1 mid-dorsal thorn behind spiracles; single row of mid-dorsal thorns to front of first dorsal fin; thorns become more apparent as fish ages.

pelvic fin

Habitat: Over soft bottoms from depths of 10′–360′ (3–110 m).

Range: From Bering Sea to Bahía de San Quintín, Baja California.

Related Species: There are 5 other species found in similar habitat on the Pacific Coast: California Skate (*R. inornata*) has orbital thorns; anterior edge of disc slightly convex; snout pointed; occurs from Strait of Juan de Fuca to Bahía Tortugas, Baja California. Sandpaper Skate (*R. kincaidi*) lacks orbital thorns, has thorn on shoulder in center of disc on each side of midline; occurs from Alaska to Cortez Banks, California. Longnose Skate (*R. rhina*) has deeply concave anterior edge of disc; pelvic fins deeply notched; occurs from SE.

pelvic fin

Alaska to central Baja California. Starry Skate (*R. stellulata*) has small ocelli; both surfaces covered with thorns; anterior edge of disc convex; occurs from Bering Sea to Coronado Bank, Baja California. Roughtail Skate (*R. trachura*) lacks large thorns on disc; black or dark gray above and below; occurs from Bering Sea to N. Baja California from 400 to 738 fathoms.

Comments: Big Skates are occasionally captured by anglers but are rarely retained. They form a minor portion of the commercial trawl catch, but only the wings are used for food.

---

263 Clearnose Skate
(*Raja eglanteria*)

Description: To 3′1″ (94 cm). Disc rhombic, depressed, wider than long, angle of snout about 100°, broadly rounded posteriorly; light to dark brown above with darker brown or black roundish spots and irregular bars, white below; *sides of snout translucent; no ocellar spots.* Thorns on shoulder region near eye and spiracle; single row of thorns along midline of back. Dorsal fins separate, same size and shape. Entire tail thorny; half of total length.

Habitat: Shallow shores.

Range: From Massachusetts to Florida and N. Gulf of Mexico.

Related Species: Rosette Skate (*R. garmani*) has scattered spots forming rosette pattern; disc has broadly rounded outer corners; occurs at 20–325 fathoms from Massachusetts to Nicaragua, including Gulf of Mexico but not West Indies. Barndoor Skate (*R. laevis*) has much broader disc; snout sharply pointed; pigmented mucous pores on lower surface; occurs from Newfoundland to Florida.

Comments: More common inshore during warm months, this skate moves into deeper water in winter.

266 Little Skate
(*Raja erinacea*)

Description: To 21″ (53 cm). Disc broadly rounded laterally and posteriorly, depressed, about as wide as long; gray to dark brown above, *usually with small irregular spots on disc;* pale below, without spots. Angle of snout about 120°; usually less than 54 series of upper teeth, never more than 66. Thorns on midline of disc between spiracles and tail, arranged in 3 or more rows. 2 dorsal fins of same size and shape, separated by narrow space lacking thorns; tail little more than half of length, with 2 or more rows of thorns.

Habitat: Shallow shore water over sand or gravel to about 80 fathoms.

Range: From Gulf of St. Lawrence to North Carolina.

Related Species: Winter Skate (*R. ocellata*) has ocellar spots on upper surface; usually 90–100 series of teeth in upper jaw; occurs in same habitat and range.

Comments: These skates feed on a variety of crustaceans, as well as clams, squids, and worms. They spawn in relatively shallow water, and the leathery egg case is partially buried in hard sand.

264 Roundel Skate
(*Raja texana*)

Description: To 24″ (61 cm). Disc greatly depressed, broader than long, outer corners abruptly rounded, anterior margins concave on sides of snout and opposite eyes and spiracles. Brownish above, with *conspicuous, round, dark ocellar spot on each side of dorsal midline;* sides of snout translucent; lower surface white. Single row of thorns on midline of disc. 2 dorsal fins separate, *thorns in intervening space.*

Habitat: Shallow waters over sand or mud.

Range: From W. Florida west to Texas.

Related Species: Ocellate Skate (*R. ackleyi*) is broadly
rounded, with oval ocellar spots; occurs
in same habitat in S. Florida and Mexico.

Comments: The Roundel Skate is frequently found
in shrimp trawls in the Gulf of Mexico.

STINGRAYS
(Family Dasyatidae)

Stingrays have a greatly depressed disc
with a tail that is distinct from the
body. The pectoral fins extend forward
beyond the mouth, and the dorsal fin is
absent. Some species have a fold of skin
on the tail. Tubercles or prickles are
present on some species, especially on
the dorsal midline of the disc. Rays in
the genera *Dasyatis* and *Urolophus* have
a long whiplike tail with a poisonous
spine. These rays are potentially
dangerous to swimmers and waders as
they can inflict wounds characterized
by intense pain and slow recovery. To
prevent an encounter with a ray, shuffle
your feet as you walk through the water
so you nudge the ray on the side or
from underneath: it is likely to swim
away. Stingrays stir the bottom with
their pectoral fins in order to dislodge
worms, mussels, and small crustaceans
on which they feed. There are 11
species in North America.

267 Southern Stingray
(*Dasyatis americana*)

Description: To 5′ (1.5 m) wide. Disc roughly
rhombic in shape; *outer corners sharply
rounded; anterior edges of disc nearly
straight.* Upper surface light brown,
gray, or olive, varies depending on
surroundings; lower surface whitish
with gray or brownish margins; ridge
and cutaneous fold of tail dark brown.
Lacks dorsal fin; long, whiplike tail

with spine near base; cutaneous fold on underside of tail about as deep as tail diameter; no conspicuous tubercles on tail.

Habitat: Near shores and in bays.

Range: From New Jersey to Brazil; rare north of Cape Hatteras; Gulf of Mexico and Caribbean.

Related Species: Roughtail Stingray (*D. centroura*) attains greater size, has conspicuous tubercles on disc and tail; occurs from Massachusetts to Florida. Diamond Stingray (*D. dipterura*) has diamond-shaped disc; whiplike tail lacks caudal fin; occurs from British Columbia to Paito, Peru. Both in similar habitat.

tail tubercle

Comments: These stingrays lie partly buried in the sand with only the eyes, spiracle, and tail exposed. Stingrays can inflict serious wounds with the tail spine.

262 Smooth Butterfly Ray
(*Gymnura micrura*)

Description: To 3′ (91 cm) wide. *Disc very broad, more than 1.5 times wider than long;* gray, brown, light green, or purplish above, with individual dots or wavy lines; tail has several dark bars; lower surface white, outer edges grayish; shading changes with surroundings. Lacks dorsal fin; *tail very short, no spine.*

Habitat: Near shore over sand in shallow water.

Range: From Massachusetts south to Brazil, including Gulf of Mexico and Caribbean. Not common north of Chesapeake Bay.

Related Species: Spiny Butterfly Ray (*G. altavela*) has tail spine and tentacle-like structure on posterior edge of spiracle; occurs over sand in shallow water south from Massachusetts to N. Argentina. California Butterfly Ray (*G. marmorata*) has short tail with spine; occurs from shore to about 30 fathoms, from Pt. Conception, California, south to Peru.

Comments: The Smooth Butterfly Ray is harmless

since it lacks a tail spine. Individuals reported to be 5 to 6′ (1.5 to 1.8 m) wide are probably another species.

268 Round Stingray
(*Urolophus halleri*)

Description: To 22″ (56 cm) long. *Disc almost circular;* tail shorter than disc; gray-brown above, sometimes with small, light spots, yellow below. Lacks dorsal fin; *long, venomous spine about halfway down tail.*

Habitat: Over sand or mud in shallow bays and off coast to 70′ (21 m).

Range: From Humboldt Bay, California, to Panama Bay.

Related Species: Yellow Stingray (*U. jamaicensis*) has variable coloration above: greenish or brownish lines, vermiculations, bands, or spots; occurs in same habitat from North Carolina to N. South America.

Similar Species: Thornback (*Platyrhinoidis triseriata*) has 2 dorsal fins and 3 rows of tubercles on back of adults. Pacific Electric Ray (*Torpedo californica*) has 2 dorsal fins and lacks venomous spine on tail.

Comments: All stingrays are ovoviviparous, the young developing within the female. Concentrations of them occasionally make some beaches in California unsafe for swimmers, as their venomous spine can cause painful wounds.

EAGLE RAYS
(Family Myliobatidae)

These rays have a robust body with roughly falcate pectoral fins, and the entire disc is wider than it is long. The anterior parts of the pectoral fins form 1 or 2 lobes, called subrostral lobes, under the snout. The eyes and spiracles are on the sides of the head, which is separate from the rest of the disc. The long tail is distinct from the body, and on its base is a fleshy dorsal fin, behind which is a venomous spine. There are 5 species in North America.

256 Spotted Eagle Ray
(*Aetobatus narinari*)

Description: To 9′ (2.8 m) wide. Disc broader than long; head distinct from body; tail very long and whiplike; dorsal fin and, usually, 2 spines at tail base. *Upper surface gray, olive-gray, or chestnut brown with whitish, yellowish, or bluish spots, variable in size and shape;* lower parts white. Eyes and spiracle dorso-lateral; teeth in both jaws like large, flat plates, arranged in single series. Pectoral fins taper to acute point, more or less falcate. Skin smooth.

upper tooth plate

lower tooth plate

Habitat: Coastal surface waters.

Range: From Chesapeake Bay to Brazil; Gulf of Mexico and Caribbean; abundant in E. Florida and Antilles.

Comments: Spotted Eagle Rays are solitary, and are found in large schools only when spawning and migrating. They are capable of sustaining long-distance travel. They are graceful swimmers and look as if they are flying through the water. When pursued, they make spectacular leaps into the air.

258 Bat Ray
(*Myliobatis californica*)

Description: To 6′ (1.8 m) wide. Disc diamond-shaped, wider than long, wings long, blunt-pointed; brown, olive, or black above, white below. *Head and eyes extend beyond front of disc.* Tail whiplike, with 1 or more spines at base. Skin smooth.

Habitat: Shallow, sandy areas in bays and on coast to 25 fathoms; kelp beds.

Range: From Oregon to Gulf of California.
Comments: Anglers consider Bat Rays excellent
fighters, but few are kept for eating.
The young develop within the female
and are released in late summer and
fall. The venomous tail spines can cause
a painful injury.

257, 261   Cownose Ray
(*Rhinoptera bonasus*)

Description: To 3' (91 cm) wide. Disc about 1.7
times wider than long; front edges
nearly straight, posterior edges of disc
concave, outer corners falcate. Brownish
above, whitish or yellowish-white
below. Front of head moderately
concave; *subrostral fin deeply notched in
middle, forming 2 lobes joined at base;*
subrostral lobes
head and subrostral lobes form shape
resembling cow's nose. Tooth plates,
usually of 7 series of teeth, in each jaw.
Tail spine immediately behind dorsal
tooth plate
fin; skin smooth.
Habitat: Primarily bottom of shallow bays and
inshore shelf.
Range: From New England to Brazil;
Caribbean and Gulf of Mexico.
Comments: Cownose Rays feed primarily on hard-
shelled mollusks that they crush with
their powerful tooth plates. They
sometimes occur in schools in bays
during the summer and disappear in
the winter. Their stinging spines make
them potentially dangerous.

**MANTAS
(Family Mobulidae)**

In contrast to eagle rays, mantas lack
large tooth plates. They also have the
anterior subdivisions of the pectoral fins
modified as 2 separate fins, known as
cephalic fins, located on the head. The
posterior edges of the pectoral fins are

falcate. Mantas have a branchial sieve apparatus and a small dorsal fin on the tail sector, but the 5 species found in North American waters lack a spine. Mantas occur in tropical and warm to temperate areas, and feed on large planktonic crustaceans or schools of small fishes that they strain with their branchial sieve.

259, 260 Atlantic Manta
(*Manta birostris*)

Description: To 22' (6.7 m) wide. Disc about twice as broad as long; upper surface varying from reddish to olive-brown to black, paler on edges. Shoulders uniform in color or with white patches or series of dark spots across them; lower surface blotched slate-gray or black. *Cephalic fins large, widely set, forward-directed, and hornlike; mouth terminal, teeth only in lower jaw.* Pectoral fins falcate. Tail relatively short; no spine at base.

Habitat: Offshore in deep water to within few miles of land.

Range: From North Carolina south to Brazil; occasionally to New England. Common in Bermuda and Gulf of Mexico.

Comments: Mantas are pelagic and are only seen when leaping out of the water or basking on the surface. The cephalic fins are used for steering and to direct food into the mouth. Regardless of their size, mantas are harmless to man.

Order Chimaeriformes

Ratfishes share many of the characteristics of sharks and rays, including a cartilaginous skeleton and a ventral mouth. They have a single gill opening on each side and the first dorsal fin is preceded by a spine. A single family occurs in North America.

CHIMAERAS
(Family Chimaeridae)

Ratfishes have a short, rounded snout and a long, pointed caudal fin. The second dorsal fin extends from just in front of the pelvic fins almost to the origin of the caudal fin. Males have a club-shaped process on the head just in front of the eyes. Ratfishes are entirely marine, and most occur offshore at great depths. There is a single species in North America.

609 Spotted Ratfish
(*Hydrolagus colliei*)

Description: To 3′2″ (96 cm). Elongate, head large, tapering to slender caudal fin; bronze above, with metallic hues, silvery below with numerous white spots; eyes green. Teeth pliable, incisorlike. Males have spiny, club-shaped process on head, sharp retracting clasping organs in front of pelvic fins, and slender claspers with expanded ends adjacent to each pelvic fin base. *First dorsal preceded by long, venomous spine; second dorsal has undulating outline.* Lateral line wavy, several branches on the head; no scales.

Habitat: Over soft bottoms to 500 fathoms.

Range: From SE. Alaska to Bahía San Sebastián Vizcaino, Baja California; isolated populations found in upper Gulf of California.

Comments: Ratfishes deposit their eggs, which are fertilized internally, in elongate, ridged, brown cases during the late summer. These distinctive fishes feed on clams, crabs, shrimps, and fishes. They are not sought by either sport or commercial fishers. Care should be taken in handling a Ratfish, as the venomous spines can cause a painful wound, and the clasping organs are quite sharp.

BONY FISHES
(Class Osteichthyes)

As their name implies, bony fishes have skeletons that are at least partially composed of bone. They have a single pair of gill openings, and most have a swim bladder or functional lung. The eggs and embryos are never enclosed in cases, and fertilization of the eggs is usually external.

This class contains most of the known marine and freshwater fishes. This group of fishes is the most valuable to people because of the large number of them that support commercial and recreational fisheries. Some fishes, such as the gobies, may live for less than a year, while others, such as some rockfishes and groupers, may live over 100 years.

This class, usually considered to be the most recent in evolutionary terms, first appeared in the Jurassic Period. Many species have become so specialized that they face extinction when some aspect of their habitat is threatened.

Bony fishes are separated into 4 major groups, but only one of these, the ray-finned fishes, occurs in North American waters. These fishes are characterized by having fins with soft rays or spines as supports. There are about 18,130 species in this class.

Order Acipenseriformes

Sturgeons and paddlefishes, forming the 2 families of this order in North America, are among the largest freshwater fishes, and are the remnants of an ancient and primitive group. They have a largely cartilaginous skeleton, an upper jaw that does not articulate with the skull, and a heterocercal tail.

STURGEONS
(Family Acipenseridae)

This family includes anadromous and freshwater fishes, and has 7 species in North America. Sturgeons are large fishes with a comparatively elongate snout. They have 5 rows of bony plates on the body (1 dorsal, 2 lateral, and 2 ventrolateral); scalelike plates on the skin between the bony plates; a head covered by bony plates; a ventral mouth without teeth; 4 barbels anterior to the mouth; and dorsal and anal fins located on the rear third of the body. Females are usually larger and mature later than males.

31 Lake Sturgeon
(*Acipenser fulvescens*)

Description: To 8' (2.4 m); 310 lbs (140.6 kg).
Elongate; dark olive to gray above, sides lighter, often reddish; off-white to yellowish below. Snout rounded above, flattened below; 4 barbels anterior to mouth; *lower lip with 2 smooth lobes;* mouth without teeth; *spiracles present above and behind eyes.* 5 rows of bony plates: 8–17 dorsal plates, 29–43 lateral, 6–12 ventrolateral; in young, bony plates with sharp spine, adjacent plates usually touching; in adults,

ventral head view

plates separated, small, more rounded. Caudal peduncle short, roundish, incompletely armored; tail heterocercal.

Habitat: Over clean bottom of firm sand, gravel, or rocks in rivers and lakes.

Range: Lower Hudson Bay west to S. Alberta; S. Canada; St. Lawrence River, Great Lakes; Mississippi River system south to Arkansas; Coosa River, Alabama.

Comments: The Lake Sturgeon is probably the largest freshwater fish in North America; the record catch, in Lake Superior in 1922, measured 7′11″ (2.4 m). They can live to be very old; one fish 154 years old and weighing 208 pounds (94.3 kg), was caught in Lake of the Woods in 1953. The population of the Lake Sturgeon has been greatly reduced by exploitation, dams, and pollution.

33, 588 White Sturgeon
(*Acipenser transmontanus*)

Description: To 12′6″ (3.8 m); 1,387 lbs (630 kg). Elongate, rounded in cross section, head slightly flattened; gray above, lighter below. Snout short, broad, pointed; mouth ventral, below eye; 4 long barbels near tip of snout. *38–48 midlateral plates.* Tail heterocercal.

Habitat: Over soft bottoms in ocean; in deep pools of large rivers.

Range: In Pacific from Gulf of Alaska south to N. Baja California; in fresh water south only to Sacramento River, N. California.

Related Species: Green Sturgeon (*A. medirostris*) has long snout, concave in profile, 4 barbels closer to mouth than to tip of snout; 23–30 sharp bony lateral plates; occurs from Gulf of Alaska south to N. Baja California. Atlantic Sturgeon (*A. oxyrhynchus*) has 24–35 lateral plates along midside; occurs from Labrador to Louisiana. Both in similar habitat.

Comments: White Sturgeons spawn in rivers

during the spring. Males do not mature until they are 11 to 22 years old; females mature between 11 and 34 years. These large game fish feed on small fishes such as Eulachon, and crustaceans, and mollusks. Sturgeons are highly regarded both commercially, for their caviar and meat, and for sport.

30, 32 Shovelnose Sturgeon
(*Scaphirhynchus platorynchus*)

Description:

ventral head view

To 3′ (91 cm); 7 lbs (3.2 kg). Elongate, *bony plates sharply keeled;* olive to yellowish-brown above, sides lighter, white below. *Bony head plates with short spines* at tip of snout and anterior to eye; snout shovel-shaped; *bases of 4 barbels in straight line; lower lip with 4 papillose lobes; no spiracles.* 5 rows of bony plates: 14–19 dorsal plates, 38–47 lateral, 10–14 ventrolateral. Caudal peduncle long, depressed, fully armored; tail heterocercal, upper lobe with long, threadlike filament.

Habitat: Channels of large, turbid rivers with moderate current over firm sand or gravel.

Range: Ohio, Mississippi, Missouri rivers; Mobile Bay drainage, Alabama; Rio Grande in Texas and New Mexico.

Related Species: Pallid Sturgeon (*S. albus*) has shorter inner barbels, their bases anterior to outer barbels; belly without small scalelike plates; occurs in Mississippi River, from Illinois south to Louisiana; Missouri River from Montana to Missouri.

Comments: The Shovelnose is the smallest and most common sturgeon in North America, rarely exceeding 3′ (91 cm) in length. It is becoming less common, but is part of the commercial fishery industry along the Mississippi and Missouri rivers.

PADDLEFISHES
(Family Polyodontidae)

This family, confined to fresh water, is represented by 2 genera, each with a single species. One occurs in the Mississippi River system and the other in the Yangtze River of China. The Paddlefish is probably the most distinctive of all North American fishes in having the snout prolonged and expanded into a thin, flat paddle. The body is covered with smooth skin that is similar in appearance to freshwater catfishes.

29 Paddlefish
(*Polyodon spathula*)

Description: To 7′1″ (2.2 m); 200 lbs (90.7 kg). Slightly compressed; *snout paddle-shaped;* back dark bluish-gray, often mottled, lighter on sides, belly white. *Mouth very large;* eyes small, above front edge of mouth; gill rakers slender, numerous; *opercular flap large, tapering, extending to pelvic fins. Caudal fin deeply forked,* lobes about equal. Scales only on caudal peduncle.

Habitat: Backwaters, sluggish pools, bayous, oxbows of large rivers, impoundments, and lakes.

Range: Throughout Mississippi River system; Mobile Bay drainage, Alabama, west to E. Texas; early records from few localities in Lakes Superior, Michigan, Huron, and W. Lake Erie.

Comments: Paddlefishes are large, reaching lengths of 7′ 1″ (2.2 m), weighing 200 pounds (90.7 kg), and living up to 30 years. They are caught by snag fishing during spawning in April and June, when they congregate below obstructions (dams) and on gravel shoals. Paddlefishes have declined recently due to pollution, channelization, dams, and intensive fishing. They are deemed good eating.

Order Semionotiformes

Gars are long, slender, predaceous fishes covered with interlocking, thick, hard, diamond-shaped ganoid scales, which protect them from most predators. The single family in North America is predominantly freshwater, but some members enter brackish and marine waters.

GARS
(Family Lepisosteidae)

Extremely hardy, gars typically inhabit quiet, weedy, often stagnant, backwater areas. They are characterized by elongate jaws with needlelike teeth; a vascularized swim bladder to permit aerial respiration; a dorsal fin placed posteriorly on the body above the anal fin; an abbreviated heterocercal tail, rounded in shape; and ganoid scales. There are 5 species in North America.

26 Spotted Gar
(*Lepisosteus oculatus*)

Description: To 3' (91 cm); 8 lbs (3.6 kg). Cylindrical; brown to olive above, sides lighter; *head, body, and all fins with olive-brown to black spots;* belly whitish; young with dark mid-dorsal and midlateral stripe. *Snout short, less than twice as long as rest of head;* teeth in upper jaw in single row; bony plates on isthmus. Caudal fin short, rounded. Scales thick, diamond-shaped, 53–59 *in lateral line.*

Habitat: Clear pools with aquatic plants in streams, swamps, and lakes; may enter brackish water along Gulf Coast.

Range: Lake Erie and S. Lake Michigan drainages; Mississippi River drainage from Illinois south to E. Oklahoma,

E. Tennessee; Gulf Coast streams from W. Florida to central Texas.

Related Species: Florida Gar (*L. platyrhincus*) lacks bony plates on isthmus; occurs in sluggish streams, canals, and lakes with vegetation in S. Georgia and Florida east of Apalachicola River drainage.

Comments: Spotted Gars spawn in shallow water over vegetation during the spring. The hatched larvae of all gars have an adhesive pad on the upper jaw, by which they attach themselves to plants.

25, 28 Longnose Gar
(*Lepisosteus osseus*)

Description: To 6′ (1.8 m); 50¼ lbs (22.8 kg). Cylindrical; dark olive to brownish above, lighter on sides with dark spots, usually on posterior, belly whitish. Median fins yellowish-brown with many dark spots; young with dark mid-dorsal and midlateral stripe. *Snout very long, more than twice as long as rest of head;* teeth large, in 1 row on upper jaw. Caudal fin short, rounded. Scales thick, diamond-shaped, *60–64 in lateral line.*

Habitat: Backwaters, large creeks, lakes, and reservoirs; may enter brackish water; near aquatic vegetation when young.

Range: St. Lawrence River drainage; along Atlantic Coast from south of New Jersey to Orlando, Florida; S. Great Lakes and Mississippi River system, south to Rio Grande drainage in Texas.

Comments: The Longnose Gar is considered a nuisance by fishers because it feeds on game fishes and damages gill nets. It may provide sport, but is rarely eaten, and the roe is poisonous. In summer, Longnose Gars can often be observed lying motionless near the surface of quiet water.

27 **Alligator Gar**
(*Lepisosteus spatula*)

Description:	To 10′ (3 m); 302 lbs (137 kg). Cylindrical; dark brown above, occasionally spotted, yellowish below. *Snout short, broad, length of jaw shorter than remainder of head; teeth large, 2 rows on each side of upper jaw.* Median fins with few dark spots; young with light mid-dorsal stripe from tip of snout to upper base of caudal fin, bordered by dark lateral stripes. Caudal fin short, rounded. *58–62 lateral line scales.*
Habitat:	Large rivers, sluggish lakes, bayous, and reservoirs; in coastal areas frequently enters brackish and marine waters.
Range:	Ohio River west from SW. Ohio; Mississippi River south from Illinois; Gulf Coastal plain from W. Florida to Veracruz, Mexico.
Related Species:	Shortnose Gar (*L. platostomus*) has jaw longer than remainder of head; head, and pectoral and pelvic fins with dark spots; occurs in backwaters and pools of streams of Mississippi River system in S. Ohio, Wisconsin, and E. Montana south to Louisiana.
Comments:	The Alligator Gar is one of the largest freshwater fishes. In some areas it is fished commercially and by anglers. There are unverified reports of attacks on humans.

Order Amiiformes

This order of ancient and highly predaceous fishes is represented by a single family, the bowfins. There is a single species, *Amia calva*, which is restricted to the fresh waters of eastern North America.

BOWFINS
(Family Amiidae)

Bowfins are a transitional group, related to the gars but possessing some characteristics of teleost (bony) fishes. For example, the primitive skeleton consists of bone and cartilage, but its vertebrae are amphicoelous (concave at each end), a characteristic of bony fishes. Other features include the abbreviated heterocercal tail, rounded in shape, thin bony plates covering the head, and a bony gular plate. A single species occurs in North America.

44 Bowfin
(*Amia calva*)

Description: To 34" (86 cm); 21½ lbs (9.8 kg). Long, moderately robust, head massive; dark olive-green above with lighter color on sides, often producing netlike pattern; cream to greenish-yellow below. *Nostrils tubular;* maxilla extends beyond eye; jaws with numerous teeth. Fins dark olive to greenish; pectoral and pelvic fins small, rounded; *dorsal fin single, long, 42–53 rays;* 9–12 anal fin rays; *caudal fin rounded,* upper base in males has dark spot and yellow to orange halo. Lateral line complete.

Habitat: Quiet, usually clear waters of low gradient, sluggish streams, swamps, and oxbow lakes with vegetation.

Range: Lake Champlain, St. Lawrence River west through Great Lakes; Mississippi River system, Minnesota to Texas; Long Island; Coastal Plain, S. Pennsylvania to Florida, west to Texas.

Comments: The Bowfin, also called mudfish, dogfish, and grinnel, is often thought of as a pest since it consumes the same food items as game fishes. It spawns in early spring in shallow waters where the male clears vegetation and excavates

a shallow nest. After spawning, the
male protects the eggs until they hatch
and guards the young for several weeks.
The Bowfin is one of the hardiest of
North American freshwater fishes.

Order Elopiformes

The Elopiformes are silvery, elongate
fishes. None of the fins have spines.
The pelvic fins are abdominal and the
pectorals are inserted below the axis of
the body. The single, short dorsal fin is
located above the middle of the body.
There are 2 families in North America.

TARPONS
(Family Elopidae)

These silvery, herring-like fishes have
either elongate, fusiform bodies, as in
Elops, or compressed and moderately
deep bodies, as in *Megalops.* Their
pelvic fins are abdominal, and both
pectoral and pelvic fins have a large
axillary scale. They have a single, short
dorsal fin, no adipose fin, and a deeply
forked caudal fin. The young pass
through a leptocephalus stage similar to
that of eels. The 3 species of tarpons
in North America are widely
distributed in warm, shallow coastal
waters, bays, estuaries, rivers, and
freshwater lakes.

579 Machete
(*Elops affinis*)

Description: To 3′ (91 cm); 10 lbs (4.5 kg). Very
elongate, slender, compressed; silvery
above and below. Snout pointed;
mouth terminal, *maxilla extends well
behind eye.* Pelvic fins abdominal;

pectoral and pelvic fins with large axillary scale; *single dorsal fin soft-rayed.* Caudal fin deeply forked.

Habitat: In shallow waters over sand.

Range: From Mondalay Beach, S. California, south to Peru.

Comments: These smaller relatives of the Tarpon are excellent fighters but are not considered edible because of their oily flesh.

---

580 Ladyfish
(*Elops saurus*)

Description: To 3'3" (99 cm). Elongate, fusiform; blue-gray above, sides silvery, belly yellowish. Mouth terminal, oblique; upper jawbone reaches well beyond eye; adipose eyelid present; 23–25 bones in gill membrane; gular plate present in lower jaw. Fins dusky with yellow tinge; pelvic fins slightly in front of dorsal fin origin; pectoral and pelvic fins have large axillary scale; single dorsal fin short, *last ray not threadlike;* anal fin short, origin well behind dorsal fin; caudal fin deeply forked. *Scales very small;* 100–120 in lateral line.

gular plate

Habitat: Primarily shallow marine and brackish waters; occasionally enters fresh water.

Range: From Cape Cod to Brazil, including Bermuda, Gulf of Mexico, and Caribbean. Occurs sporadically north of Chesapeake Bay.

Comments: The Ladyfish spawns offshore but the leptocephalus larvae transform into adults in coastal waters. Although small, when hooked the Ladyfish fights like a "tenpounder," hence one of its common names. Ladyfish are good light-tackle fishes and jump frequently. They are of no value as food for humans.

581 Tarpon
(*Megalops atlanticus*)

Description: To 8' (2.4 m); 283 lbs (128.4 kg). Large, elongate, moderately deep and compressed; back blue-gray, sides and belly silvery, fins dusky or pale. Mouth huge, oblique, superior, lower jaw projects well beyond upper; upper jawbone reaches well beyond eye; bony plate present in lower jaw. Pectoral and pelvic fins with large axillary scale; pelvic fins abdominal and in front of dorsal fin origin. Single dorsal fin short, *last ray elongate and threadlike;* anal fin origin behind dorsal fin base; caudal fin deeply forked. *Scales extremely large, cycloid;* 40–48 lateral line scales.

Habitat: Primarily shallow coastal waters and estuaries. Spawn offshore, leptocephalus larvae develop inshore; juveniles and, sometimes, adults enter fresh water.

Range: From Nova Scotia south to Brazil, including Bermuda, Gulf of Mexico, and Caribbean. Infrequently north of North Carolina.

Comments: The Tarpon is also known as the "Silverking" and is indeed the king of sport fishes. It takes an experienced angler to land a large Tarpon, for this extremely strong fish is a fast swimmer and can make spectacular leaps out of the water in an effort to throw the hook. It is not regarded as good food.

BONEFISHES
(Family Albulidae)

Bonefishes have an elongate, fusiform body with a single dorsal fin and a large caudal fin. Their eggs hatch into leptocephalus larvae. These larvae move offshore to the open ocean where they spend their early lives before returning inshore as juveniles. Bonefishes occur in warm seas throughout the world. A single species occurs in North America.

578 Bonefish
(*Albula vulpes*)

Description: To 3' (91 cm); 19 lbs (8.6 kg).
Elongate, fusiform; bluish or greenish, silvery overall, occasionally with dusky side stripes and bars that fade upon death; base of fins often yellow. *Upper jaw overhangs lower;* maxilla lacks teeth. Pelvic fins abdominal; 16–21 dorsal fin rays. *Caudal fin large, deeply forked.* Scales cycloid.

Habitat: Shallow waters over soft bottoms.

Range: In Atlantic from Bay of Fundy to Rio de Janeiro, Brazil, most common in S. Florida, Bermuda, and Bahamas; in Pacific from San Francisco, California, to Peru.

Comments: Bonefishes eat clams, snails, shrimps, and small fishes. Although they have been virtually ignored on the West Coast, they are prized game fishes on the East Coast, since they are easier to catch on shallow sand flats.

Order Anguilliformes

Eels are long, snakelike fishes without pelvic fins, premaxillary bones, or spines in the fins. Most eels lack scales; some have no pectoral fins, others lack a caudal fin. There are 9 families of eels in North America, virtually all are marine, and many are rarely seen, deep water species.

FRESHWATER EELS
(Family Anguillidae)

This family differs from most other eels in having small scales embedded in the skin. In addition, they have pectoral fins and a caudal fin that is continuous with the dorsal and anal fins. After reaching sexual maturity, freshwater eels migrate to the Sargasso Sea area of the Atlantic to spawn. The eggs hatch into leptocephalus larvae that pass through several stages as they transform to adults. Apparently only the females ascend rivers, where they remain for a number of years. There is a single North American species.

39, 445 American Eel
(*Anguilla rostrata*)

Description: To 4′11″ (1.5 m). Elongate, snakelike, circular in cross section anteriorly, compressed posteriorly. Color variable depending on habitat and age, usually dark brown or greenish above, fading to yellowish-white on belly. Head large, about one-eighth of length; mouth terminal, nearly horizontal, lower jaw projects slightly. Pectoral fins well developed; dorsal fin origin far behind pectoral fins; anal fin origin behind dorsal fin origin, both fins continuous with caudal fin. *Scales small, elliptical, deeply embedded in skin.*

Habitat: Brackish or fresh water, except when migrating and spawning at sea.

Range: Along coast and to headwaters of associated rivers from Labrador south to Guyana, including Gulf of Mexico, Antilles, and Caribbean.

Comments: Eels are eaten fresh and smoked, and elvers (young eels) are exported to Europe and Japan for use in aquaculture.

MORAYS
(Family Muraenidae)

Heavier and usually more compressed than most eels, the morays are readily distinguished by the small, round gill opening and the absence of pectoral fins. The skin is thick and leathery, the occipital region of the head is elevated, and the powerful jaws are armed with knifelike or molarlike teeth. Morays typically inhabit shallow coral reefs and rocky areas. They are most active at night; by day they hide in holes and crevices. Capable of inflicting deep wounds when disturbed, large morays are dangerous in or out of the water. Some species may cause ciguatera poisoning when eaten. There are 14 species in North America.

---

451 California Moray
(*Gymnothorax mordax*)

Description:	To 5′ (1.5 m). Elongate, eel-like; brown to green-brown. Mouth large, teeth strong, gill openings small, round; back of head elevated. *Pectoral fins absent.* Skin thick, scaleless.
Habitat:	Shallow, rocky reefs with crevices and caves to 22 fathoms.
Range:	From Pt. Conception, California, to Bahía Magdalena, Baja California.
Similar Species:	Pacific Snake Eel (*Ophichthus triserialis*) has pectoral fins; dark spots on body; occurs over soft bottoms from Humboldt Bay, California, to Peru.
Comments:	The only moray found north of Baja California, the California Moray eats crabs, shrimps, lobsters, and various fishes. Females deposit eggs that develop into leptocephalus larvae. If disturbed, California Morays may bite divers, but they are not usually aggressive unless harassed.

---

453 Spotted Moray
(*Gymnothorax moringa*)

Description:	To 3′3″ (99 cm). Robust; moderately compressed; *yellow above, white or yellow elsewhere, with dense, irregular, brownish to purplish-black spots and small blotches.*

Occipital area elevated; posterior nostril simple, without tube; rear jaw teeth not serrate. Lacks pectoral fins; anterior edge of dorsal fin black; posterior edges of dorsal, anal, and caudal fins white.

Habitat: Shallow coral reefs and rocky coasts.

Range: From North Carolina south to Rio de Janeiro, Brazil, including Gulf of Mexico, Caribbean, West Indies.

Comments: The Spotted Moray is reported to be very common in the Bahamas but is not often seen by divers due to its secretive nature.

---

452   Blackedge Moray
(*Gymnothorax nigromarginatus*)

Description: To 24″ (61 cm). Stout; brownish or purple-brown, *with numerous pale or white spots varying in size.* Forehead somewhat elevated; posterior nostril without tube; teeth serrate, sharklike. Lacks pectoral fins; dorsal and anal fins with black blotches and white interspaces. Dorsal fin origin at head.

Habitat: Over sand or mud on continental shelf to about 45 fathoms.

Range: From SW. Florida, Gulf of Mexico to Yucatán, Mexico.

Related Species: Ocellated Moray (*G. saxicola*) has geographical differences in color pattern; occurs in similar habitat from Carolinas south to Florida and Louisiana, and disjunctly to Yucatán, Mexico.

Comments: These morays probably are most active at night, when they feed primarily on fishes and squids.

SNAKE EELS
(Family Ophichthidae)

These snakelike eels have pointed snouts, and may have tubular anterior nostrils. In some genera, the dorsal and

anal fins are continuous around the tail,
and pectoral fins may be present;
certain species, however, lack all fins.
Coloration and markings vary from
striking to rather drab. The 28 species
of snake eels found in North America
occur mostly in tropical and subtropical
waters. Regardless of size, when handled
almost any snake eel is capable of
inflicting painful wounds with its teeth,
which vary from small and villiform
to fanglike, depending on the genus.

Speckled Worm Eel
(*Myrophis punctatus*)

Description: To 17″ (43 cm). Slender, wormlike;
brownish or yellowish-brown above and
on entire posterior half, belly lighter,
tiny, dark specks everywhere except belly.
Upper jaw projects beyond lower;
anterior nostril tubular, posterior
nostril on edge of lip; mouth extends
beyond oval eye. Pectoral fins short but
broad-based; no pelvic fins; origin of
dorsal fin midway between gill opening
and anus; *dorsal and anal fins continuous
around end of tail.*

Habitat: Coastal, in bays and tidal creeks,
usually over soft mud, sometimes over
sand.

Range: From Chesapeake Bay to Brazil,
including Gulf of Mexico and West
Indies.

Comments: This is one of the most common eels in
the northern Gulf of Mexico. It appears
in shrimp trawls and seine collections
made in shallow water over mud.

446 Shrimp Eel
(*Ophichthus gomesi*)

Description: To 30″ (76 cm). Elongate, snakelike,
cylindrical in front, more compressed
behind; olive-brown above, becoming

yellowish on belly; *no conspicuous markings*. Snout conical, mouth slightly inferior, eye over middle of upper lip; anterior nostril tubular, posterior one on upper lip. Pelvic fins absent, pectorals well developed; dorsal fin continuous, origin behind base of pectoral fins; anal fin present. *Caudal fin absent; end of tail stiff.*

Habitat: Inshore over mud to about 20 fathoms.

Range: From New England south to Brazil, including E. Gulf of Mexico.

Related Species: Spotted Snake Eel (*O. ophis*) has pale body with black blotches; occurs in similar habitat from S. Florida and Gulf of Mexico to N. Brazil.

Comments: This eel frequently turns up in shrimp trawl catches but is rarely caught on hook and line, and is unimportant as a food fish. It has sharp teeth that are capable of inflicting painful wounds.

Order Clupeiformes

These fishes are usually small, delicate, and silver-colored. They are noted for their schooling behavior and most species feed by filtering plankton with their numerous, long gill rakers. There are 2 families in North America.

HERRINGS
(Family Clupeidae)

This is a large, primarily saltwater family, with 27 species in North America. Herrings have variable body shapes. Typically the clupeid mouth is large and terminal, with the lower jaw projecting beyond the upper; however, the lower jaw is deep and the maxilla is broad posteriorly. The anal fin is larger than the dorsal, which is placed at about the middle of the body. There is no lateral line. The cycloid scales form scutes—modified scales with keel-like ridges—on the belly of most species.

140, 575 Alewife
(*Alosa pseudoharengus*)

mouth

Description: To 15″ (38 cm). Elongate, strongly compressed, *ventral profile more convex than dorsal,* depth less than one-quarter length. Back iridescent grayish-green or violet, sides paler, belly silvery, humeral spot dusky. Head less than one-fifth length; *eye large, diameter greater than length of snout;* mouth oblique, upper jaw deeply notched; maxilla wide, reaches middle of eye. Dorsal fin origin just before pelvic fin insertion, last dorsal ray not elongate.

Habitat: Bays, estuaries, and fresh water.

Range: From Newfoundland to South Carolina, inland along coast and in Great Lakes.

Related Species: Blueback Herring (*A. aestivalis*) has smaller eye, blue-green back; occurs in similar habitat from Nova Scotia to St. Johns River, Florida.

Comments: This is a schooling species that feeds on plankton and small crustaceans while at sea. Populations that are established in lakes remain there to spawn; all others enter freshwater streams to spawn, and then return to the sea.

123, 577 American Shad
(*Alosa sapidissima*)

Description: To 30″ (76 cm); 9¼ lbs (4.2 kg). Elongate, strongly compressed; *dorsal and ventral profiles evenly rounded;* depth about one-fourth length. Back dark bluish or greenish, sides much paler, belly silvery; dusky humeral spot usually followed by several small, less distinct dusky spots. Head one-fifth or less of length; mouth oblique, maxilla reaches to posterior margin of eye; *eye*

diameter much less than length of snout.
Dorsal fin origin slightly anterior to
pelvic fin insertion, last dorsal ray not
elongate.

Habitat: Bays, estuaries, and fresh water.

Range: From S. Labrador to St. Johns River,
Florida; introduced in Pacific from
Alaska to Mexico.

Related Species: Hickory Shad (*A. mediocris*) with dorsal
profile almost straight, well-rounded
ventrally; lower jaw projects well
beyond upper; occurs in similar habitat
from Maine to St. Johns River, Florida.

Comments: All *Alosa* are schooling species that
enter freshwater streams to spawn.
None remain long in fresh water, nor
do they go far out at sea.

---

576 Atlantic Menhaden
(*Brevoortia tyrannus*)

Description: To 18″ (46 cm). Oval, deep and
compressed; blue or green, sometimes
bluish-brown above; sides and belly
silvery, fins yellowish; distinct humeral
spot often followed by several rows of
smaller spots. *Head very large;* mouth
oblique, maxilla reaches to posterior
edge of eye. Pectoral fins slightly
falcate, near ventral profile; dorsal fin
origin slightly behind pelvic fin

exposed scales

insertion. *Exposed margin of scales almost
vertical, fringed.*

Habitat: At or near surface over continental
shelf, near large estuaries.

Range: From New Brunswick to S. Florida.

Related Species: Gulf Menhaden (*B. patronus*) has larger
head; dorsal fin further forward; occurs
in similar habitat throughout Gulf of
Mexico.

Comments: These 2 menhadens, both also called
"pogy," occur in huge schools, often
weighing hundreds of tons. They
support a large industry on the Atlantic
and Gulf coasts. Although all parts of
the fish have value, its oil is the
principal product.

574 Pacific Herring
(*Clupea harengus pallasi*)

enlarged scute

scutes

Description: To 18″ (46 cm). Laterally compressed, fusiform; dark green above, silvery-white below. Teeth present on vomer; *no striations on gill covers. Ventral scutes lack bony keel.* Single dorsal fin located directly above pelvic fins.

Habitat: Inshore waters.

Range: From Gulf of Alaska to N. Baja California.

Related Species: Pacific Sardine (*Sardinops sagax*) has black spots; ventral scutes with bony keels; no teeth on vomer; last anal fin ray elongated; occurs in similar habitat from Gulf of Alaska to Guaymas, Mexico.

Comments: The Pacific Herring spawns during the winter and early spring. The eggs are deposited on objects, such as kelp, rocks, and eel grass, in very shallow water and hatch in 10 days. Large quantities of eggs are harvested, often to be exported to Japan. Adult Pacific Herring feed on a variety of crustaceans and small fishes, and are themselves prey for many important commercial and sport fishes, such as salmons.

122 Gizzard Shad
(*Dorosoma cepedianum*)

Description: To 16″ (41 cm). Deep, moderately compressed; back dark blue or gray, sides silvery, belly white; 6 or 8 horizontal dusky stripes on upper sides; dusky humeral spot. Head small, *mouth small and inferior;* adipose eyelid present. Pelvic fin almost directly under origin of dorsal fin. *Last ray of dorsal fin elongate, filamentous.* Ventral scales scutelike, forming distinct keel.

Habitat: Fresh water in large rivers, reservoirs, lakes, and estuaries; also in salt water.

Range: Atlantic Coast and associated rivers from New York to mid-Florida, Gulf of

Mexico from mid-Florida to central Mexico; St. Lawrence River, Great Lakes, and Mississippi River system.

Related Species: Threadfin Shad (*D. petenense*) has slender body, dorsal ray almost reaches caudal fin; ridge on back before dorsal fin scaleless; occurs along coast south from Florida to Central America and in associated freshwater streams; introduced in W. United States.

Similar Species: Atlantic Thread Herring (*Opisthonema oglinum*) has scales on ridge of back before dorsal fin; occurs only in salt water from Cape Cod to Brazil, including Gulf of Mexico.

Comments: The Gizzard Shad is a very common herbivorous fish associated primarily with freshwater habitats. It has no commercial value, but is a forage fish for larger, carnivorous fishes.

ANCHOVIES
(Family Engraulidae)

maxilla

Anchovies are small, delicate fishes, almost entirely silver in color, with a broad, bright silver midlateral band. The mouth is very large with numerous long, closely set gill rakers; the maxilla extends beyond the large eye, and in some species, beyond the angle of the gill cover, known as the opercle. The snout is conical and overhangs the mouth. The large, deciduous scales do not form a keel on the belly. Anchovies are almost entirely marine, although some species enter fresh water. They are most numerous in tropical and subtropical areas, where they occur in large schools near the surface. There are 14 species in North America.

572 Striped Anchovy
(*Anchoa hepsetus*)

Description: To 6″ (15 cm). Elongate, compressed; dusky-green or greenish-blue above; broad, bright silver band on sides; whitish below. Snout conical, overhangs mouth; eye large, width greater than length of snout; maxilla long, slender, *pointed end reaches lower edge of opercle.* Pelvic fins abdominal; pectoral fins inserted well below axis of body; *anal fin origin under or behind midpoint of dorsal fin base;* caudal fin deeply forked. Scales large, deciduous; no keel on belly.

Habitat: Shallow coastal waters to about 35 fathoms.

Range: From Massachusetts to N. Brazil, including Gulf of Mexico, Caribbean, West Indies.

Related Species: Bay Anchovy (*A. mitchilli*) has smaller, deeper, more compressed body; occurs in estuaries, mouths of rivers, and on coast from Maine to Florida and throughout Gulf of Mexico.

Comments: There are 10 species of anchovies on the Atlantic Coast, and 4 on the Pacific Coast. They are similar in appearance, but differ in the number of fin rays, the position of the dorsal fin relative to the anal fin, the shape and length of the maxilla, and the number of gill rakers. Anchovies occur in large schools, filter feed on plankton, and are eaten extensively by predators such as mackerels and Bluefishes. They play an invaluable role in the marine energy web. Anchovies are also important commercially as they are widely used for bait and food.

571 Northern Anchovy
(*Engraulis mordax*)

Description: To 9″ (23 cm). Elongate, fusiform, slightly compressed; metallic blue to green above, silver below. Maxilla extends almost to rear edge of gill cover. *Pectoral axillary scale more than half of pectoral fin length.* Anal fin origin under or posterior to last few dorsal rays; 19–26 anal fin rays.

Habitat: Coastal surface waters.

Range: From N. British Columbia to Cabo San Lucas, Baja California.

Related Species: Deepbody Anchovy (*Anchoa compressa*) has pectoral axillary scale less than half of pectoral fin length; anal fin origin anterior to middle of dorsal fin base; 29–33 anal fin rays; occurs in bays and estuaries from Morro Bay, California, to Bahía de Todos Santos, Baja California. Slough Anchovy (*A. delicatissima*) has anal fin origin anterior to middle of dorsal fin base; 23–26 anal fin rays; occurs in estuaries and bay backwaters from Long Beach Harbor, California, to Bahía Magdalena, Baja California.

Comments: The Northern Anchovy spawns during the winter and early spring, and the pelagic eggs take between 2 and 4 days to hatch. This anchovy rarely lives longer than 4 years. Tagging studies indicate that schools of anchovies move fairly large distances up and down the coast. An extremely important commercial fish, this species is also a major food source for other fishes, birds, and mammals.

Order Osteoglossiformes

This small order consists of 4 families and 15 species. All inhabit tropical areas with the exception of the Hiodontidae, a freshwater family found in North America.

MOONEYES
(Family Hiodontidae)

This family consists of 2 freshwater species. They may be confused with the herrings, but they can be distinguished by the presence of teeth on the tongue and jaws and by the dorsal fin, which is positioned over the anal fin. Mooneyes have a lateral line.

124 Goldeye
(*Hiodon alosoides*)

Description: To 20″ (51 cm); 3⅛ lbs (1.4 kg). Moderately deep, compressed; bluish above; silvery below. *Mouth large, with small, sharp teeth;* eye bright golden-yellow, very large. *Keel on midline of belly from pectoral fins to anus. Dorsal fin with 9–10 rays, origin just behind anal fin origin;* 29–35 anal fin rays; caudal fin deeply forked. Lateral line complete, 55–62 scales.

Habitat: Clear to turbid water in rivers, lakes, reservoirs, and quiet backwaters.

Range: James Bay drainage, Ontario and Quebec, west to Mackenzie River, Northwest Territories, south to Alberta. Mississippi River system, SE. Ohio, W. Montana, south to N. Alabama and Louisiana.

Related Species: Mooneye (*H. tergisus*) has keel from pelvic fins to anus; dorsal fin with 11–12 rays, origin anterior to anal fin origin; occurs in same habitat in S. Canada, S. Great Lakes, Mississippi River system, south to Louisiana and Alabama.

Comments: Caught with live bait and artificial lures, Goldeyes are commercially important in Canada as a smoked fish. They appear to be more tolerant of turbid waters than are Mooneyes.

Order Salmoniformes

Most of these fishes are commercially valuable. They include freshwater, marine, anadromous, and deep-sea species. All have soft-rayed fins, an adipose fin, and abdominal pelvic fins. There are 10 families found in North American waters.

TROUTS
(Family Salmonidae)

All trouts and salmons have a pelvic axillary scale and an adipose fin, and most have well-developed teeth on both jaws. The gill membranes extend far forward and are free of the isthmus. The swim bladder is connected to the alimentary tract, allowing these fishes to change depth rapidly. Many salmonids exhibit significant sexual differences in color and morphology during the spawning season. They occur in temperate fresh and salt water in the Northern Hemisphere and have been widely introduced in North America, where there are 39 species. Many salmonids are important game fishes.

69 Lake Whitefish
(*Coregonus clupeaformis*)

nostrils

Description: To 24" (61 cm); 42 lbs (19.1 kg). Elongate, compressed; back olive to bluish-black; sides and belly silvery; fins clear to dusky. Profile of head concave behind eyes; *snout overhangs mouth; double flap between nostrils; maxilla extends past front of eye;* teeth on tongue, absent from jaws. 11–13 dorsal fin rays; adipose fin present; caudal fin forked. Lateral line complete, 70–97 scales.

Habitat: Large rivers and lakes.

Range: Alaska, Canada, N. New England, Great Lakes, N. Minnesota.

Similar Species: 14 species of *Coregonus* occur in lakes and streams of Canada and N. United States; their similar morphology and coloration make identification extremely difficult.

Comments: The Lake Whitefish, the most widely distributed whitefish, is one of the most valuable commercial freshwater fishes of North America. However, commercial landings have become much lower, especially in the Great Lakes, due to the deterioration of the habitat and depletion of stocks. Lake Whitefish are also sought for sport in some areas. They are a superlative table delicacy.

Coho Salmon
(*Oncorhynchus kisutch*)

Description: To 3'3" (99 cm). Elongate, fusiform, moderately compressed; blue-green above, silvery-white below; irregular dark spots on back and sometimes on upper lobe of caudal fin. *Gums at base of teeth white or gray.* Adipose fin present; *striations on caudal fin rays rough.*

Habitat: Inshore waters at mid-depths or near surface; spawns in coastal streams, sometimes far inland.

Range: From Bering Strait to Baja California; coastal streams south to Monterey, California. Introduced elsewhere, especially in Great Lakes.

Related Species: Pink Salmon (*O. gorbuscha*) has large, dark, oval spots on back and caudal fin; 24–35 gill rakers on first arch; more than 150 lateral line scales. Introduced from Nova Scotia and Labrador to Gulf of St. Lawrence and into upper Great Lakes. Native from Arctic Ocean to S. California; coastal streams south to Sacramento River.

Similar Species: Chinook Salmon (*O. tshawytscha*) has

oblong, black spots on back and entire caudal fin; gums at base of teeth black; striations on caudal fin rays smooth.

Comments: Like all Pacific salmons, the Coho Salmon is anadromous. The adult spawns in small streams, where the female deposits 2,500 to 5,000 eggs in the gravel during the autumn. Both the male and the female die after spawning. The young stay in the streams for about a year before migrating to the ocean, where they remain for 2 or 3 years. The Coho Salmon is a game fish prized both as a fighter and for eating. It also supports a large commercial fishery off Oregon and Washington.

499   Sockeye Salmon
(*Oncorhynchus nerka*)

Description: To 33″ (84 cm). Elongate, fusiform, moderately compressed. Marine coloration: bluish-green above, silvery below, *with fine speckling but no spots.* Freshwater coloration: bright red, head pale green; females may have green and yellow blotches. Snout bluntly pointed, mouth terminal; gill rakers long, slender, closely spaced, *28–40 on first arch.* Adipose fin present.

Habitat: Surface waters of open ocean and freshwater streams, rivers, and lakes containing tributary streams for spawning.

Range: From Bering Strait to Sacramento River, California; introduced elsewhere in northern lakes.

Related Species: Chum Salmon (*O. keta*) has all fins usually dark-tipped, dorsal can be pale at edges; has 18–26 gill rakers on first arch. Spawning adults have reddish bars and large, pale blotches on sides; tips of pelvic and anal fins white. Occurs from Arctic Ocean to S. California; coastal streams south to Sacramento River.

Comments: Sockeye Salmon spawn during summer in small tributaries of lakes, where the young spend 1 to 3 years before migrating to the ocean. After living at sea for 2 to 4 years, maturing adults return to their home stream. Sockeye Salmon have the greatest commercial value of all the Pacific salmons, although few are caught by anglers in the ocean because they rarely strike lures or trolled baits.

63, 497 Chinook Salmon
(*Oncorhynchus tshawytscha*)

Description: To 4′ 10″ (1.6 m); 126 lbs (57.2 kg). Elongate, fusiform. Marine coloration: greenish-blue to black above, silvery-white below, oblong, black spots on back and entire caudal fin; very dark overall in fresh water. *Gums at base of teeth black.* Adipose fin present; *striations on caudal fin rays smooth.*

Habitat: Ocean near surface and at mid-depths, may feed near bottom; spawns in fresh water in large rivers.

Range: Bering Strait south to S. California; in freshwater streams south to Sacramento River; widely introduced.

Similar Species: Coho Salmon (*O. kisutch*) lacks spots on lower lobe of caudal fin; gums at base of teeth white; striations on caudal fin rays strong, rough.

Comments: Chinook Salmon enter fresh water most months of the year, but their major spawning runs occur in the spring and fall. Their diet, similar to that of the Coho Salmon, consists of a variety of crustaceans, and fishes such as anchovies, herrings, young rockfishes, and sand lances. Chinook Salmon are the most highly prized ocean game fishes from Alaska to northern California. They also support a large and valuable commercial troll fishery.

68 Round Whitefish
(*Prosopium cylindraceum*)

Description: To 22″ (56 cm); 4½ lbs (2 kg).
Elongate, cylindrical; back greenish to
blue-gray with scales dark-edged, sides
silvery; young silvery, 2–3 rows of
black spots along lateral line. Snout

nostrils   narrow, pointed; *single flap of skin
between nostrils;* mouth small, ventral,
extends to eye; 13–20 gill rakers; teeth
on tongue, absent from jaws. Dorsal
and caudal fins slightly dusky, other
fins amber; adipose fin present; caudal
fin forked. *Lateral line complete, 74–108
scales.*

Habitat: Lakes to depths of 50′ (15.2 m);
streams.

Range: Canada and Alaska south and southeast
to New England and Great Lakes.

Related Species: Pygmy Whitefish (*P. coulteri*) has 55–
70 lateral line scales; inhabits upland
streams and lakes from Alaska south
to N. Montana and Washington;
Lake Superior. Mountain Whitefish
(*P. williamsoni*) has 20–25 gill rakers;
inhabits lakes and streams of
W. Canada and NW. United States.

Comments: The Round Whitefish is fished
commercially in the Great Lakes, but
is not very valuable because of its
restricted population. It is an
important forage fish for Lake Trout
in some areas.

---

59 Apache Trout
(*Salmo apache*)

Description: To 18″ (46 cm); 3 lbs (1.4 kg).

Moderately stout, compressed; dark
olive to brown above, *sides and belly
yellow to golden-yellow;* many dark spots
about one-half diameter of pupil on
head, back, sides, and fins; *large,
prominent, dark spot behind eye;* lower part
of head orange to yellow-orange.
Pelvic, dorsal, and anal fins white-

tipped; dorsal fin large; adipose fin present. Lateral line complete, 112–124 scales.

Habitat: Clear mountain streams above 7,544′ (2,300 m) with riffles and pools.

Range: Headwaters of Salt and Little Colorado rivers, E. central Arizona.

Related Species: Gila Trout (*S. gilae*) has smaller, closely spaced, dark spots extending onto belly and small, dark spots on dorsal and caudal fins; occurs in mountain streams in SW. New Mexico and central Arizona. The Gila Trout is now an endangered species.

Comments: The Apache Trout, also called the Arizona Trout, was almost totally exterminated by exotic trouts, which hybridize with it and compete for food and habitat. It is a threatened species.

60, 64, 495 Cutthroat Trout
(*Salmo clarki*)

Description: To 30″ (76 cm); 41 lbs (18.6 kg). Elongate, cylindrical or terete, moderately compressed; back dark olive; sides variable: silvery, olive, reddish to yellow-orange; belly lighter; *dark spots on back, sides, and on median fins.* Mouth extends beyond eye; basibranchial teeth present; *bright red to red-orange slash mark on each side of throat,* particularly visible in breeding males. 8–11 dorsal fin rays; 9–12 anal fin rays; adipose fin present. Caudal peduncle narrow; caudal fin slightly forked. Lateral line complete, 120–230 scales, usually 150 or more.

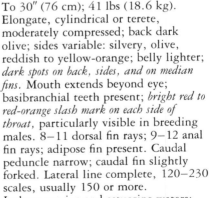

Habitat: Inshore marine and estuarine waters; lakes; coastal, inland, and alpine streams.

Range: From S. Alaska south to N. California; inland from S. British Columbia and Alberta south to New Mexico; E. California east to central Colorado. Introduced in W. United States.

Comments: There are more than 10 subspecies of

Cutthroat Trouts, locally called "native trout," which vary in coloration and size. The largest specimen, caught in Pyramid Lake, Nevada, in 1925, weighed 41 lbs (18.6 kg), but this strain is now extinct. Other cutthroats, while rarely exceeding 15" (38 cm), are important in the inland and coastal fishery, and are sought by anglers.

61, 493 Rainbow Trout
(*Salmo gairdneri*)

Description: To 3'9" (1.1 m); 42⅛ lbs (19.1 kg). Elongate, fusiform. Marine coloration: metallic-blue above, silvery-white below, with small, black spots on back, sides, and dorsal and caudal fins. Freshwater coloration: spots more prominent, distinctive red band on sides. *Mouth white; no teeth on back of tongue. 8–12 anal fin rays;* adipose fin present, usually with black edge.

Habitat: Inshore ocean at mid-depths and near surface; spawns in freshwater streams and rivers.

Range: From Bering Sea to S. California. In fresh water, native range confined to lakes and streams of western states bordering Pacific Ocean from Alaska to Baja California; introduced throughout Canada and United States in suitable streams and lakes.

Comments: Sea-run Rainbow Trout usually spend 2 to 4 years in their home stream before venturing to sea, where they remain for about 3 years. They return to their home stream in the winter to spawn, and will continue this pattern as long as they survive natural predators. Fish that exist solely in fresh water spawn in the spring. Most males spawn at 1 year, while females may take 6 years to mature. Rainbow Trout are much-sought game fish; they are rarely taken at sea by bait anglers, but do succumb readily to trolled shrimplike flies. They provide good eating and are raised for market through aquaculture. There are small commercial gill-net fisheries north of Oregon for sea-run fish.

58, 494 Atlantic Salmon
(*Salmo salar*)

Description: To 4'5" (1.3 m); 79⅛ lb (35.9 kg). Elongate, moderately compressed; *adults brownish above, sides silvery, with numerous small, black spots, sometimes X-shaped, without halos,* on head, body, and dorsal fin; males have red patches on sides; young specimens have about 11 dusky bars. Head large, depth about one-fifth length; maxilla reaches past eye; lower jaw upward-hooked in breeding males. Pectoral fins inserted well below axis of body; dorsal fin short-based, at midpoint of body; adipose fin present; caudal fin slightly forked or emarginate.

Habitat: Coastal waters; freshwater streams and lakes.

Range: Native in N. Atlantic from Arctic Circle, N. Quebec south to Delaware River; Lake Ontario. Landlocked populations in several New England states.

Comments: This anadromous species spawns in the fall in high gradient streams over gravel. After spawning, the fish are weak and emaciated but do not necessarily die like some other salmonid species. The Atlantic Salmon is a well-known and highly valued food and game fish. Specimens as large as 40 to 50 lbs (18.1 to 22.7 kg) are unusual in the Atlantic; most weigh much less.

62, 496 Brown Trout
(Salmo trutta)

Description: To 3'4" (1 m); 39¼ lbs (17.8 kg).
Elongate, fusiform, moderately
compressed; back and sides olive,
becoming lighter, belly silvery,
*numerous red or orange spots, often with
halo,* scattered on head, body, and
dorsal and adipose fins; maxilla reaches
well past eye. Pectoral fin inserted well
below axis of body; dorsal fin base
short, about midway between snout
and caudal fin base; adipose fin present;
caudal fin truncate.

Habitat: Primarily high gradient freshwater
streams; lakes; sea-run populations.

Range: From S. Canada to NE. United States,
south in Appalachians, Mississippi
Valley west in Great Lakes; W. United
States at higher elevations.

Comments: The Brown Trout, native to Europe and
western Asia, was introduced into the
United States 100 years ago and is
presently one of the most widespread
salmonids. It can tolerate higher
temperatures than the other salmons
and trouts. The young feed on aquatic
insects; adults feed to a large extent on
other fishes. Brown Trout are difficult
to catch, and as food they are not as
highly regarded as Brook or Rainbow
trouts.

65, 498 Brook Trout
(Salvelinus fontinalis)

Description: To 21" (53 cm); 14½ lbs (6.6 kg).
Elongate, fusiform, depth about one-
fifth length. Marine coloration: back
bluish-green, becoming silvery on
sides, belly white. Freshwater
coloration: back and sides have red or
yellowish tint *with lighter wavy lines;*
sides have red spots within blue halos;
belly ordinarily white, reddish in adult
males; *pectoral, pelvic, and anal fins light*

orange to red, leading edges white followed by dark, dorsal fin with dark, undulating lines. Maxilla extends well beyond eye. Fins relatively large; adipose fin present; caudal fin slightly forked.

Habitat: Clear, cool, freshwater streams; tidal streams; rarely in salt water.

Range: Native to E. Canada and NE. United States and Great Lakes region south to N. Georgia. Introduced in W. United States at higher elevations.

Comments: The Brook Trout, highly esteemed as food and game, is one of the most colorful freshwater fishes. It feeds on a variety of organisms, including other fishes, but primarily on aquatic insects. Spawning occurs in small headwater streams. The largest Brook Trout, weighing 14½ pounds (6.6 kg), was caught in 1916 in the Nipigon River, Ontario. It is also known as the Squaretail or the Speck.

66 Lake Trout
(Salvelinus namaycush)

Description: To 4′2″ (1.3 m); 102 lbs (46.3 kg). Elongate, slightly compressed; dark olive to gray-green above, blue-gray to greenish-bronze below; *creamy spots on head, body, adipose fin, and median fins;* leading edges of pectoral, pelvic, and anal fins reddish-orange with narrow, whitish margin. Mouth terminal, extends beyond eye; teeth on vomer. Adipose fin present; caudal peduncle slender; *caudal fin deeply forked.* Scales small, 175−200 in lateral series.

Habitat: Deep, cold waters of lakes; rivers in far north.

Range: Alaska; Canada, Great Lakes, Maine south to New York, west to E. Minnesota; introduced outside native range.

Comments: The Lake Trout is the largest trout native to North America. It is highly esteemed as food and is sought by anglers. A large commercial fishery for Lake Trout in the Great Lakes was decimated by pollution and by Sea Lampreys, after the rapid expansion of their population in the 1940s. Lake Trout feed on a wide range of aquatic organisms.

67 Arctic Grayling
(*Thymallus arcticus*)

Description: To 30″ (76 cm); 6 lbs (2.7 kg). Elongate, compressed; back bluish-black to purple, *sides silvery blue-gray often with pinkish cast and anterior dark spots;* lower sides have dark stripe from pectoral to pelvic fin, belly grayish. Head short, mouth extends to middle of eye; teeth small. *Fins dusky to dark; dorsal fin with light margin, 17–25 rays;* adipose fin present; caudal fin deeply forked. Lateral line complete, straight, 77–103 scales.

Habitat: Clear, cold waters of rivers, creeks, and lakes.

Range: Hudson Bay west to Alaska, south to Montana; N. Great Lakes; introduced outside native range.

Comments: The Arctic Grayling is an attractive fish and one of the most important sport fishes in northern Canada and Alaska. It has been an important food source for native Alaskans in remote areas.

SMELTS
(Family Osmeridae)

The family contains 10 freshwater, anadromous, and marine species in North American waters. They lack the axillary scale above the pelvic fin that is characteristic of trouts and salmons. During spawning smelts exhibit sexual differences, such as nuptial tubercles and a modified anal fin in the male.

Smelts are popular sport fishes and are captured in nets from shore. Used for both food and bait, they are also important commercially.

Surf Smelt
(*Hypomesus pretiosus*)

Description: To 10″ (25 cm). Elongate, fusiform, compressed; olive-green or brown above, silvery below; bright stripe along side. *Maxilla does not extend beyond midpoint of eye.* Pelvic fin insertion in front of dorsal origin; anal fin rays about one-third of head length; small sickle-shaped adipose fin.

Habitat: Close to shore off sandy beaches.

Range: From Prince William Sound, Alaska, to Long Beach, California.

Related Species: Whitebait Smelt (*Allosmerus elongatus*) has maxilla extending beyond eye; eye large, equal in size to depth of caudal peduncle; lacks close-set grooves on gill; occurs over soft bottom from S. British Columbia to San Pedro, California. Night Smelt (*Spirinchus starksi*) has maxilla reaching rear of eye; eye diameter less than caudal peduncle depth, pectoral fin extends almost to pelvic insertion; occurs in similar habitat from Shelikof Bay, Alaska to Point Arguello, California. Eulachon (*Thaleichthys pacificus*) has blue-brown above, bright silvery below; maxilla extends beyond middle of eye; close-set grooves on gill cover; occurs over soft bottoms and in coastal streams from Bering Sea to Bodega, California.

gill cover

Comments: Adult Surf Smelts spawn on beaches during daylight hours. They feed on a variety of small crustaceans.

137, 573   Rainbow Smelt
(*Osmerus mordax*)

Description: To 13″ (33 cm). Elongate, slender, moderately compressed; translucent, back purple, silvery below, sides with purplish iridescence. *Mouth has strong canine teeth on vomer,* maxilla extends to middle of eye. 8–11 dorsal fin rays, origin over or in front of pelvic fin insertion; 12–16 anal fin rays; *adipose fin over end of anal fin;* caudal fin deeply forked. *Lateral line incomplete, 14–30 pored scales;* 62–72 scales in lateral series.

Habitat: Near shore marine and estuarine areas; inland streams and lakes; anadromous and freshwater populations.

Range: From Labrador south to N. Virginia; coastal areas of Alaska; introduced in Great Lakes, Mississippi River, central Illinois south to Louisiana.

Comments: Rainbow Smelts are one of the most valuable sport and commercial fishes on the Atlantic Coast and in the Great Lakes. Anglers catch them on hook and line through the ice in winter and dip net them in small streams during the spring spawning runs. When first taken from the water, they smell similar to freshly cut cucumber.

MUDMINNOWS
(Family Umbridae)

There are 4 species of this family that occur on the Atlantic Coastal Plain, in the Great Lakes, western Washington, and Alaska. They are very hardy, withstand extreme cold, and are able to utilize atmospheric oxygen. Under adverse conditions they are reputed to become dormant in mud. Members of this family have a short snout, non-protractile jaws that bear small teeth, cycloid scales on head and body, small pelvic fins, and a rounded caudal fin.

194 Alaska Blackfish
(*Dallia pectoralis*)

Description: To 7″ (18 cm). Elongate, cylindrical anteriorly, compressed posteriorly; body dark olive-brown, sides with 4–6 bars or blotches, belly whitish. Snout short, head flattened, maxilla extends past middle of eye. Fins with reddish brown speckles; pectoral fins large, rounded; *pelvic fins small, with 3 rays; * dorsal fin with 10–14 rays, over anal fin. Scales small, cycloid, and embedded; *76–100 scales in lateral series.*

Habitat: Lowland swamps, ponds, lakes, and streams with vegetation; more abundant in tundra than forest.

Range: Arctic and sub-Arctic fresh waters of Alaska and Bering Sea Islands.

Comments: In the past, the Alaska Blackfish was an important staple in the diet of Alaskan natives and their dogs. Large quantities caught in the fall were frozen for use during the winter. The blackfishes were packed in woven grass bags in batches of 50 to 100 lbs (22.7 to 45.4 kg).

195 Central Mudminnow
(*Umbra limi*)

Description: To 5″ (12 cm). Broad anteriorly, compressed posteriorly; back brownish olive, mottled with black; *sides mottled with olive,* sometimes barred; belly yellowish. Mouth terminal, extends to middle of eye. Fins dusky; pectoral fins rounded; *anal fin under dorsal fin, about half its length; dark bar at base of caudal fin;* caudal fin rounded. Lateral line absent; 34–37 scales in lateral series.

Habitat: Cool ponds, bogs, swamps, and pools of slow moving streams with abundant vegetation.

Range: S. Manitoba, Great Lakes, and St. Lawrence drainage south to NE. Arkansas and W. Tennessee; W.

Pennsylvania west to E. South Dakota.

Related Species: Eastern Mudminnow (*U. pygmaea*) has 10–14 light stripes; occurs in Coastal Plain waters with vegetation from S. New York to N. Florida.

Similar Species: Olympic Mudminnow (*Novumbra hubbsi*) lacks dark bar at base of caudal fin, has more than 47 lateral line scales; occurs in sluggish waters of W. Washington.

Comments: The Central Mudminnow is used as bait in some areas.

PIKES
(Family Esocidae)

Pikes and pickerels are predaceous freshwater fishes with a holarctic distribution. There are 5 species in North America and most are popular game fishes. They have elongate, moderately compressed bodies with small, cycloid scales, a large head with an elongate, flattened snout, and jaws with large, sharp teeth. The dorsal and anal fins are located opposite each other far back on the body, and the caudal fin is forked.

35 Northern Pike
(*Esox lucius*)

Description: To 4′4″ (1.3 m); 46⅛ lbs (20.9 kg). Long, head one-fourth total length, tail forked; back dark olive-green to greenish-brown, sides lighter, *with irregular rows of small, oval, yellow spots and small, gold spot on exposed edge of each scale;* belly creamy-white. Lower jaw protruding, *5 large sensory pores on each side;* cheek and upper half of opercle scaled; 14–15 branchiostegal rays; median fins green to white, occasionally reddish-orange, with dark markings; lateral line complete, 105–148 scales.

sensory pores

Habitat: Lakes, reservoirs, and large streams with little current and abundant aquatic vegetation.

Range: From Alaska south throughout Canada to Missouri; New York, Pennsylvania west to Nebraska and Montana.

Comments: Because of its large size, the Northern Pike is a desirable sport fish and used to be a commercial fish as well. It is the most widely distributed freshwater fish in the world.

34 Muskellunge
(*Esox masquinongy*)

Description: To 6' (1.8 m); 100 lbs (45.4 kg). Long, head broad, flat to concave above, tail forked; back greenish to light brown; *sides greenish-gray to silvery usually with dark spots or diagonal bars;* belly creamy-white; median fins greenish to reddish-brown with dark markings. Cheeks and opercles usually scaled only on upper half; 16–19 branchiostegal rays; lower jaw has 6–9 *large sensory pores on each side;* lateral line complete, 132–167 scales.

sensory pores

Habitat: Lakes and reservoirs with thick vegetation; slow, meandering rivers and streams with abundant plant cover.

Range: SE. Manitoba, SW. Ontario east through Great Lakes to St. Lawrence River, south to Pennsylvania, West Virginia, Virginia, N. Georgia, Ohio, Kentucky; upper Mississippi River, Minnesota south to Missouri.

Comments: The largest species in the family, the "Musky" is most sought by anglers. It feeds primarily on fishes, but will eat any animal it can swallow, such as small ducks and amphibians. This species and the Northern Pike have been crossed to produce a more robust fish called the Tiger Muskellunge, commonly stocked in some areas.

36 Chain Pickerel
(*Esox niger*)

Description: To 31″ (79 cm); 9⅜ lbs (4.3 kg).
Elongate, moderately compressed; olive
to yellowish-brown above, *sides with
dark, chainlike markings;* belly whitish,
bold, dark bar under eye. Head long,
flat above; snout long, *profile concave;
lower jaw with 4 large sensory pores on each
side;* opercle fully scaled; 14–15
branchiostegal rays. Caudal fin deeply
forked. Lateral line complete, with
110–138 scales.

Habitat: Clean, clear lakes, ponds, swamps,
reservoirs, and pools of streams with
vegetation.

Range: Nova Scotia, New Brunswick, SW.
Quebec; Maine to New York south in
Atlantic Coast streams to S. Florida;
Mississippi River system, S. Indiana,
SE. Missouri south to Louisiana and
Georgia.

Related Species: Redfin Pickerel (*E. americanus
americanus*) has smaller body; snout
short; 11–12 branchiostegal rays;
inhabits lowland streams and lakes
with vegetation in SW. Quebec, SE.
Ontario, and S. Great Lakes, E. and
central United States.

Comments: In the northeastern United States Chain
Pickerels are especially popular sport
fishes in the winter and large numbers
are caught through the ice.

Order Myctophiformes

Most of these fishes occur in very deep
marine water. They are soft-rayed
fishes, with abdominal pelvic fins. Most
have an adipose fin and light-emitting
pores, called photophores, and usually
cycloid scales. There are 8 families
found in North America, and an
atypical family, the Synodontidae,
occurs in shallow waters.

LIZARDFISHES
(Family Synodontidae)

These bottom-dwelling fishes are found over sand or mud. They are oblong or elongate, cigar-shaped, and almost round in cross section. The mouth is large, wide, and a little oblique, and the maxilla extends well behind the eyes. The jaws bear numerous needlelike, or cardiform, teeth, and teeth are also present on the tongue and roof of the mouth. An adipose fin is present, the pelvic fins are abdominal, the single dorsal fin is short, and the caudal fin is forked. There are 9 species that are found in North American waters.

---

430 Inshore Lizardfish
(Synodus foetens)

Description: To 16″ (41 cm). Elongate, cylindrical; brownish or olive with greenish cast above, whitish or yellowish below; sides with obscure blotches, fading in large specimens. Snout pointed, head depressed, with light, wavy lines. *Eyes large, above midpoint of maxilla.* Pectoral fins dusky, yellowish, or light green; adipose fin with dark spot. *60 lateral line scales.*

Habitat: Bottom-dwellers, usually near shore or to about 15 fathoms.

Range: From Massachusetts to Brazil, including Bermuda, Gulf of Mexico, and West Indies. Uncommon north of South Carolina.

Comments: This is a very common lizardfish in the northeastern Gulf of Mexico, where it is often caught in shrimp trawls and discarded as a trash fish.

429 Sand Diver
(*Synodus intermedius*)

Description: To 18″ (46 cm). Elongate, cylindrical, cigar-shaped; *brown bars above* from pectoral fins to caudal fin base, thin *horizontal yellow lines above from head to tail, black humeral spot partly covered by opercle,* belly pale, fins orange. Snout relatively blunt; eyes slightly anterior to midpoint of maxilla. Adipose fin present. *Less than 52 lateral line scales.*

Habitat: Offshore over sand to depths of 175 fathoms, occasionally in shallow water and around rocks.

Range: From North Carolina to Brazil, including Bermuda, Gulf of Mexico, Caribbean, and West Indies.

Related Species: California Lizardfish (*S. lucioceps*) with brown above, belly tan; has yellow gill membranes and pelvic fins; occurs over sand and mud to 50′ (15 m) from San Francisco, California, to Guaymas, Mexico.

Comments: The Sand Diver, so called for its habit of burying itself in the sand when disturbed, is of no value as a food or game fish.

Order Cypriniformes

This is the second largest order of fishes, with about 25 families and 3,000 species. There are 4 families in North America. They are usually the dominant group of freshwater fishes, and have adapted to the most extreme environments. They are characterized by a single, rayed dorsal fin and the usual absence of fin spines. An adipose fin may be present. These fishes either have cycloid scales, or the body is naked. They also have a series of modified vertebrae connecting the swim bladder with the inner ear, which facilitates an acute sense of hearing.

CHARACINS
(Family Characidae)

This large family has more than 800 species, distributed south from Texas and New Mexico through Central and South America. It includes vegetarians as well as the carnivorous piranhas. However, only 1 species occurs in our range. Most characins have jaws with teeth and an adipose fin. They always lack barbels.

Mexican Tetra
(*Astyanax mexicanus*)

Description: To 5″ (12.5 cm). Moderately deep, compressed; back olive, sides silvery to brassy, with dusky lateral stripe, larger and more intense near caudal fin base, narrowing on caudal fin; fins yellowish to pale reddish. Head narrow, short; mouth terminal, *multicuspid teeth present. Anal fin long, 21–25 rays,* anterior tip white, middle rays dusky to black; *adipose fin present;* caudal peduncle short, deep. Lateral line almost straight, complete, 35–40 scales.

Habitat: Rivers and creeks with slow to moderate current.

Range: Native to Rio Grande, Pecos and Nueces rivers, Texas and New Mexico south into Mexico and Panama; introduced in Louisiana, Oklahoma, Texas, New Mexico, Arizona, and California.

Comments: The Mexican Tetra is the most northern representative of the family. It has been used for bait and kept by aquarists, but should not be used in this way outside its natural range, since it may cause damage to native fishes if it is released and becomes established.

CARPS AND MINNOWS
(Family Cyprinidae)

minnow

carp

Cyprinidae, the largest family of fishes in the world, has approximately 275 genera and 1,600 species worldwide, including 211 species which occur in North America. It also has the most extensive continuous distribution of any family of freshwater fishes: Cyprinids occur throughout North America, Europe, Asia, and Africa, but are absent from South America. They are characterized by jaws without teeth, the absence of an adipose fin, and the presence of cycloid scales.

128 Chiselmouth
(*Acrocheilus alutaceus*)

ventral head view

Description: To 12″ (30 cm). Elongate, caudal peduncle slender; back grayish-brown, sides lighter with small, black dots. Snout bluntly rounded, slightly overhanging wide mouth; *upper jaw has fleshy lip and straight, cartilaginous plate; lower jaw has hard sheath with straight edge;* no barbels. Anal fin reddish-orange, origin posterior to dorsal fin origin; dorsal and caudal fins grayish brown; *caudal fin deeply forked.* Scales embedded; lateral line complete, 85–93 scales.

Habitat: Rivers, creeks, and lakes with firm bottom in slow to fast water; migrates into streams to spawn.

Range: From British Columbia south to Oregon, Idaho, and NE. Nevada.

Comments: The Chiselmouth feeds by darting forward about an inch and scraping its chisel-like lower jaw over algae-covered surfaces. Other adaptations for feeding on algae include stout pharyngeal teeth with well-developed grinding surfaces and a long intestine.

142 Longfin Dace
(*Agosia chrysogaster*)

Description:

To 3½" (9 cm). Robust; head blunt; dark olive-gray above, *with dark, midlateral stripe ending in darker spot;* whitish below. Mouth terminal, reaches front of eye; *small barbel at corner of jaw.* Fins rounded except caudal forked; anterior half of anal fin elongate in females. Scales small; lateral line complete, 75–90 scales.

Habitat: Warm desert streams to cooler mountain brooks.

Range: Bill Williams and Gila rivers of central and SE. Arizona and SW. New Mexico; Sonora, Mexico.

Comments: Longfin Dace are less common in large rivers and at high elevations. They are omnivorous, feeding on detritus, aquatic invertebrates, and algae.

---

115 Central Stoneroller
(*Campostoma anomalum*)

Description:

To 9" (23 cm). Elongate, stout; dark olive to gray above, sides with dark flecks, belly whitish. *Head blunt, snout overhangs mouth;* upper lip fleshy; *lower jaw with cartilaginous ridge; no barbels.* Breeding males have tubercles on head, body, and median fins; black band through central part of pelvic, dorsal, and anal fins. Lateral line complete, 47–56 scales.

Habitat: Riffles, shallow pools in clear creeks to small rivers, with moderate to steep gradient over gravel or bedrock.

Range: Thames River, S. Ontario, south in most of E. and central United States, and San Juan River, NE. Mexico.

Related Species: Largescale Stoneroller (*C. oligolepis*) has larger scales; breeding males lack tubercles around nostrils and dark band through anal fin; occurs in streams from N. Wisconsin south to NE. Oklahoma and N. Arkansas.

Similar Species: Dace (genus *Rhinichthys*) have barbels at corner of jaw and smaller scales.

Comments: Stonerollers are common in small streams, where they feed on algae and other micro-organisms, which they scrape from the bottom using their bladelike lower jaw. They move small stones as they feed, thus the name Stoneroller.

ventral head view

120, 121 Goldfish
(*Carassius auratus*)

Description: To 16″ (41 cm); 3½ lbs (1.6 kg). Robust; usually olive, but can vary to gold, orange, or creamy-white; fins similar color; young may have dark blotches. *No barbels. Dorsal fin with 1 heavy, serrated spine, 15–18 branched rays; anal fin with 1 heavy, serrated spine, 5–6 rays;* caudal peduncle deep, short. Lateral line complete, 27–31 scales.

Habitat: Lakes, ponds, and sloughs with warm water, soft bottom, and aquatic vegetation.

Range: Introduced in warmer waters of S. Canada, United States, and Mexico.

Similar Species: Common Carp (*Cyprinus carpio*) has 2 pairs of barbels on upper lip and 32–39 smaller lateral line scales.

Comments: Goldfishes are native to China. They tolerate extreme temperatures (0° to 41° C) and low levels of dissolved oxygen, but are usually found in warmer waters where winters are not severe. Goldfish and Common Carp hybridize, making identification difficult. Since large populations of Goldfish can suppress native fishes, they should not be released into the wild.

192 Rosyside Dace
(*Clinostomus funduloides*)

Description: To 4″ (10 cm). Oblong, moderately deep and compressed; back olive, *sides light rosy with dusky, midlateral stripe, and scattered, dark scales;* belly whitish; breeding males bright red, covered with tubercles. Mouth large, extends to eye; lower jaw protrudes; barbels absent. Dorsal fin origin posterior to pelvic fin insertion. Lateral line complete, decurved, *with 48–57 scales.*

Habitat: Clear creeks with moderate current, over gravel and rocks.

Range: W. New Jersey, S. Pennsylvania south to Savannah River, Georgia, west to W. Tennessee, NE. Mississippi, SW. Kentucky; S. Ohio and E. Kentucky.

Related Species: Redside Dace (*C. elongatus*) has slender, elongate body, 59–70 lateral line scales; occurs in similar habitat from W. New York west to SE. Minnesota, south to Kentucky.

Comments: The Rosyside Dace is generally common within its range. It reaches sexual maturity after a year, and lives for 3 to 4 years.

166 Lake Chub
(*Couesius plumbeus*)

Description: To 7″ (23 cm). Elongate, somewhat rounded; bluish-gray to dark greenish above; with midlateral, lead-colored stripe, faded in older fish; silvery-white below; breeding males bright reddish orange. Snout bluntly rounded; *mouth extends to front of eye;* eye equal to snout length; *barbel present near corner of jaw.* Dorsal fin with 8 rays, origin just posterior to pelvic fin insertion; caudal fin moderately forked. Lateral line complete, *56–69 scales.*

Habitat: Clear to turbid rivers, creeks, and lakes over sand and gravel.

Range: E. Alaska, Canada, N. United States,

south to S. New York, S. Wisconsin, and N. Colorado.

Comments: Lake Chubs, which occasionally reach 9″ (22.9 cm), are used for bait in some areas. Their abundance suggests they may be an important forage fish.

---

117   Grass Carp
(*Ctenopharyngodon idella*)

Description: To 3′3″ (99 cm); 100 lbs (45.4 kg). Robust; back olive-brown, sides silvery, belly whitish; upper scales outlined with dusky pigment giving crosshatched appearance. Snout short; head blunt, broad. Dorsal fin with 8–9 rays, origin over pelvic fin insertion; *anal fin with 8–9 rays, origin nearer caudal fin base than dorsal fin origin;* fins olive to dusky; *caudal peduncle short, deep.* Lateral line complete, 40–42 scales.

Habitat: Rivers and large creeks, but adaptable to ponds and reservoirs.

Range: Introduced into more than 35 states.

Comments: This oriental carp, native to eastern Asia, was introduced into experimental ponds in Alabama and Arkansas in 1963 for aquatic weed control and as a food fish. It feeds primarily on vegetation, grows rapidly, and may eat more than its body weight daily; all are traits that could destroy fish and waterfowl habitats. Stocking of this species is prohibited in some states.

118, 119   Common Carp
(*Cyprinus carpio*)

Description: To 30″ (76 cm); 60 lbs (27.2 kg). Robust, moderately compressed; back dark olive, sides lighter, yellowish below; fins dusky-olive. *2 pairs of barbels on upper lip. Dorsal fin long, has 1 stout, serrate spine, 17–21 rays;* anal fin

with similar spine, 5–6 rays. Lateral
line complete, 32–39 scales.

Habitat: Streams, lakes, ponds, sloughs, and
reservoirs in turbid or clear water over
mud or silt with aquatic vegetation;
more common in warm waters.

Range: Introduced in S. Canada, throughout
United States, and Mexico.

Similar Species: Goldfish (*Carassius auratus*) lacks
barbels; has larger scales.

Comments: Carp were introduced into the United
States during the late 1880s by the
United States Fish Commission as a
food fish. They proved detrimental to
native fish populations and have never
become as popular as game and food
fishes in North America as they are in
Europe. Carp will take a variety of bait,
such as dough balls, cheese, corn, and
worms, and fight when hooked.

---

163 Roundnose Minnow
(*Dionda episcopa*)

Description: To 2½" (6.5 cm). Stout, rounded; back
dark olive, *sides brassy to silvery; dusky,
midlateral stripe,* less prominent on
head, terminates as caudal spot. Head
rounded; snout blunt, slightly longer
than eye; *mouth small, extends to nostril.*
Dorsal and anal fins have 8 rays; dorsal
fin base dark in middle. Lateral line
complete, *35–43 scales.*

Habitat: Rivers and creeks with low gradient, in
clear, shallow pools with vegetation.

Range: Colorado River in S. central Texas,
south and west to Rio Grande, E. New
Mexico and NE. Mexico.

Related Species: Devils River Minnow (*D. diaboli*) has
fewer lateral line scales, wedge-shaped
caudal spot separated from midlateral
stripe, dark margin on scales above
stripe give crosshatched appearance;
restricted to similar habitat in Devils
River, San Felipe and Sycamore creeks,
Val Verde County, and Las Moras
Creek, Kinney County, Texas.

Comments: This species, formerly abundant in
             eastern New Mexico, has disappeared
             from much of its range because of
             changes in its habitat.

172 Silverjaw Minnow
(*Ericymba buccata*)

Description: To 3½″ (9 cm). Cylindrical, terete;

ventral head view

pale olive-yellow above, scales dark-
edged; silvery below. Snout broad,
flattened, longer than eye; *no barbels.*
*Bones of underside and lower part of head
have cavernous channels.* Mid-dorsal stripe
narrow, most prominent anterior to
dorsal fin; fins transparent; no caudal
spot. Breeding males without
tubercles and bright colors. Lateral
line complete, almost straight,
31–36 scales.

Habitat: Small creeks to rivers, with moderate
            current over sand or fine gravel.

Range: S. Pennsylvania, SE. Michigan, N.

Illinois, south to SW. and N. Virginia,
N. Tennessee, and SE. Missouri. Gulf
Coast drainages from N. Georgia and
NE. Mississippi south to W. Florida
and E. Louisiana.

Comments: Silverjaw Minnows run in schools near
             the bottom, feed on larval insects, and
             live about 3 years.

Cutlips Minnow
(*Exoglossum maxillingua*)

Description: To 5″ (12.5 cm). Stout, thick; caudal

ventral head view

peduncle deep; back dark olive; sides
grayish-silver. Head broad, flat above;
snout blunt; *mouth ventral, without
barbel; lower jaw profile has 3 lobes, outer
lobes fleshy,* formed from lower lip. Fins
unmarked, dusky; pectoral fins short;
caudal fin shallowly forked. *Scales
crowded anteriorly;* lateral line complete,
50–53 scales.

Habitat: Clear pools and riffles of creeks and rivers over gravel or rocks.

Range: From St. Lawrence River, S. Canada, south to N. North Carolina.

Related Species: Tonguetied Minnow (*E. laurae*) has barbel near corner of upper jaw, lips not lobed; inhabits streams in SW. New York, NW. Pennsylvania, SW. Ohio, and E. West Virginia south to W. North Carolina.

Comments: During late spring and early summer the Cutlips Minnow spawns in streams, building a mound-shaped nest of gravel 12″ to 18″ (30 cm to 46 cm) in diameter and 3″ to 6″ (7.5 cm to 15 cm) high.

---

127 Tui Chub
(*Gila bicolor*)

Description:  To 16″ (41 cm). Plump, robust; back dark olive to brassy, sides lighter; lower body and fins pinkish in adults; young with dark, midlateral stripe. Head short, somewhat pointed; *mouth small, oblique, not reaching front of eye; no barbels;* eye large. 8–9 dorsal fin rays, origin usually over pelvic fin insertion; anal fin small, 7–9 rays; *caudal peduncle deep, thick.* Lateral line complete, *44–60 scales.*

Habitat: Quiet, shallow waters of large, slow streams, lakes, and ponds with vegetation.

Range: From S. Washington south through Oregon, SW. Idaho, Nevada, E. and S. California.

Comments: Tui Chubs are omnivorous, but feed primarily on invertebrates. They are a good forage fish, but have over-populated some reservoirs, adversely affecting some game fishes. Several subspecies are endangered, and most are restricted to streams and springs in isolated desert basins.

130 **Bonytail**
(*Gila elegans*)

Description: To 24″ (61 cm). Moderately elongate;
greenish-gray above, sides lighter,
whitish below. Breeding males reddish-
orange below and on paired fins. Head
short; *snout depressed, broadly rounded,
usually not overhanging upper lip;* hump
on nape in adults. Fins large, slightly
falcate; usually 10 dorsal fin rays;
10–11 anal fin rays; *caudal peduncle very
narrow;* caudal fin deeply forked. *75–
88 lateral line scales;* scales embedded or
absent on predorsal area, belly, and
caudal peduncle.

Habitat: Swift channels of large, turbid rivers.
Range: Colorado River system, SW. Wyoming
to Mexico. Presently in Green River
drainage, Utah, and Mohave Reservoir,
Arizona-Nevada border.
Related Species: Humpback Chub (*G. cypha*) has snout
slightly overhanging mouth; 9 dorsal
fin rays and 10 or more anal fin rays; in
same habitat and range.
Comments: The Bonytail Chub is an endangered
species threatened by predation and
competition from exotic fishes and by
manmade habitat changes.

---

129 **Roundtail Chub**
(*Gila robusta*)

Description: To 17″ (43 cm). Moderately thick,
streamlined; dusky to olive or silvery
above; sides of males reddish. *Mouth
terminal, reaches front of eye; no barbels;*
head flattened above; eye small. Fins
large; dorsal fin olive, 9–10 rays,
origin behind pelvic fin insertion; 9–10
anal fin rays. *Caudal peduncle moderate to
slender;* caudal fin deeply forked. *Lateral
line complete, 75–95 scales.*

Habitat: Warm, often turbid waters of large
rivers, creeks, pools, and lakes.
Range: Colorado River system, from SW.
Wyoming south to W. New Mexico.

Related Species: Utah Chub (*G. atraria*) has 50–60 lateral line scales; found in streams and reservoirs. Leatherside Chub (*G. copei*) has 8 dorsal and 8 anal fin rays, 68–85 lateral line scales; found in pools and riffles of clear, cold streams. Both occur in W. Wyoming, SE. Idaho, N. and W. Utah.

Comments: This is the most common chub in the Colorado River system. There are 4 subspecies of Roundtail Chubs, which exhibit different body forms and proportions.

186 Flame Chub
(*Hemitremia flammea*)

Description: To 3″ (7.5 cm). Moderately stout; back dark olive to brown, sides light olive to buff-colored; dusky, midlateral stripe extends from snout to caudal spot; belly whitish. Belly, and dorsal, anal, and caudal fin bases reddish in breeding males. Head short; *snout bluntly rounded; mouth small, oblique, extends to front of eye;* no barbels. Fins rounded; *lateral line incomplete, 7–24 pored scales;* 34–42 scales in lateral series.

Habitat: Clear, cool springs, creeks, and pools in small rivers with slow current.

Range: Tennessee River, N. Alabama, NW. Georgia; 1 tributary of Coosa River in Talladega County, Alabama.

Comments: Habitat alteration has reduced or eliminated some populations of the Flame Chub. It is generally rare throughout its range, but can be found in large numbers in some places.

171 California Roach
(*Hesperoleucus symmetricus*)

Description: To 4″ (10 cm). Elongate; back dusky-gray to steel-blue; sides dull silvery with small, dusky dots; breeding males red-orange on chin, opercle, base of paired fins, anal fin. Mouth slightly oblique, not reaching eye; *no barbels;* snout little longer than eye. *Dorsal fin origin far behind pelvic fin insertion; anal fin short, 6–9 rays;* caudal fin forked. Lateral line decurved, complete, 47–63 scales.

Habitat: Small, intermittent tributaries of large streams with moderate gradient.

Range: Pitt River drainage, S. Oregon; Sacramento, San Joaquin drainages, central California; coastal streams in Humboldt County south to Santa Barbara County, California.

Comments: The California Roach is one of the most common fishes in many coastal streams, partly because it can survive in isolated pools of intermittent streams, where conditions are too harsh for most other fishes. It feeds on filamentous algae, crustaceans, and aquatic insects.

167 Brassy Minnow
(*Hybognathus hankinsoni*)

Description: To 4″ (10 cm). Moderately elongate, compressed; back dark olive to blackish, *sides yellowish with brassy reflections.* Head blunt, rounded; snout slightly overhangs small mouth; no barbels. *Tips of dorsal and anal fins rounded; dorsal fin origin just in front of pelvic fin insertion;* 8 anal fin rays; fins clear, plain. Lateral line complete, 36–41 scales.

Habitat: Cool, sluggish streams and over silt and mud in dark, stained water in bogs and ponds with vegetation.

Range: SW. Quebec west to central British Columbia. New York west to Montana, south to N. Missouri and N. Kansas.

Related Species: Cypress Minnow (*H. hayi*) has dark-edged scales in crosshatched pattern on sides; occurs over mud in pools of sluggish streams from Indiana and S. Illinois to Alabama, west to E. Texas.

Comments: The Brassy Minnow is common in the
central and eastern part of its range,
where it is often used for bait. In May
it spawns over plants in quiet pools.

147 Mississippi Silvery Minnow
(*Hybognathus nuchalis*)

Description: To 7″ (18 cm). Thick, stout; back olive
to silvery with dark, mid-dorsal stripe,
silvery below without dark stripe. Snout
blunt, rounded, overhangs mouth; no
barbels; eye diameter greater than
width of mouth. Fins clear; *dorsal fin
pointed, origin anterior to pelvic fin
insertion;* 8 anal fin rays; caudal
peduncle moderately deep. Lateral line
complete, 33–41 scales.

Habitat: Clear pools and backwaters of large
creeks and rivers with slow current.

Range: Mississippi River system from
Wisconsin and Minnesota to E.
Tennessee, Alabama, and E. Texas.

Related Species: Western Silvery Minnow (*H. argyritis*)
has eye diameter less than width of
mouth; occurs in pools of large, silty
streams of S. Alberta and Montana,
southeast in Missouri and Mississippi
rivers between Illinois and Missouri.
Eastern Silvery Minnow (*H. regius*) has
deeper body, more lateral line scales;
occurs in streams on Atlantic Coast
from St. Lawrence River drainage to
central Georgia.

Comments: The Mississippi Silvery Minnow usually
stays on or near the bottom, where it
forms large schools. Its food consists
of algae and organic ooze found on the
muddy bottom.

162 Speckled Chub
(*Hybopsis aestivalis*)

Description: To 3″ (7.5 cm). Slender; olive to
brownish-yellow above; *sides yellow to*

silvery, with small, dark, rounded speckles, often with faint, dusky, midlateral stripe; belly silvery. Mouth ventral; *barbel long; snout rounded, projects far beyond upper lip;* eyes high on head, diameter much less than snout length. 7–8 anal fin rays; lateral line complete, 34–41 scales.

Habitat: Channels of large, clear to turbid streams over sand or gravel in moderate current.

Range: S. Minnesota, Ohio, Nebraska south to Rio Grande drainage in NE. Mexico, W. Florida, NW. Georgia, Alabama west to Texas.

Comments: The Speckled Chub lives on or near the bottom, and uses taste buds on the head, body, and fins to find the aquatic insects on which it feeds. It spawns in deep, swift water around midday from May through August. Its life span seldom exceeds 1½ years.

---

143 Bigeye Chub
(*Hybopsis amblops*)

Description: To 3″ (7.5 cm). Moderately slender; back olive-yellow, scales dark-edged, sides silvery, *with prominent, dusky, midlateral stripe from snout to base of caudal fin.* Head large, flattened above; mouth small, ventral, *barbel present;* snout blunt, rounded, projects beyond upper lip; *eye slightly longer than snout.* Dorsal fin origin over or just posterior to pelvic fin insertion; 8 anal fin rays. Lateral line complete, 33–38 scales.

Habitat: Pools or moderate to large, clear streams with slow current over sand, gravel, or rocks.

Range: W. New York, SE. Michigan, central Illinois south to N. Alabama, central Arkansas; NE. Oklahoma east to N. Georgia and W. North Carolina.

Related Species: Lined Chub (*H. lineapunctata*) has dusky lateral band narrowing posteriorly, terminating in caudal spot;

occurs from NW. Georgia south to
E. central Alabama. Rosyface Chub
(*H. rubrifrons*) has reddish snout and fins;
occurs from NW. South Carolina to
NE. Georgia. Clear Chub (*H. winchelli*)
has slender, more compressed body;
occurs from N. Georgia, NE.
Mississippi south to E. Louisiana, east
to W. Florida. All in similar habitat.

Comments: Its large eye and clear-water habitat
suggest that the Bigeye Chub locates
its food by sight. Intolerant of silt, it
has disappeared from some heavily
silted streams.

164 Streamline Chub
(*Hybopsis dissimilis*)

Description: To 4½" (11.5 cm). Slender; back olive-
yellow with narrow, predorsal stripe of
alternating gold and dusky areas; *sides
silvery with 6–9 large, dark, horizontal,
midlateral blotches underlaid by dusky
stripe;* belly silvery to white. Snout
extends beyond upper lip; *barbel present;*
eye large. Dorsal fin origin anterior to
pelvic fin insertion. Lateral line
complete, 44–49 scales.

Habitat: Moderate to large, clear streams over
clean gravel in moderate to swift
current.

Range: Ohio River drainage, W. New York,
N. Indiana south to N. Alabama; S.
Missouri and N. Arkansas.

Related Species: Blotched Chub (*H. insignis*) has rows of
spots above and below dusky, midlateral
stripe; vertical, midlateral blotches;
occurs from SW. Virginia, S. Kentucky
south to N. Alabama east to N.
Georgia. Gravel Chub (*H. x-punctata*)
has scattered X-shaped markings on
sides; occurs from SE. Ontario, W.
New York, SE. Minnesota south to S.
Arkansas. Both in similar habitat.

Comments: These chubs are intolerant of such
habitat alterations as impoundments,
channelization, and pollution. Their

numbers have been reduced over much of their range. They spawn during May and June, and feed on aquatic insects and snails.

126 Flathead Chub
(Hybopsis gracilis)

Description: To 12½" (32 cm). Slender; back brownish to silvery; silvery-white below, no dark spots or blotches. Head wedge-shaped; snout flattened, extends beyond upper lip; mouth somewhat oblique, extends to small eye; *barbel present. Breast scaled. Pectoral and dorsal fins falcate;* lower lobe of caudal fin dusky. Lateral line complete, 42–59 scales.

Habitat: Large, turbid rivers and lower parts of large tributaries over sand, gravel, or rocks in moderate to swift current; rarely in lakes.

Range: Great Slave Lake and Mackenzie River drainage south to S. Manitoba, west to S. Alberta; from Montana south to Mississippi River in Louisiana; west to N. New Mexico; common in Missouri River.

Comments: This is the largest species of its genus. It feeds primarily on terrestrial insects but also consumes aquatic insects, vegetation, and even small fishes.

170 Sicklefin Chub
(Hybopsis meeki)

Description: To 4" (10 cm). Cylindrical, terete; yellowish to tan with silvery reflections above; silvery-white below. Head bluntly rounded; snout extends just beyond upper lip, not depressed; mouth small, barbel present. *Breast without scales. Pectoral fin long,* extends past base of pelvic fin; *dorsal fin strongly falcate.* Caudal peduncle slender, lower lobe of caudal fin dark with white margin. Lateral line complete, 43–50 scales.

Habitat: Large, swift, warm, turbid rivers over sand or gravel.

Range: Mississippi and Missouri rivers from Montana to Louisiana; not known in Arkansas or Tennessee.

Related Species: Sturgeon Chub (*H. gelida*) has depressed head; keels present on scales above lateral line; occurs in similar habitat in Mississippi River from Missouri to Louisiana; Missouri River drainage from Montana and Wyoming to Missouri.

Comments: Both of these chubs, with their reduced eyes and external taste buds, are well adapted to turbid water.

Spotfin Chub
(*Hybopsis monacha*)

Description: To 3½" (9 cm). Elongate, compressed; back olive; *sides silvery to steel-blue,* blotches and speckles absent. Snout extends beyond upper lip; *barbels small,* sometimes absent; eyes small, laterally placed. Dark spot on posterior dorsal fin rays. *Large, dark caudal spot present.* Lateral line complete, *52–62 scales.*

Habitat: Large, clear streams over gravel or rocks in or near moderate to swift current.

Range: Tennessee River drainage, SW. Virginia south to NW. Georgia and N. Alabama.

Related Species: Thicklip Chub (*H. labrosa*) robust, with dark pigment on pelvic and median fins; 34–40 lateral line scales; occurs in similar habitat in S. Virginia, W. North Carolina, and N. South Carolina. Santee Chub (*H. zanema*) slender, elongate; lacks dark markings on pelvic, anal, and caudal fins; inhabits streams over sand or rocks in warm, clear to turbid waters in Santee River system, S. North Carolina and N. South Carolina.

Comments: The Spotfin Chub has disappeared from much of its former range and is on the United States list of threatened species. This chub feeds mainly on larval aquatic insects. It spawns in late spring and early autumn.

135 Silver Chub
(*Hybopsis storeriana*)

Description: To 9″ (23 cm). Moderately stout; back olive, *silvery-white below without dark markings.* Snout blunt, rounded, extends beyond upper lip; mouth small; *barbels present.* 7–8 dorsal fin rays, origin before pelvic fin insertion. Lower lobe of caudal fin dusky with white margin. Lateral line complete, 35–41 scales.

Habitat: Pools; in slow current of large streams over sand or gravel; occasionally in lakes and reservoirs.

Range: SE. Ontario, SE. Manitoba; W. New York west to North Dakota, south to Alabama, west to E. Texas.

Comments: The Silver Chub, the second largest species in the genus, is widespread and fairly common in the rivers of the Mississippi Valley. It feeds primarily on aquatic insects and crustaceans, and its lifespan is about 3 years.

187 Least Chub
(*Iotichthys phlegethontis*)

Description: To 2½″ (6.5 cm). Moderately deep, compressed; back olive-green; *sides steel-blue, golden stripe from upper end of gill opening to caudal fin base;* lower sides and belly golden, reddish in breeding males. Mouth very oblique, extends to front of large eye; no barbels. Fins yellowish; 8–9 dorsal fin rays, origin just posterior to pelvic fin insertion; caudal fin slightly forked. *Lateral line*

absent or only 1–3 pored scales; 34–38 scales in lateral series.

Habitat: Clear, shallow streams, springs, ponds, and swamps with abundant vegetation over clay, mud, or organic debris.

Range: Bonneville Basin of N. central Utah.

Comments: In some areas Least Chubs survive in harsh habitats with highly alkaline waters, low dissolved oxygen, and temperatures varying by 59° F (15° C) in a day. Sexually mature after 1 year and when just over 1″ (2.5 cm) long, they spawn from April to August with a peak in May. Their maximum life span is about 3 years.

125 Hitch
(*Lavinia exilicauda*)

Description: To 13″ (33 cm). Deep, compressed; caudal peduncle slender; back dark brownish-yellow; sides lighter, silvery, scale margins dusky; median fins clear to dusky. Head small; mouth terminal, oblique, not reaching eye; *no barbels.* Dorsal fin origin just posterior to pelvic fin insertion; *anal fin long, 10–14 rays;* caudal fin deeply forked. *Lateral line decurved, complete, with 54–62 scales.*

Habitat: Warm, sluggish streams, sloughs, ponds, lakes, usually with vegetation; established in some reservoirs.

Range: Sacramento, San Joaquin, Pajaro, and Salinas rivers; Clear Lake, California.

Comments: Although less common than before, the Hitch has survived habitat alterations and the introduction of exotic predators and competitors.

160 Little Colorado Spinedace
(*Lepidomeda vittata*)

Description: To 4″ (10 cm). Robust anteriorly, moderately compressed; back olive to bluish gray, *sides silvery with fine, black spots and blotches* and thin, dark, vertical lines to dorsal fin. Head broad; mouth moderately oblique; *no barbels;* eyes large. Fins clear; *dorsal fin with 2 spines,* 6 rays; 8 anal fin rays. Lateral line complete, *90–103 scales.*

Habitat: Clear streams and large pools 1–3' over rock and gravel.

Range: Upper part of Little Colorado River system, E. central Arizona.

Related Species: White River Spinedace (*L. albivallis*) has 9 anal fin rays, 79–92 lateral line scales; occurs in springs of White River system, E. central Nevada. Virgin Spinedace (*L. mollispinis*) has 9 anal fin rays, 77–90 lateral line scales; occurs in clear streams and pools over rock and gravel in Virgin River system, SW. Utah, SE. Nevada, and NW. Arizona.

Comments: The population of this species has declined in recent decades due to habitat changes, such as dams and water diversion, and the introduction of exotic minnows and game fishes.

161 Spikedace
(*Meda fulgida*)

Description: To 3" (7.5 cm). Elongate, slender, slightly compressed; back olive-brown with dark mottles; *sides silvery with scattered, black specks.* Snout short; mouth extends to below eye; *no barbels;* eye large. Base of fins, except caudal, reddish; *dorsal fin with 2 spines,* 7 branched rays, origin posterior to pelvic fin insertion; 9 anal fin rays. *Scales embedded or absent.*

Habitat: Over sand or gravel in pools of larger streams with moderate to swift current.

Range: Gila River system in central and SE. Arizona and SW. New Mexico.

Comments: The Spikedace was once widespread in the Gila River drainage, but has been displaced in many areas by the newly introduced Red Shiner.

176 Moapa Dace
(*Moapa coriacea*)

Description: To 3″ (7.5 cm). Robust, heavy
anteriorly; olive-yellow above; sides
with dusky, midlateral stripe on
posterior half of body; silvery below.
Head blunt, rounded; mouth
horizontal, extends to front of eye; *lips
thick, no barbels.* 8 dorsal fin rays, origin
over pelvic fin insertion. *Black caudal
spot present.* Scales small, embedded.
Lateral line complete, with *70–80
scales.*

Habitat: Thermal 66°–90° F (19°–32° C)
spring pools and their outflow in clear
water with moderate current.

Range: Moapa River, NE. Clark County,
Nevada.

Comments: In recent years the number of Moapa
Dace has declined because of manmade changes in its habitat and the
introduction of exotic fishes and the
bullfrog. It is on the United States list
of endangered species.

138 Peamouth
(*Mylocheilus caurinus*)

Description: To 14″ (36 cm). Elongate, somewhat
compressed; back olive-brown; lighter
below with *dark lateral stripe from near
top of head to caudal fin base,* and
sometimes another from middle of
opercle to near anal fin origin. Head
about one-fifth of length. Mouth small;
barbel present at each corner of jaw;
upper jaw protractile, *no frenum. Pelvic
axillary scales well developed;* caudal fin
deeply forked. Lateral line complete,
68–79 scales.

Habitat: Lakes, slow-flowing rivers in deeper
water; brackish water at river mouths.

Range: N. British Columbia, Vancouver Island
and other islands off British Columbia,
south to NW. Montana, SW. Idaho,
and N. Oregon.

Comments: The Peamouth is one of the few
cyprinids that tolerate salt water. A
scooling fish, it feeds on aquatic
insects and crustaceans at midwater and
on the bottom. It lives about 13 years,
unusually long for a minnow.

136 Hardhead
(*Mylopharodon conocephalus*)

Description: To 18″ (46 cm). Elongate, moderately
compressed; *back brown to dusky bronze,*
lighter below. Head broad, cone-
shaped; mouth horizontal, lips thick,
upper jaw extends to eye; *frenum present;*
no barbels. Dorsal fin has 8 rays, origin
posterior to pelvic insertion; anal fin
short, with 8–9 rays. Caudal peduncle
moderately slender and caudal fin
moderately forked. Lateral line
complete, *69–81 scales.*
Habitat: Quiet sections of large, warm, clear
streams with deep pools over rocky or
sandy bottoms.
Range: Pit, Sacramento, Russian, and San
Joaquin river systems in California.
Comments: Hardheads used to be more abundant,
prior to habitat changes and the
introduction of exotic fishes. They feed
on plant and animal matter taken on or
near the bottom. Reaching sexual
maturity after 2 years, they have a life
span of 5 to 6 years.

112 Hornyhead Chub
(*Nocomis biguttatus*)

Description: To 10″ (25 cm). Stout, heavy; olive-
brown above, sides light olive with
dusky caudal spot; young have dusky to
black lateral stripe. Head blunt, wide;
mouth almost terminal, small barbel at
corner of jaw. *Males have bright red spot*
behind eye, and head has 60–130 breeding
tubercles but no swollen crest. Dorsal fin

olive, 8 rays; 7 anal fin rays; caudal fin reddish, tips rounded. Lateral line complete, 38–46 scales.

Habitat: Creeks and small rivers in clear pools or moderate current over gravel.

Range: SE. Ontario and S. Manitoba, south to New York, N. Arkansas west to SE. Wyoming and E. Colorado.

Related Species: Redspot Chub (*N. asper*) male has breeding tubercles on front of body; occurs in similar habitat in SE. Kansas, SW. Missouri, W. Arkansas, and E. Oklahoma. Redtail Chub (*N. effusus*) has pelvic, anal, and caudal fins reddish-orange; male has breeding tubercles on head and body; occurs in similar habitat in S. Kentucky and N. Tennessee.

Comments: The Hornyhead Chub feeds on algae, other plants, aquatic insects, snails, and crustaceans. Although hardy and used as bait in some areas, it has become less abundant in silty streams.

---

116 Bluehead Chub
(*Nocomis leptocephalus*)

Description: To 8″ (20 cm). Stout, robust, not compressed; back olive-brown, sides bluish to brassy reddish orange in adults; young have dark lateral stripe and caudal spot. Head large; small barbel at corner of jaw; *males have 5–15 breeding tubercles on swollen crest between eyes,* no tubercles on snout tip. Fins rounded; *8 anal fin rays.* Breast region almost completely scaled; lateral line complete, 36–43 scales.

Habitat: Pools of small streams with widths of 10–50′ (3–15.2 m), over sand, gravel, and rocks, and in clear to slightly turbid water.

Range: Atlantic Coast streams, N. Virginia south to Georgia; Gulf Coast streams, W. Georgia west to S. Mississippi, E. Louisiana; Tennessee River system in NW. Alabama and NE. Mississippi.

Comments: The Bluehead Chub, like others in the
genus *Nocomis,* constructs a large, dome-
shaped stone nest during the spawning
period from late April to July. The
nest, up to 3' (91 cm) wide and several
inches high, is constructed by the
male, which picks up and carries stones
in its mouth to the nest site.

113, 114   River Chub
(*Nocomis micropogon*)

Description: To 10" (25 cm). Cylindrical, stout in
front; olive-brown above, sides silvery;
young have dusky lateral stripe. Head
broad; snout blunt; mouth large, small
barbel at corner of jaw; *no red spot behind
eye. Males rosy-colored, with 30–65
breeding tubercles on snout tip and between
nostrils,* none between eyes. Dorsal and
caudal fins olive-yellow to reddish-
orange. Lateral line complete, 37–43
scales.

Habitat: Clear, medium to large creeks, rivers,
and pools with moderate to swift
current over gravel and rocks.

Range: SE. Ontario; S. New York west to
Michigan and Indiana, south to S.
Virginia, and NW. South Carolina,
west to NW. Alabama.

Related Species: Bigmouth Chub (*N. platyrhynchus*) with
breast mostly scaled; male has up to
100 small tubercles from tip of snout to
top of head; occurs in SE. West
Virginia south to NW. North
Carolina. Bull Chub (*N. raneyi*) male
has over 100 tubercles from tip of snout
to top of head; occurs in S. Virginia
and N. central North Carolina. Both in
similar habitat.

Comments: Used for bait in some areas, River
Chubs live for about 5 years and reach
sexual maturity when 3 years old. Like
other *Nocomis,* spawning occurs
intermittently over the pebble nest,
which is guarded by the male. Other
small minnows often spawn on the nest

while the male chub is gathering stones. It feeds on algae, aquatic insects, crustaceans, and mollusks.

131, 141   Golden Shiner
(*Notemigonus crysoleucas*)

Description: To 12" (30 cm). Deep, compressed; back golden to olive, *sides light olive with silvery reflections,* belly silvery-yellow; some fish entirely silvery. Mouth upturned, maxilla extends to nostril; snout blunt. *Belly has pronounced keel between pelvic and anal fins.* Dorsal fin slightly falcate; breeding males have orange on pelvic and anal fins. Lateral line decurved, complete, *44–55 scales.*

keel

Habitat: Clear, quiet streams, lakes, ponds, and swamps over mud, sand, or rocks, usually near aquatic vegetation.

Range: Native to E. North America, S. Canada, and south to Texas; widely introduced elsewhere.

Comments: Golden Shiners are the most common bait fish sold in the United States and are important forage fish for several species of game fishes. They are schooling fishes that stay mainly near shore but may venture into open water.

SHINERS
(Genus *Notropis*)

The genus *Notropis,* consisting of 110 species, is the largest genus of North American freshwater fishes and represents about half of the family Cyprinidae on this continent. With the exception of a few species in northwestern Mexico, the genus is confined to fresh water east of the Rocky Mountains in Canada, the United States, and Mexico. These fishes have adapted to many habitats, including creeks, rivers, lakes, and swamps.

Shape and color vary widely, but many species appear very similar, making identification difficult. Shiners are also easily confused with other members of the family Cyprinidae. The following characteristics will help identify *Notropis* species: Their length is less than 8" (20 cm); the dorsal fin typically has 8 rays; there are usually no barbels; the scales in the lateral series are large, and there are usually fewer than 40 scales, and never more than 55. Like many other fishes, breeding males may be brightly colored (when compared to nonbreeding males and females), and may have tubercles on the head, body, and fins.

151 Satinfin Shiner
(*Notropis analostanus*)

Description: To 3½" (9 cm). Deep, moderately compressed; dark olive above; sides silvery to blue-gray; *scales dark-edged, diamond-shaped;* no caudal spot. Snout pointed, mouth slightly subterminal, oblique; eye small. *Posterior membranes of dorsal fin pigmented,* other fins plain; *13–14 pectoral fin rays; 9 anal fin rays;* edge of fins, tips of caudal fin white in breeding males. Lateral line complete, 34–37 scales.

Habitat: Clear to turbid water of small to large streams with slow to moderate current over sand or gravel.

Range: Lake Ontario drainage, New York. Atlantic Coast streams from New York south to S. North Carolina.

Related Species: Steelcolor Shiner (*N. whipplei*) has 15 pectoral fin rays; 9 anal fin rays; occurs in similar habitat from SE. Ohio west to N. Illinois, W. West Virginia to E. Oklahoma, W. central Alabama to N. Louisiana.

Comments: The Satinfin Shiner breeds from May to August. Spawning males defend their territory against other males by swimming toward them with their fins erect and making knocking sounds. Males produce a purring noise as they circle the females during courtship.

165 Emerald Shiner
(*Notropis atherinoides*)

Description: To 4″ (10 cm). Streamlined, elongate, *strongly compressed;* back yellow-olive to blue-green, *sides silvery with iridescent emerald band most visible posteriorly,* belly silvery. Snout pointed; mouth oblique, terminal, moderately large; eye large. *Fins plain;* dorsal fin origin posterior to pelvic fin insertion; *10–13 anal fin rays;* caudal fin moderately forked. Lateral line complete, with 35–43 scales.

Habitat: Clear to slightly turbid, open waters of large streams, lakes, and reservoirs.

Range: Mackenzie River drainage, S. Northwest Territories south and east through S. Canada and east to St. Lawrence River drainage. New York west through Great Lakes to Montana, south to Gulf Coast of Alabama, and west to E. Texas.

Comments: The Emerald Shiner, often found in large streams and sometimes in lakes, lives in sizable schools in midwater, where it feeds on small crustaceans and aquatic insects. It is an important forage species for a variety of game fishes and is used for bait.

148 Bigeye Shiner
(*Notropis boops*)

Description: To 3″ (7.5 cm). Cylindrical, terete, slightly compressed; greenish to olive-yellow above; scales dark-edged; sides silvery with dark lateral stripe about width of pupil extending from snout tip, unpigmented area above lateral stripe; lateral line pores outlined in black. *Eye large, diameter more than one-third head length;* mouth terminal, oblique; males with tubercles on head. Fins unpigmented; dorsal and anal fins slightly falcate; *8 anal fin rays.* Lateral line complete, 34–38 scales; *17 or fewer predorsal scales.*

Habitat: Clear pools of medium to large streams, with moderate current, over sand, gravel, or rocks.

Range: NW. Ohio, N. Illinois south to N. Alabama; NE. Missouri, SE. Kansas south to NE. Louisiana, west to SE. Oklahoma.

Comments: Bigeye Shiners are intolerant of prolonged periods in turbid water. They feed primarily on insects, which they locate by sight. On occasion, they will leap a few inches out of the water to capture insects hovering just above the surface.

191 Striped Shiner
(*Notropis chrysocephalus*)

Description: To 7″ (18 cm). Deep, compressed; back olive with broad, dusky predorsal stripe; *dusky to dark stripes above, converging behind dorsal fin;* sides silvery to bluish-gray, rosy in breeding males.

lateral scales

Mouth terminal, oblique; *chin tip dusky;* eye large. Fins pinkish, rounded; dorsal fin origin clearly in front of pelvic fin insertion; 9 anal fin rays. Lateral line complete, 37–40 scales; *lateral scales high, narrow; fewer than 22 predorsal scales.*

Habitat: Clean creeks and small rivers with moderate current, riffles, and pools over sand, gravel, or rocks.

Range: SE. Ontario; W. New York west to SE. Wisconsin, south to S. Alabama west to SW. Missouri, E. Oklahoma, and E. Texas.

Related Species: Crescent Shiner (*N. cerasinus*) has black crescent-shaped markings on sides; occurs in clear, small to medium streams in S. central Virginia and N. central North Carolina.

Comments: Until recently this fish was considered a subspecies of the Common Shiner, to which it is closely related. The Striped Shiner is common throughout most of its range and is often found in large schools.

189 Warpaint Shiner
(*Notropis coccogenis*)

Description: To 5″ (12.5 cm). Moderately elongate and compressed; back olive-yellow, sides and belly silvery, *edge of gill opening black.* Head moderately large; eye large; mouth terminal, oblique, upper lip reddish; *vertical, red line behind eye.* Pectoral fin base red; dorsal fin origin behind pelvic fin insertion; *anterior base of dorsal fin reddish, blue to black posteriorly;* other fins plain. Lateral line complete, 39–43 scales.

Habitat: Medium to large, clear, swift streams over gravel and rocks.

Range: SW. Virginia, E. Tennessee south to NW. South Carolina, N. Georgia west to S. central Tennessee and NW. Alabama.

Related Species: Bandfin Shiner (*N. zonistius*) has black band through center of dorsal fin; caudal fin bright red; occurs in similar habitat in N. and W. Georgia, E. Alabama, and N. central Florida.

Comments: The specific name *coccogenis* means berry-red cheeks, and refers to the red line on the cheeks of this colorful shiner. The common name Warpaint Shiner also calls attention to the bright red coloration.

155 Common Shiner
(*Notropis cornutus*)

Description: To 6″ (15 cm). Deep, compressed; back dusky olive with dark, wide predorsal stripe; sides silvery to bluish-purple in breeding males. Head moderately large, blunt; mouth large, terminal, oblique; *chin without dusky pigment;* eye large. *Fins clear to rosy, rounded;* dorsal fin origin over or in front of pelvic fin insertion; 8 or 9 anal fin rays. Lateral line complete, 36–44 scales; *lateral scales tall, narrow; 22–32 predorsal scales.*

Habitat: Clear, cool creeks and small rivers with moderate current in riffles and pools over firm bottom.

Range: Nova Scotia west to SE. Saskatchewan, south to central Virginia, west to SE. Wyoming, E. Colorado.

Related Species: White Shiner (*N. albeolus*) has sharp snout, posterior lateral line scales not high or narrow; occurs in streams over gravel and rock from SE. West Virginia south to N. North Carolina.

Comments: The Common Shiner, as its name implies, is found frequently in much of its range. It is often replaced by the Striped Shiner in streams that have become warm, turbid, and silty. It is often used as bait for basses and other game fishes.

150, 173 Pugnose Minnow
(*Notropis emiliae*)

Description: To 2½″ (6.5 cm). Moderately deep, compressed; back yellowish-olive, *sides silvery with dusky midlateral stripe* extending from snout, scales on sides outlined in dark pigment. *Snout blunt; mouth small, upturned, almost vertical;* barbel occasionally present. *9 dorsal fin rays,* front and rear rays dusky in males; other fins plain. Lateral line complete or interrupted, 36–40 scales.

Habitat: Clear, sluggish waters with little current and abundant vegetation over organic debris.

Range: Lake St. Clair drainage, Ontario; Coastal Plain, S. South Carolina south to Florida, west to Texas; E. Ohio west to SE. Minnesota, south to S. Texas.

Comments: The upturned mouth of the Pugnose Minnow suggests that this fish feeds in midwater or near the surface. The specific name *emiliae* honors Mrs. Emily Hay, whose husband discovered the species.

152 Whitetail Shiner
(*Notropis galacturus*)

Description: To 5″ (12.5 cm). Cylindrical, terete, slightly compressed; back olive to dusky, *sides silvery to blue-gray,* upper sides have dark, diffuse lateral stripe. Mouth terminal; eye small. Dorsal fin reddish, *posterior ray membranes black; caudal fin dusky, upper and lower base creamy-white;* anal fin reddish, 9 rays. Lateral line complete, 39–41 scales. *Scales black-edged, diamond-shaped.*

Habitat: Large creeks to small rivers with cool, clear water and moderate current over gravel or rocks.

Range: Tennessee and Cumberland river drainages, SW. Virginia, S. Kentucky, south to NW. South Carolina, west to NE. Mississippi; S. Missouri and N. Arkansas.

Related Species: Bluntface Shiner (*N. camurus*) has blunt snout, deeper body; occurs in similar habitat from SW. Kentucky south to E. Louisiana, Arkansas River system, SE. Kansas to NW. Arkansas.

Comments: The Whitetail Shiner eats aquatic and terrestrial insects. It is an active swimmer and is constantly moving.

146 Spottail Shiner
(*Notropis hudsonius*)

Description: To 6″ (15 cm). Deep, moderately robust; back yellowish, *silvery below with faint lateral stripe.* Snout blunt, rounded; eye large; mouth extends to eye. Dorsal and anal fins often slightly falcate; 8 anal fin rays; *caudal fin with black spot at base, lower rays whitish;* other fins plain. Lateral line complete, 36–42 scales.

Habitat: Creeks, rivers, and lakes with slow to moderately fast current over sand, gravel, and rocks.

Range: Mackenzie River system, Northwest Territories south to S. Canada, west from St. Lawrence River system. Massachusetts south on Atlantic Coast to central Georgia and west to North and South Dakota; Mississippi Valley south to S. Missouri.

Comments: The Spottail Shiner is one of the most widespread minnows. It is an important forage fish and is often used for bait, especially for Walleyes. The Spottail Shiner seems to be most common in large bodies of water.

177 Sailfin Shiner
(*Notropis hypselopterus*)

Description: To 2½″ (6.5 cm). Deep, compressed; back dark olive with dark predorsal stripe; upper side has golden-pink stripe, *broad steel-blue lateral band.* Dorsal fin large, slightly rounded, origin far behind pelvic fin insertion, tip clear, remainder black; anal fin olive-yellow, 10–11 rays; *caudal fin base dusky olive with 2 small, bright red spots,* outer half olive-yellow. Lateral line complete, decurved, 33–38 scales; *22–24 predorsal scales.*

Habitat: Clear to dark, stained waters of creeks with slow to moderate current and abundant aquatic vegetation.

Range: South Carolina south to peninsular
Florida west to SW. Alabama.

Related Species: Flagfin Shiner (*N. signipinnis*) has large
yellow spots at caudal fin base; occurs
in similar habitat from Apalachicola
River drainage in W. Florida west to
Pearl River drainage, E. Louisiana.

Comments: The Sailfin and Flagfin shiners are
attractive fishes that are easily kept
in aquariums. Their common and
scientific names call attention to their
very large dorsal fin.

---

190 Red Shiner
(*Notropis lutrensis*)

Description: To 3½″ (9 cm). *Very deep, compressed;*
back dark olive to bluish; *sides steel-blue
to silvery-blue with dark wedge-shaped bar
behind opercle.* Head short, deep; mouth
terminal, oblique; eye small; *border of
gill opening reddish.* Dorsal fin dusky, no
black blotch on posterior membranes;
other fins dusky to reddish-orange. 9
anal fin rays; caudal peduncle short.
Lateral line complete, 32–37 scales.

Habitat: Small to large, turbid streams with
slow to moderate current over sand or
gravel.

Range: N. Illinois west to S. South Dakota and
SE. Wyoming, southeast to Louisiana,
west to Rio Grande, Texas, New
Mexico, and Mexico; widely introduced.

Comments: The most common shiner in the turbid,
silty streams of the midwestern Plains
Region, the Red Shiner is an important
forage and bait fish. Its bright colors
and hardiness have made it a popular
aquarium fish.

---

179 Taillight Shiner
(*Notropis maculatus*)

Description: To 3″ (7.5 cm). Long, slender; olive to
yellowish-brown above, scales dark-

edged, giving crosshatched appearance; *dusky lateral stripe from snout to caudal fin ends in large, black caudal spot;* breeding males reddish. Snout rounded; mouth subterminal. Dorsal and anal fins falcate; edges of pelvic, dorsal, and anal fins dusky; leading edge of dorsal fin black; 8 anal fin rays. *Lateral line incomplete, 34–39 scales.*

Habitat: Clear or dark, stained backwaters and quiet areas of lowland rivers, streams, and lakes with some aquatic vegetation.

Range: Coastal Plain, S. North Carolina, south to S. Florida, west to E. Texas; in Mississippi River valley, S. Illinois south to E. Texas.

Comments: The total lifespan of the Taillight Shiner is 13 to 15 months. It grows rapidly, sometimes reaching sexual maturity and spawning at 6 to 9 months.

182 Ozark Minnow
(*Notropis nubilus*)

Description: To 3" (7.5 cm). Slender, slightly compressed; dusky yellow to olive above, scales dark-edged; *dark lateral stripe from snout terminating in small caudal spot;* yellow to orange below. Mouth slightly oblique; eye large. Dorsal fin origin over pelvic fin insertion; *outer half of fins clear, bases orange; fins rounded;* 8 anal fin rays. Lateral line complete, 33–38 scales; *13–14 predorsal scales.*

Habitat: Clear pools of small to medium streams with steep gradient over sand, gravel, or rocks.

Range: S. Wisconsin and SE. Minnesota, south to NE. Oklahoma and N. Arkansas.

Comments: One of the most common minnows in the Ozark Uplands, this species spawns from late April to early July over the gravel nest of chubs. Breeding males maintain a small territory during spawning.

188 Rosyface Shiner
(*Notropis rubellus*)

Description: To 3½" (9 cm). Long, slender, compressed; olive to bluish above with dusky to orange lateral stripe, darker posteriorly; *lateral line pores dark-edged; breeding males reddish.* Snout sharp; mouth terminal, slightly oblique. *Fins plain; dorsal fin origin behind pelvic fin insertion; 10–13 anal fin rays.* Lateral line complete, 36–40 scales; 17–21 predorsal scales.

Habitat: Clear pools and riffles of large creeks to small rivers with moderate current over gravel or rock.

Range: SW. Quebec west through Great Lakes drainage to S. Manitoba, south to N. Alabama, S. Arkansas, and E. Oklahoma.

Related Species: Silver Shiner (*N. photogenis*) grows to 5" (12.5 cm), has dark crescent-shaped markings between nostrils; breeding males not reddish; occurs in large, clear streams with moderate current from Lake Erie drainage, Ontario, and W. New York south to NE. Georgia and S. Tennessee.

Comments: This shiner has become less abundant in some streams that have become silty and turbid. Its specific name, *rubellus,* means reddish, describing the color of breeding males.

149 Spotfin Shiner
(*Notropis spilopterus*)

Description: To 4½" (11.5 cm). Deep, moderately compressed; back olive; *sides silvery-blue, scales dark-edged, diamond-shaped;* posterior dusky stripe below lateral line. Snout pointed; mouth slightly ventral, oblique; eye small. *Fins plain, bases yellowish, edges milky-white in breeding males; 14 pectoral fin rays; posterior dorsal fin membranes dusky,* and posterior edge straight; 8 anal fin rays.

Lateral line complete, 35–40 scales.

Habitat: Clear to slightly turbid pools and channels with moderate current over firm sand or gravel in large creeks and rivers.

Range: St. Lawrence River and Great Lakes drainage in SW. Quebec and SE. Ontario. New York south to W. North Carolina, N. Alabama west to Minnesota, SE. North Dakota south to E. Oklahoma.

Comments: The Spotfin Shiner spawns from June to late August, depositing eggs under loose bark and in crevices of submerged logs and tree roots. Prior to spawning, several males may engage in combat until a single male remains over the spawning site.

174 Weed Shiner
(*Notropis texanus*)

Description: To 3″ (7.5 cm). Elongate, moderately compressed; straw-colored above, with dusky predorsal stripe; scales dark-edged, *sides have prominent, dark lateral stripe ending as dark spot at caudal fin base;* area around stripe pale. Head short; snout blunt; mouth terminal, oblique; eye large, high on head. *Fins plain,* rosy in breeding males; *7 anal fin rays, last 2–4 rays with dusky edges.* Lateral line complete, 31–37 scales.

Habitat: Clear, open waters in slow, lowland streams over sand or gravel, often with some vegetation.

Range: Minnesota, Wisconsin, and S. Michigan south to N. Florida and west from S. Georgia along Gulf Coastal Plain to S. Texas.

Related Species: Ironcolor Shiner (*N. chalybaeus*) has 8 anal fin rays with dusky edges; occurs in similar habitat from SE. New York south on Coastal Plain to Florida, west to S. Texas; Mississippi Valley in S. Michigan and Wisconsin south to Louisiana.

Comments: The Weed Shiner is common in the southern part of its range, but rare in northern areas. It was first collected in Texas, thus its specific name *texanus*.

---

153 Redfin Shiner
(*Notropis umbratilis*)

Description: To 3½" (9 cm). *Deep, very compressed;* light olive above with overlying dusky pigment, sides silvery; reddish in breeding males. Mouth terminal, oblique; eye moderately large; top of head blue-gray, with numerous tubercles in breeding males. Fins black or black and red; dorsal fin origin posterior to pelvic fin insertion; *anterior dorsal fin rays have black spot on base;* 10–12 anal fin rays. *Lateral line decurved,* complete, 38–50 scales; *scales crowded anteriorly;* 25 predorsal scales.

Habitat: Small to moderately large streams with pools having slow to moderate current over sand, gravel, or rock, often with aquatic vegetation.

Range: SE. Ontario; W. New York, and W. Pennsylvania west to SE. Minnesota, S. Wisconsin south to S. Louisiana, E. Oklahoma, and E. Texas.

Related Species: Rosefin Shiner (*N. ardens*) has slender body, reddish fins; occurs in similar habitat in Atlantic Coast streams in S. Virginia and N. North Carolina; SW. Ohio, SE. Indiana south to NW. Georgia and N. Alabama.

Comments: Redfin Shiners spawn over the nests of sunfishes, to which they are attracted by the scent of fluids released by sunfishes during spawning. As many as 30 to 100 male Redfin Shiners have been observed over a single large Green Sunfish nest.

175   **Blacktail Shiner**
(*Notropis venustus*)

Description: To 7″ (18 cm). Deep, compressed; olive
above; *sides silvery to steel-blue, scales
dark-edged, diamond-shaped; large, black
spot on caudal peduncle* extending onto
base of caudal fin. Head pointed;
mouth slightly inferior, oblique; eye
small. Breeding males have small
tubercles on head and body. Posterior
3 dorsal fin membranes black. Lateral
line complete, 36–41 scales.

Habitat: Clear to turbid waters of medium to
large streams over sand, gravel, or
rock.

Range: S. Illinois, W. Kentucky, and SE.
Missouri south to W. Georgia and N.
Florida, west in Gulf Coast drainages to
Rio Grande drainage in Texas.

Related Species: Alabama Shiner (*N. callistius*) has blunt
snout overhanging its upper lip; occurs
in streams with moderate current over
gravel or rock in Mobile Bay drainage
of SE. Tennessee, NW. Georgia,
central Alabama, and E. Mississippi.

Comments: The common Blacktail Shiner, an
important forage species, is considered
good bait, especially for basses and
sunfishes. When it occurs in the same
area as the Red Shiner the 2 species
occasionally hybridize.

---

145   **Mimic Shiner**
(*Notropis volucellus*)

Description: To 3″ (7.5 cm). Slender, slightly
compressed; back yellowish-olive, scales
dark-edged; *sides silvery with faint dusky
lateral stripe; dark around anus.* Snout

lateral scales

rounded; mouth small, slightly
oblique; eye large. Fins plain; *tips of
pelvic fins do not reach front of anal fin;* 8
anal fin rays. Breeding males without
bright colors, small tubercles present
on head and pectoral fins. Lateral line
complete, 32–39 scales; *anterior lateral*

line scales tall and narrow.

Habitat: Clear lakes and medium to large streams with clear to turbid waters in moderate current over sand, gravel, or rocks.

Range: S. Quebec west to S. Manitoba, south to Alabama, west to S. Texas. Atlantic Coast streams in SE. Virginia and NE. North Carolina.

Related Species: Ghost Shiner (*N. buchanani*) lacks dark-edged scales on back; pelvic fins reach front of anal fin; occurs in large, turbid streams of the Mississippi River system from Ohio, S. Minnesota, and E. Kansas south to Louisiana; Gulf Coast streams, W. Louisiana and Texas.

Comments: The Mimic Shiner is common over much of its range. It is an important forage species for some fishes, especially basses, and is also preyed upon by terns and other birds.

183 Bleeding Shiner
(*Notropis zonatus*)

Description: To 4½" (11.5 cm). Elongate, slender; back olive-brown with broad, dark mid-dorsal stripe; *upper sides with dark, golden yellow, and black midlateral stripes* continuing from head to tail; *margin of gill opening black;* head of breeding males red. Mouth terminal, oblique; eye moderately large. *Fins plain, red with clear edges in breeding males;* 9 anal fin rays. Lateral line complete, 38–43 scales.

Habitat: Small to medium, clear streams with moderate to swift current over gravel or rocks.

Range: S. Missouri and NE. Arkansas.

Related Species: Duskystripe Shiner (*N. pilsbryi*) lacks dark edge along gill opening; occurs in similar habitat in SW. Missouri, NW. Arkansas, SE. Kansas, and E. Oklahoma.

Comments: Bleeding Shiners are often found in large schools with other shiners. Most

spawning takes place in May and early
June in gravel riffles, frequently over
the nests of other minnows.

---

132 Sacramento Blackfish
(*Orthodon microlepidotus*)

Description: To 18″ (46 cm). Elongate, round,
slightly compressed; back dark olive to
dark gray, sides lighter; young silvery.
Head flattened above; *mouth terminal,
maxilla not reaching small eye.* Fins rather
large; *9–11 dorsal fin rays,* origin just
anterior to pelvic fin insertion. Caudal
peduncle moderately slender; caudal fin
deeply forked. *Lateral line complete,
decurved anteriorly, up to 105 scales.*

Habitat: Streams, sloughs, lakes, and reservoirs
with shallow, warm, usually turbid
water with little or no current.

Range: Sacramento-San Joaquin river system,
Clear Lake, and Pajaro, Salinas,
Russian, and Carmel rivers, California;
Truckee River, Nevada.

Comments: The Sacramento Blackfish is unusual
among North American cyprinids in
being predominantly a filter feeder,
with adaptations such as long, slender,
fringed gill rakers and long, straight,
slender pharyngeal teeth to break up
ingested clumps. It grows rapidly to
about 14″ (36 cm) by the end of its
third year and is sold live in the
oriental fish markets in San Francisco.

---

169 Suckermouth Minnow
(*Phenacobius mirabilis*)

Description: To 4″ (10 cm). Elongate, slightly
compressed; olive above, *scales dark-
edged;* silvery below, *with dusky
midlateral stripe* ending in small caudal
spot. *Snout long, rounded; mouth
suckerlike, ventral; no barbels.* Fins plain,
rounded; 8 dorsal fin rays, origin in

ventral head view

front of pelvic fin insertion; 7 anal fin rays. Lateral line complete, 40–50 scales; 18–22 predorsal scale rows; *breast unscaled.*

Habitat: Riffles of clear to turbid water of medium to large streams over sand or gravel.

Range: S. and W. Ohio west to SE. North Dakota, and SE. Wyoming, south to NW. Alabama, southwest to N. Texas and E. New Mexico; SE. Texas.

Related Species: Kanawha Minnow (*P. teretulus*) has scales on breast, lacks caudal spot; occurs in swift, rocky streams of New River drainage, SE. West Virginia south to NW. North Carolina.

Comments: This fish has increased its range in areas where streams have become more turbid. It feeds primarily on aquatic insects obtained by rooting in gravel riffles.

168 Stargazing Minnow
(*Phenacobius uranops*)

Description: To 4½" (11.5 cm). *Elongate, slender, almost cylindrical;* olive above; dusky midlateral stripe ending in small, dusky caudal spot; silvery below. *Snout long, rounded; mouth suckerlike, ventral; eyes on upper side of head; small barbels above upper lip.* Fins plain; 8 dorsal fin rays, origin over to in front of pelvic fin insertion; 7 anal fin rays. Lateral line complete, 52–61 scales; *breast and midline of belly unscaled.*

Habitat: Over gravel or rock in riffles of moderate to swift, clear waters of medium to large streams.

Range: SW. Virginia, S. Kentucky, south to NW. Georgia and N. Alabama.

Related Species: Riffle Minnow (*P. catostomus*) has scales on belly, 59–69 lateral line scales; occurs in similar habitat in Mobile Bay drainage of SE. Tennessee, NW. Georgia, and Alabama. Fatlips Minnow

(*P. crassilabrum*) has long pelvic fins reaching anus; occurs in similar habitat in SW. Virginia, N. North Carolina, E. Tennessee, and NE. Georgia.

Comments: The Stargazing Minnow is intolerant of prolonged exposure to silty, turbid waters. Its presence generally indicates a high-quality stream habitat.

184 Southern Redbelly Dace
(*Phoxinus erythrogaster*)

Description: To 3″ (7.5 cm). Elongate; olive above with dark spots; *side has 2 black stripes separated by cream stripe, lower black stripe wider, ending in caudal spot;* lower sides and belly yellowish to bright red in breeding males. Mouth small, terminal; no barbels. Fins plain, yellowish; dorsal fin origin behind pelvic fin insertion; 7–8 anal fin rays. *Lateral line incomplete or absent;* 65–85 scales in lateral series.

Habitat: Springs and small, cool, clear streams with moderate to swift current over gravel or rocks.

Range: W. Pennsylvania, S. Michigan, and S. Minnesota south to N. Alabama and N. Arkansas; in spots in SW. Mississippi and NE. New Mexico.

Related Species: Northern Redbelly Dace (*P. eos*) grows to 2″ (5 cm); mouth more upturned; occurs in small streams, boggy ponds, and lakes of S. Canada and Nova Scotia west to British Columbia, and N. New England and N. Pennsylvania west to Montana and N. Colorado.

Comments: The Southern Redbelly Dace spawns during the spring and early summer in swift riffles over the gravel nests of other minnows. It reaches sexual maturity in 1 year and lives for about 2 to 3 years.

185 Mountain Redbelly Dace
(*Phoxinus oreas*)

Description: To 2½" (6.5 cm). Moderately deep,
robust, slightly compressed; olive above
with large, dark spots; side has light
cream lateral stripe, *narrow, black stripe
on rear half of body; black stripe from upper
edge of opercle to anal fin base;* silvery
below; breeding males bright red
below. Head small; mouth terminal,
oblique. Fins plain, yellowish; 8 anal
fin rays. *Lateral line incomplete or absent;*
65–70 scales in lateral series.

Habitat: Small, clear streams with moderate to
swift current over sand, gravel, or
rocks.

Range: Atlantic Coast drainages from N.
Virginia south to N. North Carolina.
Upper Tennessee River drainage in E.
Tennessee.

Related Species: Blackside Dace (*P. cumberlandensis*) has
1 broad, black lateral stripe; occurs in
similar habitat in the Cumberland
River drainage in SE. Kentucky and
NE. Tennessee.

Comments: Breeding males of this species are
among the most colorful fishes in
North America. Its specific name, *oreas,*
means a mountain nymph. Details of
its life history are unknown.

178 Bluntnose Minnow
(*Pimephales notatus*)

Description: To 4" (10 cm). Slender, back broad;
yellow-olive, sides silvery to bluish;
scales dark-edged forming crosshatched
pattern; narrow, dark midlateral stripe

dorsal fin ending in caudal spot; *lining of body
cavity black.* Snout blunt, rounded;
mouth small, slightly oblique. *First
dorsal fin ray short, splintlike,* dusky
blotch on first rays; 7 anal fin rays.
Lateral line complete, 39–45 scales; *scales
on back behind head crowded.*

Habitat: Clear to turbid pools of creeks, small

rivers, and lakes over sand, gravel, or rocks.

Range: SW. Quebec west to S. Manitoba; New York south to S. Virginia; through S. Great Lakes and Mississippi Valley.

Related Species: Bullhead Minnow (*P. vigilax*) has mouth terminal, slightly oblique; black spot at front of dorsal fin and caudal fin base; lining of body cavity silvery; occurs in similar habitat in Mississippi Valley; NW. Georgia; and on Gulf Coast from Alabama to S. Texas.

Comments: The Bluntnose Minnow spawns from early spring throughout the summer. The male prepares a nest by clearing a small depression beneath a flat rock. Eggs are then deposited on the underside of the rock and are guarded by the male until the young leave the nest.

154 Fathead Minnow
(*Pimephales promelas*)

Description: To 4″ (10 cm). Stout, chubby; back tan to olive; sides silvery to brassy, with dark caudal spot. Breeding males grayish-black with pale fleshy pad behind head; pale below dorsal fin. *Snout blunt; mouth nearly terminal, oblique.* Fins low, rounded; *first dorsal fin ray short, splintlike;* 7 anal fin rays. *Lateral line incomplete;* 42–48 scales in lateral series; *scales behind head crowded.*

Habitat: Clear pools of creeks, shallow ponds, and lakes over sand, gravel, or mud.

Range: SW. Quebec west to Great Slave Lake, Alberta; NE. and central United States; NE. Mexico. Widely introduced.

Related Species: Slim Minnow (*P. tenellus*) has more elongate body; prominent caudal spot; occurs in same habitat from SE. Kansas and S. Missouri to SW. Arkansas.

Comments: The Fathead Minnow, commonly sold as bait, is easily propagated in small ponds, which may yield 400,000 minnows per acre.

144 Woundfin
(Plagopterus argentissimus)

Description: To 3" (7.5 cm). Moderately slender; *back olive to silvery with minute, black dots; silvery below.* Head broad, flattened above; *snout slightly overhangs upper lip;* mouth extends to eye; *barbels present.* Pectoral fins long, reach pelvic fin base; *dorsal fin with 2 spines,* 7 rays, origin posterior to pelvic fin insertion. *Scales deeply embedded;* lateral line complete, scales thickened.

Habitat: Warm, turbid, seasonally swift streams over shifting sand.

Range: Virgin River in SW. Utah, NW. Arizona and SE. Nevada; Moapa River in SE. Nevada.

Comments: The Woundfin is an endangered species. Water storage and diversion projects eliminated the population in the Gila River drainage and, along with the introduction of exotic fishes, have reduced populations in the Virgin River. In their undisturbed habitat in the Virgin River, Woundfins are often the most common fishes.

Splittail
(Pogonichthys macrolepidotus)

Description: To 14" (36 cm). Elongate, somewhat compressed; dusky olive-gray above, *sides silvery.* Mouth extends to eye; barbel present at corner of jaw. 14–18 gill rakers. *7–9 anal fin rays, entirely posterior to dorsal fin base; caudal fin large, deeply forked,* upper lobe longer than lower; caudal and paired fins light red-orange. *Lateral line decurved,* complete, 57–66 scales.

Habitat: Large rivers and lakes with little or no current; tolerant of brackish water.

Range: Sacramento and San Joaquin rivers, California, and their delta.

Related Species: Clear Lake Splittail (*P. ciscoides*) usually has 21–23 gill rakers; mouth terminal;

barbels poorly developed or absent; caudal fin more symmetrical; occurs in open water in Clear Lake, California.

Comments: The Splittail spawns from March to May in sloughs over submerged vegetation. It was formerly widespread throughout its range, but its numbers have declined because of manmade habitat changes. There is a limited sport fishery for this species.

---

134 Sacramento Squawfish
(Ptychocheilus grandis)

Description: To 3' (91 cm). Elongate, slightly compressed; back dark olive-brown; *sides silvery-grayish;* young have dark caudal spot. Head long, flattened above; mouth terminal, large, extends to small eye; *no barbels.* Fins plain, reddish in males; *8 dorsal fin rays,* origin behind pelvic fin insertion; 8 anal fin rays; caudal fin moderately forked. *Lateral line complete, 73–86 scales; 13–15 scale rows above lateral line.*

Habitat: Clear, deep pools over sand and rocks in creeks, rivers, and lakes.

Range: Sacramento, Russian, San Joaquin, Pajaro, and Salinas rivers and Clear Lake system, N. and central California.

Related Species: Northern Squawfish *(P. oregonensis)* has 9 anal fin rays and 67–75 lateral line scales; occurs in similar habitat from W. Alberta, and N. British Columbia south to NE. Nevada and Oregon. Umpqua Squawfish *(P. umpquae)* has 9 dorsal fin rays, 8 anal fin rays, 19–24 scale rows above lateral line; occurs in similar habitat in Umpqua and Sinslaw rivers, SW. Oregon.

Comments: This fish was once considered a major predator of young salmons, but while both fishes may compete for food and space, most waters inhabited by Sacramento Squawfish are too warm for young salmons and trouts.

133 Colorado Squawfish
(*Ptychocheilus lucius*)

Description: To 5' (1.5m) long. Elongate, somewhat
compressed; back olive to dusky, *sides
silvery; young have wedge-shaped caudal
spot.* Head long, flattened; mouth
slightly oblique, *terminal, large, extends
to small eye.* Fins plain; *9 dorsal fin rays,*
origin behind pelvic fin insertion; 9
anal fin rays; caudal fin moderately
forked. *Lateral line decurved, complete,
80–95 scales.*

Habitat: Large streams with turbid to nearly
clear water and moderate current over
sand, gravel, or rock. Young in
backwater pools along stream edge.

Range: Colorado River basin, SW. Wyoming,
W. Colorado, and E. Utah south to S.
Arizona, SE. California, and NW.
Mexico.

Comments: The Colorado Squawfish is the largest
minnow in North America. During the
late 1800s, specimens 5' long and
weighing 80 lbs (36 kg) were not unusual.
Today, this species has disappeared
from the southern half of its range and
is on the United States Endangered
Species List. Its decline resulted from
impoundments, water diversions, and
the introduction of exotic fishes.

158 Blacknose Dace
(*Rhinichthys atratulus*)

Description: To 3½" (9 cm). Elongate, moderately
robust; *yellow-olive to dark brown above
with black blotches;* dusky to dark
midlateral stripe from snout to caudal
fin base. *Snout long; mouth small,
subterminal, horizontal; barbels present.*
Fins small, rounded; 8 dorsal fin rays,
origin behind pelvic fin insertion, 7
anal fin rays; caudal fin shallowly
forked. Lateral line complete, with
56–71 scales.

Habitat: Springs and cool, clear creeks with

moderate to swift current over gravel or rocks.

Range: Nova Scotia west to Manitoba; New England south to NW. South Carolina, N. Georgia, and N. Alabama and west to E. North Dakota and E. Nebraska.

Comments: The Blacknose Dace spawns during the spring and early summer in riffles over shallow gravel. Most daces spawn at 2 years and live for 3 or 4 years. Aquatic insect larvae are their primary food.

159 Longnose Dace
(*Rhinichthys cataractae*)

Description: To 7″ (18 cm). Elongate, moderately stout; dark olive to dusky above; *wide, black midlateral band extends from head.* Head flattened above; *snout long, overhangs small, ventral mouth; barbels present;* eye small. Fins plain, rosy in breeding males; pelvic axillary scale present; 8 dorsal fin rays, origin behind pelvic fin insertion; 7 anal fin rays. *Caudal peduncle long, deep.* Lateral line complete, 60–76 scales; scales small.

Habitat: Clear to turbid waters of streams and lakes, usually in swift riffles over gravel or rock.

Range: Throughout much of Canada, N. United States south in Appalachian Mountains to NE. Georgia, south in Rocky Mountains to Rio Grande, Texas and New Mexico.

Related Species: Leopard Dace (*R. falcatus*) has slender caudal peduncle; caudal fin deeply forked; 52–57 lateral line scales; inhabits slower currents of large streams from N. British Columbia south to S. Idaho and S. Oregon.

Comments: The Longnose Dace feeds almost exclusively on aquatic insects that it gleans from its riffle habitat. It is sexually mature at 3 years and lives up to 5 years. It may be an important forage fish for the Smallmouth Bass, which is found in similar habitats.

156 Speckled Dace
(*Rhinichthys osculus*)

Description: To 4″ (10 cm). Elongate, rounded, belly flattened; back dusky to dark olive; *sides gray-green with dark lateral stripe,* often obscured by dark speckles or blotches. *Snout moderately pointed; mouth small, ventral;* lips reddish in breeding males; *barbels present;* eye small. Fins plain, bases reddish in breeding males; 8 dorsal fin rays; 7 anal fin rays; caudal fin moderately forked. *Lateral line complete, 60–90 scales.*

Habitat: Cool to warm creeks, rivers, and lakes over gravel or rock; desert springs and their outflow.

Range: West of Continental Divide from S. British Columbia south to S. Arizona.

Similar Species: Desert Dace (*Eremichthys acros*) lacks barbels; has incomplete lateral line; occurs in hot springs in Soldier Meadows, NW. Nevada. Relict Dace (*Relictus solitarius*) has very robust body; lateral line incomplete; occurs in isolated spring pools in NE. Nevada.

Comments: The Speckled Dace is one of the most widespread minnows in western waters. There are several subspecies of this highly variable species. It is an important forage fish in some trout streams and is used for bait.

181 Redside Shiner
(*Richardsonius balteatus*)

Description: To 7″ (18 cm). *Deep, compressed;* back dark olive, upper sides dusky with narrow, unpigmented stripe; dark midlateral stripe; breeding males reddish below. Mouth oblique, almost reaches front of eye; *no barbel;* eye equal to snout length. Fins yellowish; *9 dorsal fin rays, origin just in front of anal fin origin; 10–22 anal fin rays.* Lateral line complete, 55–67 scales.

Habitat: Slow-flowing creeks, rivers, and

ditches; also ponds and lakes in deep water or shallow, weedy areas.

Range: N. British Columbia and W. Alberta south to Oregon, NE. Nevada, and W. Utah. Introduced in Colorado River drainage, in W. Wyoming south to NW. Arizona.

Similar Species: Lahontan Redside (*R. egregius*) has slender body, not deep; 8–9 anal fin rays; inhabits streams and lakes of Lahontan Basin, in N. Nevada and NE. California.

Comments: Increasing populations of Redside Shiners have overcrowded some lakes, reducing the trout population. Costly efforts to eradicate them with toxic chemicals have failed.

---

139 Creek Chub
(*Semotilus atromaculatus*)

Description: To 12″ (31 cm); ¾ lb (300 g). Chubby; back olive; sides silvery with greenish-purple sheen, dusky lateral stripe ending in caudal spot; margin of gill opening dusky. Head large; *mouth large, small barbel on upper lip near corner of jaw.* Fins rounded; *8 dorsal fin rays, dark spot at anterior base,* origin posterior to pelvic fin insertion. Lateral line complete, 51–69 scales, *crowded anteriorly.*

Habitat: Small, clear to turbid streams and lakes over sand, gravel, or rock.

Range: E. North America except peninsular Florida; west to Manitoba, E. Montana, Wyoming, and NE. New Mexico.

Related Species: Fallfish (*S. corporalis*) has dorsal fin origin over pelvic fin insertion, 43–50 lateral line scales; occurs in similar habitat, as well as in larger streams and lakes, on Atlantic Coast from S. Quebec south to S. Virginia.

Comments: This fish, often used for bait, is frequently caught by anglers who are flyfishing. Spawning occurs in the spring over a nest excavated by the male. Eggs are laid in the depression and covered with gravel from the downstream side of the nest, which is abandoned after spawning.

157 Loach Minnow
(*Tiaroga cobitis*)

Description: To 2½" (6.5 cm). Elongate, belly flattened; olive above with dark blotches; *2 large, light spots at base of caudal peduncle separated by black spot on caudal fin base.* Breeding males reddish around fin bases and on lower part of head. Head small, somewhat depressed; mouth small, terminal, no barbels, lips fleshy; eyes high on head. 8 dorsal fin rays; 7 anal fin rays. Lateral line complete, about 65 scales.

Habitat: Large streams in swift water over gravel riffles with algae.

Range: Restricted to Gila River in SE. Arizona, SW. New Mexico, and N. Sonora, Mexico.

Comments: Loach Minnows feed primarily on aquatic insect larvae. They have become less abundant, probably because of deteriorating habitats and the introduction of exotic fishes.

SUCKERS
(Family Catostomidae)

sucker

carpsucker or buffalofish

Suckers are small to moderately large, bottom-dwelling, freshwater fishes that inhabit rivers, creeks, and lakes. There are 59 species in North America, 22 of which are in the genus *Catostomus*. Suckers usually have ventral mouths with thick lips and toothless jaws. In most species the mouth can be extended ventrally during feeding. They lack an adipose fin and barbels. There are 10 or more soft rays in the dorsal fin, and the short anal fin is placed well back on the body. Members of the genus *Catostomus,* which occur mainly in the western United States in somewhat restricted ranges, can be distinguished by a cylindrical body with a flat or rounded head and an inferior, horizontal mouth with thick, fleshy lips that are either plicate or have papillae. The dorsal fin has a total of fewer than 20 rays. There are more than 55 lateral line scales.

---

102 Quillback
(*Carpiodes cyprinus*)

Description: To 24″ (61 cm); 12 lbs (5.4 kg). Deep, compressed, back highly arched; olive to brownish; *sides silvery.* Head small; snout blunt; mouth ventral, narrow, horizontal; lips plicate, tip of lower lip anterior to nostril. *Fins plain, median fins dusky, paired fins clear; 27–30 dorsal fin rays, anterior rays long,* longest ray almost as long as fin base; usually has 7 anal fin rays; caudal fin forked, with pointed tips. Lateral line complete, straight, 37–41 scales.

Habitat: Clear to turbid waters of large creeks, rivers, lakes, and reservoirs with firm or soft bottom.

Range: SW. Quebec and S. Ontario west to S. Alberta; Atlantic Coast drainages, NE. Pennsylvania south to South Carolina; Mississippi River system; Gulf Coast drainages, W. Florida west to Louisiana.

Related Species: River Carpsucker (*C. carpio*) has nipplelike structure at middle of lower lip; anterior dorsal fin rays about half length of fin base. Highfin Carpsucker (*C. velifer*) has nipplelike structure on lower lip; snout blunter; anterior dorsal fin rays as long as fin base. Both found in similar habitat in Mississippi Valley and Gulf Coast drainages.

Comments: Carpsuckers are rarely sought, but are occasionally taken by snag fishing. They are caught in gill nets and sold

commercially; however, they are not
important as a food fish.

106 White Sucker
(*Catostomus commersoni*)

lips

Description: To 24″ (61 cm). Elongate, cylindrical,
caudal peduncle moderately slender;
back dusky-olive, sides greenish-yellow
with brassy luster; young mottled on
sides. Head flattened above; snout
blunt; mouth large, ventral; *lips thick
with many papillae.* Fins plain; pelvic
axillary scale present; *10–13 dorsal fin
rays; 6–8 anal fin rays. Lateral line
complete, 55–74 scales;* 8–10 scale rows
above lateral line; *anterior scales crowded.*

Habitat: Cool, clear streams and lakes over sand,
gravel, or rocks.

Range: Canada and N. United States east of
Continental Divide to NW. South
Carolina, N. Alabama, N. Arkansas,
and N. New Mexico.

Related Species: Longnose Sucker (*C. catostomus*) has
long, fleshy snout extending beyond
mouth; 91–120 lateral line scales;
occurs in similar habitat throughout
Canada, N. United States to central
West Virginia, N. Illinois, central
Colorado, S. Idaho, Alaska, and
Washington.

Comments: The White Sucker is the most common
species of this genus in North America.
Anglers do not fish for it, but some are
taken during spawning runs in large
lift nets and in commercial fisheries.

100 Blue Sucker
(*Cycleptus elongatus*)

Description: To 3′4″ (1 m); 16 lbs. (7.3 kg).
Elongate, slightly compressed; back
and fins blue-black, sides light blue-
gray, belly white; breeding males dark
with tubercles on head, body, and fins.

Snout blunt, extends beyond mouth; lips with low, blunt papillae. Dorsal fin long, 28–37 rays, falcate anteriorly; 7–8 anal fin rays. Caudal peduncle long; caudal fin deeply forked. *55–58 lateral line scales.*

Habitat: Deep, moderately swift channels in rivers over firm bottom; some populations survive in reservoirs.

Range: Mississippi River system, Pennsylvania, Minnesota, and Montana, south to Louisiana; Alabama west to New Mexico; NE. Mexico.

Comments: Although never common, the Blue Sucker has declined in abundance since the early 1900s, due to siltation, pollution, and dams. It is a good food fish.

---

104 Creek Chubsucker
(Erimyzon oblongus)

Description: To 11″ (28 cm). Robust, chubby; olive-bronze above, scales dark-edged giving crosshatched appearance; 5–8 saddles across back ending in dark midlateral blotches; cream below; dorsal and caudal fins dusky olive. Mouth small, subterminal; lower lip plicate, halves meeting to form acute V-shaped angle. *Dorsal fin edge rounded; anal fin of breeding males double-lobed;* caudal peduncle narrow. *Lateral line absent, 39–41 scales in lateral series.*

Habitat: Creeks and small rivers with soft bottom, slow current, and vegetation.

Range: From S. Maine west to New York, south on Atlantic Coastal Plain to central Georgia; from W. Ohio to S. Wisconsin south to W. Florida, and west to E. Texas.

Related Species: Lake Chubsucker (*E. sucetta*) has rounded dorsal fin; 34–38 scales in lateral series; found in sluggish lowland waters from S. Great Lakes and Virginia south to Florida, and west to Texas. Sharpfin Chubsucker (*E. tenuis*) has dorsal fin edge straight and sharply pointed; anal fin in males not double-lobed; occurs in streams from NE. Mississippi south to W. Florida, west to E. Louisiana.

Comments: The Creek Chubsucker is widely distributed, but not common in most areas. It appears to be intolerant of silty streams.

109 Northern Hog Sucker
(*Hypentelium nigricans*)

snout

Description: To 24″ (61 cm). Moderately elongate, heavy anteriorly, tapering posteriorly; back dark olive to red-brown, mottled with darker brown, *3–4 dark saddles crossing back, extending obliquely forward onto sides;* sides green-yellow; belly white; fins olive. *Head large, concave between eyes;* snout long, blunt; mouth ventral, lips large, thick, fleshy, with coarse papillae. *11 dorsal fin rays; lateral line complete, 44–54 scales.*

Habitat: Riffles, pools below riffles in moderate to swift, shallow, clear streams over gravel or rocks.

Range: SE. Ontario and New York to Minnesota south to E. Louisiana and S. Mississippi; N. central North Carolina and NE. Georgia, west to NE. Oklahoma.

Related Species: Alabama Hog Sucker (*H. etowanum*) has 10 dorsal fin rays; area between eyes not concave; occurs from SE. Tennessee and NW. Georgia west to NE. Mississippi, and south to S. Alabama. Roanoke Hog Sucker (*H. roanokense*) has light streaks along upper sides, usually 40–43 lateral line scales; occurs in upper Roanoke River drainage in S. Virginia and N. North Carolina. Both in same habitat.

Comments: These 3 species are commonly found throughout their range, but they are intolerant of turbid, silty streams. They feed on aquatic invertebrates and

minute plants that they scrape off small
rocks or find under gravel.

101 Smallmouth Buffalo
(*Ictiobus bubalus*)

Description: To 3' (91 cm); 51 lbs (23.1 kg). Deep,
moderately compressed, *back arched,
often with ridge anteriorly;* dark olive to
gray, *sides grayish to bronze.* Head small;
snout bluntly rounded; *mouth small,
horizontal, ventral, below level of eye;* lips
thick, plicate. *Pelvic fins gray-black,*
other fins dusky; 24–31 dorsal fin rays,
anterior rays long, less than half length
of fin base; 8–9 anal fin rays. Lateral
line straight, with 35–39 scales.

Habitat: Clear to slightly turbid rivers with
moderate current; also lakes and
reservoirs.

Range: Throughout Mississippi River system
and Gulf Coast drainages, from
Alabama west to Rio Grande.

Related Species: Bigmouth Buffalo (*I. cyprinellus*) has
terminal mouth, tip of upper lip above
lower edge of eye; occurs in sluggish
rivers, backwaters, and lakes in Lake
Winnipeg drainage, S. Great Lakes
drainage, and Mississippi River system.
Black Buffalo (*I. niger*) has subterminal,
slightly oblique mouth; no dorsal
ridge; occurs in similar range and
habitat.

Comments: Buffalofishes are not popular for sport,
but are fished commercially in the
Mississippi River and some large lakes.
The common name refers to their large
size and humped back.

103 Spotted Sucker
(*Minytrema melanops*)

Description: To 20" (51 cm). Elongate, slightly
compressed; back olive usually with
dark blotch near base of dorsal fin; sides

and belly silvery, *scales on sides have black spots forming horizontal stripes;* median fins light olive. Lips ridged, thin; posterior margin of lower lip V-shaped. Dorsal fin short, usually 11–12 rays, posterior margin concave; caudal fin deeply forked. *No lateral line; 42–47 scales in lateral series.*

Habitat: Lowland streams with deep, clear pools and firm bottoms; overflow ponds, sloughs, lakes, and reservoirs.

Range: Coastal drainages of North Carolina south to Gulf drainages of N. and W. Florida, west to central Texas; S. Great Lakes drainage; Mississippi River system, Minnesota south to Louisiana.

Similar Species: Redhorses (genus *Moxostoma*) have lateral line; scales on sides usually without spots; occur in streams, lakes, and rivers in E. and central North America.

Comments: Spotted Suckers make spawning runs up rivers and small streams in early spring, and spawn from March to May in swift, shallow riffles. They are intolerant of silty and turbid waters.

107 River Redhorse
(*Moxostoma carinatum*)

Description: To 30″ (76 cm); 14 lbs (6.4 kg). Moderately robust, slightly compressed; back olive to dusky, *sides silvery.* Head large; snout moderately long, blunt, slightly overhangs ventral mouth; *lips fleshy, plicate, rear edge of lower lip almost straight;* eye small. Fins plain, *median fins reddish-olive, paired fins pale red;* 12–13 dorsal fin rays; anal fin long, pointed, 7–9 rays. Lateral line complete, 41–47 scales.

lips

Habitat: Large creeks and rivers with moderate to swift current in clear water over gravel or rocks.

Range: St. Lawrence River and Great Lakes drainages in S. Quebec, SE. Ontario, Ohio, and Michigan; Mississippi River system; Gulf Coast drainages of W. Florida, Alabama, and Mississippi.

Comments: The River Redhorse eats aquatic insects, crustaceans, and small mollusks. It is occasionally caught by snag fishing in shallow gravel shoals during spring spawning runs. Its numbers have declined in some areas due to siltation and pollution.

108 Golden Redhorse
(*Moxostoma erythrurum*)

lips

Description: To 24″ (61 cm); 4½ lbs (2 kg). Moderately stout, slightly compressed; back olive, *sides golden to bronze.* Head moderately large; snout blunt; mouth large, ventral; lips thick, fleshy, plicate, *rear edge of lower lip broadly V-shaped;* breeding males have tubercles on head. Fins plain, *dorsal and caudal fins grayish-olive,* other fins pale orange; 9 pelvic fin rays; 12–14 dorsal fin rays. *Lateral line complete, 39–42 scales.*

Habitat: Pools and slow to moderate current of creeks and rivers with clear to slightly turbid water over sand or gravel.

Range: SE. Ontario; Atlantic slope drainages from Maryland south to North Carolina; W. New York west to Minnesota and E. North Dakota, south to NE. Texas; S. Mississippi; Mobile Bay drainage of NW. Georgia and Alabama.

Related Species: Black Redhorse (*M. duquesnei*) has slender body; breeding males lack tubercles on head; 10 pelvic fin rays; 44–47 lateral line scales; occurs in similar habitat in S. Great Lakes drainage; Mississippi River system; Mobile Bay drainage of NW. Georgia and Alabama.

Comments: The Golden Redhorse is the most common of the 18 species of *Moxostoma* restricted to eastern North America. It is of little importance as either a sport or food fish.

111 Blacktail Redhorse
(*Moxostoma poecilurum*)

Description: To 18″ (46 cm). Elongate, moderately compressed; back yellow-olive to dusky, sides silvery to golden, *scales dark-edged, forming vague, alternating dark and light stripes.* Head short; snout blunt; mouth ventral, lips plicate, rear edge of lower lip forms broad angle. Fins plain, faint orange; *13 dorsal fin rays; lower lobe of caudal fin dusky to black, lower edge white.* Caudal peduncle slender. Lateral line complete, 39–45 scales.

Habitat: Creeks and rivers with moderate current over sand or gravel; occasionally reservoirs.

Range: W. Tennessee, NW. Georgia, Alabama, and Gulf Coast drainages from W. Florida west to E. Texas.

Related Species: Silver Redhorse (*M. anisurum*) has grooves in lower lip with transverse creases forming low papillae; 14–17 dorsal fin rays; 12 caudal peduncle scale rows; found in large streams, lakes, and impoundments over sand, silt, or rocks, from SW. Quebec west to Alberta, south through Great Lakes and St. Lawrence River; Atlantic Coast streams from S. Virginia south to S. Georgia; upper Ohio and Mississippi rivers south to N. Alabama and N. Arkansas.

Comments: The Blacktail Redhorse ascends small streams during April and May and spawns over shallow gravel shoals with swift current.

110 Striped Jumprock
(*Moxostoma rupiscartes*)

Description: To 10″ (25 cm). Elongate; back olive to yellow-brown, *sides yellowish to silver with faint striped pattern;* young have dark blotches. *Head long, wider than deep,* flattened to slightly convex between eyes; snout blunt; mouth wide, lips plicate with transverse creases. Pectoral, pelvic, and anal fins rounded; 9 pelvic fin rays with dusky edges; 12 dorsal fin rays; 7 anal fin rays; *caudal fin yellowish, lobes rounded. Lateral line complete, 45–50 scales.*

Habitat: Creeks with moderate to swift riffles over sand, gravel, or rocks.

Range: Santee River drainage, SW. North Carolina, southwest to Chattahoochee River drainage, NE. Georgia.

Related Species: Black Jumprock (*M. cervinum*) has narrow mouth; tips of dorsal and caudal fins black; 39–44 lateral line scales; occurs from James River drainage, Virginia, south to Neuse River drainage, NE. North Carolina. Greater Jumprock (*M. lachneri*) has 12 dorsal fin rays; lower edge of caudal fin white, lobes pointed; occurs in Chattahoochee and Flint rivers, NE. and W. Georgia, and E. central Alabama. Both in similar habitat.

Comments: The specific name *rupiscartes* means "rock jumper" and refers to the Striped Jumprock's habit of darting around rocks in the swift riffles where it lives.

---

105 Razorback Sucker
(*Xyrauchen texanus*)

Description: To 3′ (91 cm). Deep; *back has high, sharp ridge from head to dorsal fin;* dark olive to brownish-black above, sides lighter, belly yellowish-orange; breeding males gray-black with bright orange belly. Head long, rounded; snout long, fleshy; mouth ventral, wide; lower lip divided, 2 lobes meet at V-shaped angle. *Dorsal fin low, origin in front of pelvic fin insertion, 12–15 rays.* Lateral line complete, almost straight, 68–87 scales.

Habitat: Deep, clear to turbid waters of large rivers and some reservoirs over mud, sand, or gravel.

Range: Colorado River system from SW. Wyoming to S. Arizona and SE. California.

Comments: The Razorback Sucker, once common, is now an endangered species. Its numbers have declined throughout its range, and it has disappeared in some areas due to impoundments, water diversions, and the introduction of exotic fishes.

Order Siluriformes

This large order, with 4 families in North America, contains over 2,000 species of marine and freshwater fishes distributed in temperate and tropical waters. They are closely related to the Cypriniformes, both possessing an apparatus that, by connecting the swim bladder with the inner ear, provides an acute sense of hearing.

BULLHEAD CATFISHES
(Family Ictaluridae)

Bullhead catfishes are native to the fresh waters of North America east of the Rocky Mountains, from southern Canada south to Central America. The 5 genera and 39 species in North America range in size from 2″ (5 cm) to more than 5′ (1.5 m). They have 4 pairs of barbels, an adipose fin, and a single spine in the dorsal and pectoral fins. In some species the pectoral spines have serrations, which are short barbs along the edges. The madtoms, genus *Noturus,* are equipped with a venom gland at the base of the pectoral spine, which is often grooved, enabling them to inflict a painful, although not serious, sting.

54   Blue Catfish
(*Ictalurus furcatus*)

Description: To 3'8" (1.1 m); 100 lbs (45.4 kg).
Moderately stout, compressed
posteriorly; *head and body blue to slate
gray above,* lighter on sides; belly white.
Head small, wedge-shaped; eyes small,
situated below midline of head; 4 pairs
of barbels; mouth small, upper jaw
longer than lower. Posterior edge of
adipose fin free; *outer edge of anal fin
straight; 30–36 anal fin rays; caudal fin
deeply forked.*

Habitat: Rivers and large creeks in moderate to
swift current over rock, gravel, or clean
sand bottom.

Range: Mississippi River system, from West
Virginia west to South Dakota, south
to Gulf Coast; Alabama and Georgia
west to Texas and Mexico; widely
introduced.

Related Species: White Catfish (*I. catus*) has 18–24 anal
rays; caudal fin shallowly forked; occurs
in streams and reservoirs from S. New
York south to Florida and SE.
Alabama; widely introduced.

Comments: Its large size and firm, well-flavored
flesh have made this species a highly
valued sport and commercial food fish.
It is one of the largest North American
freshwater fishes. The decline in
abundance of the Blue Catfish has been
attributed to over-fishing and dams,
which destroy its riverine habitat and
limit its migration.

53   Black Bullhead
(*Ictalurus melas*)

Description: To 17" (43 cm); 2¾ lbs (1.2 kg).
Heavy anteriorly; back olive to black;
sides yellow-olive to black; belly
yellowish; *body not mottled;* fins dusky,
membranes darker than rays; pale bar at
base of caudal fin; 4 pairs of barbels,
chin barbels gray-black or spotted. Head

large, rounded above; eyes small; mouth terminal, short, wide. *Pectoral fin spine rough, but without serrations; 17–21 anal fin rays,* length of base less than head length; adipose fin present. Caudal peduncle short, moderately deep; caudal fin slightly notched.

Habitat: Low gradient sections of streams, backwaters, lakes, and reservoirs, frequently over silty, soft mud.

Range: From SE. Ontario west to S. Saskatchewan; central United States. Widely introduced outside native range.

Comments: The Black Bullhead is the smallest of the bullheads, and appears to be more tolerant of turbid, silty, polluted waters than other bullheads. It feeds on a variety of plant and animal material taken off the bottom.

57 Yellow Bullhead
(*Ictalurus natalis*)

Description: To 18″ (46 cm); 3 lbs (1.4 kg).

pectoral fin spine

Robust, heavy; back dark olive-brown; sides yellow-brown, *not mottled;* belly yellowish; fins dusky to olive. Head thick, long, rounded above; eyes small; mouth terminal; 4 pairs of barbels, *pair on chin yellow to white.* Serrations on rear edge of pectoral fin spine; *24–27 anal fin rays, base long, about equal to head length;* adipose fin present; caudal fin truncate to rounded.

Habitat: Pools and backwaters of sluggish streams, ponds, and lakes; sometimes in slow riffles; usually in areas with heavy vegetation.

Range: SE. Ontario; central E. United States; widely introduced outside native range.

Comments: The Yellow Bullhead is a good sport and food fish. It is active at night, searching out food along the bottom by relying on its barbels and sense of smell.

56 Brown Bullhead
(*Ictalurus nebulosus*)

pectoral fin spine

Description: To 19″ (48 cm); 5½ lbs (2.5 kg).
Robust, heavy, rounded anteriorly;
back olive to black; sides lighter,
strongly mottled with brownish blotches,
but juveniles may be black; belly
whitish; fins dusky to black. Mouth
terminal, upper jaw slightly longer
than lower; 4 pairs of barbels, *barbels on
upper jaw long, reaching past base of
pectoral fin; chin barbels dusky or black.*
Pectoral fin spine with strong serrations
on rear edge; adipose fin present; anal
fin has 21−24 rays, length of its base
shorter than head length.

Habitat: Clear water in deep pools with
submerged vegetation.

Range: Nova Scotia west to SE. Saskatchewan;
central E. United States; widely
introduced outside native range.

Related Species: Snail Bullhead (*I. brunneus*) has uniform
body color, not mottled, 17−20 anal
fin rays; inhabits moderate to swift
streams over sand or rocks from S.
Virginia south to E. Alabama and N.
Florida. Flat Bullhead (*I. platycephalus*)
has strongly depressed head; median
fins with narrow, black edge; inhabits
slow streams over sand or mud on
Atlantic Coast from S. Virginia to
central Georgia.

Comments: The Brown Bullhead appears to be
intolerant of silty, polluted waters. It
has been raised commercially and
widely stocked in ponds and lakes.

55 Channel Catfish
(*Ictalurus punctatus*)

Description: To 3′11″ (1.2 m); 58 lbs (26.3 kg).
Slender; back blue-gray; *sides light blue
to silvery with scattered dark olive to black
spots;* belly white; fins olive to dusky.
Head wide, flat to slightly rounded
above; eyes large, above midline of

head; upper jaw overhangs lower; 4 pairs of barbels. Adipose fin present; *outer edge of anal fin rounded, 24–31 rays; caudal fin deeply forked.*

Habitat: Rivers and large creeks in slow to moderate current over sand, gravel, or rocks; ponds, lakes, reservoirs.

Range: S. Quebec west to S. Alberta; central and E. central United States. Widely introduced.

Related Species: Headwater Catfish (*I. lupus*) has shorter pectoral fin spine; 22–27 anal fin rays; caudal fin less deeply forked; found in Pecos River drainage in S. and W. Texas, and E. New Mexico. Spotted Bullhead (*I. serracanthus*) has pale yellow spots, shorter anal fin, caudal fin shallowly notched; occurs in deep holes or large streams over firm bottom from SW. Georgia to N. central Florida.

Comments: The Channel Catfish, a very popular sport and food fish, is harvested commercially in some areas. It is the principal catfish reared in aquaculture.

46 Slender Madtom
(*Noturus exilis*)

Description: To 5″ (12.5 cm). Slender, *adipose fin long, low keel-like ridge;* back grayish to dark olive with *light yellow blotch under last 3 dorsal rays;* sides light gray to yellow; belly gray-white; *median fins olive to gray with black margin. Head very depressed; mouth usually terminal;* 4 pairs of barbels. 8–10 pectoral fin rays, distinct serrations on posterior spine edge, poison gland at base; adipose fin present; caudal fin truncate, slightly rounded.

pectoral fin spine

Habitat: Creeks and small rivers with moderate to swift current, clear water, riffles.

Range: Central Mississippi River system, W. Indiana, S. Minnesota, S. Wisconsin, south to N. Alabama, central Arkansas, and E. Oklahoma.

Related Species: Margined Madtom (*N. insignis*) has
median fins with dusky margin; upper
jaw overhangs lower; found in clear
streams with moderate current, gravel
and rocky riffles in Atlantic Coastal
Plain from New York to Georgia; in
upper Tennessee and New rivers.

Comments: The Slender Madtom is generally
intolerant of silty, turbid streams.
Madtoms hide under rocks or debris
during the day, becoming active at
night.

---

49 Stonecat
(*Noturus flavus*)

toothband

Description: To 12″ (30 cm). Moderately elongate;
body coloration uniform, back slate-gray
to olive-green; sides yellowish olive;
belly, lower lip, chin whitish; yellowish
blotch at end of dorsal fin base. Head
depressed; eyes small; upper jaw
overhangs lower; *toothband of upper jaw
with backward projections;* 4 pairs of
barbels. 9−11 pectoral fin rays, 1 spine
with few barbs near tip on anterior
edge, poison gland at base, adipose fin
continuous with caudal fin; *caudal fin
margin unpigmented, truncate.*

Habitat: Riffles over gravel or rocks in moderate
to large streams; also on shoals of lakes.

Range: St. Lawrence River drainage west to S.
Alberta and south to E. Arkansas; N.
New York south to N. Alabama and
W. Tennessee.

Similar Species: Orangefin Madtom (*N. gilberti*) has
median fins with broad, light margins;
inhabits clear streams over rocks in
upper Dan, Roanoke, and James rivers
in W. central Virginia and N. North
Carolina.

Comments: The Stonecat is secretive, emerging
from its cover at night to feed on
aquatic insects and crustaceans.

51 Tadpole Madtom
(*Noturus gyrinus*)

Description: To 4½" (11.5 cm). *Tadpole-shaped, robust anteriorly, strongly compressed posteriorly;* back golden-brown to olive-gray; sides gray with narrow, dark, midlateral stripe branching out to outline muscle segments; belly yellowish; median fins olive. Head deep, rounded above; eye small; *mouth terminal;* 4 pairs of barbels. *Pectoral fin spine lacks serrations,* has poison gland at base. *Adipose fin continuous with broad, rounded caudal fin.*

pectoral fin spine

Habitat: Low-gradient, quiet, slow streams, sloughs, ponds, and lakes over mud and vegetation.

Range: SW. Quebec west to SE. Manitoba and south to S. Florida and S. Texas; absent from Appalachian highlands.

Comments: The Tadpole Madtom is the most widespread species in the genus. Like most madtoms, it is secretive and frequently hides in empty cans and bottles.

52 Speckled Madtom
(*Noturus leptacanthus*)

Description: To 3½" (9 cm). Slender; back dark brown to russet; sides brownish yellow; *back, sides, median fins with scattered gray-black blotches;* belly whitish. Head narrow; eyes small, upper jaw overhangs lower; 4 pairs of barbels. Pectoral fin spine has poison gland at base, *lacks serrations;* adipose fin continuous with truncate caudal fin.

pectoral fin spine

Habitat: Creeks with moderate current over sand or gravel, often in vegetation or debris.

Range: NW. South Carolina, SE. Tennessee, and NE. Mississippi, south to N. Florida, and west to E. Louisiana.

Related Species: Black Madtom (*N. funebris*) is dark gray to black without dark blotches; occurs from W. Georgia and W. Florida west to E. Mississippi and SE. Louisiana. Brown Madtom (*N. phaeus*) is dark brown with strong serrations on rear edge of pectoral spine; occurs from W. Kentucky south to NW. Mississippi; SW. Arkansas and N. Louisiana. Both in same habitat.

Comments: Speckled Madtoms frequently nest in old cans and bottles, in which females often lay 15 to 30 large eggs during July and August. The nest is guarded by the male until the eggs hatch and the young leave.

48 Brindled Madtom
(*Noturus miurus*)

Description: To 5″ (12.5 cm). Heaviest just anterior to dorsal spine; *back dark yellow-brown with 3 saddles;* yellowish below, sides mottled. Eye large; upper jaw overhangs lower; 4 pairs of barbels.

pectoral fin spine

Pectoral spine strongly serrate, poisonous; *dorsal fin with black blotch on edge of first 4 rays;* anal fin with blotch near edge of posterior rays; adipose fin low, continuous with caudal, with shallow notch posteriorly; *dusky bands at end of caudal peduncle and near margin of caudal fin;* caudal fin rounded.

Habitat: Pools below riffles of clear, low-gradient streams, often with detritus.

Range: S. Lake Ontario drainage southwest to E. Louisiana; E. West Virginia and E. Kentucky west to SE. Kansas and NE. Oklahoma.

Similar Species: Checkered Madtom (*N. flavater*) has black blotch on edge of dorsal fin rays; adipose fin separated from caudal fin by deep notch; caudal fin with black bands at base and near edge; inhabits streams with high gradient in S. Missouri and N. Arkansas. Yellowfin Madtom (*N. flavipinnis*) has brown band near middle of dorsal fin, outer third unpigmented; inhabits pools of streams in upper Tennessee River drainage, SW.

Virginia south to NW. Georgia.
Comments: The Brindled Madtom is active at
night.

---

50 Freckled Madtom
(*Noturus nocturnus*)

Description: To 4″ (10 cm). *Moderately robust; body
color uniform,* back brown, sides lighter;
belly yellowish; *back and sides with many
dark freckles;* base of median fins dusky,
lighter towards edge, margin clear.

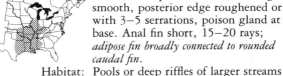

pectoral fin spine   Head depressed, rounded above; upper
jaw overhangs lower; 4 pairs of barbels.
Pectoral fin spine with anterior edge
smooth, posterior edge roughened or
with 3–5 serrations, poison gland at
base. Anal fin short, 15–20 rays;
*adipose fin broadly connected to rounded
caudal fin.*
Habitat: Pools or deep riffles of larger streams
with moderate current over gravel and
sand or rocks.
Range: From Illinois south to S. Alabama and
central Texas; E. Kentucky west to SE.
Kansas and E. Oklahoma.
Comments: The Freckled Madtom is widely
distributed, but not very common.

---

47 Flathead Catfish
(*Pylodictis olivaris*)

Description: To 4′5″ (1.4 m); 91¼ lbs (41.4 kg).
Elongate, slender; back and sides olive-
yellow to light brown with dark
mottling; belly yellowish; *caudal fin
dark brown to black, with upper lobe
unpigmented;* other fins yellowish to
light brown. *Head large, wide, very flat;*
eyes small; mouth wide, lower jaw
projecting beyond upper, 4 pairs of
short barbels. *Adipose fin large; dorsal fin
spine weak; 14–17 anal fin rays;* caudal
fin truncate, weakly notched.
Habitat: Large creeks, rivers, and reservoirs,

usually near cover of rocks, logs, or other debris.

Range: SE. Ontario; W. Pennsylvania, SW. Wisconsin and North Dakota, south to Texas and NE. Mexico; east in Gulf drainages to Mobile Bay drainage of Alabama, Georgia.

Comments: The Flathead Catfish, a good sport and food fish, is commercially important in some areas. The young feed on aquatic insects, but gradually shift their diet to fishes and crayfishes as they mature.

LABYRINTH CATFISHES
(Family Clariidae)

These catfishes are native to Africa, Syria, India, and the area encompassed by Java, Borneo, and the Philippines. The Walking Catfish has been introduced into the United States and is the family's sole representative in North America. Members of this family have a unique accessory respiratory organ, arising from the gill arches, that enables them to breathe air by increasing the surface area for absorption of oxygen. This adaptation allows some species to leave the water and move about on land.

45 Walking Catfish
(Clarias batrachus)

Description: To 14″ (36 cm). Elongate, broad anteriorly, compressed posteriorly; body dark brown to olive above, lighter below; frequent albino populations white to pinkish. *4 pairs of barbels.* Pectoral fins with 1 spine, 8–11 rays; *dorsal fin long, 60–75 rays; anal fin long, 47–58 rays;* dorsal and anal fins not joined to caudal fin.

Habitat: Lakes, swamps, and canals with little or no current, over mud with debris and aquatic plants.

Range: Established in S. Florida; introduced in Georgia, Nevada, and California.

Comments: The Walking Catfish, brought into the United States by the exotic fish business, escaped or was released from fish farms in southern Florida. It has spread rapidly, damaging native fishes in areas where this species has become established.

SEA CATFISHES
(Family Ariidae)

Unlike North American freshwater catfishes (Ictaluridae), sea catfishes do not have nasal barbels. The parents are buccal incubators: they carry eggs in the mouth for up to 3 months while the young hatch and grow into juveniles. These fishes have sharp dorsal and pectoral spines that can cause painful wounds. There are 3 species in North America.

500 Hardhead Catfish
(*Arius felis*)

Description: To 24″ (61 cm). Elongate, compressed; steel-blue or dark blue above, shading to silvery or white below. Head depressed; mouth inferior; *3 pairs of dark barbels: 1 on maxilla and 2 on chin, none notably elongate or ribbon-shaped;* rough bone exposed on top of head; pectoral and dorsal spines erect, serrated; fins dusky, anal and caudal fin tips darker, adipose fin black.

Habitat: Shallow coastal waters over sand or mud; occasionally in fresh water, but never far up rivers.

Range: From North Carolina to Florida; in Gulf of Mexico to Yucatán, Mexico.

Comments: From May to August spawning takes place in shallow back bays in the northeastern Gulf of Mexico. Fertilized eggs, .06 to .07″ (14 to 18 mm) in diameter, develop in the mouth of the male (and sometimes the female), which does not eat throughout this period. The eggs hatch in about 30 days and are carried for another 2 to 4 weeks while the larvae become juveniles. Hardhead Catfishes are not esteemed as food; commercial and sport fishers consider them pests. Their pectoral and dorsal spines can cause painful wounds.

501 Gafftopsail Catfish
(*Bagre marinus*)

Description: To 3′3″ (99 cm). Somewhat elongate; head slightly depressed; dorsal profile straight from snout to base of dorsal fin; bluish-gray above, fading to silvery on sides and white below. Mouth terminal, slightly inferior; 2 pairs of barbels: *maxillary barbels long, ribbonlike;* barbels on chin small. *Long, ribbonlike filament extending from pectoral and dorsal fin spines.* Pectoral, dorsal, and caudal fins dusky; pelvic and anal fins light dusky; adipose fin bluish black.

Habitat: Shallow coastal and bay areas; seasonal in estuaries.

Range: Uncommon north of North Carolina; ranges south to Brazil, including Gulf of Mexico; virtually absent from Antilles.

Comments: The Gafftopsail Catfish has an unusual method of reproduction, similar to that of the Hardhead Catfish. It is considered a good food and game fish in many parts of its range. Most of these fishes reach a length of about 18″ (46 cm). Their pectoral and dorsal spines can cause painful wounds.

Order Percopsiformes

These fishes are small and usually robust, with relatively large heads; their dorsal fin is preceded by up to 4 weak spines, and the anal fin by up to 3. There are 3 families confined to the fresh waters of North America.

CAVEFISHES
(Family Amblyopsidae)

This family of 6 species is restricted to the east central and eastern United States. There are 5 species that live in or around the entrance to caves. The sixth, the Swampfish, inhabits dark, stained waters in swamps. Only 2 species are pigmented, and they have reduced but functional eyes; the remaining 4, all cave dwellers, are unpigmented and blind. Interesting cave adaptations include numerous sensory papillae on the head and body, a decrease in metabolic rate, and a reproductive strategy in which the few large eggs are held in the gill chamber after being fertilized and during the early stages of development.

Northern Cavefish
(*Amblyopsis spelaea*)

Description: To 4″ (10 cm). Robust, very wide anteriorly; *pinkish-white.* Head large, somewhat depressed; eyes rudimentary, concealed beneath skin, nonfunctional; mouth moderately large, lower jaw projects beyond upper. Head and body covered with short, vertical rows of sensory papillae. Fins plain, transparent; *pelvic fins small, often absent; 9 dorsal fin rays;* anal fin under dorsal fin; *caudal fin long with 4–6 rows of sensory papillae.* Scales small, embedded.

Habitat: Over mud, sand, or rocks in caves with
clear pools.

Range: S. central Indiana and N. Kentucky
south to Mammoth Cave, Kentucky.

Related Species: Ozark Cavefish (*A. rosae*) has 7 dorsal
fin rays; no pelvic fins; occurs in similar
habitat in SW. Missouri, NW.
Arkansas, and NE. Oklahoma.

Comments: The Northern Cavefish feeds on small
crustaceans it locates with external
sensory organs that are sensitive to the
slightest vibrations. It swims very
slowly just a few inches off the bottom.

---

215 Spring Cavefish
(*Chologaster agassizi*)

Description: To 3″ (7.5 cm). Elongate, somewhat
rounded; dark brown above, *light olive-
brown on sides with pale midlateral stripe,*
belly yellowish. Head flattened above;
mouth moderately large, lower jaw
projecting; *eyes very small, functional.*
Head and body have short rows of
sensory papillae. *No pelvic fins; median
fins olive;* caudal peduncle long, deep;
*caudal fin broad, rounded, dusky bar at
base.* Scales small, embedded.

Habitat: Cool, clear waters of springs and caves.

Range: From W. Kentucky and W. central
Tennessee west to S. Illinois and SE.
Missouri.

Related Species: Swampfish (*C. cornuta*) has white dorsal
fin with dusky to black edge, caudal fin
black with 2 white blotches near base;
inhabits sluggish streams and swamps
on Coastal Plain from S. Virginia to S.
Georgia.

Comments: While the Spring Cavefish is sometimes
seen in caves and wells, it is most often
found in springs or streams flowing
from caves. It is active at night and
retreats to overhanging banks or other
cover during the day.

216 Southern Cavefish
(*Typhlichthys subterraneus*)

caudal fin

Description: To 3″ (7.5 cm). Slender, elongate; *colorless except for pinkish cast where blood vessels show through skin;* individuals exposed to light become dusky. Head blunt, broad; *eyes absent;* mouth small. *No pelvic fins;* anus considerably anterior to anal fin origin; *caudal fin rounded, with 2 rows of sensory papillae.* Scales small, somewhat embedded, body appears naked.

Habitat: Caves, underground pools at or near water table, occasionally near cave openings.

Range: S. Indiana south to NW. Georgia and N. Alabama; S. Missouri, NE. Arkansas, and NE. Oklahoma.

Similar Species: Alabama Cavefish (*Speoplatyrhinus poulsoni*) has very long, flattened snout; known only in 1 cave in Lauderdale County, Alabama.

Comments: The Southern Cavefish is the most widespread of the cavefishes, occurring east and west of the Mississippi River.

PIRATE PERCHES
(Family Aphredoderidae)

anus

This family is represented by a single species, which appears to be a remnant of a more ancient Mississippi Valley fauna. Pirate Perches are unusual because, as they mature, their anus moves forward from just in front of the anal fin in juveniles to a point anterior to the pelvic girdle in the throat region in adults.

217 Pirate Perch
(*Aphredoderus sayanus*)

Description: To 4½″ (11.5 cm). Oblong, stout anteriorly, compressed posteriorly; *head and body dark olive-grayish with dark spots;* underside of head and body yellowish to brownish. Maxilla extends to front of eye; opercle with sharp spine; preopercle strongly serrate. Fins dusky; *single dorsal fin with 2–4 spines, 10–11 soft rays; no adipose fin;* caudal peduncle deep; caudal fin has 1–2 dark bars at base. Lateral line incomplete. *Scales on head and body ctenoid.*

Habitat: Backwaters of low-gradient streams, ponds, swamps, and bayous in clear to murky water with abundant aquatic plant cover.

Range: Atlantic Coastal Plain, from Long Island south to S. Florida, west to E. Texas; S. Great Lakes drainage from W. New York to SE. Minnesota, and south in Mississippi Valley.

Comments: The Pirate Perch hides in aquatic vegetation and debris by day and emerges in darkness to feed. It is more abundant in the southern portion of its range.

TROUT-PERCHES
(Family Percopsidae)

The common name for this family was assigned to it by early naturalists, who thought it to be an intermediate form in the evolution from trouts to perches. It contains 2 species, both found only in North America. They have 8 or 9 pelvic fin rays, and 1 to 3 spines precede the dorsal and anal fins. The pectoral fin extends past the pelvic fin insertion, and an adipose fin is present. The scales are ctenoid and small.

Trout-Perch
(Percopsis omiscomaycus)

Description: To 6″ (15 cm). Moderately elongate, stout; *pale olive to straw-yellow above;*

somewhat translucent, rows of dark spots on upper half of body. Snout long; mouth small, ventral; no scales on head, cheeks, and opercles. Fins transparent; *single dorsal fin with 2–3 weak spines, 8–11 soft rays,* origin behind pelvic fin insertion; *adipose fin present;* caudal peduncle long; caudal fin forked. *Lateral line complete, 41–60 scales.*

Habitat: Lakes and streams over sand or gravel.

Range: Much of Canada and Alaska, drainages of S. Hudson and James bays; NW. Connecticut south to Potomac River; Great Lakes and upper Mississippi River system.

Related Species: Sand Roller (*P. transmontana*) has incomplete lateral line; occurs over sand or rocks in large streams in Columbia River drainage, in Washington and Oregon, and upstream to Idaho.

Comments: The Trout-Perch seeks food at night in shallow, open waters, retiring to deeper water or undercut banks during the day. In northern lakes, where it is abundant, it is an important forage fish for several species of game fishes.

Order Batrachoidiformes

This order consists of a single family, the toadfishes. They are a carnivorous species that live on the bottom. Some can survive out of water for a few hours, and can use the swim bladder to generate sound.

TOADFISHES
(Family Batrachoididae)

Toadfishes are slow-moving, bottom-dwelling fishes that prey on mollusks and crustaceans. Most species are drab brown, and variously blotched and

mottled; 1 genus has lines of
photophores on the underside of the
head and body. The eyes are near the
top of the head and directed upward.
The spinous portion of the dorsal fin
has 2 to 3 stout spines; the soft part is
long, continuous, and similar to the
anal fin. The body is naked or covered
with small cycloid scales, and 1 or
more lateral lines are present. Care
should be taken to avoid being bitten,
as their jaws are powerful. There are 6
species in North America.

460 Oyster Toadfish
(*Opsanus tau*)

Description: To 15″ (38 cm). Robust, compressed;
olive-brown above, belly paler with
pale bars or irregular blotches. Head
large and depressed; *mouth very large,
wide, fleshy flaps on upper and lower lips;*
teeth strong, blunt. Median fins dusky,
paired fins pale. Pectoral fins broad at
base, fanlike, with bars or blotches,
insertion posterior to pelvic fins. About
26 soft dorsal rays; anal fin lacks
spines, similar to soft dorsal but
shorter; caudal fin rounded. Scaleless.

Habitat: Shallow water over sand or mud, in
vegetation or among debris.

Range: From Cape Cod to S. Florida.

Related Species: Gulf Toadfish (*O. beta*) has lighter
blotches on body and pectoral fins;
fewer dorsal rays; occurs in similar
habitat in Gulf of Mexico from Cape
Sable, Florida, to Yucatán, Mexico.

Comments: All 3 North American species in this
genus have powerful jaws and should
be handled with caution. They remain
in hiding, awaiting their prey, which
includes a variety of crustaceans,
annelids, mollusks, and fishes.

463 Plainfin Midshipman
(*Porichthys notatus*)

Description:

photophores

To 15″ (38 cm). Elongate, tapering; purple-bronze above, yellow-white below. Head large, broad; *eyes widely separated, protrusible.* Rows of photophores on underside; *second row of photophores under head V-shaped with apex toward front.* Pectoral, dorsal, and anal fins lack spots.

Habitat: Over sand and mud to depths of 200 fathoms.

Range: In Pacific from Sitka, Alaska, to the Gulf of California.

Related Species: Specklefin Midshipman (*P. myriaster*) has spots on pectoral, dorsal, and anal fins; second row of photophores under head U-shaped; occurs in Pacific from Point Conception, California, to Bahía Magdalena, Baja California. Atlantic Midshipman (*P. plectrodon*) has light brown body, with saddlelike blotches on back and 10 blotches on sides; has 4 lateral lines and golden photophores; occurs in Atlantic from Virginia to Brazil, including Gulf of Mexico. Both in similar habitat.

photophores

Comments: The Plainfin Midshipman comes into shallow water during the late spring to spawn. The male becomes emaciated while guarding the eggs and young, so that the mortality rate among egg-tending males tends to be high. This species feeds at night on other fishes and crustaceans. It often appears in the catches of sport and commercial anglers.

Order Gobiesociformes

These bottom-dwellers have specialized pelvic fins that are united anteriorly and, with a fold of skin, form a large sucking disc. The dorsal and anal fins are composed only of soft rays. There is a single family in North America.

CLINGFISHES
(Family Gobiesocidae)

Members of this family have disc-shaped pelvic fins with 4 to 5 soft rays and lack scales. Clingfishes are distributed worldwide in warm seas, although a few species occur in temperate ocean waters, and several others live in fresh water. There are 9 species in North America.

---

300 Skilletfish
(Gobiesox strumosus)

Description: To 2¾" (7 cm). Very broad, greatly depressed anteriorly; tail sector becomes more compressed posteriorly; beige with dark mottling on back and sides; top of head with irregular dark brown spots. Head length and width each about two-fifths body length; mouth broad, lips with papillae; nostril has dermal flap; eyes directed upward. *Large, ventral, adhesive disc formed by modified pelvic fins and broad, apronlike dermal flap.* Pectoral fins very broad at base; caudal fin rounded. Skin smooth, lacking scales.

Habitat: On bottom, usually over mud and among oyster shells.

Range: From New Jersey to Brazil, including Bermuda, Gulf of Mexico, and West Indies.

Comments: This distinctive little fish is common around oyster reefs, where it clings so strongly to shells and other objects that it continues to grip them even when it is lifted from the water.

Order Lophiiformes

The anglerfishes have a distinctive, modified first dorsal spine called the illicium. The pectoral fins are limblike, and the gill opening is reduced to a small hole. There are 6 families that are found in North America, all marine, and all but 3 of these live in deep seas.

GOOSEFISHES
(Family Lophiidae)

Members of this family have broad, rounded, flattened heads and tapering bodies, squarish pectoral fins, and wide, superior mouths that are equipped with many long, sharp teeth. There are 2 dorsal fins, the posterior long, soft, and squarish, the anterior separated into several free spines. The foremost spine, just behind the upper lip, is modified to form a "fishing pole" complete with a fleshy lure at the tip. This structure, the illicium, attracts the smaller fishes that are part of a goosefish's diet. Goosefish flesh has an excellent flavor and is sold as a delicacy in Japan and Europe. There are 3 species in North America.

292 Goosefish
(*Lophius americanus*)

Description: To 4' (1.2 m). Tapering; tan to chocolate-brown and finely mottled above, whitish below; fin membranes behind head black, other fins darker than body. Head flattened, rounded; mouth wide, opens upward; teeth numerous, thin, sharp. Gill openings in form of round hole behind axis of pectoral fins. Lower jaw, head, and side of body have fringe of fleshy flaps. Pectoral and dorsal fins squarish; pelvic fins broad, stubby. Anterior dorsal spines present, foremost modified as "fishing lure"; *third spine on top of head shorter than width of ridge between eyes.*

Habitat: On bottom to about 200 fathoms, but

frequents shallows in north of range.

Range: From Bay of Fundy to N. Florida.

Related Species: Blackfin Goosefish (*L. gastrophysus*) with third spine on top of head longer, lacks membranes between spines behind head; posterior edges of pectoral fins not black; occurs in deep water from Cape Hatteras, North Carolina, to Gulf of Mexico and Argentina.

Comments: Goosefishes have an enormous capacity for food and eat almost any kind of fish, various species of birds (they have been reported to eat geese), turtles, and invertebrates. They apparently can swallow fishes that are equal to their own weight.

FROGFISHES
(Family Antennariidae)

Members of this family are small and globular with slightly to moderately compressed bodies. They are poor swimmers and depend on camouflage for concealment from predators. The first dorsal spine is separated from the rest of the long dorsal fin and is modified as a lure for prey. The pectoral fins are limblike, and the skin, either prickly or smooth, often has fleshy flaps. Frogfishes feed by waiting in ambush, or by enticing other fishes. The lure is wiggled to mimic a live animal, attracting potential prey. Faster than the eye can follow, the frogfish gulps the unsuspecting victim. There are 7 species found in North America.

296, 298   **Longlure Frogfish**
(*Antennarius multiocellatus*)

Description: To 6″ (15 cm). Globular, compressed; 2 color phases. Light phase: body usually pale yellow; *ocellated black spots*

on soft dorsal fin, another at base of anal
fin; 3 smaller spots on caudal fin; small
spot beneath pectoral fin and another
above, 1 at base of third dorsal spine;
other spots sometimes on median fins.
Dark phase: body darker, may be
almost black; tips of rays of pectoral
and pelvic fins pale; *whitish blotch on
caudal peduncle just behind soft dorsal fin.*
First dorsal spine elongate and delicate,
bears wormlike lure; pectoral fins
limblike, small gill opening behind
base; skin prickly.

Habitat: Reefs.

Range: Florida and West Indies.

Comments: This is probably the most common
member of the genus in the West
Indies. The 2 color phases reflect mood;
in the light phase, the fish is at rest; in
the dark phase, it is disturbed.

295 Sargassumfish
(*Histrio histrio*)

Description: To 6″ (15 cm). Short, deep, irregular in
profile, moderately compressed; *creamy
white to yellowish, mottled light and dark
spots and blotches;* blends with sargassum
plant in which it lives; coloring
changeable depending on amount of
light and on mood of fish. Mouth
relatively small, gape very wide.
Pectoral fins limblike, with long base;
small gill opening behind base. First
dorsal spine forms lure; second and
third spines large, depressible, and
covered with skin bearing fleshy cirri.
Skin smooth with numerous fleshy flaps.

Habitat: Floating sargassum weed.

Range: From New England to Brazil,
including Bermuda, Gulf of Mexico,
Caribbean, and West Indies.

Comments: The only commercial value of the
Sargassumfish is in the aquarium trade.
It is fun to watch it lurking in the
vegetation and luring prey to its
cavernous mouth.

BATFISHES
(Family Ogcocephalidae)

gill opening

These fishes have a disc-shaped body that is flattened ventrally, a small ventral mouth, limblike pectoral fins, and a distinct tail. The snout extends in front of the eyes, and the gill openings are reduced to a small hole behind the pectoral fins. The short first dorsal spine is modified to form the illicium, a retractable "fishing pole." Batfishes feed on various snails, clams, small fishes, and crustaceans, but it is not known which food is attracted to the bait. The modified scales form bucklers, which are especially large and well developed on the back. There are 7 species in North America.

---

294 Pancake Batfish
(*Halieutichthys aculeatus*)

Description: To 4″ (10 cm). Disc-shaped, fringed with fleshy papillae; light brown above with irregular, dark lines and small blotches; very small, white specks over entire dorsal surface; unpigmented and scaleless below. *Snout not protruding;* illicium retracts into depression in snout; mouth small; eyes blue. Fins dusky; pectoral and pelvic fins limblike, pectoral connected to tail by membrane. Tail sector short, broad, greatly depressed, with dorsal fin at base; caudal fin has dusky bars.

Habitat: Over sand from near shore to midcontinental shelf.

Range: From North Carolina to Florida, Gulf of Mexico, and Lesser Antilles.

Comments: This fish remains partially covered by sand during the day and becomes active at night. It swims by moving its pectoral fins in an oarlike fashion.

293 Roughback Batfish
(*Ogcocephalus parvus*)

Description: To 3¼″ (8.5 cm). Triangular, very wide, tail round in cross section. Dark brown above with light reticulate pattern; sides have uneven lavender spots; cheeks white with orange spots; tail sector with small, black dots; caudal fin with 3 bars, dark brown, white, orange. *Snout projecting, short, upturned;* illicium trilobed, fits in socket under snout; mouth small. Pectoral fins limblike, black-edged; dorsal and anal fins with 4 rays. Body and tail covered with large, rough bucklers.

Habitat: Over sand and mud to depths of about 55 fathoms.

Range: From Cape Hatteras, North Carolina, to N. Brazil, including E. Gulf of Mexico and Caribbean.

Related Species: *O. corniger* has much longer snout; ranges from North Carolina to E. Gulf of Mexico. *O. cubifrons* has more pectoral rays, greater distance between eyes; occurs in shallow water from North Carolina to Florida and disjunctly to Yucatán, Mexico. Both in similar habitat.

Comments: The recently identified related species do not yet have common names. All these fishes eat small crustaceans and fishes.

Order Gadiformes

The members of this order have an elongate, tapering body and long dorsal and anal fins. Most of these fishes are marine, although a few species live in fresh water. There are 7 families in North America.

CODFISHES
(Family Gadidae)

These fishes have 1 to 3 dorsal fins and 1 or 2 anal fins. Some species have a barbel on the lower jaw. The scales are always small and cycloid. Valuable as food, most codfishes are harvested commercially, and are sold fresh, dried, or salted. Historically, they were important as a major trading item. Some species are sought by anglers. There are 15 genera and 25 species in North America, and most occur in temperate seas. The eggs of members of this family are usually free-floating.

Cusk
(*Brosme brosme*)

Description: To 3′6″ (1.1 m); 27 lbs (12.2 kg). Moderately elongate, cylindrical anteriorly, compressed posteriorly; dark slaty to reddish-brown above, sides yellowish, sometimes mottled brown; belly whitish; *dorsal, anal, and caudal fins bordered with black stripe and white edge.* Head flattened; mouth oblique, maxilla extends beyond eye; single barbel on chin. *Single dorsal fin continuous, not elevated,* origin above anterior half of pectoral fin; caudal fin rounded.

Habitat: On bottom over hard substrates, usually at 10–100 fathoms.

Range: From Newfoundland Banks south to S. New England, occasionally extending to New Jersey.

Comments: The Cusk is an important commercial fish. In past years the annual catch totaled hundreds of tons in the United States alone. It is marketed both fresh and salted.

492 Atlantic Cod
(*Gadus morhua*)

Description: To 6' (1.8 m); 98¾ lbs (44.8 kg).
Moderately elongate, slightly
compressed, tapering to slender caudal
peduncle; variably greenish, brownish,
yellowish, whitish, or reddish; back
and sides with numerous brownish
spots; *lateral line pale; no black blotch on
shoulder.* Eye large; maxilla reaches
anterior margin of eye; *chin barbel large;*
upper jaw projects beyond lower. Fins
dark; *pelvic fins not filamentous;* 3 dorsal
fins; 2 anal fins; caudal fin emarginate.

Habitat: Usually on or near bottom of
continental shelf at depths of 6–20
fathoms, sometimes deeper, over hard,
irregular substrates.

Range: From W. Greenland south to Cape
Hatteras; most abundant from Labrador
to New York.

Comments: Reported at over 200 lbs (90 kg) but
considered large at one-third of that
weight, Atlantic Cod average 6 to
12 lbs (2.7 to 5.4 kg). They feed on a
variety of animals, mostly mollusks, sea
squirts, and other fishes. The annual
catch of this commercially important
fish amounts to tens of thousands of
tons. It is often caught on a handline
by anglers in New England.

43 Burbot
(*Lota lota*)

Description: To 3'2" (97 cm); 18½ lbs (8.4 kg).
Elongate, robust, compressed
posteriorly; yellowish-brown to dark
olive above; sides mottled light and
dark. Head broad, flattened; nostrils
tubular; mouth extends below eye;
*barbel on chin tip single, slender. Pelvic fins
placed far forward,* pale; other fins dark,
mottled; *first dorsal fin short, second dorsal
and anal fins long;* caudal fin rounded.

Habitat: In deep, cold water of rivers and lakes.

Range: Most of Canada and Alaska south to Ohio and Missouri river drainages.

Comments: The Burbot is unusual among freshwater fishes in that it spawns in winter under the ice. From December to March it spawns at night in shallow water over clean sand, gravel, or rock, where the eggs lie unattended. Fishes make up the bulk of the adult diet. The Burbot is the only exclusively freshwater species of the codfish family. It is occasionally caught by anglers.

---

491 Haddock
(*Melanogrammus aeglefinus*)

Description: To 3′8″ (1.1 m); 37 lbs (16.8 kg). Moderately elongate, slightly compressed, tapering to slender caudal peduncle; dark gray above, whitish below; *large, dark blotch on shoulder; lateral line black.* Maxilla does not reach front of eye; *chin barbel very small. Pelvic fins not filamentous;* 3 dorsal fins, anterior rays of first long, ending in sharp point; dorsal and caudal fins dusky; 2 anal fins.

Habitat: Usually at 25–75 fathoms, rarely in shoal water.

Range: Grand Banks; from Nova Scotia Banks to Cape Cod, and in deep water off Cape Hatteras.

Comments: Haddock live in deeper waters than cod and prefer smooth bottoms of sand, gravel, or clay. They feed indiscriminately on available fauna. Most specimens weigh up to 4 lbs (1.8 kg). They are somewhat more important commercially than cod.

---

488 Silver Hake
(*Merluccius bilinearis*)

Description: To 30″ (76 cm); 5 lbs (2.3 kg). Elongate, rounded to anus, compressed posteriorly; brownish with silvery iridescence, silvery below; 5–7 irregular dark bars. Lower jaw projects beyond upper, maxilla reaches middle of eye; *no barbel on chin.* Fins have light greenish borders; pelvic fins not filamentous; *first dorsal fin shorter, higher, second long with deep notch,* similar to anal fin. Caudal fin slightly truncate. *Lateral line prominent, appears double.*

Habitat: On or near bottom in deep water of continental shelf; occasionally in shallow water in pursuit of food.

Range: Continental shelf from Newfoundland Banks to offshore waters of Maryland and Virginia. Most abundant in SW. Gulf of Maine.

Similar Species: Genus *Urophycis* has chin barbel; pelvic fins long, filamentous, and consist of 2 or 3 rays; occurs from shore to depths of 110 fathoms in Atlantic and Gulf of Mexico.

Comments: The Silver Hake has a good flavor if eaten when fresh, but it deteriorates too quickly for commercial exploitation. It is not a popular sport fish.

487 Pacific Hake
(*Merluccius productus*)

Description: To 3' (91 cm). Elongate, slightly compressed; back metallic silver-gray with black speckles, silvery below. Maxilla extends to middle of eye; *lower jaw projects beyond upper; no barbel;* opercle and inside of mouth black. *2 dorsal fins, second fin and anal fin deeply notched;* caudal fin truncate.

Habitat: Surface to bottom of open sea to 500 fathoms; occasionally inshore waters.

Range: From Gulf of Alaska south to Gulf of California.

Related Species: Walleye Pollock (*Theragra chalcogramma*) with barbel weak or absent, jaws about even; 3 dorsal fins; 2 anal fins; occurs over soft bottoms from Bering Sea to Carmel Bay, California.

Comments: The Pacific Hake spawns from January to June. It feeds mostly at night, chiefly on other fishes, shrimps, and plankton. Anglers trolling for salmon commonly catch Pacific Hake, but rarely eat them. Russians eat large amounts of Pacific Hake, but in the United States these fishes are used chiefly for animal food.

490 Pacific Tomcod
(Microgadus proximus)

Description: To 12″ (30 cm). Elongate, moderately compressed; olive-green above, creamy white below, fin tips dusky. *Small chin barbel, equal in length to pupil diameter.* 3 dorsal fins and 2 anal fins present. *Anus below first dorsal fin.*

Habitat: Over soft bottoms, around piers and jetties in bays, and to depths of 120 fathoms.

Range: From Bering Sea south to Point Sal, California.

Related Species: Pacific Cod *(Gadus macrocephalus)* has larger chin barbel, equal in length to diameter of eye; anus below second dorsal fin; occurs in deeper water from Bering Sea to Santa Monica, California.

Comments: Pacific Tomcod grow fast but only live about 5 years. During "runs" of occasional abundance, they are popular with pier and skiff anglers. They are considered fine food fishes.

Atlantic Tomcod
(Microgadus tomcod)

Description: To 15″ (38 cm). Moderately elongate, tapering, slightly compressed; olive to dark green above with yellowish tinge, becoming pale on sides; *body and fins mottled with indefinite dark spots or blotches.* Snout conical, overhangs lower jaw; chin barbel relatively large; eye small. *Second pelvic fin ray filamentous;* caudal fin rounded. Lateral line pale.

Habitat: Shallow water to about 18′ (5.5 m) and in brackish and fresh water in estuaries and rivers.

Range: From Labrador to Virginia; landlocked populations in Nova Scotia and Quebec.

Comments: This small codfish usually does not exceed 1¼ lbs. It is tolerant of cold and spawns in water temperatures as low as 34° F (1° C). During the winter when other fishes may be scarce, this species provides amusement for anglers. It is an excellent food fish.

489 Pollock
(*Pollachius virens*)

Description: To 3′6″ (1.1 m); 46½ lbs (21.1 kg). Rather elongate, somewhat compressed; olive-green, brownish-green, or grayish above, sides paler, belly silvery; *lateral line white;* median fins olive-gray or greenish; paired fins have pinkish tinge. *Lower jaw projects beyond upper;* maxilla reaches anterior margin of eye; *chin barbel minute or absent.* First dorsal fin roughly triangular; pelvic fin short; caudal fin deeply emarginate or lunate.

Habitat: Over rocks to depths of 100 fathoms; sometimes at midwater or on surface.

Range: From Gulf of St. Lawrence to New Jersey, occasionally to Chesapeake Bay and North Carolina. Most abundant in Gulf of Maine.

Comments: Pollock usually run in schools and are an important part of the New England and North Atlantic fishery, but less so than Atlantic Cod and Haddock. Adults average from 4 to 15 lbs (1.8 to 6.8 kg).

473 Red Hake
(*Urophycis chuss*)

Description: To 30″ (76 cm); 7 lbs (3.2 kg). Elongate, cylindrical anteriorly, compressed posteriorly; reddish to olive-brown or almost black above, lower sides yellowish, sometimes mottled; belly whitish. *Maxilla reaches posterior of pupil; chin barbel minute. Pelvic fin reaches past anus, third ray filamentous and long.* First dorsal fin short, high; second dorsal fin and anal fin both long, straight. Caudal peduncle narrow; caudal fin rounded.

Habitat: Over mud or silt at depths of 6–60 fathoms.

Range: From Nova Scotia to Cape Hatteras.

Comments: This and the White Hake are important commercial fishes but are not highly esteemed as food or for sport. Their flesh is soft and their fighting qualities are too poor to make them attractive to anglers.

474 White Hake
(*Urophycis tenuis*)

Description: To 4′ (1.2 m). Elongate, cylindrical anteriorly, compressed posteriorly; back and dorsal fin brown or purplish brown; belly and anal fin dirty white or yellowish; dorsal and anal fins both with black edges. Head pointed, depressed; chin barbel small; *maxilla reaches posterior of eye. Pelvic fin filamentous, does not reach past anus.* First dorsal fin short, high, triangular, third ray extended; second dorsal fin and anal fin both long, straight. Caudal peduncle narrow; caudal fin rounded.

Habitat: Over mud or silt at depths of 6–60 fathoms.

Range: From Nova Scotia to Cape Hatteras.

Comments: Although not an epicurean delight, this fish tastes best in the autumn.

CUSK-EELS
(Family Ophidiidae)

These are elongate, eel-like fishes. They have a single, long-based, continuous dorsal fin that joins with the similarly shaped anal fin to form a continuous fin around the posterior end of the body. The pelvic fins consist of 2 filamentous rays, and are placed under the eye or below the opercle. Cusk-Eels have wide gill openings, and those in the genus *Brotula* have chin barbels. These fishes are usually drab, but some have distinctive spots. Cusk-Eels live over the continental shelf, but some of the brotulids range into greater depths. There are 15 species in North America.

---

450 Spotted Cusk-Eel
(*Chilara taylori*)

Description: To 14¼" (36 cm). Elongate, eel-like; light brown to cream with *small, dark spots.* No spines in fins; *pelvic fins filamentous, located on throat.* Dorsal fin single, long-based, continuous; anal fin similar in shape. Dorsal, anal, and caudal fins continuous around body.

Habitat: Over and in soft bottoms to depths of 133 fathoms.

Range: From Oregon to S. Baja California.

Related Species: Basketweave Cusk-Eel (*Ophidion scrippsae*) lacks spots, has strong crosshatched scale patterns on sides; occurs in similar habitat from Point Aguello, California, to Guaymas, Mexico.

Comments: The Spotted Cusk-Eel burrows tail-first into the sand or mud during the day, and comes out at night to feed. It is occasionally captured by divers and makes an interesting aquarium fish. A few are accidentally caught by commercial fishers in trawls and round haul nets.

449 Mottled Cusk-Eel
(*Lepophidium jeannae*)

Description: To 8″ (20 cm). Elongate, eel-like,
compressed; dusky beige or yellowish,
darker above with dusky mottling;
series of black blotches on edges of
dorsal and anal fins. Head conical;
snout has sharp spine and overhangs
mouth; gill openings wide. No spines
in fins; *pelvic fins consist of 2 filamentous
rays of equal length* inserted behind chin;
dorsal and anal fins long, continuous
with caudal fin around tip of tail. *Scales
overlapping in regular rows on body.*

Habitat: Over sand or mud, from near shore to
middle of continental shelf.

Range: From Georgia, Florida, and E. Gulf of
Mexico, disjunctly south to Yucatán,
Mexico.

Related Species: Fawn Cusk-Eel (*L. cervinum*) has large,
pale spots on upper sides; ranges from
Gulf of Maine to Florida. Blackedge
Cusk-Eel (*L. graellsi*) has continuous
black edge on dorsal and anal fins;
ranges from N. Gulf of Mexico to
Brazil. Both occur in similar habitat.

Comments: Little is known about the life history of
this fish. It probably behaves like other
members of the family, hiding during
the day and becoming active at night.

448 Bank Cusk-Eel
(*Ophidion holbrooki*)

Description: To 8″ (20 cm). Elongate, eel-like,
compressed; primarily pinkish to
brownish, with several brownish stripes
or dusky mottling on back, becoming
silvery on belly, median fins black-
edged. Head conical, has hidden spine;
mouth terminal. *Pelvic fins consist of 2
filamentous rays of unequal length* inserted
behind chin; dorsal and anal fins long,
continuous with caudal fin around tip
of tail; *scales not overlapping, in oblique
rows in herringbone pattern.*

scales

Habitat:	Continental shelf over sand.
Range:	From North Carolina to Florida, and in Gulf of Mexico west to Texas.
Comments:	This little-known fish appears in shrimp trawl collections made between shore and depths of 25 fathoms over sandy bottoms.

EELPOUTS
(Family Zoarcidae)

These eel-like fishes are found in north temperate and Arctic areas. Most of the 23 species that inhabit North American waters differ from the true eels (Anguilliformes) in having pelvic fins. These fins are small, but they are not filamentous as in cusk-eels.

---

454 Ocean Pout
(*Macrozoarces americanus*)

Description:	To 3′6″ (1.1 m). Elongate, eel-like, depth about one-eighth length; color variable: pinkish-yellow, brownish, reddish-brown, mottled with darker hues above; belly dirty white or yellowish. Head conical; teeth large, conical; maxilla reaches well beyond small eye. *Pelvic fins small, not filamentous,* insertion in front of pectoral fins, pectoral fins broad-based, fanlike. Dorsal fin origin at nape, continuous, about same height throughout, *not connected to caudal fin; anal fin long, low, continuous, connected to caudal fin.* Flesh soft, scales small, slimy.
Habitat:	On bottom over sand, mud, rocks, or seaweed from shore to 105 fathoms.
Range:	From Gulf of St. Lawrence and SE. Newfoundland to Delaware.
Related Species:	Blackbelly Eelpout (*Lycodopsis pacifica*) has black belly, black spot on anterior part of dorsal fin; occurs over soft bottoms at 5–218 fathoms from Alaska

to N. Baja California.

Comments: Though there is little demand for them as food, the flesh of Ocean Pouts is reputedly lean and wholesome. Most of the 17 species of eelpouts on the Pacific Coast live in deep water.

Order Atheriniformes

Fishes belonging to this order are morphologically diverse and are distributed worldwide in virtually all tropical and temperate, marine, brackish, and freshwater environments. There are 6 families in North America.

FLYINGFISHES
(Family Exocoetidae)

This family consists of 2 groups, the flyingfishes and the halfbeaks, which share several characteristics: a nearly cylindrical body, with pectoral fins located high on the sides, abdominal pelvic fins, and posteriorly placed dorsal and anal fins. In addition, the fins lack spines, the lower lobe of the caudal fin is longer than the upper, and the lateral line pores follow the ventral contour of the body. The flyingfishes differ in having greatly enlarged pectoral fins and elongate pelvic fins, while most halfbeaks have a very long lower jaw. Flyingfishes do not really fly, but glide above the surface of the water on their pectoral fins. There are 23 species in North America.

434 Halfbeak
(*Hyporhamphus unifasciatus*)

Description: To 10½" (27 cm). Very elongate, slightly compressed; greenish above, scales dark-edged, 3 black lines on mid-dorsal area between head and dorsal fin, silvery below. *Lower jaw very long, extends far beyond short upper jaw, tip bright orange-red.* Pectoral fins short, inserted above axis of body; pelvic fins small, abdominal; dorsal and anal fins posteriorly placed opposite each other, similar in size and shape; caudal fin not deeply forked, lower lobe slightly longer than upper. No spines in fins. Lateral line follows ventral profile. Scales cycloid, present on body, upper jaw, and bases of dorsal and anal fins.

Habitat: Usually on surface near shore; sometimes in estuaries.

Range: In Atlantic from Maine to Argentina, including Bermuda, Gulf of Mexico, and Caribbean. In Pacific from San Diego, California, to Peru.

Comments: Halfbeaks are surface dwellers that may be seen leaping and skittering across the water. They are a favorite bait for dolphins, billfishes, and larger mackerel species.

NEEDLEFISHES
(Family Belonidae)

Needlefishes are very elongate and either cylindrical or compressed. Both jaws are usually very long, beaklike, and armed with numerous, sharp teeth. Their fins are similar to those of halfbeaks and lack spines. The pelvic fins are abdominal; the dorsal and anal fins are far back on the body and similar in size and shape; and the lower lobe of the caudal fin is longer than the upper. Most species are marine, but some occasionally occur in fresh water. They are surface dwellers and skitter over the water. Needlefishes are predators that feed primarily on small fishes. There are 8 species in North America.

435 Atlantic Needlefish
(*Strongylura marina*)

Description: To 25″ (64 cm). Very elongate, round in cross section; greenish to bluish-green above, silvery below; dark stripe often on sides from above pectoral fin to caudal fin base. *Upper and lower jaws very elongate, armed with numerous sharp teeth.* No spines in fins; pelvic fins small, abdominal; pectoral fins inserted high on sides; dorsal and anal fins far posterior; caudal fin not deeply forked, lower lobe slightly longer than upper. Caudal peduncle without keels, not strongly depressed. Lateral line follows ventral profile. Scales small, cycloid.

Habitat: Coastal marine waters and into freshwater coastal streams.

Range: From Maine to Rio de Janeiro, Brazil; absent from Bahamas and Antilles.

Comments: This and other needlefishes often occur in small schools, and are most active at night. They feed primarily on small fishes. Spawning is believed to occur in both fresh and salt water.

KILLIFISHES
(Family Cyprinodontidae)

Fundulus

Cyprinodon

Killifishes are small fishes found in fresh, brackish, and coastal marine waters. Most male killifishes display striking colors, making them very popular with aquarists. Killifishes have teeth, 1 dorsal fin at the middle of the back, a rounded caudal fin, and an incomplete lateral line. The males lack external reproductive organs, and the females lay eggs; both characteristics are important in distinguishing the killifishes from the livebearers. There are 48 species in North America.

346 Diamond Killifish
(*Adinia xenica*)

Description: To 2" (5 cm). Very deep and compressed, depth about half length. *Dark green with 10–14 narrow, pearly bands with wider interspaces;* belly yellow; lower jaw orange; pelvic fins dusky, tips yellow; dorsal and anal fins dusky with pale blue or orange spots; caudal fin barred with some pale spots. Snout pointed; head flat above, anterior profile concave; mouth terminal, teeth conical. Dorsal fin origin anterior to anal fin origin. Caudal peduncle deep.

Habitat: Shallow lagoons, tide pools, ditches, and salt marshes.

Range: Gulf of Mexico from S. Florida to S. Texas.

Similar Species: Sheepshead Minnow (*Cyprinodon variegatus*) has blunter snout; humeral scale present.

Comments: This beautiful killifish is often locally abundant in shallow tidal areas of marshes and barrier islands.

205 White River Springfish
(*Crenichthys baileyi*)

Description: To 3" (7.5 cm). Deep, stout, slightly compressed; back dark olive to dusky; *sides silvery with 2 rows of dark spots,* belly yellowish to whitish. Head large, flattened above; snout blunt; mouth wide, small; *teeth bicuspid.* Fins small, edges black; pectoral fins inserted low on body, rounded; *no pelvic fins;* dorsal and anal fins placed posteriorly; caudal fin edge straight. *Lateral line absent,* 27 scales in lateral series.

biscupid tooth

Habitat: Warm desert spring pools and runs.

Range: White River drainage of SE. Nevada.

Related Species: Railroad Valley Springfish (*C. nevadae*) has 1 row of dark midlateral spots; occurs in warm springs near Duckwater, S. central Nevada.

Similar Species: Pahrump Killifish (*Empetrichthys latos*)

has conical teeth; occurs in similar habitat in Pahrump Valley, Nye County, Nevada.

Comments:

The White River Springfish feeds on microscopic and filamentous algae and aquatic invertebrates. Like many other fishes in desert springs, it is threatened by the alteration of its limited habitat and the introduction of exotic fishes.

---

209   Desert Pupfish
(*Cyprinodon macularius*)

Description: To 2½" (6.5 cm). Stout, deep, females deeper-bodied than males; back silvery to olive; *sides silvery with 6–9 dusky bars often forming irregular lateral band;* breeding males iridescent blue. Head short, scaled; mouth terminal;

tricuspid tooth   upturned; *single series of tricuspid teeth.* Dorsal and anal fins rounded, *each with 9–12 rays,* dorsal fin often with dusky blotch posteriorly; caudal fin edge slightly convex. 24–28 scales in lateral series.

Habitat: Marshy backwaters of desert streams and springs.

Range: S. Arizona, S. California, and NW. Mexico.

Related Species: Devils Hole Pupfish (*C. diabolis*) grows to ⅘" (20 mm); lacks pelvic fins, caudal fin rounded; occurs in similar habitat in Ash Meadow, Nevada.

Comments:

The Desert Pupfish grows very rapidly, sometimes reaching lengths of 2" (5 cm) in a year. Most of the 13 species of *Cyprinodon* in the United States are restricted to springs or streams in the deserts of Texas, New Mexico, Arizona, Nevada, and California. Several species are endangered by desert development and the introduction of exotic fishes. The best known is the Devils Hole Pupfish (*C. diabolis*), which was the focal point of a U.S. Supreme Court water rights case in the 1970s.

197, 349 Sheepshead Minnow
(*Cyprinodon variegatus*)

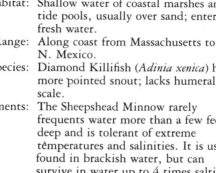

Description: To 3″ (7.5 cm). Robust, moderately
compressed. Males olive, iridescent
blue, or greenish-blue above, sides with
poorly defined bars, belly yellowish,
caudal fin edge and base with black
bar. Females olive or brassy, sometimes
light orange above, black bars on sides,
1–2 spots on rear rays of dorsal fin.
Snout blunt, mouth small, terminal.
Teeth incisor-like, tricuspid. Dorsal fin
origin midway between snout and
caudal fin, anterior to anal fin base.
Caudal peduncle deep; caudal fin
truncate. *Humeral scale present.*

Habitat: Shallow water of coastal marshes and
tide pools, usually over sand; enters
fresh water.

Range: Along coast from Massachusetts to
N. Mexico.

Similar Species: Diamond Killifish (*Adinia xenica*) has
more pointed snout; lacks humeral
scale.

Comments: The Sheepshead Minnow rarely
frequents water more than a few feet
deep and is tolerant of extreme
temperatures and salinities. It is usually
found in brackish water, but can
survive in water up to 4 times saltier
than sea water.

212 Northern Studfish
(*Fundulus catenatus*)

Description: To 5″ (12.5 cm). Elongate, moderately
stout, somewhat compressed
posteriorly; yellowish-brown to olive
above, *sides in males bluish, lighter in
females, with 7–11 rows of spots forming
stripes,* median fins with small, brown
specks, other fins plain. Head broad,
flattened above; mouth upturned.
*13–16 dorsal fin rays; 14–18 anal fin
rays; 39–52 scales in lateral series.*

Habitat: Clear streams, with moderate gradient

over clean sand, gravel, or rocks.

Range:
SW. Virginia, S. central Indiana, central Kentucky, Tennessee, NW. Georgia, N. Alabama, SW. Mississippi, S. Missouri, N. Arkansas, and E. Oklahoma.

Related Species:
Barrens Topminnow (*F. julisia*) has irregular spots on head and body; found in small spring-fed brooks in Coffee County, Tennessee. Speckled Killifish (*F. rathbuni*) has dark spots on head; body without spots or stripes; found in clear streams in extreme S. central Virginia and central North Carolina. Southern Studfish (*F. stellifer*) has 6–9 irregular rows of spots on sides; found in clear streams in Mobile Bay drainage in Tennessee, Georgia, and Alabama, and upper Chattahoochee River drainage, Georgia.

Comments:
From May to August during spawning, the colorful males establish and defend small territories in quiet, shallow water near shore, but do not prepare a nest.

211 Golden Topminnow
(*Fundulus chrysotus*)

Description:
To 3″ (7.5 cm). Robust, short; back dark olive, sides greenish-yellow; *males with reddish spots and 6–9 dusky bars on rear two-thirds of body,* median fins yellow-orange with red spots; *females with cream or golden spots.* Head short, wide, flattened above, with scales; snout short, blunt; mouth upturned. Fins small, rounded; dorsal fin origin behind anal fin origin; caudal fin rounded. Lateral line absent; 31–35 scales in lateral series.

Habitat:
Clear backwaters, sloughs, and pools of sluggish streams, lakes, and marshes with abundant vegetation.

Range:
From South Carolina south to Florida, west along coast to E. Texas; south from SW. Kentucky and SE. Missouri to Gulf Coast.

Related Species: Banded Topminnow (*F. cingulatus*) has more than 12 bars on sides; occurs in similar habitat in S. Georgia, Florida, and S. Alabama.

Comments: The Golden Topminnow feeds on a variety of aquatic invertebrates and some plant material. It spawns from March through August. The large eggs, $\frac{1}{10}''$ (2 mm) in diameter, are usually deposited in thick masses of aquatic vegetation.

210, 353 Gulf Killifish
(*Fundulus grandis*)

Description: To 6" (15 cm). Elongate, *moderately robust*. Males dark greenish-blue or olive above; sides lighter with small, pearly spots; belly yellowish; median fins with small, light spots; pelvic and anal fins yellowish. Females olive above, silvery below; sides have 12–15 narrow bars; anal fin yellow. Head rather large; snout bluntly rounded; *10 pores on lower jaw*. Dorsal fin origin over or anterior to anal fin, each has 11–12 rays. 39 or less lateral line scales.

Habitat: Over sand or mud in bays, tidal marshes, pools, and ditches.

Range: Along coast from NE. Florida to Veracruz, Mexico.

Related Species: Mummichog (*F. heteroclitus*) has 8 pores on lower jaw; occurs in shallow coastal waters over sand from S. Newfoundland to NE. Florida. Plains Killifish (*F. zebrinus*) has about 15 dark bars; scales very small; occurs in salt water from Wyoming to Texas.

Comments: The Gulf Killifish can tolerate adverse conditions such as low oxygen and great variation in salinity ranging from fresh water to salt concentration several times that of sea water. It feeds primarily on crustaceans and small fishes, and has increased in value as bait in the past few years.

202 Starhead Topminnow
(*Fundulus notti*)

Description: To 3″ (7.5 cm). Short, moderately deep; back dark, *sides olive to silvery with dark spots forming stripes;* males have faint dusky bars. Silvery spot on top of head; mouth upturned; *large, square, black blotch under eye.* Fins small; dorsal fin with 7–8 rays, origin posterior to anal fin origin. Lateral line absent; 30–35 scales in lateral series.

Habitat: Lowland marshes, ponds, swamps, and sluggish streams with vegetation.

Range: From S. Lake Michigan drainage south in Mississippi Valley to Louisiana; Gulf Coast streams from N. central Florida west to E. Texas.

Related Species: Lined Topminnow (*F. lineolatus*) has dark blotch wider than high, under eye; found in clear water of lowland streams and lakes with vegetation from SE. Virginia south to N. central and S. Florida.

Comments: Starhead Topminnows swim at the surface, feeding on aquatic as well as terrestrial insects. Spawning occurs during May and June over dense growths of aquatic plants.

203 Blackspotted Topminnow
(*Fundulus olivaceus*)

Description: To 4″ (10 cm). Elongate; back olive to tan, *sides yellowish brown with broad, black midlateral stripe extending from snout, upper sides with many discrete black spots.* Snout moderately long; head scaled, flat above. Dorsal fin has 9–10 rays, origin posterior to anal fin origin; median fins olive with discrete black spots; caudal fin rounded. 33–36 scales in lateral series.

Habitat: Clear streams with moderate current over sand, gravel, or rocks.

Range: W. Kentucky, S. Illinois, S. Missouri, E. Tennessee, Alabama, and

W. Florida west to E. Texas.

Related Species: Blackstripe Topminnow (*F. notatus*) with generally smaller body; spots absent, diffuse, or irregular in shape, larger and lighter than lateral stripe; occurs in low-gradient streams in sloughs and quiet margins of larger streams, often with vegetation in Lake Erie drainage, Ontario; from NW. Ohio west to N. Iowa, south to SW. Alabama, west to S. Texas.

Comments: The Blackspotted Topminnow feeds at the surface on small crustaceans and insects. It and the Blackstripe Topminnow are generally common throughout their range.

200, 206, 348 Bayou Killifish
(*Fundulus pulvereus*)

Description: To 3″ (7.5 cm). Elongate, rather robust anteriorly, tapering to slender caudal peduncle; olive with fine brownish spots, except on breast; *sides have 12 or more spots, each as large as pupil, sometimes joining to form oblong blotches.* Head broad, depressed; mouth superior, slightly oblique; eye diameter greater than length of snout; teeth pointed, in several series, outer ones larger. Dorsal fin origin slightly anterior to anal fin origin.

Habitat: Brackish and saltwater marshes, bayous, coastal ditches, and ponds; less often in freshwater coastal streams.

Range: From York River, Virginia, to NE. Florida; disjunctly from Mobile Bay, Alabama, to S. Texas.

Related Species: Marsh Killifish (*F. confluentus*) has about 14 distinct, irregular bars; occurs in similar habitat in peninsular Florida.

Comments: The Bayou and Marsh killifishes may represent a single species. They hybridize in northeastern Florida and on the Gulf Coast west from the Apalachicola River in Florida to Mobile Bay in Alabama.

213 Plains Topminnow
(*Fundulus sciadicus*)

Description: To 2½" (6.5 cm). Stout, short, slightly compressed; back dusky olive; *sides plain, greenish to silvery;* belly yellowish. Head scaled, flat above; mouth upturned. *Fins unspotted, reddish orange in males, yellowish in females;* 10–11 dorsal fin rays, origin behind anal fin origin; 12–15 anal fin rays. Caudal peduncle deep. Lateral line absent; 31–39 scales in lateral series.

Habitat: Over sand and gravel in clear pools and backwaters of springs and small streams with aquatic vegetation.

Range: W. Iowa, S. South Dakota, Nebraska, SE. Wyoming, and NE. Colorado; central and SW. Missouri, SE. Kansas, and NE. Oklahoma.

Comments: The Plains Topminnow is usually found near the surface. It feeds on small crustaceans, aquatic insects, and some filamentous algae. Spawning occurs from May through July in shallow water over aquatic vegetation.

---

214 Seminole Killifish
(*Fundulus seminolis*)

Description: To 6" (15 cm). Elongate, stout; back olive; *sides greenish yellow to silvery; scales dark-edged, forming stripes in males;* females with 10–15 faint dusky bars. Mouth upturned, with 2 rows of teeth. Fins large, rounded; *13–20 dorsal fin rays, origin anterior to anal fin origin;* dorsal and caudal fins of males have rows of dark spots, edges dusky. Lateral line absent; 50–55 scales in lateral series.

Habitat: Over sand in open, shallow lakes and streams with vegetation.

Range: From N. Florida to near southern tip.

Related Species: Waccamaw Killifish (*F. waccamensis*) has slender body; 54–64 lateral line scales; occurs in open water near vegetation in Phelps Lake, NE. North Carolina, and Lake Waccamaw, SE. North Carolina.

Comments: Seminole Killifishes feed on bottom-dwelling invertebrates in shallow, open, sandy areas. They spawn throughout the year, but most breeding occurs during April and May around clumps of aquatic vegetation.

347 Longnose Killifish
(*Fundulus similis*)

Description: To 6″ (15 cm). Elongate, relatively slender; olive or blue-gray above, becoming bronzy or silvery below; sides have up to 16 dark bars with wider interspaces, *last bar on caudal peduncle below distinct, black spot. Head long; snout pointed,* length greater than diameter of eye; maxilla not reaching eye. Large, dark humeral blotch. Dorsal fin origin slightly anterior to anal fin; dorsal and anal fins relatively high. About 33 lateral line scales.

Habitat: Tide pools, salt marshes, ditches, and lagoons over sand or mud.

Range: From NE. Florida along coast to Tampico, Mexico.

Related Species: Striped Killifish (*F. majalis*) female has dark stripes on sides; occurs in similar habitat from New Hampshire to NE. Florida.

Comments: The Longnose Killifish is very tolerant of low oxygen and fluctuating salinity but it does not enter fresh water. Recent evidence suggests that it and the Striped Killifish may be the same species.

201 Plains Killifish
(*Fundulus zebrinus*)

Description: To 5″ (12.5 cm). Elongate, stout anteriorly; back dark olive; *sides silvery-*

yellow to white with 12–28 dark bars,
wider, fewer, and darker in males;
belly yellowish. Head flat above,
scaled; mouth upturned, band of teeth
on jaws. *Fins large, rounded,* yellowish
to reddish; 14–15 dorsal fin rays,
origin before anal fin. Caudal peduncle
deep; *caudal fin margin straight.* Scales
small, 38–67 in lateral series.

Habitat: In shallow pools, backwaters, and along
edges of streams with slow to moderate
current over sand.

Range: Great Plains east of Rocky Mountains,
NW. Missouri and SE. Montana south
to Texas; introduced in Colorado and
upper Missouri rivers and Rio Grande.

Related Species: Banded Killifish (*F. diaphanus*) has
slender caudal peduncle; 38–48 scales
in lateral series; occurs in clear, quiet
pools of streams, ponds, and lakes with
vegetation over sand and gravel from S.
Newfoundland west to SE. Manitoba
and NE. Nebraska; south along
Atlantic Coast to South Carolina, often
in brackish water.

Comments: The Plains Killifish tolerates saline and
alkaline waters in which few, if any,
other fishes are found. This species is
occasionally used for bait.

196 Flagfish
(*Jordanella floridae*)

Description: To 2½" (6.5 cm). Short, deep,
compressed; back olive, *sides greenish-
gold to brassy,* males with 7–9 red-
orange stripes between scale rows and
dark blotch below dorsal fin origin;
belly yellowish. Head short, flat above;
mouth small, upturned; each jaw with
single row of incisorlike, tricuspid
teeth. *16–18 dorsal fin rays, first ray
short, thick, spinelike.* 25–27 scales in
lateral series.

Habitat: Quiet, shallow waters of ditches, lakes,
and ponds with vegetation; commonly
enters brackish water.

Range: From N. central Florida south throughout peninsula.

Comments: The Flagfish is primarily a herbivore. It spawns from April through August over dense mats of vegetation or in small depressions. The male fans the eggs and remains with them until they have hatched.

199 Pygmy Killifish
(*Leptolucania ommata*)

Description: To 1¼" (3 cm). Slender, compressed; *back greenish-yellow, belly yellowish.* Males have pale yellow stripe above *black lateral stripe ending in caudal spot with creamy yellow halo;* dark stripe above anal fin; 5–7 dusky bars on posterior half of body. Females have black lateral stripe ending in caudal spot. Mouth small, upturned; *eye longer than snout.* 6–7 dorsal fin rays, origin posterior to anal fin origin. 27–32 scales in lateral series.

Habitat: Dark, stained waters of swamps, slow streams, overflow ponds, and ditches with abundant vegetation.

Range: From S. Georgia south to central Florida, west to SE. Mississippi.

Comments: The Pygmy Killifish is the second smallest fish in North America. It is attractive, hardy, peaceful, and easily kept in aquariums.

207, 352 Rainwater Killifish
(*Lucania parva*)

Description: To 2" (5 cm). Small, *relatively elongate,* moderately compressed; light brown or olive above, lighter below; *scales diamond-shaped to hexagonal, margins dusky, giving crosshatched appearance;* faint lateral stripe, more intense on caudal peduncle. Pelvic and pectoral fins orange-yellow; dorsal fin dusky orange in males with black spot at front; dorsal and caudal fins have thin, black edge. Mouth small, superior, lower jaw projects beyond upper; eye diameter greater than snout length; teeth conical, in 1 series in both jaws. No large humeral scale.

Habitat: Bays, marshes, estuaries, saltwater ponds, and bayous with vegetation; enters fresh water.

Range: Along coast from Massachusetts to Mexico. Inland populations in Florida and New Mexico. Introduced in Oregon, California, NE. Nevada, and N. Utah.

Comments: Rainwater Killifishes tolerate a wide range of salinity and make good aquarium pets that require minimum attention.

LIVEBEARERS
(Family Poeciliidae)

male

female

Livebearers, unlike the closely related killifishes, give birth to live young after internal fertilization. Males transmit packets of sperm which may be held by the female for a period of months and used to fertilize several broods. There are 20 North American species of livebearers that are found in a variety of habitats in fresh, brackish, and salt water.

208, 351 Mosquitofish
(*Gambusia affinis*)

Description: To 2½" (6.5 cm). Rather robust, particularly females; compressed. Tan to olive above, pale yellowish below; *scales have small, dusky spots near edges; dark bar below eye;* many spots present on dorsal and caudal fins; females have conspicuous black spot on belly during reproductive period. Head depressed;

mouth small, oblique, lower jaw projects beyond upper; teeth small, in single villiform band on each jaw. Anal fin of male modified to form reproductive organ.

Habitat: Near surface of fresh or brackish water in ponds, lakes, ditches, backwaters, and sluggish streams.

Range: From New Jersey to central Mexico along coast and in associated freshwater streams; Mississippi River basin south from Illinois.

Similar Species: Least Killifish (*Heterandria formosa*) has 6–9 bars and midlateral stripe.

Comments: Because it eats aquatic mosquito larvae, the Mosquitofish has been introduced into many areas to control mosquitoes.

198 Least Killifish
(*Heterandria formosa*)

Description: To 1″ (2.5 cm). Moderately compressed; back golden brown to olive; *sides lighter with 6–9 indistinct bars and dusky midlateral stripe terminating in darker spot.* Snout short; mouth terminal; eye large. *Dark spot on base of dorsal fin;* females have dark spot on base of anal fin; anal fin origin anterior to dorsal fin, modified in male to form reproductive organ. 24–30 scales in lateral series.

Habitat: Fresh and brackish water in swamps, ditches, ponds, and bayous with abundant aquatic vegetation.

Range: Coastal drainages from S. North Carolina to Louisiana; throughout peninsular Florida.

Similar Species: Mosquitofish (*Gambusia affinis*) has numerous spots on dorsal and caudal fins; body color uniform; no lateral stripe or bars.

Comments: Despite its common name, this is a livebearer. It is very hardy and makes an interesting aquarium fish. It is the smallest livebearing vertebrate in the United States.

193, 350 Sailfin Molly
(*Poecilia latipinna*)

Description: To 5″ (12.5 cm). Oblong, compressed; *depth of male about same from dorsal fin posteriorly;* belly rounded in female and caudal peduncle narrower. *Olive with blackish or reddish-orange to yellowish dots on side scales forming stripes.* Head small, depressed; mouth small; teeth in several series, outer ones largest. In males, dorsal fin very tall, with blackish spots on membranes between rays forming interrupted narrow bands; caudal fin has dark spots forming bars. Anal fin of males located forward and modified as reproductive organ.

Habitat: Saltwater marshes, ponds, and ditches; also freshwater pools, ponds, and ditches.

Range: Along coast from North Carolina to Yucatán. Inland streams in Florida, Louisiana, and Texas. Introduced in lower Colorado River system.

Comments: These strikingly beautiful fishes feed primarily on plants and organic detritus. A variety with black coloring is bred as a popular aquarium fish. Like many killifishes, they are extremely tolerant of wide ranges in salinity.

204 Gila Topminnow
(*Poeciliopsis occidentalis*)

Description: To 2″ (5 cm). Moderately elongate, greatest depth anterior to dorsal fin; back dark olive, *sides olive to tan with dark lateral stripe* from upper margin of opercle to caudal fin base, scales on back and sides and *fin rays outlined with dark pigment.* Head small; *mouth small, upturned, teeth pointed.* Pelvic fins small; dorsal fin posterior to anal fin origin; anal fin modified in male to form reproductive organ; *caudal fin rounded to almost square.* Scales large, 29 in lateral series.

Habitat: Springs, pools, edges, and backwaters
of streams, usually with debris and
aquatic vegetation.

Range: Gila River drainage from S. Arizona,
SW. New Mexico to Sonora, Mexico.

Comments: Once one of the commonest fishes in
the southern Colorado River drainage,
the Gila Topminnow was added to the
list of endangered species in 1967.
Efforts are underway to remove
competitors from isolated springs.

SILVERSIDES
(Family Atherinidae)

These fishes are mostly small, delicate,
elongate, and slightly compressed; they
have a silvery lateral stripe between the
pectoral and caudal fins. The mouth is
terminal and oblique. Their 2 dorsal
fins are well separated; the first consists
of a few weak spines. A single spine
precedes the soft rays of the pelvic,
second dorsal, and anal fins. The scales
are large and cycloid and the lateral
line, if present, is placed low on the
side. The 13 members of this family
found in North America inhabit fresh,
brackish, and marine water.

570 Topsmelt
(*Atherinops affinis*)

Description: To 14½″ (37 cm). Elongate,
compressed; green-blue above with
midlateral stripe, silvery below. *Teeth
forked, in single row on each jaw.* Anal fin
origin under posterior of first dorsal fin.

forked tooth 5–8 scales on back between dorsal fins.

Habitat: Surface waters near shore, in bays, and
around kelp beds.

Range: From Vancouver Island, British
Columbia, to Gulf of California.

Related Species: Jacksmelt (*Atherinopsis californiensis*) has
unforked teeth in bands on jaws; anal

fin origin behind first dorsal fin, 10–12 scales between dorsal fins; occurs in same habitat from Yaquina, Oregon, to Bahía de Santa Maria, Baja California.

Comments: Topsmelts mature in 2 or 3 years and spawn during late winter and spring. The large eggs are attached to kelp and other algae. Topsmelts and the larger Jacksmelts are caught by anglers from piers. The annual commercial haul of both species in California weighs about 250 tons.

180 Brook Silverside
(*Labidesthes sicculus*)

Description: To 4″ (10 cm). Elongate, slender, compressed, depth one-seventh length; pale greenish-yellow, translucent with silvery lateral band bordered above by dark line; fins transparent; tips of dorsal spines black in males. Head long, flattened above, narrow below; snout longer than eye; *jaws pointed, forming beak;* maxilla not reaching eye. Dorsal fins separate, *above anal fin; anal fin long, 1 spine, 21–25 rays;* caudal fin forked. Lateral line incomplete.

Habitat: Quiet, clear waters of lakes, ponds, rivers, creeks, and reservoirs.

Range: Great Lakes and St. Lawrence River; Atlantic Coastal Plain from South Carolina to Florida; from Pennsylvania to W. Oklahoma; Mississippi River system from Minnesota to Louisiana.

Comments: Brook Silversides are adapted for living near the surface, where they form large schools during the day and feed on zooplankton and small insects. They are an important forage species and are used for bait.

569 California Grunion
(*Leuresthes tenuis*)

Description: To 7½" (19 cm). Elongate, fusiform; greenish above, silvery below with midlateral stripe. Snout bluntly rounded; *teeth minute or lacking.* First dorsal fin spiny, origin slightly in front of anal fin origin; 7–9 scales between dorsal fins.

Habitat: Off sandy beaches to depths of about 60' (18.3 m).

Range: From San Francisco, California, to Bahía de San Juanico, Baja California.

Similar Species: Surf Smelt (*Hypomesus pretiosus*) has adipose fin and single dorsal fin.

Comments: From March to September during spring high tides, the California Grunion spawns at night on beaches. The eggs are buried in the moist sand and hatch when the next spring tide occurs. Each female may spawn from 4 to 8 times during a season. Anglers are only allowed to use their hands to capture these fishes at this time.

568 Inland Silverside
(*Menidia beryllina*)

Description: To 6" (15 cm). Elongate, slender, moderately compressed; pale greenish above, pale below, *lateral band silvery,* with dark line above; posterior scale edges dusky, fins pale, *peritoneum silvery.* Mouth terminal, oblique, maxilla not reaching eye; snout shorter than eye. 2 dorsal fins well separated; anal fin long; caudal fin forked. *Scales with smooth edges, not rough to touch.*

Habitat: Along coast and in freshwater streams and rivers, usually over sand.

Range: From Massachusetts to Veracruz, Mexico, along coast, and in associated freshwater streams. Inland in lower Mississippi River drainage and Rio Grande.

Related Species: Rough Silverside (*Membras martinica*)

scale

has scalloped scales, rough to touch; occurs in salt water from New York to Mexico. Atlantic Silverside (*M. menidia*) has black peritoneum; anal fin longer; ranges in saltier water from Nova Scotia to N. Florida. Tidewater Silverside (*M. peninsulae*) has deeper body; occurs in salt water over sand from NE. Florida to E. Texas.

Comments: This fish is tolerant of wide fluctuations in salinity but is never found offshore. Until recently the freshwater form was known as the species *Menidia audens*.

Order Beryciformes

This order is made up of 15 small and little-known families, only 2 of which occur in North America. All are marine, and many live on the bottom of the ocean. The best known family is Holocentridae, the squirrelfishes.

SQUIRRELFISHES
(Family Holocentridae)

These elongate, compressed fishes are colored various shades of red. They have large eyes, often wider than the length of the snout, and large, terminal mouths. The bones around the eye and opercle are serrate. A large spine on the angle of the preopercle and another on the upper edge of the opercle can inflict wounds. Each pelvic fin consists of 1 spine and 7 rays. The dorsal fin base is long, the spinous part several times longer than the soft part. There are 4 anal spines, with the third one greatly enlarged. Most species live on shallow, tropical coral reefs; some occur over sand or mud to depths of 150 fathoms or more. They are most active at night. There are 11 species in North America.

382 Squirrelfish
(*Holocentrus ascensionis*)

Description: To 14″ (36 cm). Relatively slender; caudal peduncle narrow; *bright silvery-red with faint stripes on body; snout and top of head dark red; upper part of maxilla white;* whitish below. Eye large; mouth terminal, maxilla reaches past middle of eye; preopercular spine long and slender. Anterior rays of soft dorsal fin falcate; dorsal spines yellowish, interspinal membranes greenish; other fins pinkish; 4 anal spines; upper lobe of caudal fin slightly longer than lower lobe.

Habitat: Shallow coral and rocky reefs.

Range: From North Carolina to E. and W. Florida; Bermuda; parts of Gulf of Mexico; West Indies and Caribbean south to Brazil.

Comments: Squirrelfishes hide by day in crevices or under coral ledges, and feed by night away from the reef over sand and grass beds. The large eyes afford good night vision, and the red colors make them almost invisible in dim light. The stiff, sharp dorsal and opercular spines can inflict painful wounds.

383 Longspine Squirrelfish
(*Holocentrus rufus*)

Description: To 12″ (30 cm). Oblong and relatively slender; *caudal peduncle very narrow; bright silvery red* with diffuse red lines above becoming indistinct and pink on sides and belly; *dorsal fin membranes with white spots near upper margin.* Top of head and area below eye brick-red; maxilla extends just past anterior edge of eye; preopercular spines long, slender. 4 anal spines; anterior rays of soft dorsal fin and upper lobe of caudal fin elongate.

Habitat: Coral reefs, from near surface to about 15 fathoms.

Range: Bermuda; SE. Florida, West Indies,
W. Caribbean, and W. Gulf of
Mexico.

Comments: These squirrelfishes are active at night,
feeding away from the coral reefs where
they hide during the day. They eat a
variety of crustaceans, gastropods, and
⊘ brittle stars. The sharp spines can
inflict painful wounds.

---

385   Dusky Squirrelfish
(*Holocentrus vexillarius*)

Description: To 6″ (15 cm). Relatively deep;
alternating stripes of red and silvery white;
reddish color more prominent on upper
sides where thin, black lines separate
red and white stripes. Maxilla not
reaching middle of eye; lower jaw not
projecting beyond upper; well-
developed spines on opercle and
preopercle. *Axil of pectoral fin deep red or
dusky;* dorsal fin red, with white next to
spines; other fins reddish. Last dorsal
spine well separated from first dorsal
ray; caudal fin lobes nearly equal.

Habitat: Tide pools, coral reefs, and rocky areas.

Range: From New Jersey to Central America,
including Bermuda, Gulf of Mexico,
and West Indies.

Related Species: Reef Squirrelfish (*H. coruscus*) has longer
maxilla and large, black spot between
first 3–4 dorsal spines; occurs in
similar habitat and range.

Comments: The Dusky and Reef squirrelfishes are
reported to be the most common
inshore squirrelfishes in Bermuda,
Florida, and the West Indies. The
⊘ sharp spines can cause painful wounds.

---

384   Blackbar Soldierfish
(*Myripristis jacobus*)

Description: To 8½″ (22 cm). Oblong, relatively
deep, moderately compressed; reddish-

orange above, silvery and pinkish on sides; *broad bar from upper end of gill opening to base of pectoral fin;* median fins blue and red. Snout blunt; eye very large; mouth terminal, maxilla extends well past middle of eye; *no spines on opercle or preopercle.* Scales cover basal half of soft dorsal and anal fins; 4 anal spines.

Habitat: Shallow coral reefs and offshore to 45 fathoms.

Range: From Georgia, N. Gulf of Mexico, throughout West Indies and Caribbean to Brazil. Also Bermuda, Cape Verde Islands, and Ascension Islands.

Comments: This nocturnal species feeds mostly on planktonic organisms. It is rather common on offshore reefs.

Order Gasterosteiformes

These are primarily marine fishes, and 5 families are found in North American waters. Members of the order usually have a tubelike snout, and are often partially or completely covered with external bony plates.

STICKLEBACKS
(Family Gasterosteidae)

These fishes are characterized by the presence of 3 to 26 isolated dorsal spines followed by a soft dorsal fin. They have a fusiform body and a very long and slender caudal peduncle. Bony plates are often present along the sides. Sticklebacks are small fishes widely distributed in the Northern Hemisphere in fresh, brackish, and salt water. This family has 6 species in North America.

437 Tube-Snout
(*Aulorhynchus flavidus*)

Description: To 7″ (18 cm). Fusiform, very elongate; olive-green to tan, sometimes with silvery patch between opercle and pectoral fins; pelvic fins bright red in breeding males. Snout very long, tubular. *23–26 isolated dorsal spines in front of dorsal fin;* caudal peduncle long, slender.

Habitat: Around giant kelp and eelgrass beds in shallow bays and to 17 fathoms.

Range: From Prince William Sound, Alaska, to Punta Rompiente, Baja California.

Similar Species: Bay Pipefish (*Syngnathus leptorhynchus*) lacks isolated spines in front of dorsal fin.

Comments: The male Tube-Snout builds a nest in giant kelp fronds. The eggs, deposited in the nest by the female, adhere to these fronds. Tube-Snouts feed on small planktonic crustaceans and fish larvae, including their own young. They are rarely caught by anglers, but are familiar to most divers.

---

219 Brook Stickleback
(*Culaea inconstans*)

Description: To 2″ (5 cm). Compressed; back green to olive, sides lighter with yellowish spots or wavy lines; spawning males dusky green to black. *4–7 dorsal spines short, less than diameter of eye,* curved slightly backward. Caudal peduncle slender, without keel; *caudal fin rounded.* Minute bony plates along lateral line.

Habitat: Small streams, ponds, and lakes with clear, cold water and abundant aquatic vegetation; rarely enters brackish water.

Range: Southeast from S. Hudson Bay drainage, east from E. British Columbia, south from Northwest Territories to New England and Great Lakes; St. Lawrence River, Nova

Scotia, and upper Mississippi River
system. Introduced in Connecticut,
Alabama, and New Mexico.

Similar Species: Ninespine Stickleback (*Pungitius
pungitius*) has 9 dorsal spines; occurs in
similar habitat throughout Canada and
coastal Alaska to Great Lakes.

Comments: Brook Sticklebacks spawn in shallow
water, where the male uses vegetation
to construct a small, ball-shaped nest
with a cavity through its center.

218, 354 Threespine Stickleback
(*Gasterosteus aculeatus*)

Description: To 4″ (10 cm). Fusiform; gray to olive-
brown, sides paler, belly silvery;
breeding adults reddish on head and
belly. Head one-fourth length; lower
jaw projects beyond upper. *Usually 3
stout, widely separated dorsal spines*
preceding soft dorsal fin. Caudal
peduncle narrow; caudal fin triangular.
Sides covered with series of bony plates.

Habitat: Marine, estuarine, and fresh water,
usually in vegetation.

Range: In Atlantic, from Hudson Bay to
Chesapeake Bay; in Pacific, from
Bering Sea to N. Baja California and in
associated freshwater streams.

Related Species: Fourspine Stickleback (*Apeltes
quadracus*) has 4 dorsal spines; no bony
plates; occurs in similar habitat, less
frequently in fresh water, from Gulf of
St. Lawrence to Virginia. Blackspotted
Stickleback (*G. wheatlandi*) has black
spots, 2 soft pelvic fin rays, 3 weaker
dorsal spines, and no bony plates;
occurs in salt water south from
Newfoundland to S. Massachusetts.

Comments: These shore fishes enter brackish water
or ascend freshwater streams to spawn
from April to July. The female deposits
75 to 100 eggs on a nest built by the
male, which guards the eggs and
remains with the fry until they can
fend for themselves.

TRUMPETFISHES
(Family Aulostomidae)

Trumpetfishes are similar to cornetfishes and pipefishes in that the body is very long and the mouth is at the end of a tubular snout. They differ by having a chin barbel and a series of isolated dorsal spines that resemble small sails. There is a single North American species. The family occurs in the tropical parts of the Atlantic, Pacific, and Indian oceans.

438 Trumpetfish
(*Aulostomus maculatus*)

Description: To 30″ (76 cm). Very elongate and compressed; brown or reddish brown, with lengthwise pale lines, and irregular rows of dark spots. Head, including snout, very long, about one-third of total length; oblique mouth at end of tubular snout, single barbel on chin. Soft dorsal and anal fins similar in size and shape, anterior rays with black bar or spot near base; *dorsal fin usually has 10 isolated spines.* Caudal fin has 1–2 black spots, without long filament.

Habitat: Reefs in shallow water.

Range: From S. Florida and Gulf Coast south to Caribbean, Antilles, and Brazil.

Comments: Trumpetfishes often align themselves vertically, with head down, among sea feathers (gorgonian corals), where they cannot readily be seen. They feed on shrimps and small fishes, which they pounce on from a vertical position, taking their unwary prey by surprise as they suck it into their mouths.

CORNETFISHES
(Family Fistulariidae)

Cornetfishes are more slender than trumpetfishes and have depressed bodies. The head is long and the mouth is at the end of a tubular snout. The dorsal and anal fins are spineless, short-based, posteriorly placed, and similar in size and shape. The small caudal fin is forked, but the middle 2 rays form a long filament. There are no scales. Cornetfishes occur in tropical and subtropical coastal areas of the world; 2 species are found in North America.

436 Red Cornetfish
(*Fistularia petimba*)

Description: To 6' (1.8 m). Elongate, slender, depressed; red to reddish-brown above, sides iridescent, belly silvery, pectoral and median fins pink or red, pelvic fins orange. Head over one-third length excluding caudal filament; snout very long, tubular; mouth oblique, lower jaw extends beyond upper. *Series of embedded, elongate, bony plates on dorsal midline;* forward-projecting spines on posterior lateral line. Dorsal and anal fins small, falcate, posteriorly placed opposite each other. Caudal fin forked, 2 middle rays form long filament.

Habitat: Near shore over soft bottom to depths of about 30' (9.1 m).

Range: From Virginia south to tropical Atlantic.

Related Species: Bluespotted Cornetfish (*F. tabacaria*) lacks bony plates on dorsal midline; has blue spots on back; usually occurs in shallower waters from Nova Scotia to Rio de Janeiro, including Bermuda, Gulf of Mexico, and West Indies.

Comments: Cornetfishes tend to live among sea grasses. They apparently feed on shrimps and small fishes.

PIPEFISHES
(Family Syngnathidae)

seahorse

pipefish

Seahorses are included in this family of small, atypical fishes with bodies encased in bony rings. They have a small, toothless mouth at the end of a tubular snout. Most species have pectoral and dorsal fins; all lack pelvic fins. There are no spines in the fins, and the anal fin, when present, is very small. A unique feature of this family is the male's brood pouch (marsupium), in which the young are reared. There are 29 species of seahorses and pipefishes in North America, and most are found near shore.

---

441 Lined Seahorse
(*Hippocampus erectus*)

Description: To 5″ (13 cm). *Head perpendicular to vertical body;* body portion deep, compressed. Coloration changes with background: light brown, dusky, gray, blackish, or brick-red; unmarked or variously mottled; sometimes speckled with fine white or golden dots. Dorsal fin fan-shaped; *tail prehensile, without caudal fin.*

Habitat: Usually associated with vegetation such as eelgrasses and sargassum.

Range: From Nova Scotia to Argentina; Bermuda and Gulf of Mexico.

Related Species: Dwarf Seahorse (*H. zosterae*) grows to 3″ (7.5 cm), body green to blackish; occurs in similar habitat in Gulf of Mexico and Caribbean.

Comments: Seahorses are poor swimmers and depend on their camouflage both to hide from enemies and conceal themselves from prey. They blend so well into their background that the casual observer rarely sees them. They feed by rapid intake of water. The incubation period in the marsupium is thought to be about 2 weeks.

439 Bay Pipefish
(*Syngnathus leptorhynchus*)

Description: To 14″ (36 cm). Very elongate,
hexagonal in cross section anteriorly;
green to brown and mottled,
depending on habitat. Snout very long;
mouth small, terminal. *No pelvic fins;*
caudal fin very small. *Covered with bony*
plates, 53–63 rings.

Habitat: Eelgrass beds in bays.

Range: From Sitka, Alaska, to Baja California.

Similar Species: Tube-Snout (*Aulorhynchus flavidus*) has
23–26 isolated spines in front of dorsal
fin.

Comments: All pipefishes mate in early summer,
and the female deposits the eggs in
the brood pouch of the male. Bay
Pipefishes feed on small crustaceans.
Observers rarely notice these relatives of
the seahorse unless they are seen
swimming away from vegetation.

440 Gulf Pipefish
(*Syngnathus scovelli*)

Description: To 6″ (15 cm). Slender, very elongate;
females have deeper body and V-shaped
belly. Females usually olive-brown with
white or silvery bars, pectorals plain,
dorsal and caudal fins dusky; males
similar but usually lighter. Snout
moderately short; no pelvic fins; *dorsal*
fin usually located over 3 bony rings on body
and 5 on tail; caudal fin present.

Habitat: Shallow grass flats in salt and fresh
waters.

Range: From Florida to Mexico in Gulf of
Mexico; fresh water in Louisiana and
Florida.

Comments: There are 24 species of pipefishes on
the coasts of North America. Most are
similar in shape, and the species are
distinguished by the number of bony
rings on the body and tail and the
position of the dorsal fin relative to the
body rings. They are found primarily

near shore and prefer areas of dense
vegetation. Only the Gulf Pipefish
enters fresh water.

Order Perciformes

The largest order of vertebrates, it
includes many North American marine
and freshwater fishes, classified into 78
diverse families. These are typical
spiny-rayed, or percoid, fishes. The
pelvic fins usually consist of 1 spine
and 5 soft rays, and the anterior parts
of the dorsal and anal fins are spinous.
The scales are typically ctenoid and the
lateral line is almost always present.

SNOOKS
(Family Centropomidae)

These rather large fishes have an
elongate, compressed body with well-
separated dorsal fins. The snout is
pointed, the mouth large, and the
lower jaw projects well beyond the
upper. The anal fin has a short base and
3 spines, the second one enlarged. The
lateral line extends to the rear edge of
the caudal fin. Snooks inhabit tropical
coastal waters, estuaries, and lagoons,
and sometimes enter fresh water. This
family has 4 species in North America.

486 Snook
(Centropomus undecimalis)

Description: To 4'7" (1.4 m); 53⅜ lbs (24.3 kg).
Slender, elongate; yellowish- or
greenish-brown above, silvery below
with *dark lateral line on sides extending
through caudal fin.* Snout pointed, lower
jaw projecting; mouth large with teeth
in jaw and on roof; preopercle serrate.

Fins dusky; dorsal fins well separated, second dorsal spine very strong; anal fin with 3 spines. Scales ctenoid.

Habitat: Shallow coastal waters, estuaries, lagoons, canals, and fresh water.

Range: From Cape Fear River, North Carolina, south to S. Florida; along Gulf Coast of Florida to Destin, disjunctly to Texas; West Indies and Caribbean south to Brazil. Probably only summer migrants north of S. Florida.

Comments: The Snook, a highly esteemed food and sport fish, feeds on other fishes and various crustaceans. Sensitive to low temperatures, it avoids water cooler than about 61° F (16° C). The Snook should be handled carefully, as the sharp gill covers can cause deep cuts.

TEMPERATE BASSES
(Family Percichthyidae)

opercular spines

These fishes are found in fresh, brackish, and salt water. They are characterized by the presence of 1 or 2 opercular spines; 2 dorsal fins that are deeply divided or separate; a forked caudal fin; and a complete lateral line extending onto the caudal fin. Many species in the family are important food and sport fishes. There are 7 species in North America.

97, 524 White Perch
(*Morone americana*)

Description: To 19″ (48 cm); 4¾ lbs (2.2 kg). Oblong, moderately compressed, back elevated; *back greenish gray or nearly black; sides paler, sometimes with indistinct stripes; belly whitish.* Head depressed between eyes; lower jaw slightly projecting, maxilla reaches eye; teeth small, in bands on jaw, vomer, and palatine bones, not on base of tongue;

2 opercular spines. Dorsal fins barely
connected, first with 8–10 strong
spines. Scales extend onto base of
median fins and head.

Habitat: Brackish water in bays and estuaries;
freshwater populations in rivers and
lakes, especially in north of range.

Range: From Cape Breton Island, St. Lawrence
River, and Lake Ontario to St. Johns
River, Florida; most abundant in
Hudson River and Chesapeake Bay.

Comments: The White Perch is an important sport
and game fish. Its average size is 8″ to
10″ (20 to 25 cm), and the usual
weight is 1 lb (500 g) or less. In 1949
a record catch of 4¾ lbs (2.2 kg) was
taken in Messalonshee Lake, Maine.
The White Perch probably entered
Lake Ontario through the Erie Barge
Canal and the Oswego River. It is a
recent immigrant to Lake Erie.

95 White Bass
(*Morone chrysops*)

Description: To 18″ (46 cm); 5¼ lbs (2.4 kg).
Deep, compressed; back olive to
silvery-gray; *sides silvery to white, with
6–9 dark, narrow stripes,* sometimes
interrupted below lateral line; belly
yellowish. Mouth extends to middle of
eye; lower jaw protrudes; *single patch of
teeth on back of tongue.* First dorsal fin
separate from second; *second anal spine
about half length of third,* 11–13 soft
anal fin rays. 50–60 scales in lateral
line; scales extend onto head.

Habitat: Large streams, lakes, and reservoirs;
over firm sand, gravel, or rocks in
moderately clear water.

Range: Lake Winnipeg; St. Lawrence River,
S. Great Lakes, Mississippi River
system, Gulf Coast from Louisiana to
Texas and New Mexico. Introduced
outside native range.

Comments: The White Bass is found in schools in
open water. It feeds primarily on fishes,

but also consumes aquatic insects and crustaceans, which it locates by sight rather than scent. It is an important sport fish, especially in reservoirs. Minnows and lures are excellent bait.

93 Yellow Bass
(*Morone mississippiensis*)

Description: To 14″ (36 cm); 2¼ lbs (1 kg). Deep, compressed; back greenish-yellow, *sides silvery to brassy yellow with 7–9 dark greenish to black stripes,* those below lateral line just anterior to anal fin interrupted and offset; belly yellowish. Mouth extends to eye; lower jaw not protruding; *tongue without teeth.* Dorsal fins slightly joined at bases; 9–10 soft anal fin rays, *second anal spine about same length as third,* 49–55 lateral line scales.

Habitat: Lowland rivers, lakes, and reservoirs in backwaters and quiet pools.

Range: Central Mississippi River system; Gulf Coast from Alabama to E. Texas. Introduced outside native range.

Comments: The Yellow Bass is smaller and has a more restricted range than the White Bass, but it is a popular game fish. It lives in schools and feeds on fishes, crustaceans, and insects from midwater to the surface. During the spring it makes spawning runs up streams.

94, 510 Striped Bass
(*Morone saxatilis*)

Description: To 6′ (1.8 m); 125 lbs (56.7 kg). Elongate, moderately compressed; back olive-green to dark blue, sides silvery, belly white; *upper sides with 6–9 dark, uninterrupted stripes;* median fins dusky. Mouth large, lower jaw slightly projecting. Teeth small, in bands on jaws, vomer, and palatine bones, and in

2 parallel patches on tongue. Opercle has 2 flat spines near posterior edge. First dorsal fin with 8–10 strong spines, separated from second dorsal by deep notch. Scales extend onto all fin bases except spinous dorsal.

Habitat: Inshore over various bottoms; some permanently in fresh water.

Range: Atlantic Ocean and associated rivers from St. Lawrence River to St. Johns River, Florida; Appalachicola River, W. Florida, to Lake Ponchartrain, Louisiana. Most abundant from Hudson River to Chesapeake Bay. Widely introduced into rivers and lakes in much of Mississippi River system, Colorado River, and coastal streams in Washington, Oregon, and California.

Comments: The Striped Bass is a very important sport and commercial fish throughout its range, and large individuals are caught by surf fishing, especially on the Atlantic Coast. It is a delicious food fish. It is anadromous, and spawns prolifically in fresh water.

507 Giant Sea Bass
(*Stereolepis gigas*)

Description: To 7' 5" (2.3 m); 557 lbs (252.6 kg). Heavy, robust, slightly compressed, greatest depth near head; dark gray, *usually with large, black spots on sides;* juveniles red with black spots. *2 opercular spines present.* Dorsal fin has more spines than soft rays. Caudal fin square to slightly indented.

Habitat: Rocky areas and kelp beds.

Range: From Humboldt Bay, California, to Gulf of California.

Similar Species: Gulf Grouper (*Mycteroperca jordani*) has 3 opercular spines; posterior edge of caudal fin smooth; occurs from La Jolla, California, to Mazatlán, Mexico. Broomtail Grouper (*M. xenarcha*) has 3 opercular spines; tip of caudal fin jagged; occurs from San Francisco Bay,

California, to Paita, Peru. Both in similar habitat.

Comments: Giant Sea Basses spawn in the summer and do not mature until about 11 to 13 years of age, when they weigh 50 to 60 lbs (23 to 27 kg). These huge fishes are highly prized by anglers and divers. In recent years their numbers have declined drastically and in 1981 their capture by commercial and sport fishers was prohibited in California waters.

SEA BASSES
(Family Serranidae)

These are perchlike fishes with a single, slightly notched dorsal fin. The mouth is generally large, and the maxilla is broad and exposed. Teeth are present in the jaws and on the roof of the mouth. The upper edge of the opercle is free and usually has 3 flat spines. There are 3 anal fin spines. The lateral line is not interrupted and extends only to the base of the caudal fin. Many species change color patterns during the transformation from juvenile to adult. Coloration may also alter as the fishes move around and as the light intensity changes, so that red colors become more prominent as the light dims. There are 61 species in North America.

opercular spines

515 Black Sea Bass
(Centropristis striata)

Description: To 24" (61 cm). Elongate, moderately compressed, depth one-third length; dark brown or bluish-black, *light centers of scales form stripes above,* dorsal fin striped. Head large; maxilla reaches middle of eye, lower jaw projects beyond upper; *preopercle weakly serrate, without large spines.* Dorsal fin high, continuous, with notch between spiny and soft parts, interspinal membrane has deep notches, spines have fleshy flaps. 3 anal fin spines; caudal fin round or ending in 3 lobes, upper lobe often has elongate ray in adults. Lateral line extends to caudal fin base. Bases of dorsal and anal fins lack thick skin and scales.

Habitat: Continental shelf, over rocks around jetties, pilings, and wrecks.

Range: From Maine south to Florida Keys and E. Gulf of Mexico.

Comments: Black Sea Bass from the eastern Gulf of Mexico represent a subspecies (*C. s. melana*) that attains a length of only about half that of the Atlantic populations. The Black Sea Bass is an important food fish, especially in the mid-Atlantic states. It is often caught by anglers fishing with rods from boats for other kinds of fishes.

513 Sand Perch
(*Diplectrum formosum*)

Description: To 12″ (30 cm). Small, slender, elongate; *indistinct, dark bars and alternating blue and orange stripes,* narrow, blue lines on cheek. Head and mouth large; *preopercle has 2 bony lobes,* 1 at angle, 1 above, each with radiating spines; 3 flat opercular spines. Dorsal fin continuous; 3 anal fin spines; caudal fin slightly forked, upper rays sometimes threadlike. Lateral line continuous to caudal fin base.

Habitat: Over sand or mud in coastal waters, or near reefs or upper edges of depressions in ocean floor to about 40 fathoms.

Range: From Virginia to Florida, throughout Gulf of Mexico and West Indies to Brazil.

Related Species: Dwarf Sand Perch (*D. bivittatum*) has only 1 bony lobe on preopercle; occurs over mud or sand from North Carolina through Gulf of Mexico.

Comments: Rather common in certain areas, this

little sea bass is often caught by anglers who are pursuing something larger.

505 Rock Hind
(*Epinephelus adscensionis*)

Description: To 24" (61 cm). Robust, not strongly compressed; light olive, *body and fins covered with reddish-brown spots larger on undersides than sides; 2–3 dark saddles on back under dorsal fin, 1 on caudal peduncle;* soft dorsal, caudal, and anal fins greenish, without black margins. Head long; mouth oblique; maxilla reaches to eye. 11 dorsal fin spines, some longer than anterior soft rays, interspinal membrane notched; 3 anal fin spines; caudal fin rounded. Lateral line continuous to base of caudal fin. Bases of soft dorsal and anal fins covered with scales and thick skin.

Habitat: Over coral reefs and rocks in shallow water.

Range: Bermuda, S. Florida, Gulf Coast, West Indies, and shores of Caribbean, south to Brazil. Occasionally strays north to Massachusetts.

Similar Species: Graysby (*E. cruentatus*) has similar spotting, but with 3–4 small, distinct spots under dorsal fin base; occurs in similar habitat from Bermuda to N. Brazil, including Gulf of Mexico and Bahamas. Red Hind (*E. guttatus*) lacks spots on fins and dark saddles on back; spots on undersides and sides same size.

Comments: The Rock Hind is reported to be a better food fish than the Red Hind, but is more wary of taking bait. It is common in shallow depths, and tolerates rough inshore waters, although it has been found as deep as 16 fathoms.

503 Speckled Hind
(*Epinephelus drummondhayi*)

Description: To 18″ (46 cm). Robust, not strongly
compressed; reddish-brown above,
bluish-purple below, *covered with small,
creamy white spots.* Head long; mouth
oblique; maxilla reaches middle of eye.
11 dorsal fin spines, some longer than
anterior soft rays, interspinal membrane
notched; 3 anal fin spines; caudal fin
truncate or slightly emarginate. Lateral
line continuous to base of caudal fin.
Bases of soft dorsal and caudal fins
covered with scales and thick skin.

Habitat: Over coral reefs and rocks, usually in
deep water.

Range: Bermuda, E. coast of Florida, NE. Gulf
of Mexico, rarely to W. Gulf of
Mexico.

Comments: This beautiful grouper is unique in
having a dark background color
profusely scattered with white spots.
Apparently it is not common in most of
its range. Although Speckled Hinds
larger than 18″ (46 cm) have been
reported, these record catches have not
been documented.

502 Red Hind
(*Epinephelus guttatus*)

Description: To 24″ (61 cm). Robust, not strongly
compressed; *light pinkish with numerous
uniform, small, red spots;* no spots on
fins; soft dorsal, anal, and caudal fins
have broad, black margins. Head long,
not depressed; mouth oblique; maxilla
reaches past middle of eye. 11 dorsal
fin spines, some longer than soft
anterior rays, interspinal membranes
notched; 3 anal fin spines; caudal fin
truncate. Lateral line continuous to
base of caudal fin. Soft dorsal and anal
fins covered with scales and thick skin.

Habitat: Over coral reefs and rocks in shallow to
moderately deep water.

Range: From North Carolina south throughout
S. Gulf of Mexico, Antilles, shores of
Caribbean, and West Indies. Most
common in Bermuda.

Similar Species: Rock Hind (*E. adscensionis*) has reddish-
brown spots on fins, dark saddles under
dorsal fin and on caudal peduncle; spots
on underside larger than on sides.

Comments: The Red Hind is commonly caught off
the bottom on hook and line. The
usual size is 18″ (46 cm) or less. Like other
Epinephelus, it probably feeds primarily
on crustaceans.

508 Jewfish
(*Epinephelus itajara*)

Description: To 7′ 10″ (2.4 m); 680 lbs (308 kg).
Very robust, broad; greenish or gray with
small, black spots. *Head large, somewhat
flattened;* eye small; mouth oblique;
maxilla reaches well beyond eye. Pelvic
fins smaller than pectorals; dorsal fin
continuous, *11 spines much shorter than
foremost soft rays;* soft dorsal, anal, and
caudal fins rounded; 3 anal fin spines.
Lateral line continuous to base of
caudal fin. Scales small but strongly
ctenoid; bases of soft dorsal and anal
fins covered with scales and thick skin.

Habitat: Inshore in shallow water; also in
moderately deep water.

Range: Both coasts of Florida, Gulf of Mexico,
Greater Antilles, and SW. Caribbean.

Comments: Although the world's angling record for
Jewfishes is 680 lbs, specimens in the
90 lb (40 kg) class or under are more
likely to be caught. They are sought by
spearfishers around oil rigs in Louisiana
and Texas. Jewfishes feed mostly on
crustaceans, but are known to feed on
fishes and even on turtles.

509 Red Grouper
(*Epinephelus morio*)

Description: To 28″ (71 cm). Robust, not strongly
compressed; *reddish brown with scattered,
pale blotches,* some dark spots on cheek
and opercle, narrow, black border on
soft dorsal, anal, and caudal fins. Head
long; mouth large; maxilla reaches to
back edge of eye; eye green. 11 dorsal
fin spines, second spine longest and
longer than anterior soft rays, *interspinal
membrane not notched;* 3 anal fin spines;
caudal fin truncate or slightly lunate.
Lateral line continuous to base of
caudal fin. Bases of soft dorsal, anal,
and caudal fins covered with scales and
thick skin.

Habitat: Over variety of bottoms, but mostly
over rocks to about 75 fathoms.

Range: From Massachusetts to Florida
including Bermuda, Gulf of Mexico,
Caribbean, south to Brazil. Center of
abundance Florida and Gulf of Mexico.

Comments: The Red Grouper is one of the most
common and commercially important
groupers, especially in Florida, Cuba,
and Mexico, where thousands of tons
are caught each year. An important
sport fish, it feeds on a variety of small
fishes, squids, and crustaceans.

Warsaw Grouper
(*Epinephelus nigritus*)

Description: To 5′ (1.5 m). Robust, not strongly
compressed; *dark reddish-brown to almost
black above, dull reddish-gray below,* no
intense spots or saddles on dorsal area
or caudal peduncle. Head long; maxilla
reaches to or beyond posterior edge of
eye. 10 dorsal fin spines, second higher
than soft rays, *interspinal membrane deeply
notched.* Soft dorsal and anal fins well
rounded; 3 anal fin spines. Caudal fin
truncate or slightly rounded. Lateral
line continuous to base of caudal fin.

Bases of dorsal and anal fins covered with scales and thick skin.

Habitat: Offshore from 7–80 fathoms and near oil platforms; occasionally inshore around jetties.

Range: From Massachusetts to Florida and Gulf of Mexico; spotty distribution in Antilles.

Comments: The Warsaw Grouper seems to be most abundant in S. Florida and the Gulf of Mexico. Like the other *Epinephelus,* young Warsaw Groupers are male, and change into females as they grow older. Though reported to reach about 242 lbs (110 kg), the fishes most frequently seen in the markets are about half this weight.

516 Nassau Grouper
(*Epinephelus striatus*)

Description: To 4' (1.2 m). Robust, not strongly compressed; brownish or brownish-orange above, but often pinkish or red in deep water, 5 *dusky bars on sides; dark blotch on top of caudal peduncle,* intense dark dots around eye, *dark stripes between eye and dorsal fin origin.* Head long; maxilla reaches to posterior edge of eye. Single dorsal fin with shallow notch between spines and rays, interspinal membranes notched; 3 anal fin spines; caudal fin rounded in young, becoming truncate in adults. Small, dense scales on bases of dorsal and anal fins.

Habitat: Over coral reefs and to depths of 15 fathoms.

Range: From North Carolina to Brazil, including Bermuda, S. Gulf of Mexico, and Antilles.

Related Species: Spotted Cabrilla (*E. analogus*) has reddish-brown body with dark brown spots; 16–18 dorsal fin rays; occurs around rocky reefs from San Pedro, California, to Peru.

Comments: The Nassau Grouper changes color

phases rapidly. It is not very wary, and readily takes food from the hands of divers. It is an important sport fish, a good fighter, and will take various kinds of bait. The Nassau Grouper averages a weight of about 8 to 10 lbs (3.6 to 4.5 kg) and is considered excellent eating.

---

511   Black Grouper
(*Mycteroperca bonaci*)

Description: To 4' (1.2 m). Elongate, rather robust; color variable, usually light brown with irregular rows of darker blotches, cheeks and belly gray with hexagonal spots. Head large; mouth oblique, maxilla completely exposed, reaches beyond eye, lower jaw projects beyond upper; preopercle evenly rounded, smooth. *Pectoral fins have narrow, orange margin,* median fins have black borders; dorsal fin continuous, spiny and soft parts separated by shallow notch; 3 anal fin spines; caudal fin truncate. Dorsal and anal fins covered with thick skin and scales.

Habitat: Over rocks and coral reefs.

Range: From Bermuda, S. Florida, E. Gulf of Mexico, and West Indies to Colombia and Venezuela. Also reported from New England.

Related Species: Scamp (*M. phenax*) has body and fins tan with small, brown spots; occurs commonly at 13–25 fathoms on Snapper Banks around obstructions from Massachusetts to Caribbean, including Gulf of Mexico.

Comments: Black Groupers occupy shallow water when small. As they grow larger, they move into deeper water to depths of about 70' (21.3 m).

512 Kelp Bass
(*Paralabrax clathratus*)

Description: To 28″ (71 cm). Elongate, moderately compressed; greenish-brown above, belly white; white blotches between dorsal fin and lateral line. *10–11 dorsal fin spines, third spine about same length as fourth and fifth, 12–14 soft rays;* 3 anal fin spines. Lateral line continuous to base of caudal fin.

Habitat: Reefs, wrecks, and kelp beds to depths of 25 fathoms.

Range: From mouth of Columbia River, Oregon, to Bahía Magdalena, Baja California.

Related Species: Spotted Sand Bass (*P. maculatofasciatus*) has small, black spots on body and fins; third dorsal fin spine much longer than fourth and fifth; found from Monterey, California, to Mazatlán, Mexico. Barred Sand Bass (*P. nebulifer*) lacks spots; third dorsal fin spine very long; found from Santa Cruz, California, to Bahía Magdalena, Baja California. Both occur around rocky reefs.

Similar Species: Olive Rockfish (*Sebastes serranoides*) has 12–13 dorsal fin spines, 15–17 soft rays.

Comments: The Kelp Bass spawns from late spring through early fall. It is one of the sport fishes most sought in southern California, and the annual catch was recently estimated to have exceeded one million fishes. It feeds on crustaceans, squids, octopuses, polychaete worms, and fishes. It is a slow-growing fish that takes 4 to 6 years to reach 12″ (30 cm); a 24″ (61 cm) fish might be 20 years old.

504 Creole-Fish
(*Paranthias furcifer*)

Description: To 14″ (36 cm). Small, robust, moderately compressed, dorsal and ventral profiles equally rounded;

reddish-brown above, becoming pinkish below; *3 small, intense white spots, well separated, above lateral line;* bright orange spot at pectoral fin base. Head small; mouth moderately large, oblique. Dorsal fin continuous; 3 anal fin spines; caudal fin deeply forked. Lateral line continuous to caudal fin base. Bases of soft dorsal and anal fins covered by scales and thick skin.

Habitat: Around coral reefs, usually at depths over 18′ (5.5 m).

Range: From South Carolina, Florida, and N. Gulf of Mexico, disjunctly to Yucatán; West Indies and N. South America.

Comments: These small basses usually live in groups near the bottom, where they feed on zooplankton.

521 Tattler
(*Serranus phoebe*)

Description: To 8″ (20 cm). Oblong, robust anteriorly, dorsal profile nearly straight; light brown with lighter blotches and dusky bars, *conspicuous white bar on sides.* Head large, about one-fourth length; maxilla reaches middle of eye, lower jaw not projecting; canine teeth small; eye diameter equal to snout length. Pectoral fins long; dorsal fin not notched, spines strong, fourth longest; 3 anal fin spines; caudal fin emarginate or moderately forked. About 53 scales in lateral line series. About 8 scale rows on cheeks; scales absent on top of head, present on parts of soft dorsal fin.

Habitat: Over sand in deep offshore water.

Range: From South Carolina to Brazil, including Bermuda and Gulf of Mexico; apparently absent from Bahamas and West Indies.

Comments: This small bass has been collected in large numbers in the northeastern Gulf of Mexico at depths ranging from 42 to 67 fathoms.

514 Belted Sandfish
(*Serranus subligarius*)

Description: To 4½" (11.5 cm). Oblong, robust, deep; brownish olive, scales have light centers; broad, dark bars on sides, dark band from snout through eye to upper edge of opercle, large, white blotch on belly between pelvic and anal fins, *large, blackish spot on anterior of soft dorsal fin;* all fins except pelvics have dark spots forming bands with light interspaces, *pelvic fins blackish with white leading edges. Head small, acute, anterior dorsal profile straight;* maxilla reaches back of eye, lower jaw projects slightly beyond upper. Fins, jaws, area in front of eyes and front of head unscaled.

Habitat: Around rocky jetties and over sand.

Range: From North Carolina to Florida; Gulf of Mexico from W. Florida to Mexico.

Comments: Of no commercial value, this little bass differs from other members of its family by having 6 branchiostegal rays, rather than 7.

SOAPFISHES
(Family Grammistidae)

Soapfishes are so called because when they are handled they secrete a slimy mucus that may be toxic. They are small to medium-sized, and resemble basses or groupers. There are 2 genera and 5 species in the Atlantic off North America. The Reef Bass (*Pseudogramma gregoryi*) has 6 to 8 dorsal fin spines and 3 anal fin spines. The other species, all in the genus *Rypticus,* have only 2 to 4 dorsal fin spines and no anal fin spines.

506 Greater Soapfish
(*Rypticus saponaceus*)

Description: To 13″ (33 cm). Elongate, compressed, *anterior profile acute;* color variable, brown, gray, or almost black with irregular, lighter blotches on sides, smaller, light spots on dorsal fin, median fin edges pale. *Lower jaw projects well beyond upper;* 2 flat spines on preopercle, 3 on opercle. Dorsal fin long, continuous, with 3 spines; posterior dorsal rays longest and similar to anal fin, which has no spine; pectoral and caudal fins rounded. Scales small, embedded.

Habitat: Over sand, rocks, or reefs in relatively shallow water.

Range: From S. Florida to Brazil, including Bermuda, Central America, and Antilles.

Related Species: Whitespotted Soapfish (*R. maculatus*) has 2 dorsal fin spines; occurs in similar habitat, but less often over reefs, from North Carolina to N. Gulf of Mexico. Spotted Soapfish (*R. subbifrenatus*) has pale body with dark spots; found in similar habitat from Florida to Texas.

Comments: The Greater Soapfish is the largest and most common soapfish in the Bahamas. Its slimy mucus contains a toxic substance, and the fish is seldom used as food.

SUNFISHES
(Family Centrarchidae)

Lepomis

Micropterus

Sunfishes are one of the most widespread and popular groups of freshwater sport fishes. Their dorsal fins are joined, separated only by a notch, and the anal fin has 3 or more spines. The caudal fin is usually forked, and the gill membranes are usually separate. Except for a single species native to California, sunfishes are indigenous to warm waters of North

America east of the Rocky Mountains. However, as a result of their popularity with anglers, their range has been increased by introducing them into other areas. There are 32 species in North America.

Mud Sunfish
(*Acantharchus pomotis*)

Description: To 10″ (25 cm). Oblong, robust; back dusky green, sides greenish olive with *3−5 irregular, dull greenish-yellow stripes;* head greenish with 2−3 dark stripes. Snout short; mouth wide; *maxilla extends past middle of eye;* upper part of opercle with large, dark blotch. Fins greenish with darker edge; *4−6 anal fin spines, 9−12 soft rays.* Caudal peduncle short, deep, *caudal fin rounded.* Scales cycloid; lateral line complete, 35−43 scales.

Habitat: Sluggish Coastal Plain streams, swamps, and backwaters, usually in dark, stained water with abundant vegetation over mud.

Range: From New York to N. Florida, west to St. Marks River, W. Florida.

Comments: The Mud Sunfish spends much of the day hiding under overhanging banks, submerged debris, or vegetation. It is active at night, coming out to forage.

82 Rock Bass
(*Ambloplites rupestris*)

Description: To 13″ (33 cm); 3⅝ lbs (1.6 kg). Oblong, robust; back olive mottled with dark saddles and bronze blotches, *lighter below with rows of dusky spots. Head large; mouth extends to or past middle of large, red eye; cheeks and opercles scaled.* 10−13 dorsal fin spines; *5−7 anal fin spines.* Lateral line complete, with 36−44 scales.

Habitat: Cool, clear, rocky streams and shallow lakes with vegetation and other cover.

Range: S. Canada, S. Quebec west to Manitoba; from Great Lakes drainage south to N. Alabama and N. Georgia.

Related Species: Shadow Bass (*A. ariommus*) has deeper body; sides with dark brown blotches; occurs in creeks and small rivers from NW. Georgia and W. Florida to SE. Missouri, SW. Arkansas, south to E. Louisiana. Roanoke Bass (*A. cavifrons*) has gold spots on upper body; cheeks without scales; occurs in upland streams in Roanoke, Tar, and Neuse rivers, S. Virginia and NE. North Carolina. Ozark Bass (*A. constellatus*) has uniform color with scattered dark spots; found in upland streams in SW. Missouri and NW. Arkansas.

Comments: Although small, the Rock Bass is a popular game fish.

---

84 Sacramento Perch
(*Archoplites interruptus*)

Description: To 16″ (41 cm). Moderately elongate, compressed; back olive to black, *sides olive-brown, upper sides mottled with 6–8 irregular olive-brown bars,* belly whitish. Mouth large, extends to middle of eye; *preopercle and subopercle serrate.* 12–13 dorsal fin spines; 6–7 *anal fin spines;* caudal fin slightly forked. Lateral line complete, 38–48 scales.

Habitat: Sloughs, sluggish streams, and lakes with vegetation.

Range: Sacramento, San Joaquin, Pajaro, and Salinas rivers and Clear Lake, California. Introduced in Utah, Nevada, Oregon, and California.

Comments: The Sacramento Perch is the only sunfish native to the western United States. In its native range, it declined rapidly as exotic fishes were introduced and its habitat destroyed. It has been introduced into some western lakes that are too alkaline for other fishes.

83 Flier
(*Centrarchus macropterus*)

Description: To 6" (15 cm). Oval, strongly
compressed; caudal peduncle length
and depth about equal; dusky above,
*greenish-yellow below with 8–12 rows of
small, dark brown spots.* Snout short;
mouth small, extending to pupil of eye;
dark, wedge-shaped spot through eye;
cheeks, opercles scaled. Second dorsal
and anal fins large, mottled with
narrow, dark markings; second dorsal
fin usually has black blotch with orange
halo. *11–13 dorsal fin spines;* 7 anal fin
spines; 38–45 lateral line scales.

Habitat: Clear, quiet lowland streams, swamps,
and ditches with heavy vegetation.

Range: Atlantic Coast from S. Maryland
south to Florida, west to E. Texas;
Mississippi River valley south from
S. Illinois, SW. Indiana.

Comments: The Flier is a very attractive fish and is
locally abundant. Its small size, rarely
exceeding 6" (15 cm), makes it
unimportant as a game fish.

87 Banded Pygmy Sunfish
(*Elassoma zonatum*)

Description: To 2" (5 cm). Oblong, compressed;
dark olive-green above, *sides lighter with
8–12 irregular dark bars and black spot
below dorsal fin origin,* median fins with
dark bands. Snout short; mouth
terminal, extends to eye; cheeks and
top of head scaled. 4–5 dorsal fin
spines; 3 anal fin spines; *caudal fin
rounded. Lateral line absent;* 33–36 scales
in lateral series.

Habitat: Quiet and clear or dark, stained and
sluggish streams, sloughs, and swamps
with abundant vegetation.

Range: Atlantic Coast from North Carolina
south to Florida, west to E. Texas,
north in Mississippi River valley, S.
Illinois, SW. Indiana.

Related Species: Everglades Pygmy Sunfish (*E. evergladei*) lacks bars; has 27–30 scales in lateral series; occurs in similar habitat along coast from S. North Carolina west to S. Alabama.

Comments: The 3 species of pygmy sunfishes, genus *Elassoma,* are sometimes placed in their own family Elassomatidae. These diminutive fishes feed on crustaceans and aquatic insects. Rarely living more than 3 years, they make interesting aquarium pets.

80   Bluespotted Sunfish
(*Enneacanthus gloriosus*)

Description: To 4″ (10 cm). Short, moderately deep, compressed; back olive-brown, *sides greenish brown with bright blue spots in irregular rows,* faint in females; belly light yellow-olive. Snout short; mouth terminal, slightly oblique; pearly-edged dark spot on upper end of opercle. Dorsal fins joined, 8–9 spines, 10–11 soft rays; 3 anal fin spines, 9–10 soft rays; *caudal fin rounded.* Lateral line complete or interrupted, 30–32 scales; *16–18 caudal peduncle scale rows.*

Habitat: Clear, dark, stained waters of sluggish coastal streams, swamps, and lakes with abundant vegetation.

Range: From S. New York to S. Florida, west to S. Alabama and S. Mississippi.

Related Species: Blackbanded Sunfish (*E. chaetodon*) lacks blue spots, has 6–8 broad, dark bars; occurs from N. New Jersey to central Florida, west to SW. Georgia. Banded Sunfish (*E. obesus*) has blue spots, 4–8 dark bars; 19–22 caudal peduncle scale rows; occurs from S. New Hampshire to central Florida, west to W. Florida. Both in similar habitat.

Comments: The Bluespotted Sunfish is small, hardy, and colorful and has a mild disposition, making it a popular aquarium fish.

75 Redbreast Sunfish
(*Lepomis auritus*)

Description: To 11″ (28 cm); 1½ lbs (700 g).
Oblong, compressed; back dark olive to
dusky, sides greenish to yellowish
brown with reddish spots, belly reddish
orange. Mouth extends to eye; bluish
lines below eye. *Opercular flap "ear" very
long, no wider than eye, black, without
light border;* 11 short gill rakers. Fins
plain, median fins yellow-orange,
occasionally dusky; *pectoral fins short,
rounded, 13–15 rays;* 3 anal fin spines.
Lateral line complete, 43–50 scales.

Habitat: Streams with slow to moderate current
over sand, gravel, or rocks; also in
ponds and lakes.

Range: Atlantic Coast streams from New
Brunswick south to central Florida,
west in Gulf Coast drainages from W
Florida to E. Alabama. Introduced
outside native range.

Comments: The Redbreast Sunfish inhabits streams
more frequently than most other
sunfishes. It is usually found alone, but
it forms compact hibernating schools at
low temperatures. Unlike other
sunfishes, the Redbreast does not
produce sounds during courtship.

76 Green Sunfish
(*Lepomis cyanellus*)

Description: To 10″ (25 cm); 2¼ lbs (1 kg).
Robust, moderately elongate, depth
less than distance from snout tip to
dorsal fin origin; yellowish olive, sides
sometimes with dusky bars, belly pale
olive, median fins olive to dusky, edges
whitish to light orange. Head broad;
*opercular flap not extended; mouth extends
to middle of eye.* Pectoral fin short,
rounded; *posterior base of second dorsal and
anal fins often with black blotch.* Lateral
line complete, 40–52 scales.

Habitat: Clear to turbid water with little or no

current in smaller streams, swamps, and ponds.

Range: Native to S. Great Lakes, Mississippi River basin south to Texas; Alabama west to New Mexico; widely introduced in United States and N. Mexico.

Comments: The Green Sunfish, one of the most common sunfishes, is tolerant of a wide range of environmental conditions.

73 Pumpkinseed
(Lepomis gibbosus)

Description: To 10″ (25 cm); 1 lb (500 g). Deep, short, compressed; back dark greenish gold mottled with reddish orange, sides greenish yellow, mottled orange and blue-green, belly yellow-orange. Head small; mouth extends to eye; *opercular flap "ear" stiff, with spot, black anteriorly, bordered by white above and below, red posteriorly;* cheeks with wavy bluish lines. *Pectoral fin long, pointed; soft dorsal fin spotted,* edge yellowish to white; 3 anal fin spines. Lateral line complete, 36–47 scales.

Habitat: Cool, quiet, shallow waters of slow streams, ponds, marshes, and lakes with dense vegetation.

Range: From New Brunswick west to S. Manitoba; south along Atlantic Coast to NE. Georgia; Great Lakes and upper Mississippi River system south to S. Illinois. Widely introduced.

Related Species: Spotted Sunfish (*L. punctatus*) lacks wavy blue lines on cheeks; pectoral fin short, rounded; occurs in sluggish water with vegetation in Mississippi River valley south from Illinois to Coastal Plain drainages, and S. North Carolina west to Texas.

Comments: The Pumpkinseed is not sought by most experienced anglers, but is often caught by beginners. It is aggressive and will take a variety of bait.

86 Warmouth
(*Lepomis gulosus*)

Description: To 10″ (25 cm); 2¼ lbs (1 kg).
Oblong, robust; back and median
fins dark olive-brown with dusky
mottlings, sides lighter with scattered
dusky spots, belly yellowish. Head
large, wide; *opercular flap not extended;
teeth on tongue; mouth extends past middle
of reddish eye,* which has radiating dusky
lines, 4–5 running to edge of opercle;
dark spot on upper part of opercle.
Pectoral fin short, rounded; 9–11
dorsal fin spines; 3 anal fin spines.
Lateral line complete, 36–44 scales.

Habitat: Ponds, swamps, lakes, and sluggish
streams with vegetation or debris.

Range: From Maryland, S. Michigan, and S.
Wisconsin south to Florida, west to
Texas and New Mexico.

Comments: The Warmouth spends much of its
time in the cover of dense vegetation.
It feeds on small fishes, crayfishes, and
aquatic insects. During the late spring
and summer, it nests in shallow water.
Due to its small size, it is generally not
very important as a game fish.

85 Bluegill
(*Lepomis macrochirus*)

Description: To 12″ (30 cm); 4¾ lbs (2.2 kg).
Deep, compressed, profile rounded
under dorsal fin; body and median fins
dark olive-green; sides lighter, olive
with brassy reflections, often with
dusky bars; belly whitish. Mouth
terminal, not extending past front edge
of eye; *opercular flap broad, moderately
long,* dusky to black. *Pectoral fin long,
pointed; second dorsal fin with black blotch
near middle of posterior rays;* anal fin base
about half length of dorsal fin base.
Lateral line complete, 39–45 scales.

Habitat: Clear, warm pools of streams, lakes,
ponds, sloughs, and reservoirs, usually

in shallow water with vegetation.

Range: From S. Ontario, S. Quebec, and Great
Lakes drainage south to Florida, west to
S. Texas. Introduced throughout
United States and N. Mexico.

Comments: The Bluegill is the most common
sunfish and probably the most popular
freshwater game fish in the United
States. It is also commonly stocked in
ponds as forage for larger fishes.

74 Longear Sunfish
(*Lepomis megalotis*)

Description: To 9″ (23 cm); ½ lb (200 g). Deep,
compressed; back dark olive to blue-
green, sides light olive with yellow and
blue-green speckles, belly yellow to
reddish, cheeks reddish with wavy
blue-green stripes. Mouth extends to
eye; *opercular flap "ear" long, wider than
eye, often edged with white or red. Pectoral
fin short, rounded, 13–14 rays;* 3 anal fin
spines; soft dorsal, anal, and caudal fins
reddish-orange. Lateral line complete,
33–41 scales. *5–6 scale rows on cheeks.*

Habitat: Pools of streams with moderate current
over sand, gravel, or rocks; also
reservoirs and lakes.

Range: From SW. Quebec to SE. Manitoba;
Mississippi Valley; Gulf Coast
drainages, W. Florida west to Rio
Grande, Texas, and New Mexico.
Introduced outside native range.

Related Species: Dollar Sunfish (*L. marginatus*) has
deeper body; 12 pectoral fin rays; 4
scale rows on cheeks; occurs in slow
streams and swamps with vegetation
from E. North Carolina south to
S. Florida; W. Kentucky south to
Alabama, west to E. Texas.

Comments: The Longear Sunfish is a popular game
fish in most areas. Its food consists of
aquatic insects, snails, crustaceans, and
small fishes.

78 Redear Sunfish
(*Lepomis microlophus*)

Description: To 14″ (36 cm); 4½ lbs (2 kg).
Moderately elongate, compressed; back
olive with brown specks; sides greenish
yellow with brassy reflections and dark
speckles; young with 5–8 dusky bars;
belly yellow-orange; *opercular flap "ear"
has black spot with broad, bright reddish-
orange edge behind.* Mouth reaches eye;
sides of head have dark olive spots, no
wavy lines. *Pectoral fin long, pointed,
extends to near middle of anal fin base;* 3
anal fin spines. Lateral line complete,
35–44 scales.

Habitat: Clear, quiet pools of warm streams,
ponds, lakes, and reservoirs with
vegetation or other cover.

Range: From North Carolina and Florida to
S. Illinois, S. Missouri, south to Rio
Grande drainage. Widely introduced.

Comments: Because this fish has special molarlike
teeth for crushing snails, it is often
called the "shellcracker."

90 Smallmouth Bass
(*Micropterus dolomieui*)

Description: To 24″ (61 cm); 12 lbs (5.4 kg).
Elongate, compressed; back dark olive
to brown, *sides greenish yellow with bronze
reflections,* diffuse midlateral bars form
dark mottlings. Mouth extends to eye.
16–18 pectoral soft rays; median fins
olive; dorsal fins joined, 10 spines, 13–
14 soft rays; 3 anal fin spines, 11 soft
rays. Lateral line complete, 67–79
scales; 11–13 scale rows above lateral
line, 20–23 below; *scales on bases of soft
dorsal and anal fins;* 29–31 caudal
peduncle scale rows.

Habitat: Cool, clear streams with moderate to
swift current over gravel or rocks; lakes
and reservoirs.

Range: SW. Quebec and SE. Ontario; New
York west to Minnesota, south in

Mississippi River system to N.
Alabama, N. Arkansas, and E.
Oklahoma. Widely introduced.

Related Species: Redeye Bass (*M. coosae*) rarely exceeds
16″ (41 cm); has 12 dorsal fin rays; 7–
10 scale rows above lateral line, 16–17
below; occurs in similar habitat from
SW. North Carolina and W. South
Carolina west to W. central Alabama.

Comments: One of the most popular sport fishes in
eastern North America, this species
takes a variety of live bait, minnows,
and crayfishes, as well as artificial lures.
The Smallmouth Bass spawns earlier
than other sunfishes in the same areas.

91 Spotted Bass
(*Micropterus punctulatus*)

Description: To 24″ (61 cm); 9 lbs (4.1 kg).
Elongate, compressed; back dark olive,
sides olive to yellowish with dark,
midlateral, diamond-shaped blotches;
*lower sides have rows of dusky spots forming
stripes.* Mouth reaches middle of eye.
15–16 pectoral soft rays; median fins
olive; *dorsal fins joined,* with 10 spines,
12–13 soft rays; 3 anal fin spines, 10
soft rays. Lateral line complete, 60–75
scales; 8–9 scale rows above lateral
line, 15–18 below; *scales on bases of soft
dorsal and anal fins;* 23–28 caudal
peduncle scale rows.

Habitat: Warm, clear to slightly turbid pools of
creeks and rivers; also ponds, lakes, and
reservoirs.

Range: From W. West Virginia, SW.
Virginia, NW. Georgia, and W.
Florida west to E. Texas; S. Ohio to
SE. Kansas. Introduced outside native
range.

Related Species: Suwannee Bass (*M. notius*) grows to 12″
(30 cm); belly bluish green; occurs in
springs and rocky shoals of streams,
and in Ochlockonee and Suwannee
rivers in extreme SW. Georgia and
N. central Florida. Guadalupe Bass

(*M. treculi*) grows to 12″ (30 cm); has greenish to dusky bands from lower sides to above midline; occurs in similar habitat in S. central Texas.

Comments: There are 3 subspecies of Spotted Basses and they are often confused with the Largemouth Bass. The Spotted Bass is a prized game fish and readily takes live or artificial bait.

92 Largemouth Bass
(*Micropterus salmoides*)

Description: To 3′2″ (97 cm); 22¼ lbs (10.1 kg). Moderately deep, robust; back olive to dark green, mottled; *sides greenish yellow with dark midlateral stripe;* head greenish gold. *Mouth large, extends beyond posterior edge of eye.* 14–15 pectoral soft rays; median fins olive; *dorsal fins almost separate,* 10 spines, 12–13 soft rays; 3 anal fin spines, 11 soft rays. Lateral line complete, 59–77 scales; 7–9 scale rows above lateral line, 14–17 below; *no scales on bases of soft dorsal and anal fins;* 24–28 caudal peduncle scale rows.

dorsal fin

Habitat: Quiet, clear to slightly turbid streams, ponds, lakes, and reservoirs, often with vegetation.

Range: S. Ontario south through Great Lakes, Mississippi River system, and Coastal Plain from N. North Carolina to Texas and NE. Mexico. Also introduced throughout S. Canada and United States.

Comments: The Largemouth Bass, one of the most highly sought sport fishes in the United States, is caught with live and artificial bait. It is more tolerant of warm water than the Smallmouth Bass, but at higher temperatures it becomes less active. Adults feed primarily on other fishes. The average life span is about 16 years.

81 Black Crappie
(Pomoxis nigromaculatus)

Description: To 16" (41 cm); 5 lbs (2.3 kg). Deep,
strongly compressed, dorsal profile
rounded; back greenish, sides silvery
green with dark green to black
scattered mottlings not forming bars,
belly silvery, median fins yellowish
green with dusky, wavy lines and white
spots. Head long, concave near eye;
mouth oblique, extends past middle of
eye. *Dorsal fins connected without notch,
7–8 spines; anal fin large, 6 spines.*
Lateral line complete, 36–44 scales.

Habitat: Quiet, warm, clear streams, ponds,
lakes, and reservoirs.

Range: Quebec, Ontario, and S. Manitoba;
E. and central United States except
Atlantic Coast streams from Maine to
Virginia. Widely introduced.

Related Species: White Crappie (*P. annularis*) has more
elongate body; 6 dorsal fin spines;
occurs in same habitat in SE. Ontario
and E. central United States. Widely
introduced.

Comments: This is a very popular sport and food
fish, especially in the southern part of
its range. It is generally less abundant
than the White Crappie and less
tolerant of silty and turbid waters. It
feeds throughout the day and night,
but is most active in the evening.

PERCHES
(Family Percidae)

Perca

darters

The perches are a large freshwater
family; 5 genera and 130 species are
found in North America. They have 1
or 2 spines in the anal fin; the second
spine is not enlarged. Their dorsal fins
are usually separate. The larger species,
which reach lengths of 3' (91 cm), are
important sport fishes and have been
widely introduced. The smaller species
are among the most colorful fishes.

Darters

The 3 genera of darters, *Ammocrypta,*
Etheostoma, and *Percina,* total over 125
species and form one of the most
diverse and colorful groups of North
American freshwater fishes. The
common name, darter, describes their
habit of "darting" about, using the tail
and pectoral fins for locomotion. These
movements are largely confined to the
bottom, since most species lack a swim
bladder. Usually 2″ to 4″ (5 to 10 cm)
in length, they are found, with few
exceptions, in North America east of
the Continental Divide. *Ammocrypta*
(7 species) are translucent with a faint
orange wash, have an anal fin spine,
a complete lateral line, and lack
specialized scales on the midline of the
belly. *Etheostoma* (92 species) have 1 or
2 anal fin spines, may have a complete
lateral line, and lack specialized scales
on the belly. The males are usually
brightly colored. *Percina* (30 species)
tend to be tan or brown with darker
markings, and any bright coloration is
usually yellow or orange. There are 2
anal fin spines, a complete lateral line,
and males have specialized scales on the
midline of the belly that are used
during spawning to maintain their
position and stimulate the female.

ventral scales

---

251 Crystal Darter
(*Ammocrypta asprella*)

Description: To 5″ (12.5 cm). Very slender, length
8–10 times depth; opaque, back olive
to tan with *4 dark saddles extending
downward and forward to lateral line,*
midlateral brownish stripe usually
present, belly whitish. Head broad;
snout long, rounded; maxilla not
reaching large eye; frenum present. *Fin
membranes transparent;* dorsal and anal
fins high; caudal fin slightly forked.

Completely scaled; lateral line complete, 77–97 scales.

Habitat: Moderate to swift rivers over sand, gravel, or rocks; occasionally pools.

Range: Mississippi River system from West Virginia, Ohio, and Minnesota, south to SE. Oklahoma and Louisiana; Gulf Coast drainages from W. Florida to Louisiana.

Comments: Crystal Darters have been eliminated from much of their range because many of their habitats have been destroyed by canalization and dams.

---

255   Naked Sand Darter
(*Ammocrypta beani*)

Description: To 2½" (6.5 cm). *Elongate, cylindrical;* translucent, yellowish orange. Snout pointed; mouth extends to eye; *no opercular spine.* Pelvic fins whitish; first dorsal fin with black blotch anteriorly, dusky band posteriorly; second dorsal, caudal, and anal fins with central gray-black band. *Scaleless except 1–5 midlateral rows;* lateral line complete, 55–77 scales.

Habitat: Creeks and rivers with moderate current over clean sand.

Range: Hatchie River, W. Tennessee; from Big Black River, W. Mississippi, south to Lake Pontchartrain, east to Mobile Bay drainage of Alabama.

Related Species: Florida Sand Darter (*A. bifascia*) male has 2 black bands on dorsal and anal fins; occurs in similar habitat in S. Alabama and W. Florida.

Comments: Naked Sand Darters, like other sand darters, dive head first into the sand, emerge with only their snout and eyes protruding, and dart from this position to capture food.

254 Western Sand Darter
(*Ammocrypta clara*)

Description: To 2¾" (7 cm). Elongate, cylindrical; translucent, head and body yellowish; sides with 9–13 dark, elongate blotches centered along dusky, narrow midlateral stripe. *Opercular spine present.* Fins transparent, yellowish; pelvic fins not dusky. Body, cheeks, and opercles partially scaled; lateral line complete, 63–81 scales; *1–3 scale rows below lateral line, 1 above.*

Habitat: Medium to large rivers with moderate to slow current over sand.

Range: Ohio River drainage in Indiana, Kentucky, and Tennessee; Mississippi River system from S. Minnesota south to Mississippi, E. Texas.

Comments: The Western Sand Darter spawns from July through August. It has been found buried an inch or more below the surface of the sand.

253 Eastern Sand Darter
(*Ammocrypta pellucida*)

Description: To 2½" (6.5 cm). Slender, very elongate, length 8–11 times depth; yellowish, lighter below, *9–15 dark, oval blotches just below lateral line.* Maxilla extends to eye; *no opercular spine.* Pectoral, dorsal, and anal fin membranes transparent; anal fin origin under or just anterior to first ray of second dorsal fin. Lateral line complete, 65–84 scales, *1–4 scale rows above lateral line, 4–7 below.*

Habitat: Creeks and rivers with moderate current over sand; protected beaches of Lake Erie islands.

Range: St. Lawrence River; S. Lake Huron, Lake St. Clair, and Lake Erie islands; Ohio River drainage, Pennsylvania, south to W. Kentucky.

Related Species: Southern Sand Darter (*A. meridiana*) has more scale rows above and below lateral

line; occurs in similar habitat in Mobile
Bay drainage, Alabama and Mississippi.

Comments: Eastern Sand Darters were once fairly
common, but habitat changes have
reduced population levels. They feed
primarily on midge larvae, which are
captured as they drift over the sandy
shoals. The female probably buries
herself in the sand to deposit eggs.

---

252 Scaly Sand Darter
(*Ammocrypta vivax*)

Description: To 3″ (7.5 cm). Elongate; translucent,
yellow-orange, sides lighter with *9–16
midlateral dark, oval blotches, vertically
oriented.* Maxilla extends to front of eye;
no opercular spine. *Median fins with 2
dark bands.* Cheek and opercle scaled,
body partially scaled; lateral line
complete, 58–79 scales.

Habitat: Creeks and rivers with moderate
current over clean sand.

Range: Mississippi River system in W.
Kentucky and SE. Missouri, south to
Mississippi, Louisiana, and E. Texas.

Comments: The burying behavior of sand darters
reduces the time needed to maintain
themselves swimming, thus conserving
energy, and also offers protection from
predators.

---

243 Greenside Darter
(*Etheostoma blennioides*)

ventral head view

Description: To 6″ (15 cm). Elongate, robust; olive
above, *mottled with 6–7 dark saddles and
red-orange spots; yellowish below with dark
green V- or W-shaped markings.* Snout
blunt; mouth small, horizontal,
overhung by snout; skin over upper lip
fused with skin on snout; *middle of
upper lip has nipplelike projection;* gill
membranes broadly connected. Pectoral
fins large; dorsal fins red with greenish-

blue edge, 12–15 spines, 12–14 rays;
anal fin blue-green; pelvic and anal fins
barred. Lateral line complete, 53–83
scales.

Habitat: Riffles of large, clear creeks and rivers
with moderate to swift current over
gravel or rocks.

Range: SE. Ontario; from New York to W.
North Carolina, N. Georgia, and N.
Alabama; S. Michigan, E. Illinois; S.
Missouri and SE. Kansas to S.
Arkansas.

Related Species: Rock Darter (*E. rupestre*) lacks fusion of
skin on snout with upper lip; pelvic
and anal fins clear to dusky; occurs in
similar habitat in Mobile Bay drainage,
in NW. Georgia, Alabama, and E.
Mississippi.

Comments: The Greenside Darter is the largest
species in the genus *Etheostoma*. It lives
3 to 4 years.

221 Slackwater Darter
(*Etheostoma boschungi*)

Description: To 2½" (6.5 cm). Moderately stout,
compressed; back olive to brown with 3
dark saddles, 3–5 lighter blotches;
sides with greenish-black blotches,
often forming band posteriorly;
yellowish-olive below, orange in
breeding males. *Frenum broad; eye longer
than snout, dark blue-black bar under eye;*
gill membranes narrowly joined. First
dorsal fin orange, base blue-green,
other fins spotted; 2 anal fin spines.
*Lateral line incomplete, 30–40 pored
scales;* 43–58 scales in lateral series.

frenum

Habitat: Edges of clear, small-to-medium size
streams with moderate current around
leaf litter and detritus.

Range: Tennessee River drainage, S. central
Tennessee and N. Alabama.

Related Species: Trispot Darter (*E. trisella*) has single
anal fin spine; lateral line complete,
44–52 scales; occurs in similar habitat
in Coosa River drainage, from

SE. Tennessee to NW. Georgia and
NE. Alabama.

Comments: The Slackwater Darter leaves its stream
in January and February and moves into
the marshy seepage areas of pastures to
spawn. Eventually both the larvae,
about ½″ (1 cm) long, and the adults
return to the stream. This darter lives 2
to 3 years.

230 Rainbow Darter
(*Etheostoma caeruleum*)

Description: To 3″ (7.5 cm). Robust, deepest under
first dorsal fin; olive to yellowish-green
above, bluish-green below; *encircled by
8–11 dark blue-green bands,* space
between posterior bands reddish.
Snout pointed; frenum present; gill
membranes reddish orange, narrowly
joined. First dorsal fin reddish with
wide, blue edge; second dorsal and
caudal fins with narrow, blue edge,
reddish below; *anal fin blue-green, base
reddish. Lateral line incomplete, 12–30
pored scales.*

Habitat: Riffles of clear, swift creeks and small
rivers over gravel or rocks.

Range: SE. Ontario; from W. New York west
to S. Minnesota, south to N. Alabama
and N. Arkansas; SW. Mississippi and
E. Louisiana.

Comments: The Rainbow Darter is sensitive to
pollution and silt. It spawns in clean
gravel riffles from March through June.
Its maximum age is about 4 years.

227 Iowa Darter
(*Etheostoma exile*)

Description: To 3″ (7.5 cm). Slender; olive above
with 7–9 dark blotches; *sides have 10–
12 dark, squarish midlateral blotches* with
dark red between; belly yellow-orange.
Frenum present; gill membranes

narrowly joined. *Dorsal fins separate,* base and edge of first dorsal fin blue, center red; soft dorsal and caudal fins have brown spots forming bars. *Caudal peduncle long and slender. Lateral line incomplete,* 18–35 pored scales; 45–63 scales in lateral series; *5–6 scale rows above lateral line.*

Habitat: Quiet, cool, clear waters of streams and lakes with vegetation over sand, mud, clay, or organic detritus.

Range: From S. Quebec west to Alberta; New York west to E. Montana, south to Ohio, and west to SE. Wyoming and NE. Colorado.

Related Species: Slough Darter (*E. gracile*) has greenish bars on sides; lateral line arched anteriorly, 3–4 scale rows above it; occurs in sluggish streams over mud, silt, or detritus, from central Illinois and N. Missouri south to S. Mississippi and west to S. Texas.

Comments: The Iowa Darter spawns from April to June in quiet, shallow water, depositing eggs on the roots and stems of plants.

---

238 Fantail Darter
(*Etheostoma flabellare*)

Description: To 3″ (7.5 cm). Deep, compressed; back olive-brown, *sides lighter with narrow, dark stripes* and dusky bars, belly yellowish orange. Frenum present; gill membranes broadly connected. *First dorsal fin in adult males has fleshy knobs at tips of 6–9 low spines,* edge orange; second dorsal and caudal fins orange with dark bars; *caudal fin rounded.* Lateral line incomplete, 15–36 pored scales; 45–60 scales in lateral series.

Habitat: Clear, cool streams with moderate to swift current over gravel or rocks.

Range: SW. Quebec and SE. Ontario; from New York west to S. Minnesota, south to North Carolina, N. Alabama, and N. Arkansas.

Related Species: Stripetail Darter (*E. kennicotti*) lacks stripes on sides; has fewer than 45 scales in lateral series; occurs from S. Illinois south to SW. Virginia and N. Alabama. Spottail Darter (*E. squamiceps*) lacks stripes on sides; has 45–56 scales in lateral series; occurs from S. Illinois, and SW. Indiana south to N. Alabama. Both in similar habitat.

Comments: The Fantail Darter spawns upside down under flat rocks, which the male scrapes clean with the fleshy tips of its dorsal fin. After spawning, the male remains with the eggs until they hatch.

---

248 Swamp Darter
(*Etheostoma fusiforme*)

Description: To 2″ (5 cm). Elongate; back dark olive with 8–12 dark blotches, *sides tan to greenish, mottled, often with midlateral blotches,* belly whitish with dark specks. *Snout shorter than eye, decurved; frenum present; strong opercular spine;* gill membranes narrowly joined. 9–11 dorsal fin spines, 10–12 soft rays, first dorsal fin with dark bands; *caudal fin barred, 3 dark spots at base;* caudal peduncle long, slender. Lateral line arched upward, incomplete, 5–30 pored scales.

Habitat: Clear or dark, stained, sluggish coastal streams, ponds, and swamps with vegetation over mud, sand, and detritus.

Range: From S. Maine to Florida, west to SE. Oklahoma and E. Texas; W. Tennessee and E. Arkansas south to Louisiana.

Related Species: Sawcheek Darter (*E. serriferum*) has serrate preopercle; 13–15 second dorsal fin rays, 4 black spots at base of caudal fin; occurs in similar habitat from S. Virginia to E. Georgia.

Comments: The Swamp Darter is common over most of its range, but little is known of its life history and habits.

232 Spotted Darter
(*Etheostoma maculatum*)

Description: To 3" (7.5 cm). Deep, compressed;
dark olive-brown above; *sides lighter
with dusky spots, males with many bright
red spots.* Snout pointed, longer than
eye; frenum present; *gill membranes
narrowly joined.* Median fins olive to
reddish in males, dark-spotted with
light edges in females; paired fins
lighter. Caudal peduncle deep. *Lateral
line usually complete, 52–67 scales;* if
incomplete, last 1–5 scales unpored;
cheeks unscaled, opercles scaled.

Habitat: Clear, swift water of larger creeks and
rivers over rocks or rubble.

Range: From SW. New York and W.
Pennsylvania west to N. Indiana,
south to SW. North Carolina and E.
Tennessee.

Related Species: Bluebreast Darter (*E. camurum*) has soft
dorsal, anal, and caudal fins with black
edges; caudal peduncle has narrow,
dark lines; occurs in similar habitat
from NW. Pennsylvania west to E.
Illinois, south to S. central Tennessee.

Comments: The Spotted Darter spawns during May
and June in riffles 6" to 24" (15 to
61 cm) deep, depositing its eggs in a
wedge-shaped mass on the underside of
a rock. These nests, guarded by males,
are at least 4' (1.2 m) apart.

---

249 Johnny Darter
(*Etheostoma nigrum*)

no frenum

Description: To 2½" (6.5 cm). Slender; *yellowish to
straw-colored,* usually with 5–7 dark
saddles and *small, dark X-, V-, and W-
shaped markings on sides,* often merging
to form zigzag lines; breeding males
blackish. Snout blunt, decurved; no
frenum; dark lines from snout to eye
not joined at midline; gill membranes
narrowly joined. Fins have rows of dark
spots forming bands; spots dusky in

breeding males; pectoral fins vary from clear to barred; 1 anal fin spine, 7–9 soft rays. *Lateral line nearly complete, 40–55 scales;* cheeks usually unscaled.

Habitat: Pools near riffles in clear to slightly turbid creeks and rivers over sand, gravel, or rocks; lake shores.

Range: From S. Quebec and S. Hudson Bay drainage to E. Saskatchewan; Atlantic Coast drainages in S. Virginia and N. North Carolina; upper Mississippi River and Great Lakes drainages west to SE. Wyoming and NE. Colorado and south to SW. Arkansas; Mobile Bay drainage in Alabama and Mississippi.

Related Species: Bluntnose Darter (*E. chlorosomum*) has dark bridle around snout; lateral line incomplete, less than 25 pored scales; cheeks scaled; occurs in sluggish streams over mud, sand, or clay in Mississippi Valley from SE. Minnesota south to Louisiana; from E. Alabama to S. Texas in Gulf Coast drainages.

Comments: This is the most widespread species in the genus *Etheostoma*. It is food for game fishes, but is not an important forage fish. One of the easiest darters to maintain in captivity, it is often used in behavioral studies.

247 Tessellated Darter
(*Etheostoma olmstedi*)

Description: To 3½″ (9 cm). Elongate; olive-brown above with 6 dark saddles, upper sides mottled with zigzags and *9–11 dark midlateral X- and W-shaped markings,* yellowish below. Gill membranes narrowly joined. Fins large; pelvic and anal fins black in males; dorsal and caudal fins have thin, alternating dark and light bands; 1–2 anal fin spines, 6–9 soft rays. *Lateral line complete, 37–58 scales;* cheeks and opercles scaled or unscaled.

Habitat: Clear pools in streams with slow

current over sand, mud, or gravel; lake shores.

Range: St. Lawrence and Lake Ontario drainages in S. Quebec and SE. Ontario; Atlantic Coast drainages to NE. Florida.

Comments: The Tessellated Darter spawns in a nest cavity, usually under rocks, logs, or other debris. The eggs are deposited in a single layer over an area 1″ to 3″ (2.5 to 7.5 cm) wide. Occasionally 3 or 4 males may maintain territories under the same rock. The common name refers to the checkered pattern of the lateral markings.

220 Stippled Darter
(*Etheostoma punctulatum*)

Description: To 3½″ (9 cm). Moderately deep, compressed; brownish above with 4 prominent, dark saddles, sides have broad midlateral blue-green band posteriorly, males bright red-orange below. Snout longer than eye; frenum present; *broad, black bar under eye;* gill membranes narrowly joined, red-orange in males. First dorsal fin has orange edge and black base in males, lighter in females; other fins spotted. *Lateral line incomplete, 35–50 pored scales; 58–80 scales in lateral series.*

Habitat: Quiet pools in cool, clear creeks with moderate current over clean gravel or rocks.

Range: S. Missouri, N. Arkansas, SE. Kansas, and NE. Oklahoma.

Related Species: Arkansas Darter (*E. cragini*) has snout shorter than eye; lateral line incomplete, less than 25 pored scales; 40–55 scales in lateral series; inhabits small, clear springs and seepage areas with vegetation in Arkansas River drainage from NE. Arkansas to Colorado.

Comments: The Stippled Darter spawns during the spring and early summer. Other details of its life history are unknown.

222 Redline Darter
(*Etheostoma rufilineatum*)

Description: To 3½" (9 cm). Deep, compressed;
back olive-brown; *sides of males marked
with cream, red, orange, green, and dusky
dashes;* breast blue; females greenish
with dark bars. Snout short, pointed;
frenum present. Median fins have dark
greenish base, red band, and narrow
black edge in males; yellowish with
black spots in females. Caudal fin with
dark spot; cream spot at upper and
lower base in females. Lateral line
complete, 41–57 scales.

Habitat: Swift riffles of clear, cool creeks and
rivers over gravel or rocks.

Range: Cumberland and Tennessee river
drainages in SW. Virginia and S.
Kentucky, south to N. Georgia and N.
Alabama.

Comments: The Redline Darter is generally
common throughout its range. The
colors of the male and female are so
different that they are often thought to
be different species.

233 Tennessee Snubnose Darter
(*Etheostoma simoterum*)

Description: To 3" (7.5 cm). Robust anteriorly; back
olive with 8–10 dark saddles, *upper
sides tan with reddish scales often forming
zigzag lines,* dark, midlateral blotches
form irregular band, white below,
bright orange in males. *Snout very blunt,
strongly decurved; frenum narrow;* mouth
small, subterminal; gill membranes
broadly joined. *14 pectoral fin rays; 18–
22 caudal peduncle scale rows;* dorsal fins
dusky to black at base, dark spots or
bands near middle, outer portion
reddish.

Habitat: Riffles in clear, shallow water of creeks
and small rivers with moderate current
over sand, gravel, or rocks.

Range: SW. Virginia and W. North Carolina

south to N. Alabama.

Related Species: Blackside Snubnose Darter (*E. duryi*) lacks frenum; has 13 pectoral fin rays, 15–18 caudal peduncle scale rows; occurs in similar habitat in Tennessee River drainage in Tennessee, NW. Georgia, N. Alabama, and NE. Mississippi.

Comments: The more than 8 species of snubnose darters are closely related and therefore difficult to identify.

231 Orangethroat Darter
(*Etheostoma spectabile*)

Description: To 2½" (6.5 cm). Compressed, *deepest at dorsal fin origin;* olive above with 7–10 dark, square blotches; mottled, *sides with 7–10 blue-green bands alternating with red-orange areas;* belly pale blue-green. Cheeks ivory; gill membranes orange, narrowly joined. First dorsal fin has reddish base, center cream to orange, edge blue-green; *pelvic and anal fins blue-green;* caudal fin dusky to olive with 2 orange spots at base. *Lateral line incomplete,* 15–25 pored scales.

Habitat: Riffles in clear creeks with moderate to swift current over gravel or rock.

Range: W. Ohio, SE. Michigan, S. Iowa, and W. Nebraska south to Tennessee, west to S. Arkansas and S. central Texas.

Comments: The Orangethroat Darter spawns in shallow gravel riffles during the early spring. After hatching, the fry move into pools near the nest of a Smallmouth Bass, which defends the nest and protects them along with its own young.

229 Speckled Darter
(*Etheostoma stigmaeum*)

Description: To 2½" (6.5 cm). Slender; yellow-brown above with 5–7 dark saddles,

8–10 dark midlateral blotches becoming bright blue bars in breeding males, belly yellowish. Snout slopes downward; *no frenum;* gill membranes narrowly joined; lower side of head blue in males. First dorsal fin with 10–12 spines, blue base, orange band near center, black edge; *pelvic, second dorsal, anal, and caudal fins dusky. Lateral line incomplete, 21–50 pored scales.*

Habitat: Pools and riffles in clear creeks and small rivers with moderate current over sand, gravel, or rocks.

Range: From S. Kentucky, S. Missouri, and SE. Kansas south to W. Florida and E. Texas.

Related Species: Blueside Darter (*E. jessiae*) has frenum; found in similar habitat in Tennessee River drainage in Tennessee, NW. Georgia, and N. Alabama.

Comments: The Speckled Darter spawns from late March to May. Eggs are deposited in gravel and fertilized, then abandoned. This species is common over most of its range.

224 Gulf Darter
(*Etheostoma swaini*)

Description: To 2½" (6.5 cm). Moderately elongate, compressed; olive above, with 7–9 dark saddles; sides brownish, *males with 5–7 red-orange bars posteriorly,* belly of males yellow-orange to red. Snout short, pointed; frenum present; gill membranes narrowly joined. *Dorsal fins have red and blue bands, dusky blue edge;* bases of pelvic, anal, and caudal fins bluish; fins spotted in females. *Lateral line complete or almost so, up to 7 unpored scales;* 35–48 scales in lateral series.

Habitat: Clear creeks and small rivers over sand or gravel, vegetation, or detritus.

Range: From W. Kentucky and W. Tennessee south to SW. Georgia and W. Florida west to E. Louisiana.

Related Species: Mud Darter (*E. asprigene*) has spots

forming bars on soft dorsal fin of male;
more than 8 unpored scales in lateral
series; occurs in sluggish lowland
streams and ponds over mud, sand, or
detritus in Mississippi River valley
from Minnesota south to Louisiana and
E. Texas.

Comments: Almost nothing is known about the life
history of this species except that it
spawns during the spring.

225 Striped Darter
(*Etheostoma virgatum*)

Description: To 3″ (7.5 cm). Slender, elongate;
olive-brown above with 6–7 small,
dark saddles, *sides have 10 narrow stripes
and 9–11 dusky midlateral blotches.*
Snout pointed; frenum present; *cheeks
dusky with bicolored bar,* red above,
silvery below; gill membranes narrowly
joined. In males, first dorsal fin black
at base, edge reddish; second dorsal,
anal, and caudal fins reddish orange;
anal fin has blue edge. Fins of females
have spots forming bars. Caudal
peduncle long. *Lateral line incomplete,
6–20 pored scales.*

Habitat: Pools in creeks and small rivers with
slow to moderate current over flat
bedrock, sand, or gravel.

Range: Cumberland River drainage in SE.
Kentucky and central Tennessee.

Related Species: Teardrop Darter (*E. barbouri*) lacks
narrow stripes; has well-defined
dark bar below eye; occurs in similar
habitat and range in Green River
system. Barcheek Darter (*E. obeyense*)
lacks stripes on sides; occurs in
similar habitat and range in Cumberland
River drainage.

Comments: The Striped Darter spawns during the
spring. The female deposits the eggs on
the undersurface of a flat rock and the
male guards them until they hatch.

250 Glassy Darter
(*Etheostoma vitreum*)

Description: To 2½" (6.5 cm). Elongate; *translucent with yellowish wash,* 7–9 dark mid-dorsal blotches, upper sides have small, black spots, *6–9 dark, midlateral dashes;* breeding males dusky to black. Head pointed. *Fins plain;* pectoral fins very large; 7–9 dorsal fin spines, 11–14 soft rays; 1–2 anal fin spines, 6–9 soft rays. *Lateral line complete, 47–62 scales.* Scales strongly ctenoid, rough, *cheek and opercle scaled,* breast and back anterior to dorsal fin unscaled.

Habitat: Creeks and small rivers with moderate current over sand or gravel.

Range: Atlantic Coast streams from N. Maryland south to central North Carolina.

Comments: During spawning season in March and April, males and females gather over rocks or logs in fast currents where the eggs are deposited and fertilized. This communal spawning is unique among darters. The Glassy Darter is also the only species of *Etheostoma* that spends most of its time partially buried in the sand.

223 Redfin Darter
(*Etheostoma whipplei*)

Description: To 3½" (9 cm). Compressed; olive above with 8–10 dark saddles; sides have 6–9 dark blotches, *males with red spots;* yellow-orange below. Snout long, pointed; frenum present; gill membranes narrowly joined. *Median fins of males have reddish base and blue edge, spotted in females;* 2 red spots at base of caudal fin. Lateral line incomplete, more than 40 pored scales, *59–70 scales in lateral series.*

Habitat: Creeks and rivers with moderate to swift current over gravel or sand.

Range: From E. Alabama west to N. Arkansas,

SW. Missouri, and SE. Kansas south to
E. Texas.

Related Species: Orangebelly Darter (*E. radiosum*) lacks
red spots; has larger scales, 49–62 in
lateral series; occurs in similar habitat
in SW. Arkansas and SE. Oklahoma.

Comments: The Redfin Darter spawns in gravel
riffles during March and April. It feeds
on aquatic insects and other
invertebrates.

---

240 Banded Darter
(*Etheostoma zonale*)

Description: To 3″ (7.5 cm). Elongate; back olive
with 6–7 dark saddles, *sides greenish-
yellow, dusky midlateral band with 9–12
green bars,* belly greenish. Snout short,
blunt, decurved; frenum present; *no
dark spots on cheek and opercle;* gill
membranes broadly joined, greenish.

Pectoral fins plain, rounded, 14–15
soft rays; pelvic and anal fins greenish;
dorsal fins have reddish base, green
band, and clear to dusky edge; 2 anal
fin spines, first enlarged, 6–9 soft rays.
Lateral line complete, 38–58 scales.

Habitat: Riffles and shoals in large creeks and
rivers with moderate to swift current
over gravel, sand, or rubble.

Range: Mississippi River system from W.
New York west to Wisconsin and
Minnesota, south to E. Louisiana;
Susquehanna River drainage in
Pennsylvania; coastal streams in
Mississippi.

Comments: There are 2 subspecies of this wide-
ranging darter. Both spawn in riffles
between April and June, depositing
their eggs in the algae and on moss
growing on the surface of stones and
boulders. The Banded Darter reaches
maturity in 1 to 2 years and lives no
more than 4 years.

89 Yellow Perch
(*Perca flavescens*)

Description: To 15″ (38 cm); 4¼ lbs (1.9 kg).
Oblong, moderately compressed; brassy
green to golden yellow above with *5–8
dusky bars across back almost to belly.*
Mouth extends to middle of eye; *no
canine teeth; preopercle serrate.* Dorsal and
caudal fins dusky to olive; pelvic and
anal fins light grayish green to reddish
orange; *dorsal fins separate; 2 anal fin
spines,* 6–8 soft rays. Lateral line
complete, 53–59 scales; cheek and
opercle scaled.

Habitat: Open areas in streams, lakes, ponds,
and reservoirs with clear water and
aquatic vegetation.

Range: From Nova Scotia to Alberta; Great
Slave Lake south to Montana. Atlantic
Coast from St. Lawrence River drainage
south to South Carolina; Great Lakes
drainage; south in Mississippi River
drainage to Missouri; Gulf drainages of
W. Florida and extreme S. Alabama.
Introduced outside native range.

Comments: The Yellow Perch lives in schools in
deep water, and moves into shallower
areas to feed at dawn and dusk. It is a
sport and food fish and is harvested
commercially in parts of Canada and
the Great Lakes. Anglers use minnows,
worms, and other fishes as live bait.

239 Logperch
(*Percina caprodes*)

Description: To 7″ (18 cm). Elongate, almost
cylindrical; olive to yellowish with *15–
22 dark saddles above,* yellowish below.
*Head cone-shaped; snout pointed, extends
beyond mouth;* frenum present; gill
membranes narrowly joined. First
dorsal fin with 14–16 spines, black
base, often with orange band, narrow
black edge; second dorsal and caudal
fins have rows of dark spots; other fins

plain; *caudal spot usually present.* Lateral line complete, 71–91 scales.

Habitat: Riffles and pools of moderate to large streams over sand, gravel, or rocks; lakes and reservoirs.

Range: From Quebec west to Saskatchewan; Hudson River drainage in Vermont and New York; St. Lawrence, Great Lakes, and Mississippi River systems; Gulf Coast drainages from W. Florida west to Mississippi and E. Texas.

Related Species: Bigscale Logperch (*P. macrolepida*) lacks yellow-orange band on dorsal fin; occurs in similar habitat in S. Oklahoma, Texas, and E. New Mexico; introduced in California.

Comments: The Logperch is the most widespread species in the genus *Percina,* but has disappeared from streams contaminated by silt and pollution. It feeds on aquatic insects, frequently using its long snout to flip stones in search of prey.

235, 236 Bluestripe Darter
(*Percina cymatotaenia*)

Description: To 4″ (10 cm). Elongate, moderately compressed; dark olive-brown above, *sides have irregular, usually brownish-black midlateral band with blue-green stripe and wavy cream to yellowish stripe above,* cream to yellow below. Head short; eye large; gill membranes narrowly joined.

Fins have faint rows of dark spots forming bars; first dorsal fin has dusky edge; *base of caudal fin yellowish with black spot.* Lateral line complete, 64–73 scales.

Habitat: Pools and backwaters of large creeks and small rivers over sand, gravel, vegetation or debris.

Range: Gasconade and Osage river drainages in S. central Missouri.

Comments: The Bluestripe Darter feeds on aquatic insects and other invertebrates. It spawns during May in gravel riffles.

228 Gilt Darter
(*Percina evides*)

Description: To 3″ (7.5 cm). Moderately stout, compressed; dark olive with *6–8 dark saddles terminating in large, dark, midlateral blotches,* yellow-orange below. Head and snout short, decurved; frenum present; dark bar under eye; cheeks orange; gill membranes yellow-orange, narrowly joined. Pelvic and anal fins blue-black; first dorsal fin dusky to orange, edge transparent; soft dorsal and caudal fins dusky. Lateral line complete, 52–67 scales.

Habitat: Clear, deep, swift riffles of large creeks and rivers over gravel, rubble, or boulders.

Range: From W. New York to Mississippi River system in N. Wisconsin and E. Minnesota, south to N. Georgia, N. Alabama, and N. Arkansas.

Related Species: Bronze Darter (*P. palmaris*) has 10–11 dark saddles; occurs in similar habitat in Coosa and Tallapoosa river drainages in NW. Georgia and E. Alabama.

Comments: During the spring and summer, adult male Gilt Darters are found in deep, swift shoals, while females and young males stay in the adjacent shallows. In the winter all move into deeper pools. Their maximum life span is about 4 years.

242 Blackside Darter
(*Percina maculata*)

Description: To 4″ (10 cm). Elongate, moderately robust; back greenish brown with 7–10 dark saddles or uniformly brown, upper sides dusky to yellow, lower sides yellowish; *7–9 oval, blue-black midlateral blotches connected by dusky band.* Snout pointed; frenum present; gill membranes narrowly joined. Median fins dusky or with rows of dark spots forming bars; *black spot at base of caudal*

fin. Lateral line complete, 57–70 scales.

Habitat: Riffles and pools of large creeks and rivers over sand, gravel, or rocks, often around vegetation and debris; uncommon in lakes.

Range: From SE. Ontario to S. Manitoba and SE. Saskatchewan; Great Lakes and Mississippi River system; Gulf Coast drainages from Alabama west to Texas.

Related Species: Longhead Darter (*P. macrocephala*) has dark, broad, midlateral band with light stripe above; occurs in similar habitat from W. New York south to W. North Carolina, west to W. Kentucky.

Comments: Unlike most darters, the Blackside Darter swims in midwater during the day and rests on the bottom at night. The young feed on very small crustaceans, but change their diet to aquatic insects when they reach 1½″ to 2½″ (4 to 6.5 cm). This species lives up to 4 years.

234 Blackbanded Darter
(*Percina nigrofasciata*)

Description: To 4″ (10 cm). Elongate, stout; yellowish-tan to dark brown above with darker saddles; whitish below; *dark, midlateral band with 10–15 blotches, diamond-shaped in front, oval in back.* Snout pointed; frenum present; dusky bar under eye; gill membranes narrowly joined. Fins large, somewhat dusky; 11–13 dorsal fin spines, 11–12 soft rays; 2 anal fin spines, 8–10 soft rays; *caudal fin has 3 small, dark blotches at base.* Lateral line complete, 50–64 scales.

Habitat: Riffles of creeks and small rivers with moderate current over rocks, sand, or gravel with vegetation or detritus.

Range: Coastal Plain drainages from South Carolina to E. Louisiana; south in Florida peninsula to Lake Okeechobee.

Related Species: Dusky Darter (*P. sciera*) has oval,

midlateral blotches; 2 lower blotches on caudal fin base merge; occurs in riffles of large creeks and rivers over sand or gravel from West Virginia and N. Indiana south to N. and W. Alabama, west to SE. Oklahoma and central Texas.

Comments: The Blackbanded Darter can change its color pattern rapidly to match its background. Its diet is primarily aquatic insects. Spawning occurs during May and June.

---

237 Shield Darter
(*Percina peltata*)

Description: To 3″ (7.5 cm). Elongate, stout; yellowish to tan above, yellowish to white below, *dark blotch on nape with inner, oval, light spot;* upper sides have 6–7 blackish saddles connected by dark, wavy, narrow line; *large, dark blotches and small, lighter, squarish ones form midlateral band.* Snout moderately blunt; dark bar under eye and on midline of chin. First dorsal fin has black base with clear band, marginal band dusky; second dorsal and caudal fins spotted. Lateral line complete, 52–64 scales.

Habitat: Riffles of creeks and rivers with moderate to swift current over vegetation, and in riffles over gravel and rubble.

Range: Atlantic Coast drainages from SE. New York to S. North Carolina.

Related Species: Stripeback Darter (*P. notogramma*) lacks black bar on midline of chin, has oval midlateral blotches; occurs in similar habitat from S. Maryland south to James River drainage in S. Virginia.

Comments: The large, specialized scales on the belly of the male Shield Darter are important for stimulating the female during spawning. The spawning period extends from mid-April through May.

226 Slenderhead Darter
(*Percina phoxocephala*)

Description: To 4″ (10 cm). Elongate, slender;
yellow-brown; 14–20 dark saddles
above; *dusky midlateral band with 10–15
dark blotches.* Head long, slender; *snout
pointed, extends just beyond upper jaw;*
frenum present; gill membranes
broadly joined, 6 branchiostegal rays.
First dorsal fin has orange band, dark
edge; second dorsal and caudal fins have
dark spots; other fins plain; *caudal fin
base with black spot.* Lateral line
complete, 62–74 scales.

Habitat: Riffles over gravel or rocks and pools
over sand in rivers and larger creeks
with moderate to swift current.

Range: From Ohio to Wisconsin, S.
Minnesota, and NE. South Dakota,
south to N. Alabama, west to SE.
Kansas and E. Oklahoma.

Related Species: Longnose Darter (*P. nasuta*) has longer
snout; 6–7 branchiostegal rays; occurs
in similar habitat in White and
Arkansas river drainages from S.
Missouri to N. Arkansas and E.
Oklahoma.

Comments: The male Slenderhead Darter moves to
its spawning grounds in May and
establishes a territory in shallow, swift,
gravel riffles. After spawning in May
and June, it returns to deeper water.
The numbers of this species have
declined in some silty streams.

241 Snail Darter
(*Percina tanasi*)

Description: To 3″ (7.5 cm). Robust, thick
anteriorly; back olive-brown with 4
*broad, dark saddles extending to lateral
line, first under anterior dorsal fin spines;*
sides have midlateral blotches; pale
green to yellowish below. Head small;
snout decurved; mouth almost horizontal.
Fins large; pelvic and anal fins clear;

other fins with dark spots forming bars on rays; pectoral fins rounded, in males extend to lateral line scale 17–19; 11–12 anal fin rays. Lateral line complete, 49–56 scales.

Habitat: Clean gravel riffles and shoals in clear, medium to large streams.

Range: Tennessee River drainage in SE. Tennessee, NW. Georgia, and NE. Alabama.

Related Species: Amber Darter (*P. antesella*) has 4 narrow saddles, first anterior to dorsal fin; occurs in upper Coosa River drainage, SE. Tennessee and NW. Georgia. Saddleback Darter (*P. ouachitae*) has 5 saddles; occurs from S. Indiana, SE. Missouri south to W. Florida, west to Arkansas and Louisiana. Both in similar habitat.

Comments: The Snail Darter became the focus of a legal controversy in 1977 when its status as an endangered species delayed construction of a dam in the Tennessee Valley that threatened its habitat. Congress eventually passed legislation exempting that dam project from the Endangered Species Act.

99 Sauger
(*Stizostedion canadense*)

Description: To 28″ (71 cm); 8¾ lbs (4 kg). Elongate, almost cylindrical; gray to dull brown, sides brassy to orange with dark markings, often *with 3–4 dark saddles extending to middle of sides,* belly whitish. *Mouth extends past middle of eye;* canine teeth present; preopercle partially serrate. Dorsal fins separate; first dorsal has 2–3 rows of small, black spots and narrow, dusky edge; second dorsal fin has 2 light, narrow bands; caudal fin forked. Lateral line complete, with 85–95 scales.

Habitat: Dingy, turbid waters of large creeks and rivers with moderate to swift current; also lakes and reservoirs.

Range: From Quebec to Alberta; St. Lawrence River and Great Lakes; Mississippi River drainage south to Tennessee, N. Alabama, and Arkansas. Introduced outside native range.

Comments: The Sauger is an important sport and food fish and is harvested commercially in parts of Canada. It eats a variety of small fishes and aquatic invertebrates, which it locates with its large eyes.

---

98 Walleye
(*Stizostedion vitreum*)

Description: To 3' 5" (1 m); 25 lbs (11.3 kg). Elongate, slightly compressed; olive-brown to brassy greenish-yellow above with *dusky to black mottlings,* belly whitish with yellow-green tinge. *Mouth extends to eye,* has canine teeth; preopercle serrate. Dorsal fins separate; first dorsal fin dusky with black edge, *black blotch on membranes of last 2–3 spines;* caudal fin forked, tip of lower lobe white. Lateral line complete, 82–92 scales.

Habitat: Deep waters of large streams, lakes, and reservoirs over firm sand, gravel, or rocks.

Range: From S. Hudson Bay drainage west to MacKenzie River; south through Great Lakes and Mississippi River system to Arkansas. E. Gulf drainage, Alabama and Mississippi. Widely introduced.

Comments: The Walleye is the largest North American species in the perch family and one of the most sought sport and food fishes. The largest catch was taken in Old Hickory Lake, Tennessee, in 1960. The Walleye feeds on aquatic insects, crustaceans, amphibians, and almost any available species of fish.

BIGEYES
(Family Priacanthidae)

These small to medium-sized fishes are easily distinguished by the deep body and very big eyes. The mouth is large and quite oblique, and the lower jaw projects beyond the upper. There is a single, continuous dorsal fin, and the large, anteriorly placed pelvic fins are broadly joined to the body by a membrane. In addition, the anal fin has 3 spines, the scales are ctenoid, and the lateral line does not extend onto the caudal fin. There are 5 species in North America.

386 Bigeye
(Priacanthus arenatus)

Description: To 16″ (41 cm). Compressed, *depth one-third length; bright red, pelvic fins black.* Profile of head less curved above than below, nearly straight from snout to dorsal fin origin. Mouth large, oblique; lower jaw projects well beyond upper; *preopercular spine very small;* eyes large, diameter greater than length of snout. Pelvic fins connected to body by membrane; dorsal fin continuous, without notch; anal fin evenly rounded; caudal fin emarginate.

Habitat: Coral reefs and over rocks, to about 72′ (22 m).

Range: From Massachusetts south to Argentina, including Bermuda, Gulf of Mexico, and West Indies.

Related Species: Glasseye Snapper (*P. cruentatus*) grows to 12″ (30 cm), depth about two-fifths length; not uniformly bright red; preopercular spine strong; nocturnal; occurs in shallower water from New Jersey to Rio de Janeiro, Brazil; Bermuda and Gulf of Mexico.

Comments: The Bigeye and Glasseye Snapper are carnivores and feed on small fishes, crustaceans, and polychaete worms.

387 Short Bigeye
(*Pristigenys alta*)

Description: To 10″ (25 cm). Compressed, *depth more than one-half length,* profiles about equally rounded above and below; *bright red, including fins; median fins have black margins.* Mouth very oblique; maxilla reaches middle of eye, lower jaw projects well beyond upper; eyes very large, diameter much greater than length of snout; *preopercle with 2 small spines at its lower angle.* Pectoral fin ray length about equal to eye diameter; pelvic fins reach beyond anal fin origin, attached by membrane to body; dorsal fin continuous, notched, spines strong; soft dorsal and anal fins acute posteriorly, reach past base of caudal rays; caudal fin truncate or slightly rounded. Scales strongly ctenoid.

Habitat: Over rocks, usually at depths exceeding 30′ (9.1 m).

Range: From Gulf of Maine to Florida, including Bermuda, Gulf of Mexico, and Cuba. Apparently uncommon in West Indies.

Comments: This is a secretive, bottom-dwelling fish; its rocky habitat provides hiding places. It also occurs at depths exceeding 100 fathoms.

CARDINALFISHES
(Family Apogonidae)

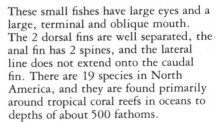

These small fishes have large eyes and a large, terminal and oblique mouth. The 2 dorsal fins are well separated, the anal fin has 2 spines, and the lateral line does not extend onto the caudal fin. There are 19 species in North America, and they are found primarily around tropical coral reefs in oceans to depths of about 500 fathoms.

378 Flamefish
(*Apogon maculatus*)

Description: To 4″ (10 cm). Elongate, caudal
peduncle deep; *bright red with dusky
band on head between eye and opercle,*
round, black spot under second dorsal
fin, *dark, dusky saddle on caudal peduncle.*
Mouth large, terminal, oblique; eyes
large; small villiform teeth in jaws and
roof of mouth; posterior edge of
preopercle finely serrate. 2 dorsal fins
separate; 2 anal fin spines. Scales
ctenoid; lateral line does not reach
caudal fin.

Habitat: Coral and rock reefs, and around oil
platforms.

Range: From New England to Venezuela,
including Bermuda and Gulf of
Mexico, but primarily in tropics.

Related Species: Guadalupe Cardinalfish (*A.
guadalupensis*) has body bluish gray to
olive or purple above, red-orange
below; occurs in crevices from San
Clemente Island to Gulf of California.

Commnents: The Flamefish occurs frequently in
shallow waters of the West Indies,
where it is the most common
cardinalfish. It hides by day and is
active at night. Like all other
cardinalfishes, this species practices oral
incubation, holding the eggs in the
mouth while they develop.

TILEFISHES
(Family Malacanthidae)

These basslike fishes have very long,
continuous dorsal and anal fins that
consist mostly of soft rays. The body
form varies from robust to elongate and
slender. Most species have some sort of
ridge or fleshy keel on the nape, and
they have a single, flat spine on the
opercle. In North America there are
7 species, which are usually found in
deep water.

553 Ocean Whitefish
(*Caulolatilus princeps*)

Description: To 3'4" (1 m). Fusiform, compressed, head profile blunt; yellow-brown above, whitish below, fins yellowish. Dorsal fin continuous, *8–9 spines, 23–26 soft rays. Anal fin long,* has blue stripe, 1–2 spines, 23–25 soft rays.

Habitat: Over soft bottoms and reefs to 50 fathoms.

Range: From Vancouver Island, British Columbia, to Peru.

Similar Species: Yellowtail (*Seriola lalandei*) has short dorsal fin, 4–8 low spines separated from 31–39 soft rays.

Comments: Ocean Whitefishes have become popular with southern California anglers. They are good fighters and their flesh is very tasty. They feed on other fishes, squids, shrimps, pelagic red crabs, and hermit crabs.

471 Sand Tilefish
(*Malacanthus plumieri*)

Description: To 24" (61 cm). Elongate, relatively slender; dark bluish-green above, fading to pale blue below; pelvic fins white, pectoral fins clear, dorsal and anal fins mostly yellow with clear bands, caudal fin lobes yellowish orange. *Head pointed, not abruptly elevated, no ridge on nape;* strong, flat spine on opercle. Dorsal fin long, low, continuous; anal fin similar; *caudal fin falcate.*

Habitat: Over sand and rubble to about 25 fathoms.

Range: From Cape Lookout, North Carolina, to Santos, Brazil, including Bermuda, Gulf of Mexico, and West Indies.

Related Species: Tilefish (*Lopholatilus chamaeleonticeps*) has more robust body; nape has fleshy flap; occurs on continental shelf to 200 fathoms from Labrador to Gulf of Mexico.

Comments: The young of the Sand Tilefish are
pelagic, but adults are bottom-dwellers
and build refuges of sand and rubble
into which they retreat when disturbed.

BLUEFISHES
(Family Pomatomidae)

This family is represented by 3 species
worldwide, 1 of which occurs in North
America. These marine fishes, known
for their voracious feeding habits, kill
more fishes than they need as food.
Bluefishes have also been known to
attack people.

556 Bluefish
(Pomatomus saltatrix)

Description: To 3′7″ (1.1 m); 31¾ lbs (14.4 kg).
Elongate, compressed; *greenish or
grayish-blue above, silvery below,* median
fins yellowish. Head large; mouth
large, terminal; *teeth prominent, sharp,
arranged in single series.* First dorsal fin
has 7–8 spines, separated from soft
dorsal fin by deep notch; anal fin with
2 spines, similar to soft dorsal; caudal
fin forked. Scales small, present on
head, body, and bases of fins; lateral
line complete, straight, follows dorsal
profile.

Habitat: Surface waters, near shore or offshore.

Range: From Nova Scotia to Argentina,
including Florida and Gulf of Mexico.

Similar Species: Cobia (*Rachycentron canadum*) has 2
narrow, silvery bands; head flattened;
dorsal fin with short, isolated spines.
Rainbow Runner (*Elagatis bipinnulata*)
has dorsal and anal finlets. Amberjacks
(*Seriola* spp.) have bands of minute teeth
in jaws; caudal peduncle has groove.

Comments: Bluefishes are voracious creatures, often
foraging on squids or schools of small
fishes. They are reported to feed until

their bellies are full, regurgitate, and feed again as long as food is present. They have been known to attack people. Bluefishes are exciting sport fishes and good food if consumed when fresh.

COBIAS
(Family Rachycentridae)

This family is represented by a single species worldwide. The depressed head, protruding lower jaw, and short, isolated dorsal spines distinguish Cobias from other species. Like their apparent relatives, the remoras, they linger around larger fishes for food scraps and protection.

586 Cobia
(*Rachycentron canadum*)

Description: To 6'7" (2 m); 110¼ lbs (50 kg). Elongate, almost cylindrical; dark brown above with 2 narrow, silvery bands, belly gray or yellowish. *Head large, broad, flattened;* mouth terminal, lower jaw projects; teeth in villiform bands in jaws, on roof of mouth and tongue. *First dorsal fin has 7–9 (usually 8) short, disconnected spines;* second dorsal fin long, elevated anteriorly; anal fin smaller, similar to second dorsal; caudal fin rounded to slightly lunate. Scales small, embedded.

Habitat: Open seas; some also found near shore around barrier islands and coral reefs.

Range: From mid-Atlantic states to Argentina, including Gulf of Mexico, Antilles, and Caribbean; rarely found off Massachusetts.

Similar Species: Bluefish (*Pomatomus saltatrix*) has bluish body, lacks silvery bands; head not flattened. Sharksucker (*Echeneis naucrates*) has sucking disc.

Comments: Cobias are often seen basking on the surface around boats or flotsam, where they will take a hook baited with almost any fish, squid, or crustacean. They may be confused with remoras when viewed from the side.

REMORAS
(Family Echeneidae)

This is the only family of fishes that has a sucking disc on top of the head. This oval disc is a modified spiny dorsal fin. Remoras are elongated fishes with a superior mouth that opens just anterior to the disc. Remoras attach themselves

sucking disc to a variety of large marine fishes, mammals, and turtles, and sometimes to ships or other floating objects. They not only save energy and get a free ride, but also feed on scraps of food left by their hosts. There are 8 species in North America.

587 Sharksucker
(*Echeneis naucrates*)

Description: To 32″ (81 cm). *Very elongate, depth about one-tenth length, head about one-fifth length;* dark gray, brown, or blackish; belly whitish; *dark band from snout through eye to caudal fin, with whitish zone on each side.* Mouth superior; *oval sucking disc* present, usually with 23 lamellae. Dorsal and anal fins same shape, with long base and whitish edges.

Habitat: Open seas.

Range: From Nova Scotia to Brazil, including Gulf of Mexico.

Similar Species: Cobia (*Rachycentron canadum*) lacks sucking disc; has short, isolated dorsal spines.

Comments: This remora, unlike some others, is indiscriminate in choosing a host. It has been observed to remain with the

Bull Shark (*Carcharhinus leucas*) even in
fresh water.

JACKS
(Family Carangidae)

This is an extremely diverse family
without obvious unifying features.
Jacks are variable in body shape,
ranging from elongate and fusiform to
deep and strongly compressed. All have
forked caudal fins. Several genera have
scutes (modified scales with ridges) on
the lateral line. Most jacks are fast
swimmers; they usually form schools,
and range in habitat from inshore
brackish waters to open seas. Some
species are highly esteemed food and
game fishes, although a few have been
linked to ciguatera poisoning. There
are 38 species in North America.

345 African Pompano
(Alectis ciliaris)

Description: To 3′ (91 cm); 41½ lbs (18.8 kg).
Deep, compressed; metallic blue-green
above, silvery below. Snout blunt; eye
moderately large, with adipose eyelid.
Pectoral fins falcate, longer than head;
pelvic fins longer than maxilla; first dorsal
fin not persistent; *second dorsal and anal
fins falcate.* Paired keels at base of
forked caudal fin. Scales minute and
embedded; scutes inconspicuous.
Arched part of lateral line follows
dorsal profile of body.

Habitat: Young in open seas; adults usually near
bottom to about 30 fathoms.

Range: From Massachusetts south to Brazil,
including Gulf of Mexico and
Caribbean. Young more common in
north of range.

Comments: Young African Pompanos, up to 3″
(7.5 cm) long, have 4 bars on the sides.

Young up to 6″ (15 cm) have long, threadlike extensions on the first dorsal and anal fins; over 6″ the 7 dorsal and 2 anal spines disappear.

551   Crevalle Jack
(*Caranx hippos*)

Description: To 3′4″ (1 m); 54½ lbs (24.7 kg). Robust, somewhat compressed; anterior profile steep, greenish-blue or bluish-black above, sides silvery, *belly yellowish*. Head large, snout blunt; mouth terminal, lower jaw projecting, *maxilla reaches posterior of eye;* adipose eyelid present; *black spot on upper edge of opercle* and on pectoral fin base. Spinous dorsal fin dusky, persistent; other fins yellow; second dorsal and anal fins similar in size and shape; 2 anal spines well separated from anal fin rays. Well-developed scutes on caudal peduncle.

Habitat: From deep water of continental shelf to inshore shallow bays and estuaries. Enters fresh water in Florida.

Range: In Atlantic from Nova Scotia to Uruguay, including Gulf of Mexico and Caribbean; irregularly in West Indies. In Pacific from San Diego to tropical South America.

Comments: The Crevalle Jack is a large, fast, strong swimmer that gives plenty of excitement to the angler. It is primarily a bottom scavenger, but also will rise to the surface.

552   Horse-eye Jack
(*Caranx latus*)

Description: To 25″ (64 cm); 23⅛ lbs (10.5 kg). Elongate, moderately deep, depth about one-third length; dark blue to bluish-gray above, silvery-white or sometimes golden below; small, diffuse black spot on opercle or pectoral fin, tip of dorsal fin black, caudal fin yellow; young have 5–6 dark bars on body, 1 on nape. Head large; snout blunt; *maxilla reaches beyond eye; eye diameter equal to snout length;* adipose eyelid present. Pectoral fin falcate, longer than head; first dorsal fin persistent; second dorsal and anal fins similar. Scales small, cycloid; *chest scaled;* scutes on caudal peduncle well developed.

Habitat: Around islands, over sand, or offshore.

Range: From New Jersey to Rio de Janeiro, Brazil, including Gulf of Mexico, West Indies, and Caribbean.

Comments: This jack is usually found in small schools and feeds primarily on shrimps and other invertebrates.

555 Bar Jack
(*Caranx ruber*)

Description: To 22″ (56 cm). Elongate, moderately compressed, *dorsal and ventral profiles about equal;* bluish-gray above, silvery below, *dark bar from base of soft dorsal fin through caudal peduncle and onto lower lobe of caudal fin.* Mouth terminal, slightly oblique; maxilla not reaching eye. Pectoral fins falcate, reaching well beyond anal fin origin. Scutes on posterior of lateral line and caudal peduncle; 2 keels on caudal peduncle.

Habitat: Shallow, clear water, often over reefs.

Range: From New Jersey to Venezuela, including Gulf of Mexico, West Indies, and Caribbean.

Related Species: Pacific Crevalle Jack (*C. caninus*) has dark spot on edge of opercle; maxilla reaches mid-eye; occurs in shallows from San Diego, California, to tropical South America.

Comments: This species, common in the Bahamas, is often seen in schools; it rarely occurs in the northern Gulf of Mexico, perhaps because of its preference for very clear water.

Round Scad
(*Decapterus punctatus*)

Description: To 12" (30 cm). Very elongate, fusiform; greenish-blue fading to silver on sides, belly white; narrow, yellowish stripe from head to caudal peduncle; *black spot on upper edge of opercle.* Eye diameter almost equals length of snout; adipose eyelid present. *Dorsal fins well developed, well separated,* second long, low; anal fin similar but shorter, *both fins followed by single finlet.* Scutes in anterior arched part of lateral line not expanded, *those in posterior straight part prominent.*

finlet

Habitat: Midwater or bottom from shallow water to about 50 fathoms; sometimes at surface, especially young.

Range: From Massachusetts and Bermuda south to Brazil, including Caribbean and Gulf of Mexico.

Comments: The 2 small papillae on the shoulder girdle, as well as the finlets distinguish scads from other carangids. Although used as food in some areas, the Round Scad is primarily a bait fish.

558 Rainbow Runner
(*Elagatis bipinnulata*)

Description: To 4' (1.2 m); 33½ lbs (15.2 kg). *Very elongate, slender,* fusiform; blue-green above, silvery below, sides have broad olive-yellow stripe between 2 narrow, light blue stripes, fins dusky with yellowish tint. Head long, pointed; maxilla not reaching eye. Pectoral fins short; dorsal fin has 6 anterior spines separated from soft portion by deep notch; *finlet consisting of 2 rays behind soft dorsal and anal fins;* caudal fin large, deeply forked. *Caudal peduncle has grooves on upper and lower sides.* No scutes in lateral line.

Habitat: On or near surface of deep water; sometimes over reefs.

Range: From Massachusetts to N. Brazil,
including most of Gulf of Mexico,
Caribbean, and West Indies. In Pacific
from Cabo San Lucas, Baja California,
to N. South America.

Comments: The Rainbow Runner resembles the
Cobia, but is readily distinguished by
its bright colors and finlets. Often
seen in the company of sharks and
pilotfishes, it is highly esteemed as a
food and game fish.

559 Bigeye Scad
(*Selar crumenophthalmus*)

Description: To 11″ (28 cm). Elongate, fusiform,
moderately compressed; blue-green or
metallic blue above, silvery below,
snout and median fins dusky, pectoral
and pelvic fins clear. Mouth relatively
large and oblique, lower jaw projects
beyond upper; *eye diameter greater than
snout length,* adipose eyelid well
developed. Pectoral fins falcate, about
same length as head; first dorsal fin
triangular; no finlets; 2 anal spines
persistent. *Straight part of lateral line
with enlarged scutes,* smaller scutes in
curved portion.

Habitat: Inshore in shallow water.

Range: From Nova Scotia to Rio de Janeiro,
Brazil, including Bermuda, Gulf of
Mexico, Caribbean, and West Indies.

Related Species: Rough Scad (*Trachurus lathami*) has
well-developed scutes in curved part of
lateral line; occurs in similar habitat
along coast from Gulf of Maine to
Argentina; rarely in West Indies.

Comments: Bigeye Scads are schooling fishes, not
highly esteemed as food but commonly
used as bait, especially for Sailfishes.
There are unsubstantiated reports of
Bigeye Scads up to 24″ (61 cm) long.

544 Atlantic Moonfish
(*Selene setapinnis*)

Description: To 15" (38 cm). *Very deep, extremely compressed,* ventral profile more convex than dorsal; silvery, sometimes metallic blue above, fins clear, dusky or olive-yellow tints on soft dorsal and caudal fin lobes. Juveniles have black spot over straight part of lateral line. *Head profile bluntly rounded above, steep and concave in front of eye;* mouth terminal, lower jaw projects beyond upper. First dorsal fin with 8 spines, persistent; second dorsal and anal fins only slightly elongate anteriorly, not falcate. Scales small, cycloid; scutes hardly differentiated.

Habitat: Inshore on bottom.

Range: From Nova Scotia to Argentina, including Bermuda, Gulf of Mexico, Caribbean, and most of West Indies except Bahamas.

Comments: The Atlantic Moonfish is a schooling fish that may be abundant within limited areas during summer months. Although edible, it is rarely used as food in North America.

545 Lookdown
(*Selene vomer*)

Description: To 16" (41 cm). *Very deep, extremely compressed; dorsal and ventral profiles anteriorly straight and almost parallel.* Mostly metallic overall; bluish on back, silvery or golden elsewhere. *Profile of head very steep; mouth ventral; terminal,* lower jaw projecting. Pelvic fins very short, much shorter than maxilla; first dorsal fin has 8 spines, persistent; *second dorsal and anal fins long, falcate,* blackish; 2 anal spines reabsorbed. Scales small, cycloid, scutes hardly visible.

Habitat: Shallow coastal waters over sand or mud.

Range: From Maine to Uruguay, including

Bermuda, Gulf of Mexico, and Caribbean.

Comments: Unlike adults, the young have long pelvic fins and long filaments extending from the first dorsal spines. In adults, the second dorsal and anal fins are greatly extended. This change is complete by the time the fish reaches 4 to 5″ (10 to 12.5 cm).

554 Greater Amberjack
(*Seriola dumerili*)

Description: To 5′ (1.5 m); 155½ lbs (70.5 kg). Elongate, fusiform, slightly compressed; bluish or olive, sides have brownish or pinkish tinge, belly silvery or whitish; olive band from eye to origin of dorsal fin; sometimes has amber stripe on side from eye to tail. Mouth large and terminal, *maxilla very broad posteriorly, reaches middle of eye. Pectoral fins shorter than head,* equal to pelvic fins; *second dorsal much longer than anal fin.* Caudal peduncle relatively deep, *grooves present above and below at base of caudal fin.* No finlets or scutes.

Habitat: Open sea to 200 fathoms. Small specimens in shallow water.

Range: From Cape Cod to Brazil, including Bermuda, Gulf of Mexico, and Caribbean.

Comments: This large fish is sought by sport and commercial fishers. Some species of amberjacks are believed responsible for ciguatera poisoning.

557 Yellowtail
(*Seriola lalandei*)

Description: To 5′ (1.5 m); 111 lbs (50.3 kg). Elongate, fusiform, compressed; olive-brown to brown above, *yellow stripe along each side,* fins yellowish. *Head longer than body depth at dorsal fin origin.*

Dorsal fin spines shorter than soft rays. Lateral line lacks bony shields.

Habitat: Near surface around reefs, islands, and kelp beds.

Range: From British Columbia to Chile.

Related Species: Green Jack (*Caranx caballus*) has pectoral fin reaching beyond origin of soft dorsal fin; soft dorsal separate from spiny portion; bony shields along lateral line; found from Santa Cruz Island, California, to Cape Agujo, Peru. Both occur in similar habitat. Pacific Amberjack (*S. colburni*) has silvery body without yellow stripes; dark bar from eye to rear of head; found from Oceanside, California, to Peru.

Similar Species: Ocean Whitefish (*Caulolatilus princeps*) has dorsal spines and soft rays of about equal height.

Comments: The Yellowtail feeds on anchovies, sardines, mackerels, squids, and pelagic red crabs. Second only to the elusive Albacore, it is one of the most popular gamefishes in southern California. Its migrations north into this area depend upon water temperature, so the annual catch fluctuates between 5,000 and 400,000 fishes. Most are caught by hook and line, as it is illegal to use purse seines for Yellowtail in California waters.

---

550 Florida Pompano
(*Trachinotus carolinus*)

Description: To 17″ (43 cm). Short, deep, moderately compressed; dorsal and ventral profiles similar; back bluish-gray or bluish-green; sides silvery; belly silvery and yellowish. Snout blunt, *mouth slightly inferior.* Fins dusky or yellowish; *pectoral fin shorter than head;* pelvic fins shorter than pectorals; first dorsal fin has 6 short spines; *base of second dorsal only slightly longer than base of anal fin. Caudal peduncle relatively deep,* without scutes or grooves at base of caudal fin; no finlets.

Habitat: Shallow water along sandy beaches.

Range: From Massachusetts to Brazil, including shores of Gulf of Mexico; occurs irregularly in West Indies. Migrates north in summer, south in winter.

Comments: The Florida Pompano is a favorite food fish and commands high prices. It is caught using light tackle over shallow sand flats. Pompanos often make long horizontal "flights" out of the water.

549 Palometa
(*Trachinotus goodei*)

Description: To 13″ (33 cm). Deep, compressed, dorsal and ventral profiles about equally rounded; silvery; sides with 4–5 bars, *leading edges of soft dorsal and anal fins and upper and lower lobes of caudal fin black*. Snout blunt; mouth slightly inferior, maxilla reaches middle of eye. Pectoral fins relatively small, not falcate; *dorsal and anal fins very long, falcate, reach past fork of caudal fin*. Caudal peduncle without grooves; no finlets or scutes. Scales small, cycloid, partially embedded.

Habitat: Surf zone and sandy beaches; also around reefs and rocky areas.

Range: From Massachusetts to Argentina, including Bermuda, Gulf of Mexico, Caribbean, and West Indies.

Related Species: Permit (*T. falcatus*) lacks bars on sides; dorsal and anal fin lobes shorter; occurs in Atlantic from Maine to Brazil, including Gulf of Mexico and most of Caribbean. Gafftopsail Pompano (*T. rhodopus*) has faint yellow bars; fins reddish yellow; occurs in Pacific from Zuma Beach, California, to Peru. Both in similar habitat.

Comments: Palometas occur in large schools, mostly in clear, tropical waters. They feed on small fishes and invertebrates.

560 Jack Mackerel
(*Trachurus symmetricus*)

Description: To 32″ (81 cm). Fusiform, compressed;
metallic blue to olive-green above;
silvery below, but darkens with age.
Pectoral fin extends to base of first soft
ray in anal fin. Dorsal fins barely
separated; no dorsal and anal finlets.
*Lateral line has 40–55 bony shields
posteriorly and a dorsal branch.*

Habitat: Offshore on surface and at midwater;
around reefs and kelp beds.

Range: From SE. Alaska to Galápagos Islands.

Related Species: Mexican Scad (*Decapterus scombrinus*) has
single dorsal and ventral finlets; lateral
line lacks dorsal branch, has bony
shields only on rear part; occurs in
similar habitat from Pacific Grove,
California, to Galápagos Islands.

Similar Species: Chub Mackerel (*Scomber japonicus*) has
dark blue back with wavy lines, 4–6
dorsal and anal finlets.

Comments: Large Jack Mackerels are important
commercially in southern California.
They feed on krill, squids, anchovies,
and lanternfishes, and are a major food
source for seals, sea lions, porpoises,
swordfishes, sea basses, and pelicans.

DOLPHINS
(Family Coryphaenidae)

Dolphins are elongate and compressed,
with a long dorsal fin that begins just
behind the eyes. The dorsal fin and the
anal fin, which begins in the middle of
the body, continue almost to the caudal
fin. Dolphins have a narrow caudal
peduncle, a long, forked tail, and
small cycloid scales. They exhibit
beautiful iridescent colors which fade
soon after they die. Adult males
develop a heavy bony crest on the
forehead, resulting in an almost vertical
anterior profile. This family has 2
species in North America.

582 Dolphin
(*Coryphaena hippurus*)

Description: To 6′6″ (2 m); 87 lbs (39.5 kg).
Elongate, compressed, greatest depth at
nape; iridescent blues, greens, and
tinges of yellow with scattered, small,
dark or golden blotches and spots.
Head blunt; mouth large, terminal;
lower jaw projecting. Pectoral and
pelvic fins about equal length, fit into
depressions; *dorsal fin single, black, begins
at nape, reaches almost to caudal fin; anal
fin black with white border, long and low,*
similar to posterior half of dorsal fin;
caudal fin deeply forked.

Habitat: Surface of open sea, usually over deep
water, but sometimes near shore.

Range: From Nova Scotia to Brazil, including
Bermuda and Gulf of Mexico.

Related Species: Pompano Dolphin (*C. equisetis*) grows
to 30″ (76 cm); body deeper, occurs
farther offshore from New Jersey to
Brazil, including Bermuda, Gulf of
Mexico, and Caribbean.

Comments: Dolphins are found near rafts of
sargassum, where they apparently feed.
Young Dolphins, to about 3″ (7.5 cm),
are part of the sargassum fauna. Their
iridescent colors are lost soon after
death.

SNAPPERS
(Family Lutjanidae)

Snappers are oblong, moderately
compressed fishes. The large mouth is
terminal, and the maxilla is partly
hidden by the area before the eyes. The
teeth are conical and sharp, and never
molarlike, and there are teeth in the
roof of the mouth. The chin has no
barbels or pores, and the opercle lacks
spines. The dorsal fin is single and
continuous, and the caudal fin varies
from deeply forked to truncate. Small
ctenoid scales cover the body, except

no scales

between the mouth and eyes. Lateral
line scales extend onto the caudal fin
base, but not to its edge. Most
snappers are carnivorous and live
around reefs and on the continental
slope. They are very important
economically as commercial and sport
fishes. This family has 17 species in
North America.

538 Schoolmaster
(*Lutjanus apodus*)

Description: To 24″ (61 cm). Moderately deep;
olive-gray with yellow tinge above,
lighter below. *8 narrow, pale bars on back
and upper sides* under base of dorsal fin,
fins yellow or yellow-green. Snout
long, pointed; upper profile of head
nearly straight; *solid or broken blue line
under eye, canine teeth visible in upper jaw
when mouth closed.* Anal fin rounded;
caudal fin emarginate.

Habitat: Coastal waters around coral reefs and
over rocks; in mangrove swamps,
tidepools, and estuaries.

Range: From Maine to Brazil, including
Bermuda, Gulf of Mexico, and
Caribbean.

Related Species: Amarillo Snapper (*L. argentiventris*) has
body rose-red anteriorly, light yellow
posteriorly, with blue spots or streaks
under eye; occurs in shallow, inshore
waters, usually around reefs or
mangrove swamps, from S. California
to Peru, including Galápagos Islands.

Comments: The Schoolmaster is very common on
coral reefs, where it associates with the
Gray Snapper during the day, but goes
its separate way at night to feed, like
other snappers, mainly on fishes and
crabs.

522 Red Snapper
(*Lutjanus campechanus*)

Description: To 31" (79 cm). Rather deep, depth one-fourth length; *scarlet above fading to rosy red below, sometimes with silvery sheen; fins red or reddish orange, some with dusky borders;* small specimens, to 12" (30 cm), have dark spot on upper sides below anterior dorsal fin soft rays. Head large, anterior profile steep, rounded behind eye; snout long; eye small; maxilla not reaching below front edge of eye. Single dorsal fin long; caudal fin emarginate.

Habitat: Over rocks and natural and artificial reefs at 5–100 fathoms.

Range: From Massachusetts south to Florida, but rare north of Carolinas; Gulf of Mexico to Yucatán, Mexico. Absent in Antilles and Caribbean.

Comments: Red Snappers account for a substantial part of the food fishery on the Gulf Coast of the United States and Mexico. In the northeastern Gulf, artificial reefs have been constructed to attract these and other fishes for sport fishing.

539 Gray Snapper
(*Lutjanus griseus*)

Description: To 3' (91 cm). Relatively slender; *gray or olive above with reddish tinge or blotches,* grayish or yellowish-pink below; scale centers sometimes orange, edges white; *no black spot on sides;* spinous dorsal fin edge red. Snout long, pointed; lower jaw projects slightly beyond upper; dorsal profile of head slightly concave; large pair of canine teeth in upper jaw. *Pectoral fin relatively short, not reaching anus;* soft dorsal with 14 rays, it and anal fin rounded; caudal fin emarginate.

Habitat: Juveniles and young inshore, even in fresh water; adults offshore to about 90 fathoms, around estuaries, mangrove swamps and coral reefs, and over rocks.

Range: From Massachusetts to Rio de Janeiro, Brazil, including Bermuda, Gulf of Mexico, Antilles, and Caribbean.

Related Species: Mutton Snapper (*L. analis*) has conspicuous black spot on sides below dorsal fin; ranges from Massachusetts to Brazil. Mahogany Snapper (*L. mahogoni*) has similar spot; angle of preopercle strongly serrate; ranges from North Carolina to Brazil. Both in similar habitat.

Comments: This species can change color instantly to match its background. Although the Gray Snapper is reported to reach 3' (91 cm) in length, most are less than half that long. It is an excellent food fish.

540 Dog Snapper
(*Lutjanus jocu*)

Description: To 29" (74 cm). Deep body, depth and head length each about one-third length; *olive-brown with bronzy tinge above, pinkish with coppery cast below,* no spots or bars on sides. Profile more or less straight from snout to nape; snout pointed; mouth terminal, slightly oblique; *canine teeth in upper jaw large, visible when mouth closed;* eye large with *pale, narrow, triangular patch and row of blue dots below eye. Fins orange;* anal fin rounded; caudal fin emarginate or slightly forked.

Habitat: Young inshore and around estuaries; adults around coral reefs over continental and island shelves.

Range: From Massachusetts to Brazil; Bermuda, N. Gulf of Mexico, Yucatán, Mexico, Antilles, and Caribbean.

Comments: The Dog Snapper is a voracious predator that feeds mainly on fishes and bottom-dwelling invertebrates. It has been implicated in ciguatera poisoning.

534 Lane Snapper
(*Lutjanus synagris*)

Description: To 14″ (36 cm). Moderately deep; pinkish above with green tinge and, when resting, diffuse dusky bars; silvery with yellow tinge below, *8 or 10 yellow or golden stripes on body, 3–4 on head.* Snout pointed; mouth rather large; *canine teeth not visible when mouth closed.* 12 dorsal fin rays; *black spot between lateral line and anterior soft dorsal rays;* anal fin rounded; outer margins of dorsal, anal, and pelvic fins yellow; caudal fin light red.

Habitat: Continental and island shelf waters to about 200 fathoms.

Range: From North Carolina to Brazil, including Gulf of Mexico, Antilles, and Caribbean.

Comments: The Lane Snapper is often found in large schools and is most common in the Antilles and off Yucatán, Mexico, and northern South America. It is a food fish, although it is less important than most snappers because of its smaller size.

536 Yellowtail Snapper
(*Ocyurus chrysurus*)

Description: To 24″ (61 cm). *Fusiform,* dorsal and ventral profiles evenly rounded; back and sides olive, blue, or blue-gray, *with yellow spots; prominent midlateral yellow band* begins on snout and becomes progressively broader to cover entire caudal peduncle; lower sides and belly have alternating narrow reddish and pale yellow stripes. Head and mouth relatively small; *no canine teeth. Caudal fin yellow, deeply forked.*

Habitat: Most common in coastal waters to about 60′ (18.3 m), usually around coral reefs and over rocks.

Range: From Gulf of Maine to S. Brazil, including Bermuda, Gulf of Mexico,

Caribbean, and West Indies.

Comments: This excellent food fish is a schooling species abundant off southern Florida and throughout the Caribbean.

TRIPLETAILS
(Family Lobotidae)

Tripletails are so called because the long, rounded posterior lobes of the dorsal and anal fins extend back to the caudal fin, giving the appearance of 3 tails. The body is deep and compressed. The dorsal fin has stiff spines that are continuous with the soft rays. Adult tripletails float on their sides in the shade of flotsam; the young do the same, mimicking drifting leaves. There is a single species found worldwide.

517 Tripletail
(*Lobotes surinamensis*)

Description: To 3'4" (1 m). Deep, compressed, *soft dorsal and anal fins long, with rounded caudal fin giving appearance of 3 tails;* dark brown to bronzy to yellow-brown, often blotched or mottled, especially in young. Teeth in jaws pointed; preopercle strongly serrate. Pectoral fins pale, other fins dark; single dorsal fin without pronounced notch; 3 anal fin spines. Scales adherent, strongly ctenoid.

Habitat: Inshore in bays and estuaries near buoys and channel markers; offshore.

Range: From Cape Cod to Argentina, including Gulf of Mexico, Caribbean, and tropics; most abundant south of Cape Hatteras.

Comments: This excellent food fish can be caught around piers, pilings, wrecks, or flotsam using live shrimps for bait. It feeds primarily on crustaceans.

MOJARRAS
(Family Gerreidae)

jaws

protrusible jaws

Most of these small fishes are entirely covered with shiny silver scales. They have a rather deep and compressed body, a pointed snout, and extremely protrusible jaws. When projected, they point downward. The ventral profile of the head is concave. The single dorsal fin is interrupted by a shallow notch; it and the anal fin can fold into a deep sheath of scales. The caudal fin is deeply forked. Mojarras are bottom-dwelling fishes, usually found over mud and sand in relatively shallow water. This family has 10 species in North America.

542 Spotfin Mojarra
(*Eucinostomus argenteus*)

Description: To 8″ (20 cm). Oblong, compressed; silvery; grayish-green when viewed from above; dusky oblique bars or stripes. Jaws strongly protrusible; *premaxillary groove slender, not interrupted by transverse row of scales.* Spinous dorsal fin sometimes has black spots, folds into deep sheath of scales; 3 anal fin spines.

Habitat: Coastal waters over shallow sand flats.

Range: From New Jersey to SE. Brazil, including Bermuda, Gulf of Mexico, Antilles, and Caribbean.

Related Species: Silver Jenny (*E. gula*) has deeper body and 3 anal spines; premaxillary groove interrupted by transverse row of scales; found from Maine to Argentina. Mottled Mojarra (*E. lefroyi*) has 2 anal fin spines; found from Chesapeake Bay to Florida and Caribbean. Both in similar habitats.

Comments: The greatly protrusible jaws, directed downward, enable this and other mojarras to feed on bottom-dwelling invertebrates.

518   **Yellowfin Mojarra**
(*Gerres cinereus*)

Description: To 16″ (41 cm). Deep, compressed;
*silvery with 7–8 dark bluish or pinkish
bars on sides, fins yellow,* dorsal
and caudal fins dusky. Jaws very
protrusible, maxilla barely reaches eye;
posterior part of premaxillary groove
broad. Pectoral fin reaches anal fin
origin; dorsal fin slightly notched;
dorsal and anal fins have sheath of
scales at bases; 3 anal fin spines, second
greatly enlarged.

Habitat: Shallow coastal waters, usually over
sand near coral reefs; known to enter
fresh water.

Range: From NE. Florida to Texas along coast;
Caribbean and West Indies south to
Rio de Janeiro, Brazil.

Comments: Reef-dwelling fish have pinkish bars on
their sides. This species feeds primarily
on worms and crustaceans that it grubs
from bottom sediments.

GRUNTS
(Family Haemulidae)

head scaled

These perchlike fishes have an oblong
body and a relatively large head. They
have teeth in the jaws and on the
pharyngeal bones, but none in the roof
of the mouth. There are 2 small pores
under the chin. The scales are ctenoid
and cover the body, opercles, cheeks,
and the area between the eye and
mouth. Grunts inhabit shallow inshore
waters in warm seas, in a variety of
habitats from coral reefs to sand, grass
flats, and over mud. They produce
a grunting sound by rubbing the
pharyngeal teeth together, hence their
common name. This family has 20
species in North America.

537 Porkfish
(*Anisotremus virginicus*)

Description: To 14″ (36 cm). Deep, compressed; alternating silvery blue and yellow stripes on sides, *diagonal black band from chin through eye to nape, another from below first dorsal spine to base of pectoral fin;* spiny dorsal and pelvic fins dusky to black, other fins yellow. Head short; snout blunt; mouth small, lips thick. Scales only on bases of soft dorsal and anal fins.

Habitat: Shallow water over reefs and rocks.

Range: From Florida to Brazil, including Bermuda, E. and W. Gulf of Mexico, Caribbean, and West Indies.

Related Species: Black Margate (*A. surinamensis*) has silvery-gray body without bright coloration or dark bands on head; occurs in similar habitat from S. Florida to Brazil, including Bermuda, Gulf of Mexico, Caribbean, and West Indies.

Comments: Adult Porkfishes feed on a variety of invertebrates; the young, however, are known to pick parasites from the skin of larger fishes.

535 Tomtate
(*Haemulon aurolineatum*)

Description: To 10″ (25 cm). Oblong, compressed; silvery white, head dusky; *broad bronze to yellow stripe from eye to dusky spot at base of caudal fin,* narrow yellow stripe just above lateral line, fins chalky to light gray. Snout pointed; upper jaw extends beyond lower; mouth red inside; maxilla reaches past middle of eye. Scales above and below lateral line about same size.

Habitat: From shallow water over sand and grass beds to outer reefs.

Range: From Chesapeake Bay to Brazil, including Bermuda, Gulf of Mexico, and Caribbean.

Related Species: French Grunt (*H. flavolineatum*) has
bronze stripes above, oblique lines
below; larger scales below lateral line
than above; occurs in similar habitat in
SE. Florida.

Comments: The Tomtate is common over
shrimping grounds in the Tortugas and
the Gulf of Mexico, as well as around
reefs and oil platforms. Its species name
aurolineatum refers to the golden lateral
stripe.

---

532   White Grunt
(*Haemulon plumieri*)

Description: To 16″ (41 cm). Oblong, compressed;
light yellowish or bronze with
alternating blue and bronze stripes on head;
paired fins pale, dorsal fin chalky or
yellow-white, anal and caudal fins
grayish brown, *scales have white or blue
spot, bronze edges.* Snout long, pointed;
mouth terminal, red inside; maxilla
reaches to eye; preopercle often has
black blotch beneath edge. Soft dorsal
and anal fins scaled; *larger scales above
lateral line than below.*

Habitat: Grass beds, sand flats, and nearby reefs.

Range: From Chesapeake Bay to Brazil,
including Bermuda, Gulf of Mexico,
Caribbean, and West Indies.

Related Species: Bluestriped Grunt (*H. sciurus*) has pale
blue stripes; scales above and below
lateral line of same size; occurs over
reefs to about 16 fathoms. Striped
Grunt (*H. striatum*) has slender body;
yellow with 4 dark brown stripes;
occurs over reefs to about 54 fathoms.
Both in SE. Florida.

Comments: The White Grunt, like other grunts,
displays "kissing" behavior, that is, 2
individuals will face each other and
push with open mouths.

PORGIES
(Family Sparidae)

Porgies have an oblong, compressed body and a large head with a steep profile. The mouth is small and terminal; the maxilla never reaches beyond the center of the eye. The opercle is scaled but has no spines or serrations. Well-developed, the teeth include incisors or canines in the front of the jaw and molars in the sides. The pectoral fins are long and there is a single dorsal fin. Some porgies live on hard bottoms, others over mud. Practically all occur inshore, but some are found in brackish or fresh water. There are 16 species in North America.

395 Sheepshead
(*Archosargus probatocephalus*)

Description: To 30″ (76 cm). Deep, compressed; gray, *5–6 dark bars on body, 1 on nape,* with slightly wider pale interspaces; bars darker in young than adults. Head profile very steep; snout pointed; mouth terminal; jaws have *broad incisor teeth in front,* molars on sides. Pectoral fin long; single dorsal fin preceded by small, forward-directed spine embedded in skin.

teeth

Habitat: In muddy, shallow water or over oyster beds; frequently around piles and piers of bridges; occasionally enters fresh water in Florida.

Range: From Cape Cod to Brazil, including Gulf of Mexico, but absent from the Caribbean.

Comments: The Sheepshead gets its name from its large incisor teeth, which protrude a little beyond the lips. Its stout dorsal and anal spines can cause punctures. This excellent food fish is a bottom-dweller; it does not school, although it forms feeding groups.

547 Jolthead Porgy
(*Calamus bajonado*)

Description: To 27" (69 cm). Deep, compressed, oblong; *brassy or silvery, scale centers shiny blue, blue stripe below eye, 2 white stripes on each cheek;* lower jaw and corner of mouth purplish, isthmus orange, fins usually plain. Snout long, rather pointed; eye midway between snout and dorsal fin origin; posterior nostril slitlike; mouth terminal, maxilla not reaching to eye; *teeth slender, caninelike in front of jaw,* molarlike on sides. Pectoral fins long, 15 rays; single dorsal fin; 3 anal fin spines, 10 rays. 51–57 lateral line scales.

nostril

teeth

Habitat: Along coast, over coral or sand with vegetation to 100 fathoms.

Range: From Rhode Island to Brazil, including most of Gulf of Mexico, Caribbean, and Antilles.

Related Species: Red Porgy (*Pagrus pagrus*) has reddish body; posterior nostril oval; occurs in similar habitat along coast from New York to Argentina.

nostril

Comments: One of the largest species of porgies, the Jolthead Porgy feeds on hard-bodied invertebrates such as sea urchins and crabs. The sharp front teeth are used to dislodge mollusks and crustaceans that are then crushed with the strong molarlike teeth.

548 Saucereye Porgy
(*Calamus calamus*)

Description: To 16" (41 cm). Deep, oval; depth about half length; *silver with bluish reflections* and brassy stripes alternating with pearly or bluish stripes, *deep blue streak below eye,* cheeks blue with yellowish spots in a netlike pattern, *lips and isthmus orange.* Snout rather long; anterior profile steep with hump opposite eye; posterior nostril slitlike;

nostril

teeth

maxilla not reaching eye; *teeth slender, caninelike in front of jaw,* molarlike on sides. Pectoral fins large, 14 rays; dorsal fin single, third and fourth spines longest; 3 anal fin spines, 11 rays. 51–55 lateral line scales.

Habitat: Over coral and sand with vegetation to 40 fathoms.

Range: From North Carolina and Bermuda south to Gulf of Mexico, Caribbean, and West Indies.

Related Species: Knobbed Porgy (*C. nodosus*) has deeper body; anterior profile steeper; occurs in similar habitat south from North Carolina to NW. Florida along coast, and in all but W. Gulf of Mexico.

Comments: This and other species of the genus *Calamus* contribute significantly to the commercial fishing industry in southern Florida and the West Indies. Like most other porgies, the Saucereye Porgy produces free-floating eggs and gives no parental care.

533 Pinfish
(*Lagodon rhomboides*)

Description: To 15″ (38 cm). Oval, compressed; *back olive, sides bluish with yellow stripes and 5–6 faint dusky bars, silvery sheen overall, dark spot on shoulder,* fins yellow, *no dark blotch on caudal peduncle.* Head profile slightly concave at eye; snout relatively short, rather pointed; posterior nostril oval; mouth terminal, maxilla just reaches eye; front teeth strongly flattened, incisorlike, deeply notched; side teeth molarlike, in 2½ rows in each jaw. Pectoral fins long; dorsal fin single, *forward-directed spine at origin.*

teeth

Habitat: Primarily shallow water around vegetation.

Range: From Cape Cod south along coast to Yucatán, Mexico; possibly including N. Cuba.

Related Species: Spottail Pinfish (*Diplodus holbrooki*) has dark blotch on caudal peduncle;

occurs along coast from North Carolina to Texas. Longspine Porgy (*Stenotomus caprinus*) has much deeper body; dorsal spines very long; occurs along coast from Gulf coast of N. Florida to Yucatán, Mexico. Scup (*S. chrysops*) lacks bars and humeral spot; occurs from Nova Scotia to North Carolina. All in similar habitat.

Comments: This is a very common porgy, but because of its small size it is seldom used as food. Its greatest value is as forage for larger fishes.

DRUMS
(Family Sciaenidae)

These elongate and moderately compressed fishes occur in a variety of habitats, but most live close to the bottom. They often have chin and rostral pores, and may possess chin barbels. Teeth are present in the jaws, but absent on the roof of the mouth; however, molarlike teeth may be on the pharyngeal bones. The 2 dorsal fins are separated by a distinct notch. The anal fin usually has 2 spines. Drums have ctenoid scales, often covering the bases of the fins, and the lateral line extends to the posterior edge of the caudal fin. This is one of the most commercially important families in North America, and is represented by 33 species, that occur in both the Atlantic and Pacific.

---

96   Freshwater Drum
(*Aplodinotus grunniens*)

Description: To 35″ (89 cm); 54½ lbs (24.7 kg). Oblong, robust; greatest depth at dorsal fin origin; *silvery-bluish above, sides silvery;* whitish below. Mouth ventral. Pelvic fins whitish, median fins dusky. 2 dorsal fins almost completely

anal fin

caudal fin

separated by deep notch, with scaly sheath at base; *2 anal fin spines, second enlarged, 7 rays;* caudal fin moderately pointed. Scales ctenoid; lateral line extends to tip of caudal fin.

Habitat: Small to large rivers with slow to moderate current; lakes and reservoirs, in deeper water.

Range: Hudson Bay drainage in Manitoba and SW. Saskatchewan; St. Lawrence River, S. Great Lakes; Mississippi River drainage, Alabama west to Texas, south to Guatemala.

Comments: The Freshwater Drum, the only North American freshwater member of the Sciaenidae, has the widest distribution in latitude of any freshwater fish in the United States and Canada, and is fished commercially and for sport throughout much of its range. Like other species of Sciaenidae, this fish makes the drumming sound that gives the family its common name by vibrating the muscles attached to the swim bladder.

White Seabass
(*Atractoscion nobilis*)

Description: To 5' (1.5 m); 83¾ lbs (38 kg). Fusiform, elongate, slightly compressed; blue-gray above, silvery below; black spot at base of pectoral fin. *No large canine teeth in middle of upper jaw;* no chin barbel; pores on chin and snout. 2 dorsal fins slightly joined by membrane; anal fin with 2 spines, base less than one-half length of rayed dorsal fin base. Lateral line extends to tip of caudal fin.

Habitat: Inshore waters to 67 fathoms.

Range: From Juneau, Alaska, to Bahía Magdalena, Baja California, and upper Gulf of California.

Comments: White Seabasses spawn from April to August, congregating inshore. These large fishes, also known as croakers, are important sport and commercial fishes,

and feed on squids, sardines, and
anchovies. They migrate north along
the coast in spring, return south in fall,
and generally spend the winter off Baja
California.

476 Spotted Seatrout
(*Cynoscion nebulosus*)

Description: To 28″ (71 cm); 16 lbs (7.3 kg).
Elongate, fusiform, moderately
compressed; dark gray above with
bluish iridescence and *black dots
extending onto dorsal and caudal fins;*
spiny dorsal fin dusky, other fins pale
yellowish; silvery below. Mouth
oblique; lower jaw projects beyond
upper, which extends past eye; *2 large
canine teeth in front of upper jaw; no
barbels or pores on chin;* preopercular
margin smooth. Dorsal fins completely
separated by deep notch; soft dorsal fin
unscaled, base much longer than anal
fin base; *caudal fin truncate or emarginate.*
Scales ctenoid, large; lateral line
extends to caudal fin tip.

Habitat: Juveniles in estuaries, tidal mud flats,
grass beds, and salt marshes; larger
specimens mostly in shallow coastal
waters over sand.

Range: From Cape Cod to Florida; Gulf of
Mexico from W. Florida to Laguna
Madre, Mexico; absent from West
Indies and Caribbean.

Comments: The Spotted Seatrout, often called
"speck," is a valued food and game
fish, especially in the shallow sand flats
around barrier islands off Florida and
the Gulf Coast.

482 Silver Seatrout
(*Cynoscion nothus*)

Description: To 14″ (36 cm). Elongate, fusiform,
moderately compressed; grayish above,

silvery below, *no conspicuous markings, dorsal fin dusky, other fins pale. Maxilla reaches middle of eye;* no barbels or pores on chin. First dorsal fin separated from second by deep notch; caudal fin either truncate or *lower lobe rounded, longer than upper.* Lateral line extends to caudal fin tip; *scales extend beyond basal half of soft dorsal fin.*

Habitat: Offshore over sand at depths of more than 36' (11 m); moves inshore and into bays during winter.

Range: From Chesapeake Bay to Florida and SW. Texas.

Related Species: Sand Seatrout (*C. arenarius*) has firmer flesh; scales fall off more easily; occurs nearer shore in Gulf of Mexico.

Comments: The Silver Seatrout is used for pet food. It is not of much interest to anglers due to its relatively small size and because it occupies deep waters well outside the reach of the cane-pole angler.

483 Weakfish
(*Cynoscion regalis*)

Description: To 35" (89 cm); 18 lbs (8 kg). Elongate, fusiform, moderately compressed; greenish-olive above, sides iridescent, silvery below, *small, irregular dark dots on back form oblique streaks on scale rows,* pelvic and anal fins usually yellow, other fins dusky, tinged with yellow. Mouth oblique; lower jaw projecting, maxilla extends to back of eye; 2 large canine teeth in upper jaw; no barbels or pores; preopercular margin smooth. *Soft dorsal fin covered with scales up to basal half;* caudal fin truncate or emarginate. Lateral line extends to caudal fin tip; scales ctenoid, large, cycloid on head.

Habitat: Shallow coastal waters over sand or mud; summer feeding and nursery grounds in estuaries.

Range: From Nova Scotia to Florida, and W. Florida to Tampa Bay. Most abundant from New Jersey to Chesapeake Bay.

Related Species: Shortfin Corvina (*C. parvipinnis*) has large canine teeth in middle of upper jaw; found in shallow inshore waters over soft bottoms from Santa Barbara Island, California, to Mazatlán, Mexico.

Comments: Although this important game and commercial fish is reported to reach about 35″ (89 cm), the majority caught by anglers are 18″ (46 cm) or smaller.

343 Jackknife-Fish
(*Equetus lanceolatus*)

Description: To 9″ (23 cm). Compressed, deep anteriorly, tapering to narrow caudal peduncle; *white with 3 broad, dark bands, each bordered by thin, silvery stripes,* first band through eye, second obliquely from forehead to pelvic fin base, third from first dorsal fin lengthwise to end of caudal fin; broad, dark band on leading edges of first dorsal and pelvic fins. *Head profile very steep;* mouth small, inferior. *First dorsal fin very tall;* caudal fin pointed. Lateral line extends to tip of caudal fin.

Habitat: Coral reefs or over mud or rocks in relatively shallow waters.

Range: From South Carolina to West Indies and Brazil; also in S. Gulf of Mexico.

Comments: Small specimens have relatively tall first dorsal fins; that of a 3″ (7.5 cm) specimen is as high as the fish is long. This species is valued as an aquarium fish.

481 Southern Kingfish
(*Menticirrhus americanus*)

Description: To 20″ (51 cm). Elongate, fusiform, moderately compressed; dusky, darker above, lighter below, almost white on belly, sides with 7 or 8 dark, dusky oblique bands. Pelvic, anal, and caudal fins dusky, sometimes tinged with yellow; pectoral fins dusky, outer edges black; spiny dorsal fin dusky, apex black; soft dorsal fin plain. Snout conical; mouth small, horizontal, inferior; *chin with single, short, stout barbel.* When depressed, longest dorsal spine falls short of first soft ray; 1 anal fin spine. Scales small, ctenoid, adherent. Lateral line extends to caudal fin edge.

Habitat: Usually over sand but also over mud or silt at depths of at least 60' (18 m).

Range: From Cape Cod to Florida, Gulf of Mexico, and W. Caribbean.

Related Species: Gulf Kingfish (*M. littoralis*) has silvery body; occurs in surf zone from Virginia to Florida and Gulf of Mexico. Northern Kingfish (*M. saxatilis*) has V-shaped mark on shoulders; occurs in similar habitat from Cape Cod to Florida and in Gulf of Mexico to Yucatán, Mexico.

Comments: One of several kingfishes called "ground mullets," the tasty Southern Kingfish is caught in the northeastern Gulf of Mexico by baitcasting in the surf.

479 Atlantic Croaker
(*Micropogonias undulatus*)

Description: To 24" (61 cm). Moderately elongate and compressed; dusky bluish or grayish above, silvery-bronze below, small brownish dots form irregular lines on sides and 1–2 horizontal rows on soft dorsal, other fins clear or pale yellowish. Snout conical; *mouth small, slightly oblique, inferior; chin with 3–5 pairs of minute barbels and 5 pores;* preopercle serrate, with strong spines at angle. 2 anal fin spines; caudal fin doubly emarginate in adults. Lateral line extends to tip of caudal fin.

Habitat: Over mud or sand in coastal waters and estuaries.

Range: Along coast from Cape Cod to Texas,
south to Yucatán, Mexico; not common
north of New Jersey or in S. Florida.

Comments: In the southern part of its range, the
Atlantic Croaker matures in 1 year and
lives another 1 or 2 years; in the north
it matures later and survives longer.
Important commercially, it is caught
by the thousands of tons.

477   Reef Croaker
(*Odontoscion dentex*)

Description: To 10″ (25 cm). Oblong, compressed;
*brownish silver with dark dots on scales,
large, black blotch at pectoral fin base.
Mouth terminal, oblique;* maxilla reaches
posterior margin of pupil; teeth large,
conical, 2 canine teeth at tip of lower
jaw; no chin barbels. Lateral line
extends to tip of truncate caudal fin.

Habitat: Rocks or coral reefs in shallow water.

Range: S. Florida, reefs off Texas, south from
Caribbean to Brazil; apparently absent
from Bahamas.

Comments: The Reef Croaker is active at night,
feeding on shrimps and small fishes.
During the day it retreats to crevices in
coral reefs and caves.

475   Black Drum
(*Pogonias cromis*)

Description: To 3′3″ (99 cm); 113 lbs (51.3 kg).
Deep, moderately compressed, back
elevated, ventral profile nearly straight;
silvery to dark gray; *4–5 broad, black
bars on sides,* bars less intense in large
fish; all fins dusky or black. Mouth
nearly horizontal, inferior; maxilla
reaches middle of eye; pharyngeal teeth
large; *chin has numerous small barbels,*
longer posteriorly on chin; *preopercle
smooth.* 2 anal fin spines, *second much
larger than first;* caudal fin truncate to

slightly emarginate. Lateral line extends to tip of caudal fin; scales large, ctenoid.

Habitat: Over sand or sandy mud in bays and estuaries.

Range: From Gulf of Maine to S. Florida; Gulf of Mexico west from S. Florida to Laguna Madre, Mexico; Brazil.

Comments: Black Drums feed on fishes, crustaceans, and oysters, which they crush with their huge pharyngeal teeth. Although they may weigh more than 100 pounds (45.4 kg), and are often caught, they are not popular as game or food fishes.

478 Red Drum
(*Sciaenops ocellatus*)

Description: To 5′ (1.5 m); 90 lbs (41 kg). Elongate, moderately compressed, ventral profile nearly straight; *iridescent silvery gray, copper, bronze, or reddish; 1 or more large, black, ocellated spots on caudal peduncle;* dorsal and caudal fins dusky; anal and pelvic fins pale. Snout conical; mouth horizontal, inferior; maxilla reaches back of eye; *no chin barbels;* preopercular margin smooth. Third and fourth dorsal spines longest; caudal fin truncate in adults. Lateral line extends to tip of caudal fin; scales large, ctenoid.

Habitat: Surf zone to offshore waters, depending on season and age of individuals; also occasionally enters fresh water.

Range: Along coast from New York to Florida, west to Laguna Madre, Mexico. Most abundant from Florida to Texas.

Comments: Red Drums run in schools during their spring and fall migrations, which makes them popular with anglers. Large specimens, usually much smaller than 5′ (1.5 m), are called "bullreds," small ones "ratreds." They migrate in response to temperature, salinity, and food availability.

480 Yellowfin Croaker
(*Umbrina roncador*)

Description: To 18" (46 cm); 4 lbs (1.8 kg).
Elongate, compressed, greatest depth
under origin of first dorsal fin;
iridescent blue to gray above, sides
silvery with dark, wavy lines, *fins
yellowish*. Snout bluntly rounded; upper
jaw projects beyond tip of lower; *chin
has single barbel, preopercle serrate*. Dorsal
fins contiguous, 10–11 spines in first;
1 spine, 25–30 rays in second. Caudal
fin emarginate. Lateral line extends to
tip of caudal fin.

Habitat: Over sand, in surf zone, near rocks or
kelp, and to 25' (8 m) in bays.

Range: From Point Conception, California, to
Gulf of California.

Related Species: White Croaker (*Genyonemus lineatus*)
lacks wavy lines on sides; chin barbels
minute or absent; 12–16 dorsal fin
spines, 10–12 soft rays; found near
shore over soft bottoms from Vancouver
Island, British Columbia, to Bahía
Magdalena, Baja California. Queenfish
(*Seriphus politus*) has snout not
extending beyond tip of lower jaw;
mouth terminal; found near shore over
soft bottoms from Yaquina Bay,
Oregon, to Uncle Sam Bank, Baja
California.

Comments: Yellowfin Croakers spawn during the
summer. They are caught by surf
anglers and speared by skin divers.
This fish has been recorded to a length
of 20" (51 cm).

GOATFISHES
(Family Mullidae)

These rather elongate fishes have 2
well-separated dorsal fins and 2
large barbels that trail from the chin
or fit into a groove on the throat.
Goatfishes are bottom dwellers, usually
colored bright red or yellow. There are

6 species in North American waters, 4 found in the Atlantic Ocean and 2 found in the Pacific Ocean.

415 Red Goatfish
(*Mullus auratus*)

Description: To 8″ (20 cm). Elongate, depth greatest at nape, then tapering posteriorly; *bright red and yellow along sides;* pelvic fin plain; pectorals reddish; first dorsal fin pale with 2 reddish-orange or yellowish stripes; caudal fin scarlet, sometimes with white markings. Head profile steep; mouth terminal, horizontal; maxilla reaches eye; small teeth on roof of mouth and in lower jaw. *2 large barbels on chin;* no opercular spine. 8 dorsal fin spines, well separated from soft dorsal.

Habitat: Coastal waters over mud to about 40 fathoms.

Range: From Cape Cod to Guyana, including Gulf of Mexico, Caribbean, and West Indies.

Comments: Goatfishes use their long chin barbels to probe the bottom for food. When not in use, the barbels are retracted under the throat. Red Goatfishes feed primarily on invertebrates. In some areas they are highly prized as food.

SEA CHUBS
(Family Kyphosidae)

These are oval, compressed fishes. They have a dorsal fin composed of spines and rays, 3 anal fin spines, and a caudal fin that is lunate to almost truncate. These perchlike fishes have small mouths and most eat algae. Some are referred to as rudderfishes because of their penchant for following ships. Sea chubs occur in tropical waters. There are 7 species in North America.

327   Opaleye
(*Girella nigricans*)

Description: To 26″ (66 cm). Deep, compressed; dark olive-green, usually with *2 yellow-white spots below dorsal fin,* eyes blue. Snout rounded. 12−14 dorsal fin spines, 12−15 rays; anal fin with 3 spines, 17−21 rays, rear profile rounded; caudal fin almost square in profile. Scales prominent.

Habitat: Shallow reefs and kelp beds to 16 fathoms.

Range: From San Francisco, California, to Cabo San Lucas, Baja California.

Related Species: Zebra Perch (*Hermosilla azurea*) has about 10 dark bars on sides, bright blue spot on opercle; 11 dorsal fin spines, 11 rays; found in similar habitat from Monterey Bay, California, to Gulf of California.

Comments: Opaleyes spawn during April, May, and June and are mature at 2 to 3 years, reaching 8″ to 9″ (20 to 23 cm) in length. They feed on algae and eelgrass, apparently taking most of their nourishment from small animals living on the plants. Anglers fishing from shore and skiffs take about 74,000 Opaleyes annually. Commercial fishers using round haul nets or purse seines catch only small amounts.

526   Bermuda Chub
(*Kyphosus sectatrix*)

Description: To 20″ (51 cm). Oval, compressed; *bluish gray to dark gray with pale yellow stripes,* horizontal yellow bands on head, *upper part of opercular membrane blackish;* young have pale spots same size as eyes on head, body, and fins. Head short; snout blunt; mouth small, horizontal; maxilla partly hidden. *Roots of incisorlike teeth horizontal, visible in mouth.* Pectoral fin short; dorsal fin continuous, interrupted by shallow notch, with 12 rays, spiny portion retractable into sheath of scales; 11 anal fin rays; caudal fin forked. Scales ctenoid, cover most of head, body, and all fins except spiny dorsal.

Habitat: Near shore on coral reefs and over rocks, occasionally in sargassum.

Range: In Atlantic from Massachusetts to Brazil, including Bermuda, Gulf of Mexico, and Caribbean.

Related Species: Blue-bronze Chub (*K. analogus*) has brassy stripes on sides, prominent stripe under eye; occurs in shallow reefs and kelp beds to 16 fathoms in Pacific from Oceanside, California, to Peru. Yellow Chub (*K. incisor*) has brighter yellow stripes; 1–2 more rays in dorsal and anal fins; occurs in habitat and range similar to Bermuda Chub south from Virginia.

Comments: The Bermuda Chub and Yellow Chub are herbivorous schooling fishes that feed primarily on bottom-dwelling algae. Neither of these fishes is highly regarded as food.

541 Halfmoon
(*Medialuna californiensis*)

Description: To 19″ (48 cm). Compressed, deep; dark blue above, light blue below, dark spot above gill opening. 9–10 dorsal fin spines, 22–27 longer soft rays; 3 anal fin spines, 17–21 rays; *caudal fin lunate. Scales extend onto soft rays of dorsal fin.*

Habitat: Reefs and kelp beds from near surface to depths of 22 fathoms.

Range: From Vancouver Island, British Columbia, to Gulf of California.

Comments: Halfmoons probably spawn during the summer and fall. At 2 years of age, most are mature and about 8″ (20 cm) long; the maximum known age is 8 years. Halfmoons feed on small invertebrates, particularly those living among algae. The sport catch in

California amounts to about 67,000 fishes annually with an average weight of about ½ lb (200 g).

SPADEFISHES
(Family Ephippidae)

The members of this family are similar to butterflyfishes in that their bodies are very deep and compressed. Their small mouth is not protractile. The stout dorsal fin spines are separate from the soft rays. The deep, short body of spadefishes allows them to make quick and easy lateral movements in confined places such as shipwrecks. There are 2 species in North America.

344 Atlantic Spadefish
(*Chaetodipterus faber*)

Description: To 3' (91 cm). *Short, very deep, disc-shaped,* compressed; *bronze or silvery gray with 3–4 dark bars on sides;* larger fishes more silvery with fading bars; juveniles almost black. *Snout blunt;* mouth terminal, small, ending below nostrils; *opercle ends in blunt point.* Pectoral fins shorter than head; 9 dorsal fin spines, strong, slightly connected to soft dorsal; *anterior rays of soft dorsal and anal fins falcate,* similar in size and shape, densely covered with scales; caudal fin emarginate.

Habitat: Shallow water near rocks, reefs, pilings, and wrecks.

Range: In Atlantic from Cape Cod to Brazil, including Gulf of Mexico and Caribbean; rare north of Chesapeake Bay; introduced in Bermuda.

Related Species: Pacific Spadefish (*C. zonatus*) has 6 dark bars, first passing through eye; occurs in bays over sand or rubble in Pacific from San Diego, California, to N. Peru, including Gulf of California.

Comments: The Atlantic Spadefish is reported to reach 3′ (91 cm), but most specimens are less than half that length. It is popular with anglers and spear fishers, and its flesh is tasty. It feeds on a variety of invertebrates.

BUTTERFLYFISHES
(Family Chaetodontidae)

These small fishes have deep, disc-shaped, compressed bodies. Yellow colors dominate in many species, and most have a dark band through the eye. The color pattern on juveniles is sometimes different from that on adults. The snout is pointed, and the small mouth has protractile jaws. The opercle lacks a strong spine. The dorsal fin is long and continuous. The lateral line extends onto the caudal peduncle. For the most part, Butterflyfishes are a shallow-water, reef-dwelling family. Some species are solitary; others pair off early and for life. There are 7 species in North America.

339 Foureye Butterflyfish
(*Chaetodon capistratus*)

Description: To 6″ (15 cm). Deep, compressed, disc-shaped; silvery gray to pale yellow or whitish with *dark, oblique lines above and horizontal lines below, meeting to form chevrons;* black bar on head through eye; pelvic fins mostly yellow; *large, ocellated black spot below back end of dorsal fin.* Snout pointed; mouth small; jaws protractile. Dorsal fin continuous, long. Lateral line extends onto caudal peduncle.
Habitat: Coral and rocky reefs.
Range: From New England to Panama, including Gulf of Mexico and West Indies.

Related Species: Scythe Butterflyfish (*C. falcifer*) has yellow body with black scythe-shaped stripe; occurs on deep, rocky reefs from Santa Catalina Island, California, to Galápagos Islands.

Comments: The Foureye Butterflyfish, one of the most common butterflyfishes, rarely exceeds 4″ (10 cm). It feeds primarily on coral polyps, sea anemones, tubeworms, and algae.

338   Spotfin Butterflyfish
(*Chaetodon ocellatus*)

Description: To 8″ (20 cm). Deep, strongly compressed, disc-shaped; *whitish with dark bar from cheek through eye and onto front of dorsal fin; soft dorsal has dark blotch at base, smaller spot on tip;* median fins yellow with thin, blue line near edges; pectoral fins pale with yellow stripe running from base to edge of opercle; pelvic fins yellow. Juveniles have dark bar between soft dorsal and anal fins. Head profile steep, concave in front of eye; snout pointed. Soft dorsal and anal fins similar size and shape.

Habitat: Coral and rocky reefs in shallow water; rock jetties in areas without reefs.

Range: From Massachusetts to Brazil, including Gulf of Mexico and Caribbean; most abundant in Central and South America; rare in West Indies.

Comments: Well adapted to their habitat, the body form of butterflyfishes allows them to dart through crevices with agility.

340   Reef Butterflyfish
(*Chaetodon sedentarius*)

Description: To 6″ (15 cm). Deep, compressed, disc-shaped; yellow above shading to white below, dark bar on head through eye; *broad, black bar extending from dorsal and anal fins to caudal peduncle.* Snout pointed; mouth small, jaws protractile. *Soft dorsal and anal fins more rounded posteriorly.* Lateral line extends onto caudal peduncle.

Habitat: Coral and rocky reefs.

Range: From North Carolina to S. Florida, E. Gulf of Mexico, and Caribbean.

Comments: The adult Reef Butterflyfish is probably seen less often than some other butterflyfishes because it frequents deeper water. In the Tortugas it has been reported at 40 fathoms. The young are often seen in shallow water.

---

341 Banded Butterflyfish
(*Chaetodon striatus*)

Description: To 6″ (15 cm). Deep, compressed, disc-shaped; whitish with lines forming chevrons, black band on head through eye, *2 broad, black bars on sides; black or dusky bar from soft dorsal fin base to caudal peduncle; median fins with black submarginal bands,* white edges; pelvic fin spine white, rays black. Soft dorsal and anal fins not noticeably rounded.

Habitat: Coral and rocky reefs.

Range: From New Jersey to Brazil, including Gulf of Mexico and Caribbean.

Comments: In the Gulf of Mexico the Banded Butterflyfish is known only around offshore reefs.

ANGELFISHES
(Family Pomacanthidae)

These brightly colored fishes have a deep, compressed body. They are so close anatomically to the butterflyfishes that some experts classify them together. Angelfishes differ in having a blunter snout and a large spine on the angle of the preopercle. In addition, the rays of the dorsal and anal fins are often long and filamentous. Active during the day and lethargic at night, most species inhabit shallow reefs. Some feed on the ectoparasites of other fishes. There are 6 species in North America.

321   Cherubfish
(*Centropyge argi*)

Description: To 2¾″ (7 cm). Oval; *deep blue, head and chest yellow; narrow, blue ring around eye; pectoral fins pale yellowish,* other fins deep blue, edges pale blue. Head blunt, not concave over eye; eye diameter greater than length of snout; bone anterior to eye with 2 large, decurved spines; large spine at corner of strongly serrate preopercle. Dorsal and anal fins not filamentous; caudal fin rounded.

Habitat: Coral and rocky reefs, usually at depths of over 16 fathoms.

Range: Bermuda, S. Gulf of Mexico, and West Indies.

Comments: This beautiful little fish is apparently not often encountered because it seems to prefer deep water.

331, 336   Queen Angelfish
(*Holacanthus ciliaris*)

Description: To 18″ (46 cm). Deep, compressed; *bluish, scale edges yellow-orange; head yellowish with blue markings on snout, opercle, and chest; large, black spot encircled by blue ring (crown) on nape;* pectoral, pelvic, and caudal fins yellow, black blotch at base of pectorals; dorsal and anal fins with narrow, light blue edges. Juveniles yellowish green with narrow, light blue bars; bluish-black band through eye. Upper profile of head nearly straight to slightly concave above eye; no spine on bone anterior to eye; preopercular spine present. *Dorsal and anal fins long, filamentous, extending beyond end of caudal fin;* caudal fin rounded, without upper filament.

Habitat: Coral reefs in shallow water.

Range: From Florida to Brazil, including Gulf of Mexico and Caribbean.

Related Species: Blue Angelfish (*H. bermudensis*) lacks crown on nape; most of caudal fin dark; occurs in similar habitat in Bermuda, Florida, Gulf of Mexico, and West Indies.

Comments: Queen Angelfishes blend well with their natural habitat, despite their bright colors. Juveniles may exhibit cleaning behavior typical of some wrasses. The Queen and Blue angelfishes commonly hybridize, producing offspring that are intermediate in appearance.

333 Rock Beauty
(*Holacanthus tricolor*)

Description: To 14″ (36 cm). Deep, compressed; *head, chest, and belly yellow, remainder of body black; first few dorsal spines,* posterior edges of dorsal and anal fins, and *pectoral, pelvic, and caudal fins yellow;* lips black or blue. Head profile concave in front of eye; *preopercular spine very long.* Dorsal and anal fins not filamentous, posterior edges straight; *caudal fin rounded with short filament at upper corner.*

Habitat: Shallow water over coral and rocky reefs, sometimes offshore.

Range: Bermuda; from Georgia to Brazil, including West Indies; offshore reefs in NW. Gulf of Mexico.

Comments: This attractive species is very common on the West Indian reefs. The Rock Beauty is a conspicuous fish that, like many other angelfishes, feeds on sponges, tunicates, and algae.

334 Gray Angelfish
(*Pomacanthus arcuatus*)

Description: To 24″ (61 cm). Compressed, depth about three-fourths length; *gray or brown, most large scales dark with pale edges, median fin edges light blue or white, chin and mouth area white;* juveniles black with 5 yellow bars across head and body. Head profile very steep; mouth small, lower jaw projects beyond upper; preopercular spine well developed. Soft dorsal and anal fins filamentous; usually 9 dorsal spines; caudal fin truncate.

Habitat: Shallow reefs.

Range: From New England to SE. Brazil, including West Indies; rare on offshore reefs in Gulf of Mexico.

Similar Species: French Angelfish (*P. paru*) has narrow yellowish margin completely encircling caudal fin with large, dark area in center; caudal fin more rounded.

Comments: The Gray Angelfish, perhaps the largest of the angelfishes, is reported to be among the least wary of the reef fishes. Apparently it is also hardy, as it is known to straggle north as far as New England. The species has been introduced in Bermuda.

332, 335 French Angelfish
(*Pomacanthus paru*)

Description: To 14″ (36 cm). Deep, compressed; *blackish, most scales with crescent-shaped yellow marks, yellow ring around eye, yellow bar at pectoral fin base, dorsal fin filament yellow;* juveniles black with 5 yellow bars on head, body, and caudal fin base. Head profile very steep; mouth small, lower jaw projects beyond upper; preopercular spine well developed. Usually 10 dorsal spines; dorsal and anal fins filamentous; caudal fin rounded.

Habitat: Shallow reefs.

Range: Bermuda; from N. Florida and West Indies to N. South America. Reported in Gulf of Mexico around West Flower Gardens Reef.

Similar Species: Gray Angelfish (*P. arcuatus*) has broad yellow margin not entirely circling caudal fin, with less extensive black center; caudal fin more truncate.

Comments: Juvenile specimens of the French Angelfish and the Gray Angelfish are very similar, and this has undoubtedly led to some confusion regarding the geographical distribution and relative abundance of the 2 species.

CICHLIDS
(Family Cichlidae)

Noted for their elaborate breeding behavior and bright colors, cichlids are important aquarium fishes. They are a widespread, abundant, and diverse group of primarily freshwater fishes that superficially resemble the sunfishes. Cichlids have a single nostril on each side of the snout, and the lateral line is interrupted posteriorly. Several species have been introduced for the purpose of weed control and pond culture, frequently adversely affecting native fishes. There are 12 species in North America, 11 of which were introduced.

79 Rio Grande Cichlid
(*Cichlasoma cyanoguttatum*)

Description: To 12″ (30 cm). Deep, compressed, dorsal profile gently curved; breeding males have hump at nape; dusky to olive above, sides greenish gray with *numerous small, blue or blue-green to whitish spots* and 4–6 dusky bars, dark spots below middle of dorsal fin and near caudal fin base, dusky below.

Maxilla does not reach eye; single
nostril each side of snout. Dorsal fins
joined, spiny portion much longer; anal
fin has 5–6 spines, 8–9 rays. Lateral
line interrupted, *27–30 scales in series.*

Habitat: Warm streams in pools and slack
water, usually with aquatic vegetation.

Range: Gulf of Mexico drainages from Rio
Grande, Texas, to N. Mexico;
introduced in W. central Florida, S.
Texas, and other southern states.

Similar Species: Sunfishes (Centrarchidae) have nostrils
with 2 openings on each side of snout;
lateral line complete.

Comments: This very attractive fish is easy to keep
in an aquarium, but like other cichlids,
it digs up the bottom, uproots plants,
and is somewhat aggressive if kept with
other fishes.

78, 523   Mozambique Tilapia
(*Tilapia mossambica*)

Description: To 15″ (38 cm). Deep, compressed;
dark olive to gray above, sides gray-
green to yellowish, yellowish below;
dorsal and caudal fins have reddish
edges; breeding males bluish to black;
young silvery with 6–8 bars. Mouth
small; lips of breeding males large,
blue; single nostril on each side of
snout. *Dorsal fins joined, 15–17 spines,*
10–12 rays; anal fin has 3–4 spines,
9–10 rays; *dorsal and anal fins pointed
posteriorly.* Caudal peduncle short, deep;
caudal fin rounded. Lateral line
interrupted posteriorly, 29–33 scales in
series.

Habitat: Warm, sluggish streams, ponds,
and canals with abundant aquatic
vegetation; also enters brackish coastal
waters.

Range: Widely introduced in S. United States
south of North Carolina, Missouri, and
central California.

Comments: The Mozambique Tilapia has been
introduced for the purpose of weed

control and has escaped from ponds where it was cultured for the tropical fish trade. It feeds on aquatic insects and small fishes as well as aquatic weeds, and competes with native game fishes for food and space.

SURFPERCHES
(Family Embiotocidae)

These deep, very compressed fishes have an anal fin with 3 spines and 15 to 35 soft rays. The single dorsal fin is composed of spines and rays, and the caudal fin is indented or deeply forked. The maxilla is fully exposed. Cycloid scales are present, and there is usually a sheath of scales extending onto the dorsal fin. There are 20 surfperches in North America, and all but a single species are limited to the northern Pacific. They are viviparous, and the developing embryos receive nourishment from the female through a series of capillaries in their enlarged dorsal and anal fins.

528 Redtail Surfperch
(Amphistichus rhodoterus)

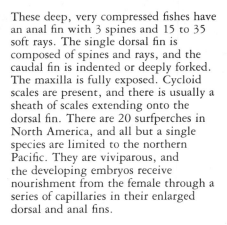

Description: To 16″ (41 cm). Deep, very compressed; silver with light reddish bars on sides, caudal fin reddish. Lower edge of eye below top of upper lip; maxilla fully exposed; 10–14 rakers on lower limb of first gill arch. *Longest dorsal fin spine longer than rays;* 3 anal fin spines, 28–31 soft rays.

Habitat: Steeply sloping sandy beaches and other sandy areas to about 25′ (8 m).

Range: From Vancouver Island, British Columbia, to Monterey Bay, California.

Related Species: Barred Surfperch (*A. argenteus*) has lower edge of eye above upper lip;

dorsal fin spines shorter than soft rays; found from Bodega Bay, California, to Bahía Playa Maria, Baja California. Calico Surfperch (*A. koelzi*) has lower edge of eye below top of upper lip; longest dorsal spine about equal to longest soft ray; found from Shi Shi Beach, Washington, to Arroyo San Isidro, Baja California. Both in similar habitat.

Comments: Redtail Surfperches feed on sand-dwelling crustaceans and mollusks. Highly sought by surf anglers in northern California, they also support a small, hook-and-line commercial fishery.

---

530 Kelp Perch
(*Brachyistius frenatus*)

Description: To 8½" (22 cm). Elongate, compressed; golden above with elongate, white blotches, silvery below. *Snout long, pointed, upturned; tip of lower jaw projects beyond upper jaw;* maxilla exposed. 7–10 dorsal fin spines, 13–17 rays; 3 anal fin spines, 20–25 rays. Caudal peduncle long; caudal fin shallowly forked.

Habitat: In kelp beds among fronds; near surface to 17 fathoms.

Range: From N. British Columbia to Bahía Tortugas, Baja California.

Related Species: Reef Perch (*Micrometrus aurora*) has series of half rings on scales just posterior to pectoral fins; 15–19 soft dorsal rays; found from Tomales Bay, California, to Punta Baja, Baja California. Dwarf Perch (*M. minimus*) has black area at pectoral fin base, dark stripes just behind it below lateral line; mouth horizontal; jaws equal; 12–16 soft dorsal rays; found from Bodega Bay, California, to Isla Cedros, Baja California. Both occur in tidepools and shallow water over rocks.

Comments: Kelp Perches breed in the fall and give

birth to fully developed young in
the spring. These small perches are
cleaners; much of their food consists of
ectoparasites picked off other fishes.
Kelp Perches are too small to be sought
by anglers.

543 Shiner Perch
(*Cymatogaster aggregata*)

Description: To 8" (20 cm). Elongate, depth one-
third length, compressed; light
greenish above, silvery below, *3 yellow
bars on sides interspersed with black;*
breeding males nearly all black, with
speckles covering yellow areas. Maxilla
exposed, not reaching eye. *Distance from
pectoral fin insertion to dorsal fin origin one-
third of standard length;* 8–11 dorsal
spines, 18–23 rays; 3 anal fin spines.

Habitat: In bays around piers; on outer coast
over soft bottoms, and near reefs and
kelp beds to 80 fathoms.

Range: From Wrangell, Alaska, to Bahía de
San Quintín, Baja California.

Similar Species: Island Seaperch (*C. gracilis*) more
slender; distance from pectoral fin
insertion to dorsal fin origin about one-
quarter standard length; in similar
habitat in Channel Islands, California.

Comments: Anglers fishing from piers catch large
numbers of these abundant perches.

519 Black Perch
(*Embiotoca jacksoni*)

Description: To 15½" (39 cm). Deep, very
compressed; usually dark brown to
reddish-brown above, yellowish below,
dark bars on sides, *blue bar on anal fin
base.* Maxilla exposed; lower lip has
frenum. 3 anal fin spines, 23–27 rays.
*Patch of enlarged scales adjacent to pectoral
fin insertion;* row of scales extends onto
anal fin rays.

Habitat: Nearshore reefs and kelp beds.
Range: From Fort Bragg, California, south to Punta Abreojos, Baja California.
Similar Species: Barred Surfperch (*Amphistichus argenteus*) lacks enlarged scales adjacent to pectoral fins.
Comments: This fish feeds on worms, crustaceans, and mollusks; some are cleaners that pick parasites off both their own and other species of fishes. The peak breeding season is in the summer, and most young are born in the spring. Anglers fishing from shore and skiffs off southern California harvest about 125,000 Black Perches each year.

---

531 Striped Seaperch
(*Embiotoca lateralis*)

Description: To 15″ (38 cm). Deep, very compressed; red, blue, and yellow stripes on sides, pelvic fins dusky, *caudal fin base orange.* Upper jaw extends beyond lower; maxilla exposed. *Base of anal fin longer than distance from pelvic fin insertion to anal fin origin;* 3 anal fin spines, 29–33 rays.
Habitat: Reefs, piers, and kelp beds; in bays and offshore areas to depths of 70′ (21 m).
Range: From Wrangell, Alaska, to Punta Cabros, Baja California.
Similar Species: Rainbow Seaperch (*Hypsurus caryi*) has pelvic fins red-orange, edges blue; base of anal fin shorter than distance from pelvic fin insertion to anal fin origin.
Comments: Anglers fishing from rocky shores, piers, and small boats catch about 100,000 Striped Seaperches each year in northern and central California. They are also harvested in small numbers by commercial hook-and-line fishers.

525 Walleye Surfperch
(*Hyperprosopon argenteum*)

Description: To 12″ (30 cm). Deep, very compressed; silver, back faintly dusky, *pelvic fin tips black, caudal fin edge black.* Lower lip lacks frenum; maxilla exposed. 20–23 rakers on lower limb of first gill arch. 3 anal fin spines, 30–35 rays.

Habitat: In surf, over sand, and around piers, reefs, and kelp beds; bays and outer coast to depths of 60′ (18.3 m).

Range: From Vancouver Island, British Columbia, to Punta Rosarito, Baja California.

Related Species: Spotfin Surfperch (*H. anale*) has black blotch on dorsal fin spines and anal fin soft rays; found from Seal Rock, Oregon, south to Bahía Blanca, Baja California. Silver Surfperch (*H. ellipticum*) with caudal fin pinkish, pelvic fin tips not black; found from Vancouver Island, British Columbia, to Rio San Vicente, Baja California. Both in similar habitat.

Comments: The Walleye Surfperch breeds from October through December, giving birth to 5 to 12 young in the spring. This species feeds on small crustaceans. Shore anglers in southern California bays and on the outer coast catch between 150,000 and 200,000 Walleye Surfperches annually. The species is also part of the commercial surfperch catch.

520 Rainbow Seaperch
(*Hypsurus caryi*)

Description: To 12″ (30 cm). Deep, very compressed; sides have red and blue stripes, about 10 red-brown bars on upper body, *pelvic and anal fins usually red-orange, edges blue,* dark blotch on soft dorsal fin. *Anal fin base shorter than distance from pelvic fin insertion to anal fin* origin; 3 anal fin spines, 20–24 rays.

Habitat: Reefs, piers, and kelp beds; bays and
outer coast to depths of 22 fathoms.

Range: From Cape Mendocino, California, to
Isla San Martin, Baja California.

Similar Species: Striped Seaperch (*Embiotoca lateralis*)
with pelvic fins dusky; 29–33 anal fin
rays; anal fin base longer than distance
from pelvic fin insertion to anal fin
origin.

Comments: Rainbow Seaperches gather in large
aggregations to breed in the fall; the
young are born the following summer.
Members of this species occasionally act
as cleaners, picking parasites off other
fishes. Anglers catch 10,000 to 20,000
Rainbow Seaperches annually along the
California coast.

527 Sharpnose Seaperch
(*Phanerodon atripes*)

Description: To 12″ (30 cm). Elongate, very
compressed; silvery with *reddish-brown
marks on upper scales; pelvic fins dusky,
black-tipped.* Maxilla exposed. 3 anal fin
spines, 27–30 rays.

Habitat: Deep reefs, kelp beds, sometimes
shallow reefs and piers; to depths of
125 fathoms.

Range: From Bodega Bay, California, to Islas
San Benito, Baja California.

Similar Species: White Seaperch (*P. furcatus*) has thin,
black line at base of soft dorsal fin;
lacks reddish-brown marks on scales
and black-tipped pelvic fins; occurs in
similar habitat from Vancouver Island,
British Columbia, to Punta Cabros,
Baja California.

Comments: The Sharpnose Seaperch obtains some of
its food by picking parasites off other
fishes such as the Ocean Sunfish and
various species of rockfishes. It is less
common than the White Seaperch,
although it becomes abundant every
few years.

529 Rubberlip Seaperch
(*Rhacochilus toxotes*)

Description: To 18″ (46 cm). Deep, very
                compressed; brassy above, tan below,
                occasionally with wide, tapering, light
                bar below middle of dorsal fin. *Lips
                large, pink, fleshy;* lower lip with 2
                fleshy ventral lobes; maxilla exposed.
                First dorsal fin soft ray shorter than
                third; base of spiny part shorter than
                smooth part; spines shorter than
                longest ray; origin of first dorsal above
                pectoral insertion. 3 anal fin spines,
                27–30 rays. Caudal fin moderately
                forked.

Habitat: Reefs, piers, and kelp beds, from
                shallow bays to depths of 25 fathoms.

Range: From Russian Gulch State Beach,
                California, to Thurloe Head, Baja
                California.

Related Species: Pile Perch (*R. vacca*) with lips not
                fleshy or pink; pelvic fins black-tipped;
                dark bar below middle of dorsal fin;
                found in similar habitat from
                Wrangell, Alaska, south to Isla de
                Guadalupe, Baja California.

Comments: A large female Rubberlip Seaperch
                produces about 20 young each summer.
                Adults feed on shrimp, amphipods,
                small crabs, and other crustaceans.
                Numbers of Rubberlip Seaperches are
                taken by anglers in California, and
                commercial fishers catch about 10 tons
                (9,000 kg) each year on hook and line
                and in gill nets.

DAMSELFISHES
(Family Pomacentridae)

single nostril

Most of these small, deep-bodied, and
compressed fishes are brightly colored,
especially when young. The mouth is
small, but the jaws are very protractile.
There is a single nostril on each side of
the snout, a characteristic that
distinguishes this family from all

similar ones except the Cichlidae,
which are found mostly in fresh water.
The shallowly notched dorsal fin
usually has 10 to 14 spines; the anal fin
has 2 spines. The scales are ctenoid,
and the lateral line scales end under the
soft dorsal fin. There are 16 species in
North America, all marine.

342   Sergeant Major
(*Abudefduf saxatilis*)

Description: To 7″ (18 cm). Oblong, deep,
compressed; *bluish white, back under
spiny dorsal fin yellow or greenish yellow, 5
prominent dark bars on sides with wider,
light interspaces,* dark spot at pectoral fin
base. Mouth small, terminal, slightly
oblique; 1 nostril on each side of snout.
Dorsal fin spines continuous with soft
rays; soft dorsal and anal fins pointed,
similar in size and shape; 12–13 anal
soft rays; caudal fin forked. Lateral line
ends under soft dorsal fin.

Habitat: Shallow reefs, rock jetties, grass beds,
and around pilings. Juveniles part of
sargassum fauna.

Range: From Rhode Island to Uruguay,
including Bermuda, Gulf of Mexico,
and Caribbean.

Related Species: Night Sergeant (*A. taurus*) has pale
interspaces narrower than dark bars,
9–10 soft anal rays; occurs in similar
habitat from S. Florida to Caribbean.

Comments: The Sergeant Major is apparently most
abundant on shallow reefs in the
Caribbean; far fewer occur north of
Florida. It feeds on plankton, deep-sea
invertebrates, and even plants.

326   Blacksmith
(*Chromis punctipinnis*)

Description: To 12″ (30 cm). Deep, elongate, very
compressed; *back dark blackish blue, sides*

gray-blue; black spots posteriorly and on dorsal fin; juveniles purplish blue anteriorly, yellowish posteriorly. Mouth slightly upturned; maxilla does not reach eye; single nostril on each side of snout. Lateral line ends under soft dorsal fin.

Habitat: Reefs and kelp beds to 45 fathoms.
Range: From Monterey Bay, California, to Punta San Pablo, Baja California.
Related Species: Blue Chromis (*C. cyaneus*) mostly blue or black; occurs on reefs in S. Florida and the Caribbean.
Comments: Blacksmiths spawn during the summer; the male cleans the nesting site, then herds a ripe female to it. After spawning, the male guards the eggs until they hatch. Because of their small size, Blacksmiths are not sought by anglers, but they are occasionally taken on small hooks, and by spear fishers.

319, 320 Garibaldi
(*Hypsypops rubicundus*)

Description: To 14″ (36 cm). Deep, compressed; *adults bright orange, juveniles have iridescent blue markings on head, body, and fins.* 1 nostril on each side of snout. 11–13 dorsal fin spines, 12–15 rays; extends from above pectoral fin insertion to posterior of anal fin base, caudal fin forked, tips rounded. Lateral line ends under soft dorsal fin.
Habitat: Reefs and kelp beds to 16 fathoms.
Range: From Monterey Bay, California, to Bahía Magdalena, Baja California; rare north of Point Conception, California.
Comments: Garibaldis spawn from March through July. The male prepares the nest and guards the eggs until they hatch in 2 or 3 weeks. They feed on a variety of invertebrates. Garibaldis are protected by law in California, and may not be taken for either sport or commercial purposes.

322 Yellowtail Damselfish
(*Microspathodon chrysurus*)

Description: To 7½" (19 cm). Depth about one-half
length; *entire body and all fins except
caudal dark blue to almost black, bronzy on
cheeks and breast, light blue spots on back
and dorsal fin,* caudal fin either
yellowish or white. Young have more
blue spots on back and dorsal fin,
caudal fin dark. Upper profile of head
steep; mouth small, terminal; eye
small, relatively high on head; teeth in
upper jaw flexible, brushlike; deep
notch anterior to eyes next to exposed
maxilla; preopercular bone smooth; 1
nostril on each side of snout. Posterior
edges of soft dorsal and anal fin
truncate. Lateral line ends under soft
dorsal fin.

Habitat: Reefs in shallow water or offshore.

Range: From N. Florida to Venezuela; Gulf of
Mexico, West Indies, and Caribbean.

Comments: This species feeds on algae, organic
detritus, and certain corals. The young
pick parasites from larger fishes.

323 Beaugregory
(*Pomacentrus leucostictus*)

Description: To 4" (10 cm). Relatively slender,
compressed, depth about two-fifths
length; *yellow, top of head and back
bluish;* light blue dots and wavy lines
on head, back, and spiny part of dorsal
fin; large, black spot in bluish portion
of dorsal fin; small, black spot on upper
bases of pectoral fins. Mouth small,
terminal; eye diameter greater than
length of snout; *preopercle strongly serrate;*
nostril on each side of snout. Dorsal fin
long, continuous, 12 spines, 14–15
rays; rays of dorsal and anal fins taper to
acute point. Lateral line ends under soft
dorsal fin.

Habitat: Shallow water in rocky tide pools, or
over coral or sand.

Range: From Maine to Brazil, including Bermuda and West Indies; possibly Gulf of Mexico.

Similar Species: Cocoa Damselfish (*P. variabilis*) juveniles have small, dark spot on dorsal fin not extending onto back; small, dark spot on top of caudal peduncle.

Comments: This is one of the most common damselfishes in shallow rocky areas of the Bahamas and the Caribbean. As individuals approach maximum size, they lose their bright colors and become dusky.

324 Cocoa Damselfish
(*Pomacentrus variabilis*)

Description: To 4¼" (11 cm). Relatively slender, compressed, depth little less than half length; top of head, back, and most of dorsal fin bluish or brownish, streaking into yellow on upper sides and forming vertical lines; remainder of body yellow; spiny dorsal fin with posterior dark spot; *dark spot on upper part of caudal peduncle.* Upper profile of head slightly convex; snout pointed; nostril on each side of snout. Soft dorsal and anal fins bluntly rounded posteriorly. Lateral line ends under soft dorsal fin.

Habitat: Coral reefs, rocks, wrecks, and oil platforms.

Range: From Florida to Brazil, including Gulf of Mexico, Caribbean, and West Indies.

Similar Species: Beaugregory (*P. leucostictus*) juveniles have obvious small, dark spots along back and dorsal fin; lack small, dark spot on caudal peduncle.

Comments: As in the Beaugregory, large adults become dusky, and it is consequently difficult to see the subtle differences that distinguish these species unless specimens are in hand.

WRASSES
(Family Labridae)

As they mature, some of these brightly colored fishes may change sex and their patterning. Additionally, males and females are often shaded differently. They may have a deep, compressed body or be cigar-shaped. The mouth is terminal and protractile, with conspicuously thick lips. Most wrasses have strong canine teeth in the jaws and conical teeth in the pharynx, but none on the roof of the mouth. There is a single dorsal fin and its spines are weak. The lateral line, following the dorsal contour, may be continuous or interrupted. Many wrasses are tropical and live on coral reefs. There are 24 North American species.

369 Spanish Hogfish
(*Bodianus rufus*)

Description: To 24″ (61 cm). Moderately deep, depth about one-third length; *anterior two-thirds, including dorsal fin and upper part of head, bluish purple; posterior third and entire belly yellow;* pectoral fins unpigmented. Head pointed, forehead not steep in profile; maxilla reaches eye; jaws have canine teeth anteriorly; *upper jaw has large canine tooth, curved backwards, on each side.* Dorsal fin continuous, with 12 spines; upper and lower caudal fin rays form short filaments. Lateral line not interrupted.

Habitat: Coral and rocky reefs to depths of about 16 fathoms.

Range: Bermuda; from S. Florida to N. Brazil, including offshore reefs in Gulf of Mexico; Caribbean.

Related Species: Spotfin Hogfish (*B. pulchellus*) has red body with broad, white band on sides from chin to above middle of anal fin; yellow on posterior rays of soft dorsal fin, upper half of caudal peduncle, caudal fin base, and upper lobe; found in deeper water from South Carolina to Florida, N. Gulf of Mexico, and West Indies.

Comments: The young of the Spanish Hogfish pick parasitic crustaceans off other fishes. As a defense mechanism, the bluish-purple color becomes reddish in deep water, protecting the fishes from predators because red is not visible at great depths.

366 Creole Wrasse
(*Clepticus parrai*)

Description: To 12″ (30 cm). Moderately deep, depth about one-third length; *deep purple or violet above, becoming lighter violet or purple below;* snout and nape black; yellow area above anal fin and on caudal peduncle. *Snout blunt; mouth small, very oblique;* lower jaw projects beyond upper; canine teeth pale blue, small, weak, none in posterior of jaws. Dorsal fin single, with 12 spines; caudal fin forked.

Habitat: Outer reefs to depths of 70′ (21 m).

Range: Bermuda; from North Carolina to Florida and West Indies; Flower Gardens Reef in N. Gulf of Mexico.

Comments: Creole Wrasses are common on the outer reefs, where they form large feeding assemblies well off the bottom. They feed on copepods, small jellyfishes, tunicates, and other invertebrates. Like most wrasses, they are usually most active during the day, and at night may bury themselves in the sand or hide in crevices of reefs.

374 Slippery Dick
(*Halichoeres bivittatus*)

Description: To 9″ (23 cm). Moderately slender, cigar-shaped; *green above, becoming light greenish-yellow or whitish on sides; sides with 2 purplish or blackish stripes* from eye to caudal fin base and from pectoral fin base to caudal peduncle; stripes overlaid with red, and lower stripe may be yellow; sometimes pinkish marking on head; upper and lower caudal fin tips black, with irregular red bands. Head somewhat pointed; mouth terminal, not oblique; jaws with canine teeth, 2 large pairs anteriorly. Dorsal fin single, with 9 spines; caudal fin squarish. Lateral line continuous, abruptly decurved below soft dorsal fin.

Habitat: Around shallow coral and rocky reefs and over nearby sand.

Range: Bermuda; from North Carolina to Brazil, including N. Gulf of Mexico, West Indies, and Central America.

Related Species: Rock Wrasse (*H. semicinctus*) has body yellow above, lighter below; male has dark blue bar behind pectoral fin; female has large, black spots on scales adjacent to lateral line. 12 anal fin soft rays; occurs in similar habitat from Point Conception, California, to Gulf of California.

Comments: The Slippery Dick is perhaps the most common wrasse around shallow-water reefs. It is less fastidious about its habitat and food selection than are other wrasses.

367, 372   Yellowhead Wrasse
(*Halichoeres garnoti*)

Description: To 7½" (19 cm). Moderately slender, depth about one-quarter length. *Males bisected by oblique, black girdle* extending onto soft dorsal and caudal fins; *anterior to girdle bright yellow above, blue below; posterior to girdle bluish green;* anal fin usually reddish orange. Females reddish orange. Juveniles yellow with narrow, blue stripe down middle; both have dark lines radiating posteriorly from eye. Head somewhat pointed; mouth terminal, not oblique; jaws with canine teeth, 2 large pairs anteriorly. Dorsal fin single, with 9 spines; caudal fin slightly rounded. Lateral line continuous, curves downwards below soft dorsal fin.

Habitat: Coral and rocky reefs to depths of 27 fathoms.

Range: Bermuda; Florida south to SE. Brazil, including parts of Gulf of Mexico and West Indies.

Comments: The Yellowhead Wrasse is apparently common on the Bahama reefs, but rather rare in the peripheral areas of its range. It is named for Garnot, an early fish collector from Martinique.

363, 373 **Puddingwife**
(*Halichoeres radiatus*)

Description: To 20″ (51 cm). *Depth about one-third length,* greatest just in front of dorsal fin; in smaller individuals dorsal and ventral profiles about equally rounded. *Adults olive-yellow on back; sides yellowish orange with round or crescent-shaped blue spots; blue lines on snout and through eye;* 3–5 blue bars on back, more conspicuous in young, becoming blotches in adults. Juveniles with 2 orange or yellow stripes on side separated by blue stripe. Mouth small, terminal; jaws have canine teeth. Dorsal fin single, with 9 spines, 11 rays; caudal fin truncate with rounded corners. Lateral line abruptly decurved before beginning of caudal peduncle.

Habitat: Rocks and coral reefs; young to 18′ (5.5 m), adults to 30 fathoms.

Range: Bermuda; from North Carolina to Brazil, including Gulf of Mexico, Caribbean, and West Indies.

Comments: This is one of the largest wrasses in North America, distinguished from all others in the genus by its deeper body. It feeds on mollusks and echinoderms.

371   Señorita
(*Oxyjulis californica*)

Description: To 10″ (25 cm). Elongate, cigar-
shaped; yellow-orange above, cream
below; *caudal fin with large, black spot.*
Snout pointed; mouth small; teeth
small, protruding. Dorsal fin single,
elongate, with 10 spines, 13 rays; *13
anal fin rays.* Caudal fin truncate to
slightly rounded. Scales large, cycloid.

Habitat: Reefs and kelp beds to depths of 55
fathoms.

Range: From Salt Point, Sonoma County,
California, to Isla Cedros, Baja
California.

Comments: Señoritas occur in large aggregations
and singly. They spawn from May
through August and feed on small
snails, crustaceans, worms, and larval
fishes. Some pick parasites from other
fishes; they are the most common
parasite-cleaners off southern
California. Anglers catch Señoritas
using very small hooks, but few are
retained because they are not
considered edible.

377, 380   California Sheephead
(*Semicossyphus pulcher*)

Description: To 3′ (91 cm). Fusiform, deep,
compressed. Males with head, posterior
body, and caudal fin black, mid-body
brick-red, chin white. Females reddish
brown; *juveniles brick-red on sides with
white stripe; pectoral, dorsal, and caudal
fins with large, black spots.* Forehead
steeply sloping in adults; large canines
present. Single dorsal fin extends from
pectoral fin insertion to rear of anal fin
base; caudal fin almost square.

Habitat: Reefs and kelp beds to depths of 48
fathoms.

Range: From Monterey Bay, California, to
Cabo San Lucas, Baja California; also in
Gulf of California.

Comments: Adult California Sheepheads are female until they are 7 or 8 years old, when the ovaries become testes; fishes then function as males for the rest of their lives. California Sheepheads spawn in spring and summer and feed on crustaceans, echinoderms, and mollusks. They are popular with anglers and spear fishers, but the annual catch in California is no more than about 50,000 fish.

381 Tautog
(*Tautoga onitis*)

Description: To 3′ (91 cm); 21½ lbs (9.8 kg). Depth one-third length; color varies with background; *dull-colored: mousy, chocolate-gray, deep dusky green, brownish, or dull black,* sides irregularly mottled with paler shades; chin white in large specimens. *Head profile steep; snout blunt; mouth terminal; lips thick;* jaws stout, conical teeth anteriorly, molarlike posteriorly. Long-based dorsal fin notched, with 16–17 spines, 10 rays; caudal fin truncate, slightly rounded at corners. *Cheeks scaleless,* velvety to touch.

Habitat: Coastal waters, usually at depths of less than 60′ (18 m); near wrecks, piers, docks, mussel beds, and steep, rocky shores.

Range: From Nova Scotia to South Carolina; most abundant from Cape Cod to Delaware.

Comments: Despite reported lengths of 3′ (91 cm), most catches are less than half that size. Tautogs feed by crushing shelled invertebrates with their strong teeth. Although considered good food and sport fishes, they are not sufficiently plentiful anywhere in their range to be of great importance as either.

357   Cunner
(*Tautogolabrus adspersus*)

Description: To 10″ (25 cm). *Moderately slender;*
reddish-brown above with bluish or
brownish tinge, mottled with blue,
brown, and red; some specimens
uniformly brown, others deep sepia;
color varies with background. *Snout
pointed; lips moderately thick;* teeth
conical anteriorly, molarlike
posteriorly. Dorsal fin notched, base
long. *Cheek scaled.*

Habitat: Shallow coastal waters, in eelgrass,
around pilings, piers, and rock piles.

Range: From Newfoundland to New Jersey,
occasionally to Chesapeake Bay.

Comments: Cunners are so variably colored that it
is difficult to describe them. Those that
live among red seaweeds or in deep
water are reddish or rust-colored;
whereas over sand they are pale and
speckled with blackish dots. Cunners
are omnivorous. Popular with anglers,
they are good pan fishes.

368, 370   Bluehead
(*Thalassoma bifasciatum*)

Description: To 6″ (15 cm). Elongate, depth about
one-quarter length. *Large males blue
anteriorly, green posteriorly, colors separated
by 2 broad, black bands enclosing light
area;* soft dorsal and anal fins blue;
upper and lower caudal fin rays
blackish. Small males, females, and
juveniles yellow, usually with broad,
blackish lateral stripe from opercle to
caudal fin base; red band from snout
through eye to end of opercle. Head
somewhat pointed; mouth terminal; no
posterior canine teeth. *8 dorsal fin spines;
caudal fin lobes elongate.* Lateral line
abruptly decurved under soft dorsal fin.

Habitat: Coral and rocky reefs.

Range: Bermuda; from S. Florida to Caribbean;
Gulf of Mexico and West Indies.

Similar Species: Wrasse Blenny (*Hemiemblemaria simulus*)
has more elongate body; snout more
pointed; found in similar habitat in S.
Florida and Bahamas.

Comments: Most Blueheads are yellow, and are
sexually mature at 1½" (4 cm). The
blue head, seen only in some large,
sexually mature males, is less common.
The Wrasse Blenny mimics this species
and enjoys protection from predators
that assume that it, like the Bluehead,
is a parasite picker.

PARROTFISHES
(Family Scaridae)

These striking fishes have an unusual
sexual development. The young are, for
the most part, drably colored females;
this is known as the primary phase. In
the terminal phase the fishes turn into
males, and are colored gaudy greens
and blues. Parrotfishes have uncommon
teeth that are fused to form beaklike

teeth   plates in both jaws. They have a single,
uninterrupted dorsal fin, and large,
cycloid scales. Very common on coral
reefs, they are herbivores and are
therefore restricted to relatively shallow
water. There are 14 species in North
America.

365 Blue Parrotfish
(*Scarus coeruleus*)

Description: To 4' (1.2 m). Moderately deep, depth
more than one-third length; *large adults
deep blue; smaller specimens light blue, head
yellow, bases of scales yellowish pink. Teeth
white,* forming beaklike plates, lower
plate hidden by upper when mouth
closed. Single dorsal fin long; caudal fin
truncate, upper and lower lobes become
longer as size increases. 3 scale rows on
cheek; 6 predorsal scales.

Habitat: Coral reefs.
Range: From Maryland to Rio de Janeiro, Brazil, including Bermuda, Caribbean, and West Indies.
Related Species: Emerald Parrotfish (*Nicholsina usta*) has teeth incompletely fused, more slender; occurs from New Jersey to Brazil. Midnight Parrotfish (*S. coelestinus*) has blackish body, scale centers bright blue, teeth blue-green; 2 scale rows on cheek; occurs from S. Florida to Brazil, including Bermuda and Bahamas, but apparently not in Gulf of Mexico. Both in similar habitat.
Comments: The Blue Parrotfish, like other parrotfishes, uses the molarlike teeth on its upper and lower pharyngeal bones to grind algae along with soft coral.

360, 375   Princess Parrotfish
(*Scarus taeniopterus*)

Description: To 13″ (33 cm). Moderately deep, depth about one-third length. *Terminal males blue-green and orange with broad, pale yellow stripe above pectoral fin, 2 narrow blue-green stripes on head;* dorsal and anal fins blue with orange band through middle, *caudal fin blue, edges orange.* Primary female has 3 dark brown stripes alternating with white, fins pale blue. Teeth form beaklike plates, lower plates hidden by upper when mouth closed. Single dorsal fin long; caudal fin truncate or slightly rounded. 3 scale rows on cheek; 7 scales in series under eye; 7–8 predorsal scales.
Habitat: Coral reefs.
Range: Bermuda, S. Florida, Florida Keys, NW. Gulf of Mexico, Bahamas, and throughout Caribbean to NW. Brazil.
Similar Species: Striped Parrotfish (*S. croicensis*) has orange caudal fin, with edges blue in terminal phase; snout yellow in primary phase; 6 scales in series under eye; occurs on coral reefs near S. Florida;

Comments: may stray to Massachusetts.
It is difficult to determine the exact geographical limits of this and other parrotfishes due to the similarity of the species and the many color phases. Undoubtedly this species has sometimes been confused with the Striped Parrotfish.

362 Queen Parrotfish
(*Scarus vetula*)

Description: To 24" (61 cm). Moderately deep, depth one-third length. *Terminal males blue-green, scale edges red-orange; head green with alternating orange and blue-green stripes on lower snout and chin, caudal fin green, orange band on upper and lower rays.* Primary females dark reddish to purplish brown with broad, whitish band on lower sides. Teeth form beaklike plates, lower plate hidden by upper when mouth closed. Single dorsal fin long, caudal fin truncate, lunate in adult males. 4 scale rows on cheek, 7 predorsal scales.
Habitat: Coral reefs.
Range: Bermuda; from S. Florida to Colombia, including NW. Gulf of Mexico and Caribbean.
Comments: This fish is one of the most noticeable members of the coral reef community. This and other parrotfishes are believed to be the major factor in reef attrition and sand production in calm areas.

355, 358, 359 Redband Parrotfish
(*Sparisoma aurofrenatum*)

Description: To 11" (28 cm). Moderately deep, depth about two-fifths length. *Terminal males greenish-gray above, sides and fins reddish, sometimes tinged with blue.* Primary females brown to greenish brown with deep bluish cast on sides, reddish below, *small, light saddle behind soft dorsal fin.* Teeth form beaklike plates, upper plate hidden by lower when mouth closed. Single dorsal fin long; caudal fin rounded in young, truncate in intermediate sizes, emarginate in adults. 1 scale row on cheek; 4 predorsal scales.

Habitat: Coral reefs.

Range: Bermuda; from Florida to Brazil, including Gulf of Mexico, Caribbean, and West Indies.

Related Species: Redtail Parrotfish (*S. chrysopterum*) has large, black spot on upper pectoral fin base; caudal fin slightly emarginate to lunate; occurs on coral reefs in S. Florida, Bahamas, Caribbean, and West Indies.

Comments: The young feed off seagrass beds adjacent to coral reefs.

356, 376   Bucktooth Parrotfish
(*Sparisoma radians*)

Description: To 8″ (20 cm). Depth one-third length. Terminal males greenish brown with pale dots and netlike markings, *some scale edges reddish; blue and orange band from mouth to eye; black bar at pectoral fin base; broad, black border on posterior part of caudal fin.* Primary phase olive to yellowish brown with many pale dots. Teeth form beaklike plates, upper plate hidden by lower when mouth closed, canine teeth prominent. Single dorsal fin long; caudal fin slightly rounded.

Habitat: Seagrass beds.

Range: From Bermuda, S. Florida to Central America, including Bahamas, Lesser Antilles, and part of Gulf of Mexico.

Comments: This parrotfish can change colors rapidly to blend with its surroundings. The genus name derives from the Greek words "spairo," meaning "I gasp," and "soma," meaning "body," and describes the viewer's reaction to these brightly colored fishes.

364 Redfin Parrotfish
(*Sparisoma rubripinne*)

Description: To 18″ (46 cm). Robust, depth about two-fifths length. Terminal males dull green, *scales dark-edged, black spot on upper half of pectoral fin base.* Primary phase light greenish-brown, scales darker-edged, 2 pale bands on chin, caudal peduncle and caudal fin yellowish. Teeth form beaklike plates; upper plate hidden by lower when mouth closed. Single dorsal fin long; caudal fin rounded in young, truncate in intermediate sizes, deeply emarginate in terminal males; 1 scale row on cheek; 4 median predorsal scales.

Habitat: Reefs in shallow water.

Range: From Massachusetts (as a straggler) south to Florida and Rio de Janeiro, including Bermuda and Caribbean. Apparently not in Gulf of Mexico.

Comments: When pursued, the Redfin Parrotfish can hide by rapidly changing its colors to match its surroundings. It is common on inshore reefs.

361, 379 Stoplight Parrotfish
(*Sparisoma viride*)

Description: To 24″ (61 cm). Deep, depth about two-fifths length. Terminal males mostly green, *scale edges dull green, 3 diagonal, yellow-orange bands on head, opercle edge orange with small, bright spot on top; large, yellow spot at caudal fin base.* Primary phase brown above and on head, lower third and fins bright red, scale centers lighter. Teeth form beaklike plates, upper plate included in lower when mouth closed. Single dorsal fin long; caudal fin truncate in young, emarginate in medium sizes, lunate in large males. 1 scale row on cheek; 4 median predorsal scales.

Habitat: Coral reefs and adjacent seagrass beds.

Range: Bermuda; from S. Florida to NE.
           Brazil, including Gulf of Mexico,
           Caribbean, and West Indies.
Comments: This rather large species is most
           abundant in the Florida Keys and on
           West Indian reefs. The specific name
           viride calls attention to its green color.

MULLETS
(Family Mugilidae)

These elongate fishes are almost
cylindrical near the head, but become
compressed posteriorly. The snout is
blunt, the mouth is small and wide,
and the premaxilla is protractile. The
adipose eyelid is well developed. The
pelvic fins are abdominal, and the
pectoral fins are inserted above the axis
of the body. The dorsal fins are well
separated, the first consisting of 4 weak
spines. Mullets have cycloid scales and
lack a lateral line. They are primarily
marine and estuarine fishes, but some
enter fresh water and ascend rivers for
considerable distances. There are 6
species in North America.

484, 485 Striped Mullet
(*Mugil cephalus*)

Description: To 18″ (46 cm). Elongate, cylindrical
              anteriorly, compressed posteriorly;
              silvery, back olive- or bluish-green,
              6–7 *darker stripes on sides*. Head flat
              between eyes; adipose eyelid well
              developed; mouth small, wide,
              terminal, *lower jaw has fleshy knob at tip*.
              Pectoral fins inserted high on shoulders;
              pelvic fins abdominal; dorsal fin has 4
              weak spines well separated from soft
              dorsal; 3 anal fin spines, *usually 8 rays;*
              caudal fin forked. Scales cycloid, cover
              body, top of head, and bases of soft
              dorsal and anal fins. No lateral line.

Habitat: Coasts, estuaries, and fresh water.
Range: In Atlantic from Cape Cod to Brazil, including Gulf of Mexico, Caribbean, and West Indies. In Pacific from San Francisco Bay, California, to Chile.
Related Species: White Mullet (*M. curema*) lacks lateral stripes; has 9 anal fin soft rays; soft dorsal and anal fins densely scaled; occurs in similar habitat and range.
Comments: These important food fishes occur in schools. Striped Mullets are known to travel several hundred miles up rivers, but spawning always takes place in the sea. They feed on small algae and detritus that they glean from the mud.

BARRACUDAS
(Family Sphyraenidae)

These elongate fishes have 2 dorsal fins that are widely separated; the first consists of 5 spines, the second has a spine in front of the soft rays. The second dorsal and anal fins are mirror images. The small pectoral fins are inserted anterior to the pelvic fin base. The pelvic fins are also small and are inserted more or less under the dorsal fin origin. Barracudas may have dark bars, chevrons, stripes, or dark blotches. They are voracious predators that feed mainly on fishes. They may be solitary or gregarious, largely depending on the species and the size of the individual fish. The 5 species in North America may be dangerous.

Pacific Barracuda
(*Sphyraena argentea*)

Description: To 4' (1.2 m); 18 lbs (8 kg). Very

elongate, cylindrical, cigar-shaped; bluish to brownish above, silvery below, *caudal fin yellow. Snout long, pointed; tip of lower jaw extends beyond upper*. Large canine teeth present. Pelvic fin inserted under first dorsal fin origin. Spinous dorsal fin widely separated from soft dorsal fin, soft dorsal fin mirror image of anal fin.

Habitat: Near shore in surface waters and around outer edges of kelp beds to 60′ (18 m).

Range: From Kodiak Island, Alaska, to Cabo San Lucas, Baja California.

Comments: After they mature at about 2 years of age, Pacific Barracudas spawn during the summer. Also known as California Barracudas, they are deemed excellent food and are highly prized by anglers. They are more abundant off Southern California during warm-water years. The annual sport catch has fluctuated from 100,000 to 1 million fish.

583, 584 Great Barracuda
(*Sphyraena barracuda*)

Description: To 6′ (1.8 m); 83 lbs (37.6 kg). Elongate, torpedo-shaped, robust. Color varies with surroundings; deep green to steel-gray above, possibly with purplish cast; sides silvery; belly white; oblique, dark bars on sides of adults, and dark, irregular blotches on lower posterior sides; second dorsal, anal, and caudal fins violet to black with whitish tips. Jaw lacks distinct fleshy flap. *Vertical line drawn from origin of dorsal fin would touch pectoral and pelvic fins. 75–87 scales in lateral line.*

Habitat: Inshore along coast and offshore.

Range: From Massachusetts to S. Brazil, including Bermuda, Gulf of Mexico, Caribbean, and Antilles.

Related Species: Northern Sennet (*S. borealis*) has pelvic and dorsal fins set farther back; occurs from Massachusetts to Uruguay. Guaguanche (*S. guachancho*) has elongate last ray of soft dorsal and anal fins; 108–114 lateral line scales; occurs from Massachusetts to Brazil. Both in similar habitat.

Comments: Specimens under 24″ (61 cm) occur in shallow inshore waters over sandy bottoms, frequently in schools, whereas larger ones are more often found offshore and are usually solitary. Great Barracudas feed chiefly on fishes and occasionally on squids and shrimps. Their large, shearlike, palatine teeth are capable of cutting great lumps of flesh. Divers should be cautious: Great Barracudas can attack people. This species may also cause ciguatera poisoning when eaten.

CLINIDS
(Family Clinidae)

These are small, elongate fishes with long-based dorsal and anal fins. The head usually has cirri, or fleshy flaps, on the nostrils, above the eyes, and at the rear of the head on the side. The pelvic fins are inserted anterior to the pectoral fins and consist of an inconspicuous spine and only 2 or 3 rays. The dorsal fin spines are generally flexible and outnumber the soft rays, and there are only 2 anal fin spines. The body may be naked, although in most species it is covered with cycloid scales. Clinids live on the bottom, usually around rocky or coral reefs in shallow water. There are 46 species in North America.

467 Island Kelpfish
(*Alloclinus holderi*)

Description: To 4″ (10 cm). Elongate, slender; gray with red stripes, iridescent blue spots, 6–8 dark bars; *dorsal fin with green spot anteriorly*. Snout bluntly rounded with 2–3 small cirri above each eye. Pelvic fins almost as long as pectoral fins; dorsal fin with first 4 spines longer than remainder, soft rays longer than spines; caudal fin profile straight. *Abrupt arch in lateral line just behind pectoral fin tip.*

Habitat: Rocky reefs to depths of 27 fathoms.

Range: From Santa Cruz Island, California, to Punta San Pablo, Baja California.

Related Species: Deepwater Blenny (*Cryptotrema corallinum*) has first 3–4 dorsal spines not longer than others; no abrupt arch in lateral line; occurs from Santa Cruz Island, California, to Bahía de San Quintín, Baja California. Reef Finspot (*Paraclinus integripinnis*) has dorsal fin with single ocellus posteriorly; occurs from Santa Cruz Island, California, to Bahía Almejas, Baja California. Both in similar habitat; Deepwater Blenny to 50 fathoms.

Comments: Island Kelpfishes make good aquarium dwellers. Because they are easily approached, they are frequently photographed by scuba divers.

---

466 Sailfin Blenny
(*Emblemaria pandionis*)

Description: To 2″ (5 cm). Elongate, slightly compressed; immature males and females straw-colored with scattered small spots and dark flecks; adult males generally darker; all have dorsal fin with alternating diagonal dark and light lines. Head blunt; snout short; *cirrus above eye 3-lobed at tip;* cirrus at edge of nostril; *no spines on top of head;* lower jaw projects slightly beyond upper; lips thick. Pelvic fin long; *spiny dorsal fin elevated anteriorly,* more so in males, 21 spines. *No lateral line canals or tubes; scaleless.*

Habitat: On bottom over coral rubble, sand, or shells.

Range: S. Florida, NW. Gulf of Mexico, Bahamas, and Caribbean; Central America.

Related Species: Roughhead Blenny (*Acanthemblemaria aspera*) has spines and elongate, fleshy

ninth spines; occurs to 33 fathoms from San Francisco, California, to Isla Cedros, Baja California. Yellowfin Fringehead (*N. stephensae*) has maxilla extending almost halfway to rear edge of opercle; no ocelli; occurs from Monterey Bay, California, to Punta San Hipolito, Baja California. Both in similar habitat.

Comments: Onespot Fringeheads are very aggressive and threaten intruders by opening their large mouths or by lunging. Anglers occasionally catch them, and usually have trouble removing the hook because the fish will attempt to bite.

COMBTOOTH BLENNIES
(Family Blenniidae)

These bottom-dwelling fishes are small, scaleless, and usually drably colored. Robust and deep-bodied, they have a blunt snout and a steep head profile. Both jaws have a single row of incisor teeth, and some species also have canine teeth. Fleshy, featherlike flaps called cirri are present above the eyes and sometimes on the nape. The pelvic fins are inserted anterior to the pectoral fins, and each has only 2 to 4 visible rays. The dorsal fin may be long and continuous or slightly notched; the base of the spiny section is shorter than that of the soft rays. There are 2 flexible anal fin spines. Blennies usually occur in shallow water. There are 17 species in North America.

459 Striped Blenny
(*Chasmodes bosquianus*)

Description: To 3″ (7.5 cm). Elongate, compressed; brownish; sides with dark blotches forming wide irregular bands, dark spots sometimes forming horizontal lines; breeding males have blue spot or band on anterior part of dorsal fin, and orange streak extending posteriorly. *Snout pointed;* maxilla reaches beyond eye; teeth in single row, slender, curved backward, *jaws lack large canine teeth posteriorly.* 12 pectoral fin rays; dorsal fin long, continuous, spines slightly shorter than soft rays, *last ray attached to caudal fin by membrane;* usually 2 anal fin spines, with fleshy knobs at ends in males.

Habitat: Shallow grassflats over sand.

Range: From New York to NE. Florida, disjunctly to Pensacola, Florida, and south to Veracruz, Mexico; rarely north of Maryland.

Related Species: Florida Blenny (*C. saburrae*) has blunter snout and smaller mouth; occurs in similar habitat from NE. Florida west to W. Mississippi.

Comments: The Striped Blenny has an interesting distribution because it is found on the Atlantic and Gulf coasts but not off peninsular Florida.

462 Barred Blenny
(*Hypleurochilus bermudensis*)

Description: To 3½" (9 cm). Elongate, robust anteriorly, depth greatest at dorsal fin origin; grayish, olive, or reddish-brown with darker bars on sides; males darker than females; colors sometimes highly contrasted and vary with substrate. *Snout blunt; head profile steep;* mouth small, terminal, horizontal; *canine teeth in posterior part of jaws; gill openings restricted;* cirri over each eye relatively short. 14 pectoral fin rays; dorsal fin shallowly notched, spines and rays total 25, last ray attached to caudal peduncle; anal fin spines and rays total 16.

Habitat: Rocky areas and jetties; less common on coral reefs.

Range: Bermuda; Florida, Gulf of Mexico, and Bahamas.

Related Species: Crested Blenny (*H. geminatus*) has larger cirrus over eye; more total spines and rays in dorsal and anal fins; occurs in similar habitat from North Carolina to Brazil, including Gulf of Mexico.

Comments: Both of these fishes can be observed by snorklers wherever rock jetties occur. They feed freely on almost any kind of flesh and make good aquarium pets.

461 Feather Blenny
(*Hypsoblennius hentzi*)

Description: To 4″ (10 cm). Elongate, robust anteriorly; brownish with darker blotches or spots; fins variously spotted, pelvics darkest, males have blue spot on anterior part of dorsal fin. Head short, profile rounded; mouth small, terminal; lips fleshy, *upper lip attached to snout;* teeth incisorlike, *no canine teeth;* cirrus over each eye larger in males. 14 pectoral fin rays; usually 12 dorsal fin spines, 14 rays, last ray attached to caudal peduncle by membrane; 2 anal fin spines, 16–17 rays.

Habitat: Over mud in grassflats and oyster reefs.

Range: From Nova Scotia along coast to Yucatán, Mexico.

Related Species: Freckled Blenny (*H. ionthas*) has upper lip free of snout; occurs in similar habitat from North Carolina to NE. Florida, disjunctly to NW. Florida, west to Texas.

Comments: These fishes lay their eggs in "oyster boxes"—empty oyster shells with the hinge intact and the interior relatively clear of silt or mud. Both species are suitable for aquariums.

464 Molly Miller
(*Scartella cristata*)

Description: To 4½" (11 cm). Elongate, robust
anteriorly, deepest at nape; usually
olive with darker blotches, some
extending onto dorsal fin; sometimes
with pearly spots along dorsal fin base;
lighter below with almost no spots or
blotches. Head short, blunt; mouth
small, terminal, lips fleshy; teeth
incisorlike, *canines only in posterior of
lower jaw; median row of cirri on top of
head and nape.* 14 pectoral fin rays;
dorsal fin long, continuous, with 12
spines, 14–15 rays; 2 anal fin spines,
16–17 rays.

Habitat: Rocky areas near shore.

Range: Bermuda; from Florida to Brazil,
including Gulf of Mexico.

Comments: The Molly Miller is the only blenny in
North America with a median row of
cirri on top of the head. It may be
found in very shallow water around
rocks and jetties, or in sandy tide
pools. It is primarily herbivorous.

PRICKLEBACKS
(Family Stichaeidae)

These fishes are eel-like, elongate and
compressed, with long dorsal and anal
fins. The dorsal fin usually consists only
of spines. The pelvic fins, if present,
have branched rays. Pricklebacks may
have brown, red, or yellow coloring,
and, in some species, faint bars or
stripes. The lateral line may be faint,
incomplete, or entirely absent;
occasionally, it will have 4 main
branches with vertical side branches.
These marine fishes occur primarily
in the northern Pacific; there are 29
species in North America, but most are
rarely encountered.

456 Monkeyface Prickleback
(*Cebidichthys violaceus*)

Description: To 30″ (76 cm). Elongate, eel-like, compressed; color highly variable, generally light to dark brown, 2 dark bars below each eye. Snout bluntly rounded; *lips fleshy, prominent; 2 fleshy humps on head;* gill membranes free of isthmus. No pelvic fins; dorsal fin origin above gill openings, 22–25 spines, 40–43 rays, joined to caudal fin. Single lateral line high on sides near dorsal fin base.

Habitat: Crevices and holes in shallow rocky areas to depths of 80′ (24 m).

Range: From Brooking, Oregon, to Bahía de San Quintín, Baja California.

Related Species: Black Prickleback (*Xiphister atropurpureus*) has white band on caudal peduncle; dorsal fin composed entirely of spines, origin about half-way between snout and anal fin origin; occurs from Kodiak Island, Alaska, to Punta China, Baja California. Rock Prickleback (*X. mucosus*) has dorsal fin origin about one-third distance from snout to anal fin origin; occurs from Port San Juan, Alaska, to Point Arguello, California. Both in similar habitat.

Similar Species: High Cockscomb (*Anoplarchus purpurescens*) has gill membranes attached to isthmus; 54–60 dorsal fin spines, no soft rays; single lateral line at middle of side; found in similar habitat from Bering Sea to Santa Rosa Island, California.

Comments: The Monkeyface Prickleback is the target of a specialized sport fishery called "poke poling." Anglers use long cane poles with a 6″ (15 cm) piece of wire attached to the tip; a short leader and hook are attached to the wire. The hook, baited with a crustacean or worm, is poked into crevices at low tide.

GUNNELS
(Family Pholidae)

These eel-like fishes have a long, slender, compressed body. Their teeth are small and conical. The pectoral and pelvic fins are very small or absent. The long dorsal fin, usually joined to the caudal fin, has 75 to 100 flexible spines and no soft rays, and is twice the length of the anal fin. The lateral line, if present, is short. Most gunnels live in the intertidal region or in shallow waters. There are 11 species found in North America.

---

447 Penpoint Gunnel
(Apodichthys flavidus)

Description: To 18″ (46 cm). Elongate, eel-like, compressed; green, yellow, light brown, or red. Head bluntly rounded; mouth terminal, small. *Pectoral fin length about twice eye diameter;* no pelvic fins; dorsal fin contains only spines, extending from pectoral fin insertion to caudal peduncle, connected to caudal fin. *Anal fin spine strong, has deep groove.*

Habitat: Intertidal areas over rocks and shallow eelgrass beds.

Range: From Kodiak Island, Alaska, to S. California.

Related Species: Saddleback Gunnel (*Pholis ornata*) has series of V- or U-shaped dark marks along dorsal fin base; pelvic fins small; 34–38 anal soft rays; occurs from Vancouver Island, British Columbia, to Carmel Bay, California. Red Gunnel (*P. schultzi*) has bars on anal fin; 40–44 anal soft rays; occurs from Queen Charlotte Islands, British Columbia, to San Luis Obispo County, California. Rockweed Gunnel (*Xererpes fucorum*) has pectoral fin same length as eye diameter; anal fin spine without groove; occurs from Vancouver Island, British Columbia, to Punta Escartada, Baja

Comments: California. All in similar habitat. The rarely seen Penpoint Gunnel spawns in January. Its diet consists of small crustaceans and mollusks.

WOLFFISHES
(Family Anarhichadidae)

These eel-like fishes have strong jaws with large canine or conical teeth in front and molarlike teeth in the rear. The gill membranes are attached to the isthmus. The pectoral fins are large, but the pelvic fins are absent. The dorsal fin consists only of flexible spines, and the small caudal fin is usually pointed. Wolffishes do not have a lateral line, and usually lack scales; if present, the scales are small and cycloid. There are 5 species of this marine family in North America.
Wolffishes can cause serious wounds with their teeth.

457 Atlantic Wolffish
(*Anarhichas lupus*)

Description: To 5′ (1.5 m). Elongate, greatest depth at nape, tapering to slender caudal peduncle; color varies with substrate: purplish, brownish, bluish-gray, olive, or combinations of these; 10 or more irregular bars on sides. Maxilla reaches beyond small eye; *teeth conical anteriorly, molarlike posteriorly*. Pectoral fin broad at base, fanlike; no pelvic fins; *dorsal fin spines numerous, flexible;* dorsal fin long, continuous, begins at nape and of uniform height throughout; dorsal and anal fins separate from caudal fin.

Habitat: Over hard bottoms from near shore to depths of 85 fathoms.

Range: From Greenland and Davis Strait to Cape Cod, occasionally to New Jersey.

Comments: This solitary species is not abundant

anywhere. Its large jaws, formidable teeth, and habit of attacking objects and people—in the water or when caught—make it a potentially dangerous species. It feeds on a variety of shelled mollusks, echinoderms, and crustaceans.

455 Wolf-Eel
(*Anarrhichthys ocellatus*)

Description: To 6′8″ (2 m). Eel-like, elongate, compressed, tapering to pointed caudal fin; light gray or gray-brown with *dark mottling and spots surrounded by lighter coloration.* Snout blunt; *front of jaws with large, strong, canine teeth.* Pelvic fins absent; dorsal fin long, continuous, consists of spines. Lateral line absent.

Habitat: Reefs and wrecks with large crevices, to depths of 106 fathoms.

Range: From Kodiak Island, Alaska, to Imperial Beach, San Diego County, California.

Similar Species: California Moray (*Gymnothorax mordax*) lacks both pectoral and pelvic fins.

Comments: The Wolf-Eel spawns during the winter, when the eggs are deposited in crevices or caves and are guarded by both parents. This large predator feeds on crabs taken from traps and on fishes, sea urchins, sea cucumbers, and snails. Anglers and spear fishers catch a few Wolf-Eels. If molested, these fishes may bite and cause serious wounds.

SAND LANCES
(Family Ammodytidae)

These small, eel-like fishes are quite long, lack pelvic fins, and swim with an undulating motion. Unlike eels, they have wide gill openings, a large opercle, a forked caudal fin, and scales. There are 3 species in North America.

American Sand Lance
(*Ammodytes americanus*)

Description: To 7" (18 cm). Very elongate, depth
one-tenth or less of length; variably
bluish-green to olive-brown above,
sides silvery, belly white; sides often
with steel-blue iridescence. Head large,
snout sharply pointed; mouth large, lower
jaw projects well beyond upper jaw.
Pectoral fins inserted well below axis of
body; *no pelvic fins;* dorsal fin long, low,
has only soft rays, origin over pectoral
fins, extends almost to caudal fin base;
anal fin similar but much shorter;
caudal fin forked.

Habitat: Primarily sandy shores, seldom in
deep water over mud or rocks of
continental shelf.

Range: From N. Labrador to Cape Hatteras,
North Carolina.

Related Species: Pacific Sand Lance (*A. hexapterus*) has
metallic blue on back; occurs from
Bering Sea to Los Angeles, California.

Comments: American Sand Lances are often seen in
schools consisting of several thousand
individuals. They swim with an
undulating motion similar to that of
eels. Sand lances are the primary prey
of terns, and are also eaten by other
seabirds, predatory fishes, and
cetaceans. To escape predators they
burrow rapidly into the sand.

SLEEPERS
(Family Eleotridae)

These elongate, robust fishes are drably
colored and often have irregular
mottling. The pelvic fins are inserted
close to each other and, unlike those of
gobies, are not united to form a disc.
The distance from the end of the
second dorsal fin to the base of the
caudal fin rays is equal to or longer
than the length of the second dorsal
base. Sleepers are mostly found in

brackish and fresh water. The family Eleotridae has, in the past, often been included within the Gobiidae, but is now recognized as a distinct family. There are 6 species in North America.

88, 431 **Fat Sleeper**
(*Dormitator maculatus*)

Description: To 10″ (25 cm). Robust, depth one-fourth length; dark brown with light bluish spots and inconspicuous dark stripe on sides; top of head to dorsal fin origin dark; large blotch, usually dark blue, above pectoral fin base; rusty spots on dorsal fin, anal fin dusky; gill membranes dark, sometimes dusky. *Head broad, flat above, fully scaled;* mouth oblique; lower jaw projects beyond upper, which barely reaches eye. Pelvic fins separate; *7 dorsal fin spines well separated from rays;* soft dorsal fin base shorter than caudal peduncle. 30–33 scales in lateral series.

Habitat: Brackish ponds and ditches, saltwater marshes, and freshwater streams near coast.

Range: From New York to Brazil, including Bahamas, Gulf of Mexico, and West Indies; rare north of South Carolina.

Related Species: Spinycheek Sleeper (*Eleotris pisonis*) has more elongate body; twice as many lateral scales; occurs in same habitat and range.

Comments: The Fat Sleeper is used for food in some areas. It is locally common along the Gulf Coast, where there is abundant aquatic vegetation.

GOBIES
(Family Gobiidae)

These small fishes have an elongate, robust body and are variably colored and marked. The pelvic fins are usually

pelvic fin

connected to form a suction disc. The broad-based pectoral fins are inserted just above the pelvic fins. The dorsal fin is single or double; if single it is deeply notched. The distance between the end of the second dorsal fin and the caudal fin base is less than the length of the second dorsal fin base. Scales are usually present but do not form a lateral line. There are 70 species in North America, occurring in both fresh and salt water.

469 Blackeye Goby
(*Coryphopterus nicholsi*)

Description: To 6″ (15 cm). Elongate, almost round in cross section; tan to olive, usually with brown mottling and speckles, *first dorsal fin edge black; iridescent blue spot beneath each eye.* Snout rounded. Tips of pectoral fins reach anus; pelvic fins form ventral sucking disc; 2 dorsal fins, second long, almost reaches caudal fin; anal fin almost one-third length; caudal fin rounded. Scales large, cycloid.

Habitat: Over sand and mud near reefs, in bays and off coast to depths of 70 fathoms.

Range: From Queen Charlotte Islands, British Columbia, to Punta Rompiente, Baja California.

Related Species: Arrow Goby (*Clevelandia ios*) has mouth extending beyond eye; dorsal fins separated by distance greater than eye diameter; occurs from Vancouver Island, British Columbia, to Gulf of California. Tidewater Goby (*Eucyclogobius newberryi*) lacks black edging on first dorsal fin; 2 pores between eyes; occurs from Del Norte County to San Diego County, California. Longjaw Mudsucker (*Gillichthys mirabilis*) has huge maxilla extending almost to rear edge of opercle; occurs from Tomales Bay, California, to Gulf of California. Bay Goby (*Lepidogobius lepidus*) has black edge on first dorsal fin; pectoral fin extends half-way to anus; dorsal fins widely separated; occurs from Welcome Harbor, British Columbia, to Isla Cedros, Baja California. All in similar habitat.

Comments: Spawning occurs from April to October, when the males lure females into their resting cave. The eggs are guarded by the male.

470 Sharptail Goby
(*Gobionellus hastatus*)

Description: To 8″ (20 cm). Very elongate, slender; brown above, sides lighter, belly pale, opercle dusky; *distinct, dark, oval spot on sides below spiny dorsal fin; small, dark spot at caudal fin base;* fin rays dusky, fin membranes pale; paler overall in lighter surroundings. Head bluntly rounded, scaleless; mouth terminal, oblique. Pelvic fins form ventral sucking disc, connected to belly only anteriorly; first dorsal fin high, with 6 spines reaching well past origin of soft dorsal; *caudal fin very long, lancelike.*

Habitat: Over mud in bays and sounds, and near shore.

Range: From North Carolina along coast to Yucatán, Mexico.

Comments: Most gobies are tolerant of wide fluctuations in salinity, and seem to prefer mud bottoms strewn with shells and debris, or sandy and silty areas with vegetation.

468 Bluebanded Goby
(*Lythrypnus dalli*)

Description: To 2½″ (6.5 cm). Elongate, compressed; *bright orange-red with 4–9 blue bands,* blue marks around eyes. Snout rounded. Tips of pectoral fins reach anal fin origin; pelvic fins form

ventral sucking disc; 2 dorsal fins,
second about same length as anal fin;
second and third dorsal spine ends free
from membrane, longer than other
spines. Caudal fin rounded.

Habitat: Shallow rocky areas with crevices, to
depths of 41 fathoms.

Range: From Morro Bay, California, to Gulf of
California.

Similar Species: Zebra Goby (*L. zebra*) has 10 or more
slender, light blue bands, body red;
occurs in same habitat from Carmel
Bay, California, to Clarian Island,
California.

Comments: The Bluebanded Goby spawns from
around May through August. The
courtship of the male involves his
darting at the female several times in
rapid succession, with his dorsal fin
fully extended before she deposits the
eggs, which he guards until they
hatch. This fish was considered rare
before the advent of scuba diving; it is
now known to be abundant around
islands off southern California. It makes
an excellent aquarium pet.

SURGEONFISHES
(Family Acanthuridae)

scalpel-like spine

Surgeonfishes are so-called because of a
hinged scalpel-like spine, actually a
highly modified scale, that folds into a
groove on each side of the caudal
peduncle. They are also known as
doctorfishes or tangs. They have a deep,
compressed body; the eyes are high on
the head; and the small mouth has
spatula-shaped, finely serrate teeth.
Surgeons have an uninterrupted dorsal
fin with 9 spines. The caudal fin is
emarginate. When the fish is moving,
the spine can be slashed out at other
fishes, either to warn or injure. These
fishes are not known to attack divers,
but they should be handled carefully.
There are 4 species in North America.

329   Ocean Surgeon
(*Acanthurus bahianus*)

Description: To 14″ (36 cm). Deep, compressed, depth half length; *grayish brown to yellow with pale bluish- to greenish-gray lengthwise lines; opercular membrane purple or black;* pelvic fin rays pale blue; dorsal fin has alternating narrow bands of dull orange and light bluish green; anal fin has dark gray to grayish-blue bands; *area around blade violet;* caudal fin olive to yellow-brown to dark blue with edge bluish white. Mouth small, slightly inferior. Dorsal fin continuous, without notch; bladelike spine on caudal peduncle; *caudal fin emarginate or lunate.*

Habitat: Shallow reefs and rocky areas, and nearby sand.

Range: From Massachusetts to Rio de Janeiro, Brazil, including Caribbean and West Indies; absent from Gulf of Mexico.

Related Species: Doctorfish (*A. chirurgus*) has 10 narrow, dark bars on sides; caudal fin less emarginate; occurs in same range. Gulf Surgeonfish (*A. randalli*) has pearly white saddle on caudal peduncle; caudal fin slightly emarginate; occurs in Gulf of Mexico. Both in similar habitat.

Comments: The Ocean Surgeon is a bottom dweller. The algae that it scrapes off hard substrates is ground in its gizzardlike stomach.

328, 337   Blue Tang
(*Acanthurus coeruleus*)

Description: To 14″ (36 cm). Deep, almost disc-shaped, compressed, depth more than half length; *adults blue to purplish gray, frequently with narrow, gray bands; sheath of blade white;* narrow, purplish-gray bands on dorsal and anal fins. Juveniles lemon-yellow; preadults sometimes part yellow, part blue, or blue with yellow fins. Eyes high on head; mouth small.

Dorsal fin continuous, uninterrupted;
bladelike spines on caudal peduncle;
caudal fin distinctly concave in adults,
emarginate in juveniles.

Habitat: Shallow coral and rock reefs.

Range: From New York to Brazil; center of
abundance West Indies; stragglers in
N. and S. parts of range; known off
Louisiana in Gulf of Mexico.

Comments: Surgeonfishes have 3 color phases:
juvenile, preadult, and adult. They are
active during the day and often occur
in rather large groups. Their teeth are
adapted for feeding on algae that grow
on or among coral and rocks.

CUTLASSFISHES
(Family Trichiuridae)

These silvery, elongate fishes have long
jaws armed with large canine or
lancelike teeth. The pelvic fins, when
present, are small. The dorsal fin
continues from just behind the head to
the tip of the tail. There are 5 species
in North America.

433 Atlantic Cutlassfish
(*Trichiurus lepturus*)

Description: To 5′ (1.5 m). *Very elongate, ribbonlike,
highly compressed, tail tapering to point;*
silver with light blue iridescence,
dorsal fin yellowish gray. Mouth large,
terminal; lower jaw projects beyond
upper; teeth large, fanglike. Dorsal fin
long, begins at nape, continues to near
tip of tail; *anal fin reduced to long series of
very short, separate spines;* no pelvic or
caudal fins; no finlets. Lateral line near
ventral profile; no scales.

Habitat: Estuaries or open sea over mud.

Range: From Gulf of Maine to Florida, Gulf of
Mexico, Antilles, and Caribbean, south
to Argentina.

Related Species:	Pacific Cutlassfish (*T. nitens*) has eye larger relative to length of snout; maxilla shorter; fewer dorsal fin rays; found in seas at mid-depth to 210 fathoms from S. California to Peru.
Similar Species:	Snake Mackerel (*Gempylus serpens*) has 5–6 finlets; first dorsal with 28–32 spines, second dorsal with 1 spine, 11–14 rays; obvious anal fin; tail forked; occurs near surface to 109 fathoms in open ocean in Atlantic from New York to Brazil; in Pacific from San Pedro, California, to Chile.
Comments:	The Atlantic Cutlassfish is voracious, feeding on almost any kind of fish. It is quite edible, but not often used as food in North America.

MACKERELS
(Family Scombridae)

These torpedo-shaped fishes are prized commercially and for sport. In mackerels and tunas the pectoral fins are inserted high above the axis of the body. There are 2 dorsal fins that fit into grooves when depressed, and a series of finlets from the second dorsal and anal fins to the caudal fin. The caudal peduncle has 2 or 3 pairs of keels. The scales are small and cycloid. Scombrids are fast-swimming schooling fishes that occur in open oceans. There are 23 species that are found in North America.

Wahoo
(Acanthocybium solanderi)

Description:	To 6′ (1.8 m); 149 lbs (67.6 kg). Long, slender, slightly compressed; dark greenish- or steel-blue above, paler below, *numerous narrow, dark bars extending below axis on sides.* Head pointed; *snout half length of head;*

pòsterior part of maxilla hidden under preorbital area; teeth compressed, strong, knifelike. Dorsal fins not well separated, first has 24–26 spines; 9 dorsal and 9 anal finlets. Caudal peduncle with 1 large and 2 small median keels. Corselet of scales obscure.

Habitat: Surface of open seas, usually well offshore.

Range: In Atlantic from New York to N. South America, including Caribbean and Gulf of Mexico. In Pacific from California to tropical South America.

Similar Species: King Mackerel (*Scomberomorus cavalla*) and Cero (*S. regalis*) lack bars on sides; snouts shorter.

Comments: The Wahoo, a very swift swimmer, feeds on squids and small fishes. It is esteemed by anglers for its speed, fighting qualities, and excellent flavor.

Bullet Mackerel
(*Auxis rochei*)

Description: To 20″ (51 cm). Elongate, fusiform, slightly compressed; bluish-green to black above, silvery below, *12 or more irregular, dark bars on scaleless area above lateral line.* Snout much shorter than rest of head; teeth slender, conical, slightly compressed. Pectoral fin not reaching to below dorsal scaleless area; first dorsal fin with 10–12 spines, *well separated from second;* 8 dorsal and 7 anal finlets. Caudal peduncle has large median keel between and anterior to 2 smaller ones. Scaleless except for corselet of well-developed scales.

Habitat: Surface of open seas, usually offshore; adults inshore near islands.

Range: Migratory. In Atlantic from Massachusetts to N. South America. In Pacific from Redondo Beach, California, to Peru.

Similar Species: Frigate Mackerel (*A. thazard*) has longer pectoral fins, extending to below dorsal scaleless area; occurs in similar habitat in Atlantic from Massachusetts south to Colombia, including Gulf of Mexico; in Pacific from Santa Catalina California, to Peru.

Comments: The Bullet and Frigate mackerels are difficult to distinguish from one another, and distribution data are consequently confused.

566 Little Tunny
(*Euthynnus alletteratus*)

Description: To 4′ (1.2 m); 27 lbs (12.2 kg). Robust, fusiform, slightly compressed; dark blue to steel-blue above, silvery below; dark, wavy stripes on scaleless area above lateral line; *dark spots between pectoral and pelvic fin bases.* Snout shorter than rest of head. *First dorsal fin, narrowly separated from second,* with 15 spines, *first spine longest.* 8 dorsal and 7 anal finlets. Caudal peduncle has large median keel between and anterior to 2 smaller keels. Scaleless except for corselet of well-developed scales.

Habitat: Surface of open seas; turbid inshore waters over continental shelf.

Range: From Gulf of Maine south to Brazil, including Bermuda, N. and E. Gulf of Mexico, and Caribbean. Common off S. Florida in summer.

Similar Species: Skipjack Tuna (*E. pelamis*) has conspicuous dark bands on scaleless area below lateral line.

Comments: Abundant inshore, the Little Tunny is popular as both an edible sport fish and as bait for sailfishes.

Skipjack Tuna
(*Euthynnus pelamis*)

Description: To 3′3″ (1 m); 50 lbs (22.7 kg). Robust, fusiform, slightly compressed; dark blue above with metallic reflections, silvery below; *4–6 lengthwise, broad, dark bands on scaleless area below lateral line.* Snout shorter than rest of head. *First dorsal fin narrowly separated from second, has 15–16 spines, first spine longest.* 7–9 dorsal and 7–8 anal finlets. Caudal peduncle has 3 median keels, 1 large, 2 small. Scaleless except for corselet of scales well-developed anteriorly.

Habitat: Tropical and subtropical open seas with maximum salinity, near 68° F (20° C).

Range: Migratory. In Atlantic from Gulf of Maine to Argentina, including blue waters of Gulf of Mexico. In Pacific from Vancouver Island, British Columbia, to Peru.

Comments: Since this species is canned for human consumption, it is of considerable commercial importance. A schooling fish, it is also popular with anglers.

Atlantic Bonito
(*Sarda sarda*)

Description: To 3′ (91 cm); 16¾ lbs (7.6 kg). Elongate, fusiform, somewhat compressed; steel-blue above, silvery below, *5–11 dark, slightly slanted stripes on upper sides.* Head large, compressed, tapering to pointed snout; maxilla reaches to or beyond rear edge of eye. Teeth in jaws slender, conical, slightly compressed. *First dorsal fin straight in profile,* 20–23 spines, *second spine longest;* 7–9 dorsal and 6–8 anal finlets. 1 smaller keel above and 1 below large median keel on each side of caudal peduncle. *Lateral line distinctly wavy; scales overall* with corselet of well-developed scales.

Habitat: Near surface of tropical and temperate open seas and inshore waters.

Range: Migratory. From Nova Scotia to Florida; N. Gulf of Mexico, and off Yucatán, Mexico; disjunctly to Argentina.

Related Species: Pacific Bonito (*S. chiliensis*) has slanted
lines on back; scaled overall; occurs
near surface of open seas from Gulf of
Alaska to Chile.

Comments: This fish is often found in schools and
is important commercially. It feeds on
herrings and other fishes, including
mackerels.

564 Chub Mackerel
(*Scomber japonicus*)

Description: To 25″ (64 cm). Elongate, fusiform,
slightly compressed; dark green to
blue-black above with many wavy, dark
streaks extending to just below lateral
line, *silvery below with numerous dusky
blotches*. Head pointed, depressed
between eyes; snout conical, shorter
than rest of head; *adipose eyelid present*.
2 dorsal fins widely separated, first
triangular, with 8–10 spines; second
slightly concave; *5 dorsal and 5 anal
finlets. 2 small keels on each side of caudal
peduncle, no large median keel.* Lacks
corselet of scales, largest scales around
pectoral fins.

Habitat: Mostly warm coastal waters over
continental shelf.

Range: In Atlantic from Nova Scotia south
to Florida, Gulf of Mexico, and
Venezuela. In Pacific from Gulf of
Alaska to Chile.

Comments: Chub Mackerels, usually schooling
fishes themselves, feed on other
schooling fishes like anchovies and
herrings, and on invertebrates. This
species is an excellent food fish.

565 Atlantic Mackerel
(*Scomber scombrus*)

Description: To 22″ (56 cm). Elongate, fusiform,
slightly compressed; dark bluish-green
to blue-black above, top of head

darker; *usually 27–30 transverse, wavy, dark bands to just below lateral line;* silvery below. Head large, pointed; maxilla reaches middle of eye; adipose eyelid present. First dorsal fin triangular, second slightly concave, with 11–12 spines depressible into dorsal groove; 5 dorsal and 5 anal finlets. *2 small keels on each side of caudal peduncle, no large median keel.* Scales minute, barely visible except around pectoral fin base, lacks corselet of scales.

Habitat: Open seas and over continental shelf in temperate water below 68° F (20°C).

Range: Migratory. From Newfoundland to Cape Hatteras.

Comments: The Atlantic Mackerel, an extremely abundant fish that travels in large schools, is important commercially for food. The fishing industry makes no distinction between the Atlantic and Chub mackerels.

King Mackerel
(*Scomberomorus cavalla*)

Description: To 5' (1.5 m); 90 lbs (40.8 kg). Elongate, fusiform, strongly compressed; iridescent bluish-green or iron-gray above, silvery below, *spiny dorsal fin pale, other fins dusky;* young have spots on sides. Snout shorter than rest of head; lower jaw protrudes beyond upper; maxilla exposed, extends to middle of eye. First dorsal fin has 14–16 weak spines; 8–9 dorsal and 9–10 anal finlets. 3 keels on each side of caudal peduncle. *Lateral line abruptly decurved below second dorsal fin.* Small scales overall, no corselet.

Habitat: Open ocean in warm waters; young in bays and near shore.

Range: Migratory. From Gulf of Maine to Florida and NE. Gulf of Mexico; Antilles.

Similar Species: Spanish Mackerel (*S. maculatus*) has

dorsal fin with anterior part black; no abrupt curve in lateral line.

Comments: King Mackerels are popular sport fishes throughout their range. Although reported to reach up to 5' (1.5 m) in length and to weigh 100 lbs (45.4 kg), they are commonly about half that size.

563 Spanish Mackerel
(*Scomberomorus maculatus*)

Description: To 3' (91 cm); 8⅞ lbs (4.4 kg). Elongate, fusiform, strongly compressed; iridescent bluish-green or dark blue above, silvery below, *yellowish-brown or golden spots evenly distributed on mid-sides,* anterior third of spiny dorsal fin black, pelvic fins and remainder of dorsal and anal fins white, other fins dusky, tinged with yellow and green. Snout shorter than rest of head; maxilla exposed posteriorly, extends to rear edge of eye. 2 dorsal fins barely separated, first with 17–19 (usually 19) spines; 8–9 dorsal and 8–9 anal finlets. *Lateral line not abruptly decurved, gradually undulating from opercle to caudal peduncle.* Small scales overall, no corselet.

Habitat: Surface of open seas; near shore in bays and estuaries.

Range: Atlantic and Gulf coasts from Maine to Yucatán, Mexico.

Similar Species: King Mackerel (*S. cavalla*) young lack black pigment on dorsal fin; lateral line abruptly decurved. Cero (*S. regalis*) has yellow stripe on sides, with yellow spotting above and below.

Comments: Spanish Mackerels are important commercially, and are caught with gill nets and purse seines. Anglers also troll with artificial lures. This fish swims in large schools whose presence is often given away by excited birds overhead. The Spanish Mackerel feeds on schooling bait fishes such as anchovies.

562 Cero
(*Scomberomorus regalis*)

Description: To 32″ (81 cm). Elongate, fusiform, strongly compressed; bluish-green to dark blue above, silvery below, yellowish-bronze oval spots on sides above and below *darker yellow midlateral stripe,* anterior third of spiny dorsal fin black. Snout shorter than rest of head; maxilla, exposed posteriorly, reaches almost to rear edge of eye. 17–19 dorsal fin spines; 8–9 dorsal and 8–9 anal finlets; soft dorsal and anal fins somewhat falcate; caudal fin deeply forked. 3 keels on each side of caudal peduncle. Lateral line gently decurved under soft dorsal fin, then undulating to caudal fin base. *Small scales overall, including on pectoral fins,* no corselet.

Habitat: Over reefs and turtlegrass beds, or in shallow open waters.

Range: From Massachusetts to Brazil, including parts of Gulf of Mexico, West Indies, and E. Caribbean.

Similar Species: Spanish Mackerel (*S. maculatus*) lacks small yellow dots above and below midlateral stripe.

Comments: This fish occurs infrequently north of Florida. The Cero, unlike the Spanish Mackerel which it resembles, tends to be found singly or in small groups.

567 Albacore
(*Thunnus alalunga*)

Description: To 5′ (1.5 m); 96 lbs (43 kg). Fusiform, compressed; depth greatest at pelvic fins; dark blue or gray above and on fins, light gray below, rear edge of caudal fin whitish. Snout pointed; mouth terminal; palatine teeth present. *Pectoral fin extends beyond rear of soft dorsal fin and anal fin origin;* dorsal fins barely separated; 7–8 finlets behind second dorsal fin; 7–8 anal finlets. Tail slender, lunate. Lateral line straight.

Habitat: On surface and at mid-depths in open
           seas.

Range: In Atlantic from Nova Scotia to Brazil.
           In Pacific from SE. Alaska to Isla
           Clarion, Mexico.

Similar Species: Yellowfin Tuna (*T. albacares*) has
           pectoral fin not reaching beyond origin
           of second dorsal fin. Bigeye Tuna
           (*T. obesus*) has 8–10 dorsal and 7–10
           anal finlets, all yellow.

Comments: The Albacore, which feeds on small
           bait fishes, squids, and surface-
           dwelling crustaceans, is one of the most
           prized fishes on the Pacific Coast; the
           annual catch by anglers has reached
           230,000 fishes. It migrates to the
           middle Pacific, sometimes as far as
           Japan in the winter, and returns to the
           California coast in the summer.

---

561   Yellowfin Tuna
        (*Thunnus albacares*)

Description: To 6' (1.8 m); 450 lbs (204.1 kg).
           Fusiform, compressed; dark blue above,
           gray below, fins tinged yellow, finlets
           yellow, edges black. Snout moderately
           sharp, mouth terminal. *Pectoral fin tip
           not extending beyond second dorsal fin
           origin;* dorsal fins about same height,
           second dorsal greatly elongate in large
           individuals; 8–9 dorsal and 7–9 anal
           finlets; caudal fin lobes slender, rear
           profile lunate.

Habitat: On surface and at mid-depths in open
           seas.

Range: In Atlantic from Massachusetts to
           Brazil. In Pacific from Point Buchon,
           California, to Chile.

Similar Species: Albacore (*T. alalunga*) has pectoral fins
           extending beyond anal fin origin.

Comments: This is the most valuable of all tunas
           worldwide. Schools of Yellowfin Tunas
           are pursued by fleets of purse-seine
           boats from around the world. Dolphins
           are frequently caught in large numbers
           with the tunas, and these large,

expensive boats have had to modify their nets and fishing methods to resolve this problem. The Yellowfin Tuna is also a highly prized game fish.

Bigeye Tuna
(*Thunnus obesus*)

Description:	To 7′9″ (2.4 m); 435 lbs (197.3 kg). Robust, fusiform, slightly compressed; metallic dark blue above, whitish below, first dorsal fin deep yellow, second dorsal and anal fins light yellow, *finlets bright yellow, edges black.* Head large; length of snout less than distance from eye to back of head; mouth reaches front of eye. *Pectoral fin long, pointed at tip, reaches past origin of second dorsal fin;* 2 dorsal fins barely separated, first with 13−15 spines; 8−10 dorsal and 7−10 anal finlets. Scales very small, corselet indistinct.
Habitat:	In ocean from surface to depths of 138 fathoms.
Range:	In Atlantic from Nova Scotia to Argentina, including deep waters of Gulf of Mexico and Caribbean; rare north of Cape Hatteras, North Carolina. In Pacific from Iron Springs, Washington, to Peru.
Related Species:	Blackfin Tuna (*T. atlanticus*) grows to 3′ (91 cm); first dorsal fin dusky, second dorsal and anal fins silvery, finlets dusky with yellow tinge; in similar habitat from Massachusetts to Brazil, including Bermuda.
Similar Species:	Albacore (*T. alalunga*) has pectoral fin extending beyond rear of soft dorsal fin.
Comments:	The Bigeye Tuna is caught for human consumption using commercial longlines. This method, developed by the Japanese, involves using a line, tracked by radar, which may be 20 or more miles long.

Bluefin Tuna
(*Thunnus thynnus*)

Description: To 10′ (3 m); 1,496 lbs (678.6 kg). Robust, fusiform; *dark blue or black above, silvery-white below with pale lines alternating with rows of light dots, first dorsal fin yellow or bluish,* second dorsal reddish brown, anal fin and all finlets dusky yellow, edges black, *median keels black.* Snout conical, shorter than rest of head; maxilla reaches pupil of eye. *Pectoral fin tip falls well short of second dorsal fin.* 2 dorsal fins hardly separated, first with 14 (rarely 12) spines; 8–10 dorsal and 7–9 anal finlets. Caudal peduncle has large, lateral keel, 2 smaller keels at caudal fin base. Minute scales overall, corselet indistinct.

Habitat: Surface of open ocean; young in warm waters, adults move into colder waters.

Range: In Atlantic from Labrador to NE. Brazil, including Gulf of Mexico and Caribbean. In Pacific from Shelikof Strait, Alaska, to Peru.

Comments: The Bluefin Tuna is a very important part of the commercial longline fishery. The heaviest Bluefin Tuna on record weighed 1,496 lbs (678.6 kg), and was caught off Nova Scotia in 1979.

SWORDFISHES
(Family Xiphiidae)

These large, distinctive fishes have a long snout with the anterior upper jaw and nasal bones modified to form a sword. The jaws lack teeth and the gill membranes are free from the isthmus. Adult swordfishes lack pelvic fins, and have 2 widely separated dorsal fins, the first much larger than the second. The caudal peduncle has a single keel. Adults lack scales. The single species occurs in temperate and tropical seas in North America.

Swordfish
(*Xiphias gladius*)

Description: To 15' (4.6 m); 1,182 lbs (536.2 kg).
Elongate, fusiform, compressed,
greatest depth near first dorsal fin; dark
gray or black above; gray, sometimes
yellowish, below. Snout very elongate,
forming flattened beak or sword; *no
teeth in jaws.* Pectoral fin length about
equal to first dorsal fin height. *No pelvic
fins;* first dorsal fin large, widely
separated from second. Single keel on
caudal peduncle. Caudal fin lunate,
lobes very long. *Adults lack scales.*

Habitat: Surface near shore and in open seas to
depths of at least 33 fathoms.

Range: In Atlantic from Newfoundland south
to Argentina. In Pacific from Oregon
south to Chile.

Comments: Swordfishes feed on crustaceans, squids,
anchovies, hakes, mackerels, rockfishes,
and other fishes. Although the
Swordfish is highly prized as a game
fish, few are taken by anglers because of
the great expense involved in their
pursuit. The annual commercial catch
off southern California has grown to
over 500 tons (453,590 kg). Most of
the catch is now taken with gill nets,
and a smaller portion with harpoons.

BILLFISHES
(Family Istiophoridae)

These fishes resemble swordfishes in
having an elongate snout that forms a
sword or spear. They differ, however, in
possessing jaws with teeth, pelvic fins,
scales, and, in adults, 2 keels on the
caudal peduncle. Their first dorsal fin
has a very long base, and the fin is
depressible into a groove. The lateral
line is usually single, but may be
branched to form a chainlike pattern.
There are 7 species that are found in
North American waters.

585   Sailfish
(*Istiophorus platypterus*)

Description: To 10'9" (3.3 m); 182 lbs (82.6 kg).
Elongate, tapering, compressed; dark
blue above, silvery below; adults have
vertical rows of gold spots on sides.
Snout modified to form sword; jaws
with teeth. Distance from nostril to
rear edge of opercle less than either
sword length from nostril to tip, or
pectoral fin length. Pelvic fins rodlike;
dorsal fin depressible into groove,
*middle rays longer than greatest body depth,
and longer than anterior rays.* Caudal
peduncle has 2 keels in adults. Scales
present.

Habitat: At surface and mid-depth in open seas.

Range: In Atlantic from Rhode Island to
Brazil. In Pacific from San Diego,
California, to Chile.

Similar Species: Shortbill Spearfish (*Tetrapturus
angustirostris*) with length of middle
rays of dorsal fin about equal to greatest
body depth; occurs near surface of open
seas from Cape Mendocino, California,
to Chile.

Comments: Sailfishes grow most during their first 2
or 3 years and live to only 4 or 5 years
of age. They are rarely caught off
southern California, but are very
popular sport fishes off Mexico.

Blue Marlin
(*Makaira nigricans*)

Description: To 14'8" (4.5 m); 1,805 lbs (818 kg).
Deep, moderately compressed; deep
blue to rich brown above, silvery
below, 15 bars formed by pale blue
spots on sides; first dorsal fin blue-
black, usually without spots, other fins
brownish black. Head profile steep;
snout elongate, forms spear. Tips of
pectoral, first dorsal, and anal fins
pointed; pectorals can be folded against
body; pelvic fins long, slender, shorter

than pectorals; first dorsal fin long, tall anteriorly, abruptly becoming lower, height less than body depth. *Lateral line in netlike pattern; scales dense, embedded, ending in 1–2 long spines.*

Habitat: Usually near surface of open seas.

Range: Migratory. In Atlantic from New England to Gulf of Mexico, Caribbean, and Uruguay; uncommon in Gulf of Maine. In Pacific rarely from S. California to Chile.

Related Species: Black Marlin (*M. indica*) has pectoral fins not folding against body; occurs near surface of open, warm seas from S. California to South America.

Similar Species: Striped Marlin (*Tetrapturus audax*) has pelvic fins much longer than pectorals.

Comments: The Blue Marlin is highly prized as a large game fish; it is also caught in significant numbers on commercial longlines. Although the record size is reported to be about a ton, most Blue Marlins weigh between 200 and 400 lbs (91 to 181 kg). The females attain much larger sizes than males.

White Marlin
(*Tetrapturus albidus*)

Description: To 10′ (3.3 m); 181⅞ lbs (82.5 kg). Elongate, compressed, snout elongate, forms spear; blue to rich brown above, silvery-white below, *usually no bars or spots.* Tips of pectoral, first dorsal, and anal fins rounded; pelvic fins long, slender; first dorsal fin blue-black, covered with numerous small, black spots, higher anteriorly, becoming quite low posteriorly, its height greater than body depth; other fins brown-black. *Anus immediately in front of first anal fin. Lateral line continuous, not forming netlike pattern.* Scales dense, embedded, *end in single point.*

Habitat: Usually near surface of open seas.

Range: Migratory. Gulf of Maine; from Long Island, New York, to Brazil, including

Gulf of Mexico and Caribbean.

Comments: The White Marlin feeds on squids and a variety of fishes, including Round Herrings and jacks. This species is fished primarily between New Jersey and Cape Hatteras, and in the Gulf of Mexico. It is also frequently caught accidentally on commercial longlines. Most specimens weigh about 50 lbs (22.6 kg).

Striped Marlin
(*Tetrapturus audax*)

Description: To 13'5" (4 m); 692 lbs (313.8 kg). Slender, elongate, compressed posteriorly; snout elongate, forms spear; dark blue above, silvery below, *dark blue bars on sides.* Pectoral fins fold back along sides; *pelvic fins much longer than pectoral fins;* first dorsal fin falcate, anterior height equal to or greater than body depth, anterior spines and rays much longer than posterior spines. Scales present; lateral line single.

Habitat: Surface and mid-depth in open seas.

Range: From Oregon to Chile.

Related Species: Shortbill Spearfish (*T. angustirostris*) has short spear, lower jaw more than two-thirds length of upper; length of middle rays of dorsal fin about equal to body depth; occurs from Cape Mendocino, California, to Chile.

Similar Species: Black Marlin (*Makaira indica*) has rigid, pectoral fins. Blue Marlin (*M. nigricans*) has pelvic fins shorter than pectoral fins; dorsal fin height less than body depth; chainlike lateral line.

Comments: Striped Marlins spawn from May to August in the northern Pacific. These greatly prized game fishes feed on Jack Mackerels, flyingfishes, sauries, sardines, and squids. A small, highly specialized sport fishery for the Striped Marlin has existed off southern California since the early 1900s. It is also an excellent food fish.

Longbill Spearfish
(*Tetrapturus pfluegeri*)

Description: To 6' (1.8 m). Elongate, highly
compressed, snout elongate, forms
spear; dark blue above, blending to
brownish-white on sides, silvery-white
below, *usually no bars or spots.* Pectoral,
first dorsal, and anal fin tips rounded;
first dorsal fin blue-black, no spots,
twice as tall anteriorly as posteriorly,
height equal to or slightly greater than
body depth; other fins brown-black.
Anus well in front of first anal fin.
Lateral line continuous, not forming
netlike pattern; *scales dense, embedded,
end in several sharp points.*

Habitat: Usually near surface of open seas.

Range: Migratory; from New Jersey to Florida;
Gulf of Mexico west to Texas; from
Antilles south to Venezuela.

Comments: The Longbill Spearfish is apparently
found mostly off southeastern Florida
and the Florida Keys.

BUTTERFISHES
(Family Stromateidae)

These fishes are short, deep, and
compressed; the upper profile is a
mirror image of the lower. Butterfishes
are gray to blue or green above and
have intense silvery reflections,
especially on the lower sides and the
belly. The mouth is small, not
protractile, and at the end of a blunt
snout. The pectoral fins are long and
pointed and the pelvic fins are absent in
adults. The dorsal and anal fins have a
long base and only 2 to 6 weak spines.
The caudal peduncle is narrow and
lacks keels. The scales are cycloid and
the lateral line is parallel to the dorsal
profile. This family has 20 species in
North America.

546 Harvestfish
(Peprilus alepidotus)

Description: To 12″ (30 cm). Very deep, compressed, upper and lower profiles similar; pale blue or greenish above, silvery with yellowish tinge below. Snout short, length less than diameter of eye; maxilla not reaching eye. Pectoral fin longer than head; no pelvic fins; *anterior edges of dorsal and anal fins falcate;* caudal fin deeply forked. *No pores below dorsal fin;* scales small, deciduous, extend to cheeks and bases of median fins.

Habitat: Surface of inshore and offshore waters over continental shelf to depths of about 15 fathoms.

Range: From Maine to Uruguay, including Gulf of Mexico and West Indies, but not W. Caribbean; infrequent north of Chesapeake Bay.

Related Species: Butterfish (*P. triacanthus*) has row of pores below dorsal fin; occurs in similar habitat from S. Newfoundland to E. coast of Florida.

Comments: Adult Harvestfishes swim in large schools and feed on jellyfishes, crustaceans, worms, and small fishes. The juveniles are plankton feeders and often live among floating weeds or large jellyfishes. Although most individuals are less than 6″ (15 cm) long the Harvestfish is an excellent food fish.

SCORPIONFISHES
(Family Scorpaenidae)

spiny head

These fishes are fusiform and compressed. They have ridges and spines on the head, and there are usually 5 preopercular and 2 opercular spines. All members of the family possess a suborbital stay, a bone beneath the eye that extends across the cheek. They have a single dorsal fin, often notched, containing 11 to 17 spines and 8 to 18 rays. The anal fin contains 1 to 3 spines and 3 to 9 soft rays. The pelvic, dorsal, and anal fin spines often contain venom glands that may cause very painful wounds. The scales, if present, are ctenoid or cycloid. Fertilization is internal, and some species lay eggs. There are 90 species in North America, with more members of this family occurring on the Pacific Coast than of any other family. There are 65 species in the genus *Sebastes,* and many are difficult to identify. They all have palatine teeth, 12 to 15, usually 13, dorsal fin spines, and 9 to 16 rays. All *Sebastes* are viviparous.

422 Barbfish
(*Scorpaena brasiliensis*)

Description: To 8″ (20 cm). Robust, depth about one-third length; pinkish or reddish with lighter mottling. Head large, with numerous spines; pit between eyes; mouth terminal, maxilla reaches beyond eye; usually large tentacle over eye. Pectoral fins broad and fanlike, *axil pale with small, brown spots; 2–3 large, brown spots on sides between pectoral and anal fins;* dorsal fin continuous, deeply notched, 12 spines, 9 rays; caudal peduncle pale; caudal fin truncate or slightly rounded. Lateral line complete; scales cycloid.

Habitat: Inshore waters to about 50 fathoms, over mud, silt, sand, rocks, or coral.

Range: From Virginia to Brazil, including Gulf of Mexico; sparsely in West Indies.

Comments: This is a common scorpionfish species in Florida waters. It has the most toxic spines, so anglers should be cautious when handling this and other scorpionfishes.

417   California Scorpionfish
(Scorpaena guttata)

Description: To 17″ (43 cm). Elongate, rounded in
cross section, slightly depressed; red to
brown with spots overall. Head robust,
with ridges; maxilla reaches middle of
eye; *palatine teeth present;* snout rounded.
Opercular and preopercular spines
present. Pectoral fin large, broad,
rounded; dorsal fin continuous,
notched, *12 spines,* 8–10 rays; caudal
fin truncate. Lateral line straight; scales
large, ctenoid.

Habitat: Shallow reefs and kelp beds to depths
of 100 fathoms.

Range: From Santa Cruz, California, to Uncle
Sam Bank, Baja California; upper Gulf
of California.

Similar Species: Sculpins (Cottidae) lack anal fin spines.
Rainbow Scorpionfish (*Scorpaenodes xyris*)
lacks palatine teeth; has 13 dorsal fin
spines; occurs in caves and crevices to
depths of about 84′ (26 m) from San
Clemente Island, California, to Peru.

Comments: Unlike most other members of the
family, this fish deposits eggs
embedded in transparent, pear-shaped
cases. It is considered an excellent food
fish and makes up a minor portion of
the southern California sport and
commercial catch. All of its spines are
venomous.

421   Spotted Scorpionfish
(Scorpaena plumieri)

Description: To 17″ (43 cm). Robust, depth about
one-third length; dark brown or black
blotches on pale background above,
reddish below; colors in variegated
pattern. Head large, with numerous
spines; *deep pit under eye,* another
between eyes; mouth terminal, maxilla
reaches past eye. *Axil of pectoral fins
black with white spots or blotches;* pectoral
fin broad-based, fanlike; dorsal fin

continuous, deeply notched, 12 spines,
9 rays; caudal fin truncate. Lateral line
complete; scales cycloid.

Habitat: Reefs in shallow waters, rocky areas,
and oil platforms to about 30 fathoms.

Range: From Massachusetts to Rio de Janeiro,
Brazil, including Bermuda, Gulf of
Mexico, West Indies, and Caribbean.

Related Species: Plumed Scorpionfish (*S. grandicornis*)
has tan pectoral fin axil with small,
white dots; occurs in grassy areas and
bays in Bermuda, Bahamas, S. Florida,
south along coast to Central America
and Brazil.

Comments: The Spotted Scorpionfish preys on small
fishes and crustaceans. Its spines are
very venomous. When disturbed, it
spreads its pectoral fins, apparently to
display the characteristic black and
white coloration underneath, as a
warning.

Pacific Ocean Perch
(*Sebastes alutus*)

Description: To 20″ (51 cm). Elongate, fusiform,
compressed; light red with dark areas
under soft dorsal fin and on caudal
peduncle. *Lower jaw projects, has
prominent knob;* 1 pair of spines above
eyes, usually 5 additional pairs of
small, weak spines. Dorsal fins
continuous, deeply notched, spiny
portion longer-based, with incised
membrane; 8–9 anal fin soft rays, rarely
6–7.

Habitat: Over soft bottoms and near reefs at
30–350 fathoms.

Range: From Bering Sea to La Jolla, California.

Related Species: Darkblotched Rockfish (*S. crameri*) has
depth at pelvic fin insertion greater
than head length; 5 dark bars or
blotches on back; occurs at 16–300
fathoms from Bering Sea to Santa
Catalina Island, California. Stripetail
Rockfish (*S. saxicola*) has green stripes
on caudal fin membranes; occurs at

25–230 fathoms from S. central Alaska to Bahía Sebastián Vizcaíno, Baja California. Halfbanded Rockfish (*S. semicinctus*) has single blackish-red bar below each dorsal fin, dark red-brown spots on dorsal and caudal fins; occurs at 32–220 fathoms from Point Pinos, California, to Bahía Sebastián Vizcaíno, Baja California. Sharpchin Rockfish (*S. zacentrus*) has dark, forked bar from eye to edge of opercle; 7 anal fin soft rays; occurs at 50–175 fathoms from Sanak Island, Alaska, to San Diego, California. All in similar habitat.

Comments: The Pacific Ocean Perch is the most important commercial rockfish on the Pacific Coast, with annual foreign and domestic landings of over 50,000 tons. It has mildly venomous spines.

406 Kelp Rockfish
(*Sebastes atrovirens*)

Description: To 17″ (43 cm). Deep, fusiform, compressed; body and fin membranes *light gray and brown to golden brown with mottling.* Snout moderately sharp, lower jaw scaled; 5 or more pairs of head spines; no coronal spines; *gill rakers on first arch long and slender.* Spiny and soft dorsal fin portions same height; continuous, deeply notched, spiny portion longer-based, with incised membranes. Caudal fin rounded.

gill rakers

Habitat: Rocky reefs and kelp beds to depths of 25 fathoms.

Range: From Timber Cove, California, to Punta de San Pablo, Baja California.

Similar Species: Brown Rockfish (*S. auriculatus*) has coronal spines; dark blotch on rear edge of opercle; membranes of pectoral, pelvic, and caudal fins pinkish. Grass Rockfish (*S. rastrelliger*) has short, blunt gill rakers on first arch; lower jaw unscaled; occurs in shallow rocky areas from Yaquina Bay, Oregon, to Bahía Playa Maria, Baja California.

gill rakers

Comments: Kelp Rockfishes occur singly or in large aggregations. They feed on small crabs, shrimps, squids, and some fishes. They form a small proportion of the catches of sport anglers and scuba divers. The sharp head spines and the mildly venomous dorsal and anal spines should be handled with caution.

407 Brown Rockfish
(*Sebastes auriculatus*)

Description: To 21½" (55 cm). Deep, fusiform, compressed; olive-brown above with light orange-brown mottling, lighter below, *dark brown spot on rear of opercle,* pectoral, pelvic, and caudal fins pinkish. Snout moderately sharp; top of head flat between eyes; 6 pairs of head spines, *including coronals.* Dorsal fins continuous, deeply notched, spiny portion longer-based, with incised membranes; spines and rays about same length; caudal fin truncate.

Habitat: Shallow, low-profile reefs; occasionally over soft bottoms to 70 fathoms.

Range: From Prince William Sound, Alaska, to Bahía Hipolito, Baja California.

Similar Species: Kelp Rockfish (*S. atrovirens*) lacks spot on rear edge of opercle; has no coronal spines; pectoral, pelvic, and caudal fin membranes not pinkish. Grass Rockfish (*S. rastrelliger*) lacks spot on rear edge of opercle; gill rakers on first arch short, blunt.

Comments: Brown Rockfishes are born in the late spring, and after a short period during which they float with the plankton community, they settle to the bottom, usually in calm areas such as bays. Brown Rockfishes make up a minor portion of the sport and commercial rockfish catch. The sharp head spines and mildly venomous dorsal and anal spines should be avoided.

399 Gopher Rockfish
(*Sebastes carnatus*)

Description: To 15″ (38 cm). Deep, elongate,
fusiform; *dark olive-brown or brown with
pinkish or white blotches and spots.* Snout
moderately sharp; *lower lip yellow to
orange;* no knob on lower jaw. Top of
head concave between eyes; 5 pairs of
head spines. Dorsal fins continuous,
deeply notched, spiny portion longer-
based, with incised membranes; usually
5–7 anal fin soft rays, occasionally 7–
10; caudal fin slightly rounded.

Habitat: Shallow rocky areas to depths of 30
fathoms.

Range: From Eureka, California, to San Roque,
Baja California.

Similar Species: Black-and-yellow Rockfish
(*S. chrysomelas*) has black body with
orange-yellow to light yellow blotches;
lower lip dark gray.

Comments: The Gopher Rockfish feeds on crabs,
squids, and small fishes. Anglers catch
a fair number from charter boats and
skiffs. It is considered fine eating,
particularly when freshly caught.

⚠ Anglers should avoid handling the
mildly venomous dorsal and anal
spines.

393 Copper Rockfish
(*Sebastes caurinus*)

Description: To 22″ (56 cm). Deep, fusiform,
compressed; orange-brown, olive, dull
yellow or copper above, white below
and on head, posterior *two-thirds of
lateral line whitish or pinkish with white
blotches.* Snout moderately sharp; 5 pairs
of head spines; lower jaw unscaled.
Dorsal fins continuous, deeply notched,
spiny portion longer-based, with
incised membranes, spines at least as
long as rays. Caudal fin truncate.

Habitat: Over low-profile rock and shale reefs to
depths of 100 fathoms.

Range: From Kenai Peninsula, Alaska, to Islas San Benito, Baja California.

Similar Species: Calico Rockfish (*S. dalli*) has orange-brown bars extending down sides from dorsal fin, orange-brown spots on and below dorsal fin; occurs near reefs and over soft bottoms from San Francisco, California, to Bahía San Sebastián Vizcaíno, Baja California.

Comments: The Copper Rockfish feeds on fishes and crustaceans. It is a popular sport fish, although not abundant on any reef. Caution should be used to avoid touching their mildly venomous dorsal and anal spines.

398 Black-and-yellow Rockfish
(*Sebastes chrysomelas*)

Description: To 15″ (38 cm). Deep, elongate, fusiform, compressed; *black with yellow or yellow-orange blotches and spots, lower lip dark gray.* Snout moderately sharp; lower jaw lacks knob at tip; top of head concave between eyes; 5 pairs of head spines. Dorsal fin continuous, deeply notched, spiny portion longer-based, with incised membranes; 6–7 anal fin soft rays.

Habitat: Shallow intertidal rocky areas to depths of 20 fathoms.

Range: From Eureka, California, to Isla Natividad, Baja California.

Similar Species: Gopher Rockfish (*S. carnatus*) has brown or olive-brown body with pinkish or whitish blotches. China Rockfish (*S. nebulosus*) has continuous yellow stripe extending from third and fourth dorsal fin spine membranes along lateral line to caudal fin.

Comments: Black-and-yellow Rockfishes are often caught by anglers. Like most scorpionfishes, they are ovoviviparous: Fertilization is internal and the embryos develop within the female. The mildly venomous dorsal and anal spines can cause a painful wound.

408 Widow Rockfish
(*Sebastes entomelas*)

Description: To 21″ (53 cm). Elongate, fusiform,
compressed; brassy brown above, often
whitish below, *membranes of pectoral,
pelvic, and anal fins black.* Snout fairly
sharp; top of head convex between eyes;
head spines not prominent; maxilla
extends to middle of eye. Dorsal fins
continuous, deeply notched, spiny
portion longer-based, with incised
membranes; spines and rays about same
length. *Rear profile of anal fin straight;*
caudal fin emarginate.

Habitat: Over deep, rocky reefs and soft bottoms
from surface to depths of 200 fathoms.

Range: From Kodiak Island, Alaska, to Bahía
de Todos Santos, Baja California.

Related Species: Squarespot Rockfish (*S. hopkinsi*) has
dark, squarish blotches on back and
sides; second anal fin spine extends
beyond tip of third; occurs at depths of
10–100 fathoms from Farallon Islands,
California, to Isla de Guadalupe, Baja
California. Speckled Rockfish (*S. ovalis*)
covered with small, black spots;
orange-brown above, yellow-tan below;
occurs at depths of 17–200 fathoms
from San Francisco, California, to Cabo
Colnett, Baja California. Both in
similar habitat.

Comments: Widow Rockfishes occur in huge
groups in mid-water, where they feed
on plankton. They contribute to the
catches of anglers, and are now one of
the most important commercial
rockfishes on the Pacific Coast. A single
trawler has been known to catch over
50 tons (45,359 kg) in one day. Mildly
venomous spines are present in the
dorsal and anal fins.

401 Yellowtail Rockfish
(*Sebastes flavidus*)

Description: To 26" (66 cm). Deep, fusiform, compressed; brown to dark gray, *reddish-brown speckles on scales;* pectoral, pelvic, anal, and caudal fins yellowish. *Head spines not prominent;* head convex between eyes; *33–39 gill rakers on first arch.* Dorsal fin continuous, deeply notched, spiny portion longer-based with incised membranes; spines and rays about same length; *8 anal fin soft rays,* rarely 7 or 9; rear edge of anal fin straight, vertical; caudal fin slightly emarginate or forked.

Habitat: Over deep reefs and soft bottoms from surface to depths of 150 fathoms; often over bottom.

Range: From Kodiak Island, Alaska, to San Diego, California.

Related Species: Puget Sound Rockfish (*S. emphaeus*) has copper-red body with greenish-brown bars and blotches; rear lobe of anal fin rounded; occurs at 6–200 fathoms from Prince William Sound, Alaska, to Punta Gorda, California. Bank Rockfish (*S. rufus*) has dusky back, black spots on red body and dorsal fin; anal fin membranes black; occurs at 17–135 fathoms from Mad River, California, to Isla de Guadalupe, Baja California. Both in similar habitat.

Similar Species: Olive Rockfish (*S. serranoides*) has light blotches on back; no reddish-brown speckles on scales; 29–36 gill rakers on first arch; 9 anal fin soft rays, rarely 8 or 10.

Comments: Yellowtail Rockfishes are born in January, February, and March. Large aggregations occur in mid-water, usually over deep reefs. They feed on crustaceans, squids, and small fishes. This species is one of the 3 most important rockfishes caught for sport in central and northern California. The dorsal and anal fins contain mildly venomous spines.

Cowcod
(*Sebastes levis*)

Description: To 3'1" (94 cm); 28 lbs (12.7 kg).
Deep, fusiform, compressed; adults
yellow-red or pink with faint dark bars;
juveniles yellow with dark bars. Head
ridges not serrate; 5–6 pairs of head
spines; lower jaw projects slightly
beyond upper; *wide space between bottom
of eye and upper lip.* Dorsal fins
continuous, deeply notched; spines
longer than rays; *membranes between
dorsal spines deeply incised.* Caudal fin
slightly forked.

Habitat: Adults around deep reefs at 84–200
fathoms. Juveniles over sand at 10–17
fathoms.

Range: From Usal, California, to Isla de
Guadalupe, Baja California.

Similar Species: Yelloweye Rockfish (*S. ruberrimus*) has
bright yellow eyes; head ridges serrate
on older fishes more than 12" (30 cm)
long; edges of pelvic, anal, and caudal
fins black.

Comments: The Cowcod releases its young during
the winter and early spring. A single
female may produce 2 million young.
Adults feed on fishes, octopuses, and
squids. This species is a very popular
sport fish off southern California
because of its large size, and is
marketed by commercial longline
fishers. Mildly venomous spines are
present in the dorsal and anal fins.

396 Quillback Rockfish
(*Sebastes maliger*)

Description: To 24" (61 cm). Fusiform, deep,
compressed; brown with orange spots
and blotches on back and dorsal fin,
rear of head to pectoral fin insertion
yellow with brown spots, orange spots below.
Head flat between eyes; 5 pairs of
spines on head. Pectoral and pelvic fins
blackish. Dorsal fin continuous, deeply

notched; spines cream-colored, longer than rays, membranes of spiny dorsal deeply incised.

Habitat: Rocky reefs with caves and crevices to depths of 150 fathoms.

Range: From Gulf of Alaska to Point Conception, California.

Similar Species: China Rockfish (*S. nebulosus*) has black body with yellow stripe from dorsal spines to and along lateral line, bluish-white spots below.

Comments: This is a common inshore, solitary rockfish north from British Columbia. It is caught in small numbers by anglers and commercial fishers. It has mildly venomous spines.

409 Black Rockfish
(*Sebastes melanops*)

Description: To 24″ (61 cm); 10½ lbs (4.8 kg). Deep, fusiform, compressed; black with gray mottling, *gray to white stripe along lateral line usually present;* black spots on dorsal fin. Maxilla extends to rear of eye; head convex between eyes; *head spines not prominent;* no knob at tip of lower jaw. Dorsal fin continuous, deeply notched, spiny portion longer-based, with incised membranes, rear profile of anal fin rounded; caudal fin truncate to emarginate.

Habitat: Over rocks and soft bottoms to depths of 200 fathoms.

Range: From Amchitka Island, Alaska, to Huntington Beach, California.

Related Species: Dusky Rockfish (*S. ciliatus*) has body blackish-brown with brown speckles; medium-sized knob at tip of lower jaw; rear edge of anal fin straight; occurs in similar habitat from Bering Sea to Dixon Entrance, British Columbia.

Similar Species: Blue Rockfish (*S. mystinus*) has dark blue body with light blue mottling, lacks gray stripe on lateral line; maxilla not reaching rear of eye; rear edge of anal fin straight.

Comments: The Black Rockfish occurs both singly
and in large groups near the bottom or
at mid-water. It feeds on crabs and
other crustaceans as well as on fishes,
and may weigh as much as 10½ lbs
(4.8 kg). This species is an important
Ⓐ   sport and commercial fish. The mildly
venomous spines in the dorsal and
anal fins should be avoided.

388   Vermilion Rockfish
(*Sebastes miniatus*)

Description: To 30″ (76 cm). Deep, fusiform,
compressed; red to orange with gray
mottling, mouth and fins reddish,
posterior two-thirds of lateral line gray
to white, fin edges usually black. *Rough
scales on underside of jaw;* head convex
between eyes; 6 pairs of head spines.
Dorsal fin continuous, deeply notched,
spiny portion longer-based, with
incised membranes. Caudal fin
truncate.

Habitat: Over rocky reefs and soft bottoms to
depths of 150 fathoms.

Range: From Queen Charlotte Islands, British
Columbia, to Islas San Benito, Baja
California.

Related Species: Rougheye Rockfish (*S. aleutianus*) has
2–10 sharp spines on ridge below eye,
no gray mottling; occurs in similar
habitat from Aleutian Islands to San
Diego, California.

Similar Species: Canary Rockfish (*S. pinniger*) has gray
band along lateral line; underside of
jaw smooth, unscaled; young have
black blotch on rear of spiny dorsal fin.

Comments: The Vermilion Rockfish is popular with
anglers because it is large and makes
good eating. It is also an important
commercial species caught with hook
Ⓐ   and line off southern California. Mildly
venomous spines in the dorsal and anal
fins can cause painful wounds.

410 Blue Rockfish
(*Sebastes mystinus*)

Description: To 21″ (53 cm). Fusiform, deep, elongate, compressed; dark blue with light blue mottling, *no spots on dorsal fin membranes.* Snout moderately sharp; *maxilla not reaching rear edge of eye;* up to 4 pairs of weak head spines. Dorsal fins continuous, deeply notched, spiny portion longer-based, with incised membranes; rear edge of anal fin straight or slightly indented; caudal fin emarginate.

Habitat: Shallow and deep reefs and kelp beds to 300 fathoms; usually off the bottom.

Range: From Bering Sea to Punta Santo Tomás, Baja California.

Similar Species: Dusky Rockfish (*S. ciliatus*) has blackish-brown body with brown speckles; occurs in similar habitat from Bering Sea to Dixon Entrance, British Columbia. Black Rockfish (*S. melanops*) has black spots on dorsal fin; maxilla reaching rear edge of eye; rear edge of anal fin rounded.

Comments: In late winter, the Blue Rockfish bears its young, which spend several weeks as part of the plankton community. Large aggregations of adults occur in mid-water, where they feed on small crustaceans, jellyfishes, pelagic tunicates, algae, and small fishes. The Blue Rockfish is usually the most abundant rockfish in the catches of charter boat and skiff anglers. The annual sport catch in California is close to 500,000 fishes. The dorsal and anal fins contain mildly venomous spines.

397 China Rockfish
(*Sebastes nebulosus*)

Description: To 17″ (43 cm). Deep, fusiform, compressed; black with yellow mottling and *yellow stripe extending from spiny dorsal fin down to and along lateral line, bluish-white spots below.* Snout moderately sharp; head deeply concave between eyes; 5 pairs of head spines prominent. Dorsal fin continuous, deeply notched, with incised membranes; some spines longer than rays. Usually 7 anal fin soft rays; caudal fin slightly rounded.

Habitat: Rocky areas with caves and crevices at depths of 2–70 fathoms.

Range: From Prince William Sound, Alaska, to San Miguel Island, California.

Similar Species: Black-and-yellow Rockfish (*S. chrysomelas*) lacks yellow stripe and bluish-white spots; head convex between eyes. Quillback Rockfish (*S. maliger*) lacks yellow stripe and blue spots.

Comments: This solitary rockfish spends most of its time in or near crevices or caves, where its large pectoral fins enable it to support itself on the cave floor and maneuver in crevices. Its food consists of brittle stars, crabs, and shrimps. China Rockfishes make up a minor portion of sport and commercial hook-and-line catches. The dorsal and anal fins contain mildly venomous spines.

391 Tiger Rockfish
(*Sebastes nigrocinctus*)

Description: To 24″ (61 cm). Fusiform, deep, compressed; pink, rose, or gray, with 5 *red or black bars, 2 red or black stripes radiate posteriorly from eyes to rear edge of opercle.* Snout moderately sharp; lower jaw projects beyond upper; head concave between eyes; 6 pairs of head spines prominent. Dorsal fin deeply notched, continuous, spiny portion longer-based, with incised membranes. Caudal fin rear profile rounded.

Habitat: Deep reefs with caves and crevices at depths of 13–150 fathoms.

Range: From Prince William Sound, Alaska, to Point Buchon, California.

Similar Species: Redbanded Rockfish (*S. babcocki*) has 4 dark bars, first mostly behind opercle; occurs in similar habitat from Amchitka Island, Alaska, to San Diego, California. Flag Rockfish (*S. rubrivinctus*) has white or light pink body with 4 dark red bars, first mostly on opercle.

Comments: This solitary rockfish prefers caves and other hiding places, and is seldom part of either sport or commercial catches. However, it is commonly observed by divers at 13 to 17 fathoms off British Columbia and Alaska. Its dorsal and anal spines are mildly venomous.

405 Bocaccio
(*Sebastes paucispinis*)

Description: To 3′ (91 cm). Elongate, fusiform, compressed; brown to dusky red or bronze above, lighter below; *young have dark brown spots.* Snout sharp; lower jaw projects beyond upper; head convex between eyes; 3 pairs of head spines, not prominent; *maxilla extends beyond eye;* 28–31 gill rakers. Dorsal fin continuous, deeply notched, spiny portion longer-based, with incised membranes. Usually 9 anal fin soft rays; caudal fin slightly forked.

Habitat: Adults over rocky reefs and soft bottoms to 175 fathoms. Juveniles around shallow reefs and in bays.

Range: From Kodiak Island, Alaska, to Punta Blanca, Baja California.

Related Species: Silvergray Rockfish (*S. brevispinis*) has body dark gray above, silvery below; 4 pairs of head spines, not prominent; occurs at 17–200 fathoms from Bering Sea to Santa Barbara Island, California. Bronzespotted Rockfish (*S. gilli*) has brown spots on back; usually 8 anal fin soft rays; occurs at 41–205 fathoms from Monterey Bay, California, to Ensenada, Baja California. Chilipepper (*S. goodei*) has bright red stripe along lateral line; maxilla not reaching rear edge of eye; usually 8 anal fin soft rays; occurs to 180 fathoms from Cape Scott, Vancouver Island, British Columbia, to Bahía Magdalena, Baja California. All in similar habitat.

Comments: A single Bocaccio female will release 20,000 to 2,000,000 larvae in the winter. This species feeds on a variety of fishes, crabs, and squids. Small numbers are taken by ocean anglers. The dorsal and anal fins contain mildly venomous spines.

389 Canary Rockfish
(*Sebastes pinniger*)

Description: To 30″ (76 cm). Deep, fusiform, compressed; orange with gray blotches and bands along lateral line; pectoral, pelvic, and anal fins yellow-orange, fin edges not black; *young have dark blotch on spiny dorsal fin.* Snout moderately sharp; head convex between eyes; 6 pairs of head spines; *lower jaw projects slightly,* no knob at tip, *underside of jaw smooth, unscaled.* Dorsal fin continuous, deeply notched, spiny portion longer-based, with incised membranes. Rear edge of anal fin straight; caudal fin moderately forked.

Habitat: Around deep reefs and over soft bottoms to depths of 150 fathoms.

Range: From Cape San Bartoleme, Alaska, to Cabo Colnett, Baja California.

Similar Species: Vermilion Rockfish (*S. miniatus*) has deep red dorsal, pectoral, pelvic, and anal fins with edges usually black; underside of lower jaw rough, scaled.

Comments: During winter months, the Canary Rockfish releases its young, which become part of the plankton community. Mildly venomous spines are present in the dorsal and anal fins.

404 Rosy Rockfish
(*Sebastes rosaceus*)

Description: To 14″ (36 cm). Fusiform, deep, compressed; back bright red or orange-red with lavender blotches and 3–6 *white blotches ringed by pale purplish red,* purple bar across nape. Snout moderately sharp; head concave between eyes; 6 pairs of prominent head spines; lower jaw smooth, unscaled. *Usually 17 pectoral fin rays.* Dorsal fin continuous, deeply notched, spiny portion longer-based, with incised membranes. Caudal fin truncate.

Habitat: Around reefs with crevices and caves at depths of 8–70 fathoms.

Range: From Puget Sound, Washington, to Bahía Tortugas, Baja California.

Related Species: Greenspotted Rockfish (*S. chlorostictus*) has bright green spots and vermiculations; occurs at 27–110 fathoms from Copalis Head, Washington, to Isla Cedros, Baja California. Starry Rockfish (*S. constellatus*) has white spots overall; occurs at 13–150 fathoms from San Francisco, California, to Thetis Bank, Baja California. Rosethorn Rockfish (*S. helvomaculatus*) has white blotches on back not ringed by purplish red; usually 16 pectoral fin rays; occurs at 65–300 fathoms from Kodiak Island, Alaska, to Point Loma, California. All in similar habitat.

Comments: The small and distinctive Rosy Rockfish makes excellent eating, but because of its small size it is discarded by many anglers. The dorsal and anal fins contain mildly venomous spines.

390 Yelloweye Rockfish
(*Sebastes ruberrimus*)

Description: To 3′ (91 cm). Deep, fusiform, compressed; orange-yellow above, paler below, *eyes bright yellow, fin edges black; juveniles have 2 silvery-white stripes on sides.* Mouth terminal, large; lower jaw unscaled, knob at tip broad, low, rounded; head concave between eyes, *with serrated ridges on older individuals;* 6 or more pairs of head spines. Dorsal fins continuous, deeply notched, spiny portion longer-based, with incised membranes. Caudal fin rounded.

Habitat: Around reefs with caves and crevices at depths of 10–300 fathoms.

Range: From Gulf of Alaska to Ensenada, Baja California.

Similar Species: Cowcod (*S. levis*) has unserrated ridges on head; eyes not yellow; spiny dorsal fin membrane deeply incised. Redstripe Rockfish (*S. proriger*) has pectoral and pelvic fin membranes light red or yellow; lateral line gray bordered by red stripes; 5 pairs of head spines, no serrated ridges on head; occurs at depths of 7–150 fathoms from Bering Sea to San Diego, California.

Comments: A female may release up to 3 million young in late spring. The Yelloweye Rockfish feeds on fishes and crustaceans. Because it is large and makes fine eating, this rockfish is highly prized by both sport and commercial bottom fishers. However, since it remains in a single location and is solitary, not many catches are sizable. The dorsal and anal fins contain mildly venomous spines.

392 Flag Rockfish
(*Sebastes rubrivinctus*)

Description: To 25″ (64 cm). Deep, fusiform, compressed; white or light pink with 4 dark red to reddish-brown bars, *first extending over rear of opercle anterior to pectoral fin,* second and third to dorsal fin. Snout moderately sharp; 5 pairs of head spines, sometimes additional pair at nape; *lower jaw smooth, unscaled.*

Dorsal fin continuous, deeply notched, spiny portion longer-based, with incised membranes. Caudal fin truncate to slightly rounded.

Habitat: Around reefs and over soft bottoms at 17–100 fathoms.

Range: From San Francisco, California, to Cabo Colnett, Baja California.

Related Species: Redbanded Rockfish (*S. babcocki*) has first red bar extending across body behind pectoral fin insertion; lower jaw scaled; occurs at 50–260 fathoms from Amchitka Island, Alaska, to San Diego, California.

Similar Species: Tiger Rockfish (*S. nigrocinctus*) has pink or light yellow body with 5–6 dark red bars.

Comments: The Flag Rockfish is occasionally caught by anglers as well as by commercial trawlers and hook-and-line fishers. The dorsal and anal fins contain mildly venomous spines.

403 Olive Rockfish
(*Sebastes serranoides*)

Description: To 24″ (61 cm). Elongate, fusiform, compressed; olive-brown with *light blotches under dorsal fin,* ivory below, pectoral, pelvic, and anal fins yellowish. Snout moderately sharp; head usually lacks spines; 29–36 gill rakers on first arch. Dorsal fin continuous, deeply notched, spiny portion longer-based, with incised membranes, 13 spines. *Usually 9 anal fin soft rays;* caudal fin emarginate.

Habitat: Shallow reefs and kelp beds to 80 fathoms.

Range: From Redding Rock, California, to Islas San Benito, Baja California.

Similar Species: Kelp Bass (*Paralabrax clathratus*) has 10–11 dorsal fin spines, 12–14 soft rays, with longest spine longer than longest ray. Yellowtail Rockfish (*S. flavidus*) has reddish-brown speckles on scales; usually 8 anal fin soft rays;

33−39 gill rakers on first arch.

Comments: The young are born during winter and late spring. Adults occur singly as well as in small aggregations, and are often confused with Kelp Basses. They are excellent sport fishes, readily take surface lures, and feed on crustaceans and small fishes. The dorsal and anal fins contain mildly venomous spines.

394 Treefish
(*Sebastes serriceps*)

Description: To 16″ (41 cm). Deep, fusiform, compressed; *bright yellow to olive-yellow with 6 black bars.* Snout moderately sharp; *lips thick, pinkish or red;* 6 pairs of head spines, sharp, prominent. Dorsal fin continuous, deeply notched, spiny portion longer-based, with incised membranes. Caudal fin rounded.

Habitat: Around shallow reefs with crevices and caves to depths of 25 fathoms.

Range: From San Francisco, California, to Isla Cedros, Baja California.

Comments: The Treefish is often observed by divers off southern California. This solitary species is territorial, defining its area by its constant presence. Mildly venomous spines are present in the dorsal and anal fins.

402 Honeycomb Rockfish
(*Sebastes umbrosus*)

Description: To 10½″ (27 cm). Elongate, fusiform, compressed; back orange-brown with 5 or fewer white blotches, light orange below; *scales on sides have dark edges, giving honeycomb appearance; all fin edges white.* Lower jaw scaled; 6 pairs of head spines sharp; 33−38 gill rakers on first arch. 15−18 pectoral fin rays; Dorsal fin continuous, deeply notched, spiny portion longer-based, with incised membranes. Caudal fin truncate.

Habitat: Around moderately deep reefs and sometimes over soft bottoms at depths of 15–265 fathoms.

Range: From Monterey Bay, California, to Punta San Juanico, Baja California.

Related Species: Swordspine Rockfish (*S. ensifer*) lower jaw projects slightly; second anal fin spine equal to or longer than anal soft rays; scales lack dark edges; occurs from San Francisco, California, to Ranger Bank, Baja California. Pink Rockfish (*S. eos*) has 26–31 gill rakers on first arch, 4–7 of these rudimentary and spiny; usually 18 pectoral fin rays; scales lack dark edges; occurs at 42–201 fathoms from Monterey, California, to Bahía San Sebastián Vizcaíno, Baja California. Freckled Rockfish (*S. lentiginosus*) has green freckles; front of upper jaw extends forward, forming 2 toothed knobs; scales lack dark edges; occurs at 22–92 fathoms from Santa Catalina Island, California, to Isla Coronados, Baja California. Greenblotched Rockfish (*S. rosenblatti*) has green spots; 29–34 gill rakers on first arch; usually 17 pectoral fin rays; scales lack dark edges; occurs at 34–218 fathoms from San Francisco, California, to Ranger Bank, Baja California. All in same habitat.

Comments: Very few Honeycomb Rockfishes are caught by sport or commercial fishers. Divers occasionally encounter a solitary fish around low-profile reefs at 15 to 17 fathoms. The dorsal and anal fins contain mildly venomous spines.

---

412 Shortspine Thornyhead
(*Sebastolobus alascanus*)

Description: To 30″ (76 cm). Elongate, fusiform; red with some black on fins. Snout rounded; 7 pairs of head spines, very strong, sharp. *Branchiostegal rays unscaled.* Pectoral fins deeply notched in

profile. Dorsal fin continuous, deeply
notched, spiny portion longer-based,
with incised membranes; *16–17 spines,
fourth and fifth longest.* 4–5 anal fin soft
rays; caudal fin truncate.

Habitat: Over deep, soft bottoms and sometimes
around reefs to depths of 838 fathoms.

Range: From Bering Sea to N. Baja California.

Similar Species: Longspine Thornyhead (*S. altivelis*)
usually has 15 dorsal fin spines, third
longest; scales on branchiostegal rays;
occurs at 182–838 fathoms from
Aleutian Islands to Cabo San Lucas,
Baja California.

Comments: Both of these fishes lay eggs that float
in masses near the surface. The
Shortspine Thornyhead feeds on
crustaceans and other invertebrates. It
is rarely caught by anglers, but makes
up a major share of the catches of
commercial trawlers working deeper
than 100 fathoms.

SEAROBINS
(Family Triglidae)

The bottom-dwelling searobins are
small to medium-sized fishes, variably
colored, and easily recognized by the
large head with many ridges and
spines, which tend to wear down with
age; the broad, flat snout and equally
broad mouth that is terminal or
slightly inferior; and the usually large,
winglike pectoral fins with the first 3
rays free and detached from the rest of
the fin. The spiny dorsal fin is
triangular, with 10 spines in the genus
Prionotus and 11 in *Bellator*. The soft
dorsal fin and the anal fins are long
and continuous. Searobins inhabit
continental and insular shelves of
tropical and temperate seas to depths of
about 95 fathoms. There are 21 species
in North America.

426 Northern Searobin
(*Prionotus carolinus*)

Description: To 17″ (43 cm). Elongate, robust anteriorly, tapering posteriorly; grayish or reddish above, pale below. Head large with many ridges and spines, some disappearing with growth; branchiostegal membranes black. Pectoral fins winglike, reddish-brown to black above, grayish or whitish below, extend to middle of soft dorsal fin; pelvic fins white. *Black spot between fourth and sixth dorsal spines, surrounded by light halo extending through membrane between third and fourth, sixth and seventh spines.*

Habitat: On bottom in shallow to deep coastal waters.

Range: From Bay of Fundy to Palm Beach, Florida; most common north of Bermuda. Migrates offshore and south in winter.

Comments: This is thought to be the most common searobin in Chesapeake Bay. It feeds on various crustaceans, including shrimps and crabs, and on bivalves, squids, and fishes. Searobins are a good food fish rather similar to goosefishes in taste.

424 Bandtail Searobin
(*Prionotus ophryas*)

Description: To 7″ (18 cm). Elongate, slightly compressed; usually brownish or coppery with several dark, oblique bands, lateral area of snout has light areas between dark blotches; pectoral fins brown, sometimes with spots and bands; free pectoral rays have alternating light and dark bands. *3 dark bars on caudal fin.* Head broad, ridged, profile very steep; preopercular spine well developed, other spines on head and snout relatively small or absent; *long filament on nostril; tentacle above eye.* Pectoral fin relatively long, winglike, reaches well past middle of soft dorsal fin.

Habitat: On bottom in shallow, grassy areas and in deep water over sand.

Range: From Georgia to Florida, Bahamas, and Gulf of Mexico.

Comments: The Bandtail Searobin has been recorded at depths of 95 fathoms in the Gulf of Mexico. Rarely seen elsewhere, it is the only searobin in North America with a nasal filament and a tentacle above the eye. Like other searobins, it has free pectoral rays that it uses for support on the bottom.

---

425 Leopard Searobin
(*Prionotus scitulus*)

Description: To 8″ (20 cm). Elongate, *relatively slender,* slightly compressed; brown or olive-brown above, abruptly lighter below lateral line, *darker spots on back and upper sides and on dorsal, pectoral, and caudal fins;* no markings below; black spot on membrane between first and second dorsal fin spines, larger spot between fourth and fifth. Head relatively small; *snout relatively narrow, dorsal profile rounded,* no prominent spines. Pectoral fins winglike, not greatly expanded, usually extending to third anal fin ray.

Habitat: Bays and near shore, often over sand.

Range: From Virginia to Texas and Venezuela.

Comments: This distinctively marked searobin is usually found in bays and near shore. As other searobins do, it lives on the bottom and feeds primarily on invertebrates.

---

423 Bighead Searobin
(*Prionotus tribulus*)

Description: To 14″ (36 cm). *Robust,* slightly compressed, depth one-fourth length;

light to olive-brown above with darker spots, especially on head; often with irregular, oblique bands, especially noticeable under soft dorsal fin and on caudal peduncle; whitish below, no conspicuous markings; black spot on membranes between fourth and sixth dorsal fin spines; dark lines across pectoral fins; pelvic fins pale. *Head large, two-fifths length;* snout broad, flat; maxilla reaches front of eye; *spines on snout, head, and shoulders very large, well developed,* become worn with age. Pectoral fins large, winglike, reach well past anal fin origin.

Habitat: Over sand or mud, near shore and in bays and sounds.

Range: From New York along coast to Mexico.

Comments: Young fishes less than 3" (7.5 cm) long, with their oversized heads armed with large spines, make interesting aquarium pets.

SABLEFISHES
(Family Anoplopomatidae)

Members of this family have an elongate, fusiform body that is only slightly compressed. They lack spines, ridges, and cirri on the head. The first dorsal fin is rounded, and the anal and second dorsal fins are smaller and triangular. The anal fin has up to 3 weak spines and 11–23 soft rays. The caudal fin is truncate or indented. The scales are ctenoid. A lateral line is present. There are only 2 species worldwide in the family; both are in North America off the Pacific Coast.

432 **Sablefish**
(*Anoplopoma fimbria*)

Description: To 3'4" (1 m); 126 lbs (57.2 kg). Elongate, fusiform, almost round in cross section; *blackish-gray above, gray to white below.* Snout moderately sharp; maxilla projects slightly beyond lower jaw, does not reach posterior of eye. First dorsal fin rounded, *17–30 spines,* second dorsal triangular, wide space between them; anal fin has no spines, 16–23 rays; caudal fin indented.

Habitat: Over soft bottoms in deep water to depths of 1,000 fathoms.

Range: From Bering Sea to Isla Cedros, Baja California.

Related Species: Skilfish (*Erilepis zonifer*) has light blotches on head and anterior part of body; 12–14 dorsal fin spines; 2–3 anal fin spines, 11–14 rays; occurs in similar habitat from Bering Sea to Moss Landing, California.

Comments: The Sablefish spawns during the winter, and the eggs drift near the surface. This species feeds on fishes, worms, and crustaceans. Smoked and sold for food, it is very important commercially, although of minor interest to anglers.

GREENLINGS
(Family Hexagrammidae)

These colorful fishes have cirri, but no ridges or spines, on the head, and a sharp, blunt, or rounded snout. They are elongate, slender, and slightly compressed, with a single, long dorsal fin, usually with a notch separating the 15 to 27 spines from the 11 to 26 soft rays. They may have up to 4 spines in the long anal fin, which may be longer than one-third of the body length. The caudal fin is truncate or forked. There are 1 to 5 lateral lines, and the scales can be either ctenoid or cycloid. This entirely marine family is comprised of 9 species in North America, most of which occur only on the Pacific Coast.

400, 411 Kelp Greenling
(*Hexagrammos decagrammus*)

Description: To 21" (53 cm). Elongate, fusiform, slightly compressed; males dark gray with bright blue spots, occasionally black-edged; females gray-brown with golden or brown spots. Snout moderately sharp; mouth yellowish inside; lips fleshy; palatine teeth present; *pair of cirri over eyes with length less than three-fourths eye diameter, pair on nape very small, occasionally absent.* Dorsal fin long, single, deeply notched; caudal fin slightly indented. 5 lateral lines, *fourth extends well beyond anal fin origin.* Ctenoid scales covering opercle.

Habitat: Shallow reefs to depths of 25 fathoms.

Range: From Aleutian Islands, Alaska, to La Jolla, California.

Related Species: Rock Greenling (*H. lagocephalus*) has single pair of cirri over eyes with length more than three-fourths eye diameter; mouth bluish inside; occurs from Bering Sea to Point Conception, California. Whitespotted Greenling (*H. stelleri*) has white spots on back; no palatine teeth; fourth lateral line not extending beyond anal fin origin; occurs from Gulf of Alaska to Puget Sound, Washington. Both in similar habitat.

Comments: The Kelp Greenling spawns in the fall. Its mass of blue eggs is attached to rocks and guarded by the male. This very colorful fish, popular among anglers, feeds on shrimps, small crabs, polychaete worms, small fishes, and the siphons of clams.

---

428 Lingcod
(*Ophiodon elongatus*)

Description: To 5' (1.5 m); 105 lbs (47.6 kg). Elongate, fusiform, almost round in cross section; gray-brown to green with darker spots and mottling. *Snout sharp;*

mouth large; lower jaw projects beyond upper, jaws with very sharp, large canine and smaller conical teeth; cirrus over each eye. Dorsal fin long, continuous, deeply notched, with 25–28 spines, 19–24 soft rays; 0–2 visible anal fin spines, 21 or more soft rays; caudal fin truncate. *1 lateral line.*

Habitat: Over reefs and soft bottoms, in shallow and deep water to 233 fathoms.

Range: From Kodiak Island, Alaska, to Punta San Carlos, Baja California.

Related Species: Painted Greenling (*Oxylebius pictus*) has very small mouth; 15–17 dorsal fin spines; 3–4 anal fin spines, 12–13 rays; occurs in similar habitat from Kodiak Island, Alaska, to Punta San Carlos, Baja California. Shortspine Combfish (*Zaniolepis frenata*) has 21 dorsal fin spines, second slightly longer than third; 15–16 anal fin rays; occurs over soft bottoms from S. Oregon to Bahía Tortugas, Baja California.

Comments: Lingcods feed on various large fishes, crustaceans, and mollusks. This voracious predator is one of the most highly esteemed sport fishes, primarily because it makes excellent eating. It is also a valuable commercial species.

SCULPINS
(Family Cottidae)

Most members of this family have a large head and an elongate, tapering body, partly covered with scales or prickles, but a few are scaleless. The eyes are placed high on the head. The pelvic fins have a single spine and 2 to 5 soft rays. Most species have separate spiny and soft-rayed dorsal fins. The anal fin is usually about as long as the soft dorsal fin and has no spines. A lateral line is present. There are 111 species in North America, which occur in both fresh and salt water and also frequently in rocky intertidal areas.

246 Mottled Sculpin
(*Cottus bairdi*)

Description: To 4" (10 cm). Robust, thick anteriorly, *caudal peduncle deep, compressed;* back olive to tan, dusky in adult males, sides lighter with dark mottlings, belly whitish; traces of 2 dark saddles sometimes under second dorsal fin, *first dorsal fin of males black, edge bright orange,* other fins dusky or have faint, narrow, dusky to brown bands. Head broad, depressed; palatine teeth present; mouth extends to below eye. Pelvic fin has 1 slender spine, 3–4 soft rays. *Lateral line incomplete,* 18–25 pores.

Habitat: Clear, cool or cold creeks, rivers, and lakes over gravel or rocks.

Range: Quebec, Ontario, central Manitoba south to N. Georgia, west to N. Arkansas; S. Alberta and British Columbia south to W. Colorado, NW. New Mexico, and Utah, west to Oregon.

Related Species: Black Sculpin (*C. baileyi*) grows to 2½" (6.5 cm); no palatine teeth; inhabits headwater spring creeks of Clinch, Holston, and Watauga rivers in SW. Virginia, NE. Tennessee. Pygmy Sculpin (*C. pygmaeus*) has 2 dorsal fins broadly joined; restricted to Coldwater Spring, Calhoun County, Alabama.

Comments: The Mottled Sculpin, which feeds on aquatic insects, is frequently cited as a major predator of trout eggs, but this does not appear to be true. Trouts, however, may prey on sculpins.

245 Banded Sculpin
(*Cottus carolinae*)

Description: To 5" (12.5 cm). Robust, depressed anteriorly, compressed posteriorly, *caudal peduncle slender;* back reddish brown to olive-gray, *sides lighter, 3 dark saddles,* 2 under second dorsal fin, 1 on caudal peduncle. Head large, broad, depressed; mouth wide; *chin mottled.* Pelvic fin has 1 slender spine and 4 soft rays. *First dorsal fin has dark blotches;* pectoral, second dorsal, anal, and caudal fins have rows of spots forming bands. *Lateral line complete.*

Habitat: Clear creeks and rivers in moderate to swift current over gravel or rocks.

Range: SE. West Virginia, S. Indiana, and W. central Illinois south to SW. Alabama; W. North Carolina west to N. Arkansas and NE. Oklahoma.

Related Species: Potomac Sculpin (*C. girardi*) has incomplete lateral line, 17–25 pores; occurs in streams of upper Potomac River drainage and headwaters of James River in Pennsylvania, Maryland, Virginia, and West Virginia.

Comments: The Banded Sculpin occurs farther south than any other freshwater species in this family and appears to be more tolerant of turbidity and warm waters than most sculpins.

244 Slimy Sculpin
(*Cottus cognatus*)

Description: To 4″ (10 cm). Moderately elongate, *caudal peduncle slender;* back and sides dark brown to olive-gray, mottled; First dorsal fin base dark, edge clear. 2–3 faint dark saddles, if present, under second dorsal fin. Head flattened, wide; mouth wide, extends to eye; *chin lightly pigmented; 3 preopercular spines,* larger points upward, smaller 2 decurved. Pelvic fin has 1 slender spine and often 3 soft rays, usually 4 in Northwest. *Lateral line incomplete, usually ends at middle of second dorsal fin.*

Habitat: Cold streams with moderate current and clear springs over gravel, rocks, or sand; in lakes from rocky shoals to deeper water.

Range: Alaska and throughout Canada; Great Lakes south to N. Virginia; Maine west to Minnesota, Iowa, W. Montana, W. central Idaho, and Oregon.

Comments: Common throughout its range, especially in the northern part, the Slimy Sculpin is the most widespread species of the genus *Cottus* in North America. It feeds primarily on aquatic insects and is preyed upon by game fishes such as Lake Trout, Burbot, and Northern Pike.

419 Buffalo Sculpin
(*Enophrys bison*)

Description: To 15″ (38 cm). Elongate, tapering, almost round in cross section, greatest depth at pectoral fin insertion; dark gray, green, or brown above, often with light blotches. Snout rounded; head large; *preopercular spine long, sharp,* reaches rear of opercle. Pelvic fin with 1 spine, 3 soft rays; 2 dorsal fins, second with 9–13 rays; 8–10 anal fin rays; caudal fin truncate. *Heavy bony plates on lateral line.*

Habitat: Over shallow reefs and soft bottoms around piers and wrecks.

Range: From Kodiak Island, Alaska, to Monterey Bay, California.

Related Species: Bull Sculpin (*E. taurina*) has preopercular spine extending beyond opercle; 6–7 anal fin rays; occurs from San Francisco to Santa Catalina Island, California. Pacific Staghorn Sculpin (*Leptocottus armatus*) has antlerlike preopercular spine, not reaching rear edge of opercle; no bony plates; occurs from Chignik, Alaska, to Bahía San Quintín, Baja California. Both in similar habitat.

Comments: Buffalo Sculpins eat shrimps, crabs, and young fishes. A few are caught by anglers but are seldom retained because they lack sufficient flesh to be edible.

413 Red Irish Lord
(Hemilepidotus hemilepidotus)

Description: To 20″ (51 cm). Elongate, tapering, almost round in cross section; body and fins red and brown with black mottling and spots. Head depressed; cirri present; snout moderately sharp; 2–3 pairs of simple preopercular spines. *Gill membranes united, narrowly joined to isthmus.* Dorsal fin single with 2 notches, 10–13 spines, 17–20 rays; 13–16 anal fin soft rays; caudal fin slightly rounded. *Band of 4–5 scale rows just below dorsal fin.*

Habitat: Shallow, rocky reefs to 26 fathoms.

Range: From Bering Sea south to Monterey Bay, California.

Related Species: Coralline Sculpin (*Artedius corallinus*) has 2 dorsal fins, first with 9 spines, second with 15–16 rays; head unscaled; 39–49 scale rows in dorsal band; occurs from Orcas Island, Washington, south to Isla San Martin, Baja California. Smoothhead Sculpin (*A. lateralis*) has 18–29 scale rows in dorsal band; head unscaled; occurs from Bering Sea south to Sulphur Point, San Quintín, Baja California. Brown Irish Lord (*H. spinosus*) has light to dark brown body; band of 7–8 scale rows below dorsal fin; occurs from Puffin Bay, Alaska, south to Santa Barbara Island, California. All in similar habitat.

Comments: The colorful Red Irish Lord lays its egg masses in intertidal areas during the spring. Adults feed on crabs, barnacles, and mussels. Anglers only occasionally catch this edible sculpin.

416 Lavender Sculpin
(Leiocottus hirundo)

Description: To 10″ (25 cm). Elongate, slightly compressed; olive-green with blue blotches, mottled with red; iridescent blue stripes on dorsal fin. Snout moderately sharp; *no cirrus over eye;* preopercular spines present. Anterior of spiny dorsal much higher than rest of fin, *first dorsal spine twice as long as third;* anus midway between pelvic and anal fins; caudal fin truncate.

Habitat: In shallow water over rocks and soft bottoms; around kelp beds to depths of 20 fathoms.

Range: From Point Conception, California, to Punta Banda, Baja California.

Related Species: Roughback Sculpin (*Chitonotus pugetensis*) has spiny dorsal fin with deep notch, first spine twice length of second; occurs from Ucluelet, British Columbia, to Bahía Santa Maria, Baja California. Threadfin Sculpin (*Icelinus filamentosus*) has first 2 dorsal spines greatly elongated, about two-thirds free of membrane; occurs from N. British Columbia to Cortez Banks, California. Sailfin Sculpin (*Nautichthys oculofasciatus*) has very high spiny dorsal fin, first 4 spines almost 3 times height of soft rays; occurs from Bering Sea to San Miguel Island, California. All in shallow water around rocks.

Comments: Although anglers rarely catch the distinctive Lavender Sculpin, it is commonly encountered by divers.

Deepwater Sculpin
(*Myoxocephalus thompsoni*)

Description: To 8″ (20 cm). Moderately elongate; caudal peduncle slender; grayish-brown above with dark speckles or mottling; 4–7 thin, dark saddles; light gray to white below. Head flattened, very broad; mouth extends past middle of eye; 4 preopercular spines, upper 2 larger. *Gill membranes meet at acute angle. Dorsal fins separated by distance equal to eye diameter;* pectoral and second dorsal fins very large. *Prickles present only above usually complete lateral line; no scales.*

Habitat: Deep, cold inland lakes; occasionally streams in far north.

Range: From Great Bear Lake, Mackenzie, south to Quebec; throughout Great Lakes west to S. Manitoba and S. Alberta.

Related Species: Great Sculpin (*M. polyacanthocephalus*) has 1 simple, long preopercular spine; 11–13 anal fin soft rays; no bony plates on lateral line; occurs on shallow reefs and over soft bottoms around piers and wrecks from Bering Sea to S. Puget Sound, Washington. Fourhorn Sculpin (*M. quadricornis*) has prickles above and below lateral line; inhabits shallow salt, brackish, and fresh water in coastal NW. Canada and N. Alaska.

Comments: The Deepwater Sculpin eats crustaceans and aquatic insects; it, in turn, is preyed upon by the Lake Trout and the Burbot. This fish has been captured to depths of 200 fathoms.

414 Snubnose Sculpin
(*Orthonopias triacis*)

Description: To 4″ (10 cm). Elongate, slightly compressed; brown with light and dark mottling and bright red patches. Head large, *snout very blunt;* preopercular spines present. Pelvic fins with 1 spine, 3 soft rays; *anus much closer to pelvic fin base than to anal fin;* caudal fin rounded. Cirri along lateral line; scales between lateral line and dorsal fin.

Habitat: Rocks between high and low tide levels and reefs below intertidal zone to depths of 17 fathoms.

Range: From Monterey Bay, California, to Isla San Geronimo, Baja California.

Related Species: Woolly Sculpin (*Clinocottus analis*) has anus midway between pelvic and anal fins; cirri and minute scales between dorsal fin and lateral line; occurs from Cape Mendocino, California, to Punta Asunción, Baja California. Mosshead Sculpin (*C. globiceps*) has cirri in front of and between eyes; head bluntly rounded; no scales between lateral line and dorsal fin; occurs from Kodiak Island, Alaska, to Gaviota, California. Bald Sculpin (*C. recalvus*) has head bluntly rounded; no scales between lateral line and dorsal fin; occurs from Brookings, Oregon, to Punta Rompiente, Baja California. Fluffy Sculpin (*Oligocottus snyderi*) has anus close to anal fin; first anal fin soft rays longest in males; no visible scales; occurs from Sitka, Alaska, to Rio Socorro, Baja California. All in similar habitat.

Comments: This small sculpin is rarely caught by anglers, but is familiar to divers.

---

418 Grunt Sculpin
(*Rhamphocottus richardsoni*)

Description: To 3¼″ (8.5 cm). Deep, compressed; creamy yellow with brown bars and streaks; caudal peduncle and all fins except pelvics bright red. *Snout long, sharp;* mouth small, terminal; cirrus on upper lip of adults small, flaplike. *Lowest pectoral rays free;* spiny and soft dorsal fins separated by notch; 6–7 anal fin rays; caudal fin rounded. Scales reduced to plates bearing minute spines.

Habitat: Rocks and reefs in intertidal zone and below low tide level; over soft bottoms to depths of 90 fathoms.

Range: From Bering Sea to Santa Monica Bay, California.

Comments: The Grunt Sculpin is thought to spawn in the winter. It feeds on the larvae of both small crustaceans and fishes. This distinctive sculpin makes an amusing aquarium pet because of the way it uses its pectoral fins to crawl over rocks.

420 Cabezon
(*Scorpaenichthys marmoratus*)

Description: To 3'3" (99 cm). Elongate, slightly
compressed; variably red to olive-green
to brown with dark and light mottling.
Snout moderately blunt, with *large,
fleshy cirri on midline of snout* and over
each eye. Pelvic fin with 1 spine, 5 soft
rays; 11–14 anal fin soft rays; caudal
fin truncate. *No visible scales.*

Habitat: Rocks and reefs in intertidal zone and
below low tide level to 42 fathoms.

Range: From Sitka, Alaska, to Punta Abreojos,
Baja California.

Similar Species: Rosylip Sculpin (*Ascelichthys rhodorus*)
grows to 6" (15 cm); has head bluntly
rounded; no pelvic fins; occurs from
Sitka, Alaska, to Moss Beach, San
Mateo County, California. Blackfin
Sculpin (*Malacocottus kincaidi*) grows to
8" (20 cm); lacks large cirri on head;
has 3 pelvic fin soft rays; skin thin,
loose; occurs from Bird Island, Alaska,
to Puget Sound, Washington. Both in
shallow water around rocks.

Comments: The Cabezon spawns in winter, and the
male guards the mass of greenish to
purplish eggs until they hatch. The
eggs are poisonous if eaten. This large,
tasty sculpin is highly desired by
anglers, who catch it from the shore.

POACHERS
(Family Agonidae)

These fishes have an elongate, slender
body tapering to a small caudal fin, and
either 1 or 2 dorsal fins. When
separated, the first dorsal fin is spiny,
and the second is soft-rayed. The pelvic
fins have 1 spine and 2 soft rays and are
below the pectoral fins. There are no
spines in the anal fin. A few specimens
have cirri, usually on the lower jaw.
Poachers are often confused with
juvenile sturgeons, since they are both

covered with scales modified as bony plates. This entirely marine family has 29 North American species.

427 Sturgeon Poacher
(*Agonus acipenserinus*)

Description: To 12″ (30 cm). Elongate, tapering, caudal peduncle long, slender; gray-brown above, light yellow to orange below, orange spot under each eye, dark saddles across back. Snout long, sharp; *mouth ventral, with patch of long, yellow to cream cirri in front and at corners.* 2 projecting rostral spines, widely separated. Pelvic fin with 1 spine, 2 rays; 16–18 pectoral soft rays. 2 dorsal fins; 6–9 anal fin rays; caudal fin rounded. 4 rows of bony plates on each side.

Habitat: In shallow water over soft bottoms and on reefs to 30 fathoms.

Range: From Bering Sea to Eureka, California.

Related Species: Northern Spearnose Poacher (*Agonopsis vulsa*) lacks large, yellow cirri on snout; mouth terminal; 2 projecting rostral spines close together; occurs from SE. Alaska to Point Loma, California. Rockhead (*Bothragonus swani*) has deep pit on head behind eyes; body deep, robust; occurs from Kodiak Island, Alaska, to Lion Rock, California. Warty Poacher (*Occella verrucosa*) has terminal mouth; pelvic fins as long as pectoral fins in males; 15 pectoral fin soft rays; knobby, platelike scales on breast in front of pelvic fins; occurs' from Shelikof Strait, Alaska, to Point Montara, California. Pygmy Poacher (*Odontopyxis trispinosa*) has upright rostral spines; shallow pit on top of head behind eyes; occurs from SE. Alaska to Isla Cedros, Baja California. Pricklebreast Poacher (*Stellerina xyosterna*) has terminal mouth; breast smooth with minute spines; 17–19 pectoral soft rays; occurs from Queen

Charlotte Islands, British Columbia, to
Bahía San Carlos, Baja California. All
in similar habitat.

Comments: This fish, rarely caught by anglers, is
often netted by trawlers, but not kept.

SNAILFISHES
(Family Cyclopteridae)

This family is divided into 2 groups,
the snailfishes and the lumpfishes.
Some experts place the snailfishes in a
separate family, the Liparidae. All of
these fishes have a ventral sucking disc.
The snailfishes are tadpole-shaped with
soft bodies and smooth skins, while
lumpfishes are short and robust and
covered with blunt tubercles. There are
30 species in North America.

297, 299 Lumpfish
(*Cyclopterus lumpus*)

Description: To 23″ (58 cm). *Very robust, more or less
triangular-shaped in cross section;* variably
bluish, olive, brownish, reddish,
greenish; paler below, often with
darker blotches and black dots. Mouth
small, terminal, oblique. *Pectoral fins
broad-based, almost meet at throat; pelvic
fins inserted just behind throat, modified to
ventral sucking disc;* dorsal and anal fins
similar, posteriorly placed opposite
each other, not attached to truncate
caudal fin. Skin rough with 7 lengthwise ridges formed by large tubercles,
tips of largest sometimes black.

Habitat: Primarily over rocks in shallow water.

Range: From Newfoundland to Hudson Bay,
and along coast to Chesapeake Bay.

Related Species: Showy Snailfish (*Liparis pulchellus*) has
dorsal and anal fins connected to caudal
fin; rear edge of sucking disc under
pectoral fin behind gill opening; occurs
over soft bottoms to 100 fathoms from

Bering Sea to Monterey, California.
Comments: This ungainly fish clings to rocks or debris. Males make good eating, and this species is noted for its tasty roe, but females are inedible while breeding.

Order Pleuronectiformes

All of these fishes have a highly compressed body and are called flatfishes. They live on the bottom. In adult flatfishes both eyes are on the same side of the head, and they swim with the blind side downward. There are 4 North American families.

LEFTEYE FLOUNDERS
(Family Bothidae)

The eyes and color of these highly compressed flatfishes are usually on the left side of the body. Their pigmented side is usually brownish, often with markings, and the blind side is white; they are capable of changing color patterns to match the substrate. The edge of the preopercle is visible and not hidden by skin. The dorsal fin base is long, beginning over or in front of the eyes, and, like the anal fin it is not connected to the caudal fin. Some species exhibit sexual dimorphism: The males may have a greater distance between the eyes and longer pectoral fins. There are 38 species in North America. Most are marine, but a few may enter brackish to fresh water.

287 **Three-eye Flounder**
(*Ancylopsetta dilecta*)

Description: To 7″ (18 cm). Highly compressed, depth about half length, eyes on left side; eyed side light brown with numerous small spots and blotches; *3 large, ocellated spots form triangle, with apex on lateral line near caudal peduncle;* blind side white. Head long; lower jaw not projecting; preopercle visible. Pectoral fins on both sides; pelvic fin bases symmetrical, fin on eyed side longer than head length; dorsal fin origin over eye, *anterior soft rays longer than others, have fleshy tips.* Lateral line highly arched anteriorly.

Habitat: Continental shelf at 32–200 fathoms.

Range: From North Carolina along coast to Texas and Yucatán, Mexico.

Related Species: Ocellated Flounder (*A. quadrocellata*) has 4 ocellated spots, fourth above arched part of lateral line; usually occurs at depths of less than 25 fathoms in similar range.

Comments: This is the only North American genus of lefteye flounder with a spot on the lateral line near the caudal peduncle. It feeds primarily on crustaceans and small fishes.

283 Eyed Flounder
(*Bothus ocellatus*)

Description: To 7″ (18 cm). Highly compressed, depth two-thirds length, eyes on left side; light tan or gray, usually with rings or blotches; 3 diffuse, dark blotches along lateral line; *caudal fin has 2 small, vertically placed, black dots;* blind side white. Maxilla not reaching center of lower eye; eyes well separated, more so in males; preopercle free, visible. *Pectoral fin base on eyed side twice as long as on blind side;* dorsal fin origin anterior to eyes, anterior rays not branched. Lateral line distinctly arched over pectoral fin.

Habitat: Shallow water in protected areas over sand; less frequently over mud.

Range: From Long Island to Rio de Janeiro, Brazil, including Bermuda, parts of

Gulf of Mexico, Caribbean, and West Indies.

Related Species: Peacock Flounder (*B. lunatus*) lacks conspicuous spots on caudal fin; occurs from S. Florida to Brazil, including Bermuda, Caribbean, and West Indies. Twospot Flounder (*B. robinsi*) has 2 horizontally placed, black spots on caudal fin; occurs from New York to Brazil. Both in similar habitat.

Comments: These 3 species are good food fishes, but they are of little commercial value due to their small size and the fact that they are infrequently caught by anglers. They burrow into sand or mud, behavior shared with other lefteye flounders.

288 Spotted Whiff
(*Citharichthys macrops*)

Description: To 6″ (15 cm). Highly compressed, depth half length, eyes on left side; *eyed side tan to dark brown with numerous small spots or blotches on body and median fins;* blind side white. Maxilla reaches middle of eye; single row of teeth in each jaw, front teeth larger than lateral; preopercle visible. Pectoral fins short; bases of pelvic fins about equal length; dorsal fin origin anterior to eye, first ray longer than second or third. Lateral line nearly straight.

Habitat: Shallow water over sand or crushed shells.

Range: From North Carolina to Florida, Gulf of Mexico, and along coast to Honduras.

Comments: The Spotted Whiff is usually found in shallow water, but has been collected at depths of 50 fathoms. Like most lefteye flounders, it can move rapidly over short distances in pursuit of prey.

284 Pacific Sanddab
(*Citharichthys sordidus*)

Description: To 16″ (41 cm). Extremely compressed, deep, eyes on left side; eyed side brown, with darker brown mottling and sometimes dull orange spots; blind side off-white to pale brown. Snout moderately sharp; *ridge between eyes concave; diameter of lower eye longer than snout length;* preopercle visible. Pelvic fins asymmetrical, attached to ventral ridge on eyed side; dorsal fin origin over eyes; anal fin origin below pectoral fin; anal and dorsal fins extend almost to caudal fin. Lateral line straight.

Habitat: Over soft bottoms to 300 fathoms.

Range: From Bering Sea to Cabo San Lucas, Baja California.

Related Species: Speckled Sanddab (*C. stigmaeus*) has 11–15 gill rakers on first arch; short pectoral fin; occurs from Montague Island, Alaska, to Bahía Magdalena, Baja California. Longfin Sanddab (*C. xanthostigma*) has very long pectoral fin, upper soft rays longer than head; occurs from Monterey Bay, California, to Costa Rica. Both in similar habitat.

Comments: The Pacific Sanddab spawns during the winter; some females may spawn twice a season. Highly regarded as food, this flatfish is sought by anglers as well as commercial trawlers.

286 Spotfin Flounder
(*Cyclopsetta fimbriata*)

Description: To 15″ (38 cm). Highly compressed, depth two-fifths to half length, eyes on left side; eyed side uniformly brown, no conspicuous spots or blotches on head or body; blind side white; outer half of pectoral fin covered by large, dusky or black blotch; *dorsal and anal fins each have 2 large spots; large, dark spot enclosing irregularly-shaped lightish area in center of caudal fin;* sometimes 3 smaller spots on rear edge. Lower jaw not projecting, maxilla reaches rear edge of eye; preopercle visible. Pectoral fins on both sides; pelvic fins symmetrical, relatively short; dorsal fin origin over eye. Lateral line not highly arched anteriorly.

Habitat: Near shore to about 125 fathoms.

Range: From North Carolina along coast to Texas; Caribbean.

Related Species: Mexican Flounder (*C. chittendeni*) has large, black blotch under pectoral fin on eyed side; no large spot in middle of caudal fin, 3 distinct spots on rear edge; occurs in similar habitat from W. Gulf of Mexico to Brazil; Caribbean.

Comments: The Spotfin Flounder is more common in the eastern Gulf of Mexico and is largely replaced by the Mexican Flounder to the west. Both feed on bottom-dwelling invertebrates and small fishes.

71, 285 Gulf Flounder
(*Paralichthys albigutta*)

Description: To 15″ (38 cm). Oval, depth less than half length, eyes on left side. Eyed side light to dark brown, olive-brown or dark gray, with diffuse black, dark brown, or dusky spots and blotches disappearing with age; *3 small, distinct ocellated spots* form triangle, 2 vertically placed spots, just posterior to pectoral fin, 1 to rear of lateral line; blind side white or dusky. Maxilla reaches past pupil of lower eye; no bony ridge between eyes; preopercle visible. Pectoral fins on both sides; pelvic fin bases on each side about equal length, soft rays on each side of equal length, pelvic fin on eyed side inserted off median line; dorsal fin origin slightly anterior to eye, first soft ray shorter than second. *Lateral line highly arched above pectoral fin.*

Habitat: Over mud in estuaries and coastal

waters to depths of 70 fathoms.

Range: From North Carolina to Texas coast.
Related Species: Southern Flounder (*P. lethostigma*)
grows to 3′ (91 cm); lacks 3 ocellated
spots; occurs in similar habitat and
range; sometimes enters fresh water.
Comments: The Gulf Flounder is an important food
and game fish, but its comparatively
small size makes it less valuable than
other flounders. It is a voracious
predator and will take live and artificial
baits. Many are caught at night in
shallow water with a fishing spear.

282   California Halibut
(*Paralichthys californicus*)

Description: To 5′ (1.5 m); 72 lbs (32.7 kg).
Elongate, deep, highly compressed;
eyes usually on left side, occasionally
on right. Eyed side light to dark brown
with lighter mottling, blind side
lighter. Snout moderately sharp; mouth
large; *maxilla extends beyond rear edge of
lower eye;* numerous sharp teeth in jaws;
preopercle visible. Dorsal fin origin
over eye; caudal fin truncate or
indented. *Lateral line highly arched over
pectoral fin.*
Habitat: Over soft bottoms to 100 fathoms.
Range: From Quillayute River, Washington,
to Bahía Magdalena, Baja California.
Related Species: Bigmouth Sole (*Hippoglossina stomata*)
has maxilla almost reaching rear edge
of eye; caudal fin rounded, occurs from
Monterey Bay to Gulf of California.
Fantail Sole (*Xystreurys liolepis*) has
maxilla not reaching rear of lower eye;
mouth small; pectoral fin longer than
head; caudal fin rounded; occurs from
Monterey Bay, California, to Gulf of
California. Both in similar habitat.
Comments: This is a very popular sport fish; the
annual catch may exceed 300,000. It is
also an important commercial species,
with annual landings of 500 to 1,000
tons (454,000 to 908,000 kg).

289 **Windowpane**
(*Scophthalmus aquosus*)

Description: To 18″ (46 cm). Highly compressed;
depth about two-thirds length, eyes on
left side. Eyed side translucent, olive,
brownish, reddish, or grayish, mottled
with *numerous small, irregular, lighter or
darker blotches on head, sides, and fins;*
blind side white, sometimes with
dusky blotches. Lower jaw projects
slightly beyond upper; maxilla reaches
middle of eye; preopercle visible. *Pelvic
fin bases very long,* extend toward head;
*dorsal fin origin over snout, first few rays
free* without membrane between them.
Lateral line highly arched anteriorly.

Habitat: Over sand, from near shore to depths of
about 25 fathoms.

Range: From Gulf of St. Lawrence and Nova
Scotia to Florida.

Comments: The Windowpane is most common in
the New England states, where it is a
year-round resident. It is of little
importance as a food or game fish.

RIGHTEYE FLOUNDERS
(Family Pleuronectidae)

These flatfishes almost always have their
eyes on the right side. Righteye
flounders have a deep, very compressed
body. The pelvic fins are symmetrically
placed, and the dorsal and anal fins are
elongate. The dorsal fin usually
originates near the eyes, and the anal fin
origin is below the pectoral fin; both
extend to near the base of the caudal
fin and are composed of soft rays only.
The lateral line may be straight or
highly arched over the pectoral fin;
some species have a dorsal branch off
the lateral line. The scales may be
cycloid or ctenoid, and in some species
they are ctenoid on the eyed side and
cycloid on the blind side. The caudal
fin is truncate, rounded, pointed, or

slightly indented. All the members of this family are marine, and there are 31 species in North America. Most are found over soft bottoms.

280 Pacific Halibut
(*Hippoglossus stenolepis*)

Description: To 8′9″ (2.7 m); 800 lbs (363 kg). Elongate, highly compressed, diamond-shaped, eyes on right side; eyed side dark brown with fine mottling, blind side pigmented, lighter brown. Snout moderately sharp; mouth medium-sized; double row of teeth in upper jaw sharp, conical; *maxilla not extending beyond anterior edge of lower eye.* Pelvic fins symmetrically placed; dorsal fin origin over middle of eye, *longest soft rays of dorsal and anal fins at about middle of body;* caudal fin slightly forked. Lateral line arched above pectoral fin; scales numerous, smooth.

Habitat: Over soft bottoms at 3–600 fathoms.

Range: From Bering Sea to Santa Rosa Island, California.

Similar Species: Arrowtooth Flounder (*Atheresthes stomias*) lacks pigment on blind side; each jaw has 2 rows of sharp, strong teeth; dorsal fin origin over middle of upper eye; occurs from Bering Sea to San Pedro, California. Greenland Halibut (*Reinhardtius hippoglossoides*) has dark to light brown on blind side; maxilla extends to rear edge of lower eye; teeth strong, sharp, simple, in single row on jaws; dorsal fin origin behind upper eye; lateral line straight; occurs in Atlantic from Arctic Ocean to Bay of Fundy; in Pacific from Bering Sea to N. Baja California. Both in similar habitat.

Comments: The Pacific Halibut supports one of the oldest and most valuable fisheries on the Pacific Coast. It is a highly desirable sport fish off Washington, British Columbia, and Alaska.

281 Diamond Turbot
(*Hypsopsetta guttulata*)

Description: To 18" (46 cm). Deep, *diamond-shaped,* highly compressed, eyes on right side; eyed side dark gray with *numerous blue spots,* blind side not pigmented, yellow around mouth. Snout short, moderately sharp. Dorsal fin origin over eyes; middle soft rays of dorsal and anal fins longest; caudal fin rounded. *Dorsal branch of lateral line extends more than halfway to caudal fin.*

Habitat: Over soft bottoms at 1–25 fathoms.

Range: From Cape Mendocino, California, to Bahía Magdalena, Baja California.

Similar Species: Sand Sole (*Psettichthys melanostictus*) lacks blue spots; eyes usually on right side; first 4–5 dorsal soft rays free of membrane; occurs in similar habitat from Bering Sea to Redondo Beach, California.

Comments: This distinctively shaped flatfish is commonly encountered by divers off southern California.

277 Rock Sole
(*Lepidopsetta bilineata*)

Description: To 24" (61 cm). Moderately deep, compressed, eyes on right side; eyed side dark brown or gray with mottling, blind side whitish. Snout short, bluntly sharp; maxilla not reaching middle of lower eye; teeth in both jaws, better developed on blind side. Dorsal fin origin over eyes; caudal fin slightly rounded. *Lateral line arched over pectoral fin, has short dorsal branch not extending beyond posterior edge of opercle.* Scales ctenoid on eyed side, cycloid on blind side, extend onto dorsal, anal, and caudal fin rays.

Habitat: Over rocks and soft bottoms at 2–200 fathoms.

Range: From Bering Sea to Tanner Bank, California.

Related Species: Petrale Sole (*Eopsetta jordani*) has
maxilla reaching middle of lower eye;
no arch in lateral line over pectoral fin;
occurs from Bering Sea to Isla
Coronados, Baja California. Butter Sole
(*Isopsetta isolepis*) has maxilla not
reaching middle of lower eye; dorsal
and anal fins with yellow edges; rough
scales on body, head, and fins on eyed
side; occurs from Bering Sea to
Ventura, California. Yellowfin Sole
(*Limanda aspera*) has no dorsal branch of
lateral line; occurs from Bering Sea to
Barkley Sound, S. British Columbia.
All in similar habitat.

Comments: The female Rock Sole releases between
400,000 and 1,300,000 eggs during
the spawning period from February to
April. Adults feed on clam siphons,
polychaete worms, shrimps, small
crabs, brittle stars, and sand lances, all
of which can be used as bait by anglers.

276 English Sole
(*Parophrys vetulus*)

Description: To 22″ (56 cm). Deep, elongate,
highly compressed, almost diamond-
shaped, eyes on right side; eyed side
dark to light brown, occasionally with
brown spots, blind side pale yellow to
white. Snout moderately long, sharp;
mouth small; *upper eye visible from blind
side.* Dorsal fin origin above middle of
upper eye, longest dorsal soft rays at
middle of body; caudal fin indented.
Lateral line almost straight, with short
dorsal branch; *no scales on fins.*

Habitat: Over soft bottoms to 300 fathoms.

Range: From Bering Sea to Bahía de San
Cristobal, Baja California.

Comments: The migratory English Sole may travel
up to 700 miles (1,160 km). It ranks
among the top 3 flatfishes in terms of
pounds caught by commercial trawlers,
although very few are caught for sport.

72, 278, 279 Starry Flounder
(*Platichthys stellatus*)

Description: To 3' (91 cm). Deep, compressed, almost diamond-shaped, eyes on either left or right side; eyed side dark brown to nearly black with vague blotches, blind side white to creamy white, occasionally blotched. *Dorsal, anal, and caudal fins have distinctive black and white or black and orange bars.* Mouth small. Dorsal and anal fin soft rays longest posterior to middle of body; caudal fin straight or rounded. Lateral line only slightly curved over pectoral fin, no dorsal branch; scales star-shaped, very rough to touch.

Habitat: In bays and estuaries over soft bottoms, and off open coast to 150 fathoms.

Range: From Arctic Ocean off Alaska to Santa Barbara, California.

Comments: The Starry Flounder feeds on crabs, shrimps, worms, clams, and small fishes. It can tolerate very low salinity and is often captured in major rivers, well away from the open ocean. Small numbers are taken by anglers and commercial trawlers. Like all flatfishes, it is edible.

274 C-O Sole
(*Pleuronichthys coenosus*)

Description: To 14" (36 cm). Deep, highly compressed, eyes on right side; eyed side brown with darker mottling, blind side creamy white; *prominent C- and O-shaped marks on caudal fin.* Snout rounded; mouth small, almost hidden by eyes when viewed from above. Dorsal fin origin anterior to middle of upper eye; *4–6 anterior soft rays of dorsal fin extend onto blind side but not beyond mouth;* caudal peduncle about one-fourth body depth; caudal fin rounded, cycloid scales on both sides. Lateral line lacks abrupt arch over pectoral fin, dorsal branch extends posteriorly to about middle of body.

Habitat: Over soft bottoms and rocks to depths of 191 fathoms.

Range: From SE. Alaska to Cabo Colnett, Baja California.

Related Species: Curlfin Sole (*P. decurrens*) has at least 9 dorsal fin soft rays extending onto blind side, reaching below mouth; occurs from Prince William Sound, Alaska, to Bahía San Quintín, Baja California. Spotted Turbot (*P. ritteri*) has 1–2 black spots on middle of lateral line; caudal peduncle less than one-fourth body depth; occurs from Morro Bay, California, to Bahía Magdalena, Baja California. Hornyhead Turbot (*P. verticalis*) has 2 prominent spines between eyes; occurs from Point Reyes, California, to Bahía Magdalena, Baja California. All in similar habitat.

Comments: This flatfish probably spawns during late winter and early spring; its eggs float near the surface. Small numbers of C-O Soles are caught by anglers with hook and line and by commercial trawlers. Like other flatfishes, the C-O Sole is edible.

---

275 **Winter Flounder**
(*Pseudopleuronectes americanus*)

Description: To 23″ (58 cm). Highly compressed, elliptical, eyes on right side, dorsal and ventral profiles evenly curved. Color varies with substrate from reddish-brown to olive-green to almost black, sometimes mottled; fins plain; blind side white. *Head small; maxilla barely reaches front edge of lower eye;* preopercle visible. Dorsal fin origin over front edge of upper eye. Lateral line almost straight, slightly arched above pectoral fins; scales strongly ctenoid on eyed side, smoother on blind side.

Habitat: Over mud or sand, with or without vegetation, to 20 fathoms or more.

Range: From Labrador to Georgia; rarely south of Chesapeake Bay; most abundant in Gulf of Maine.

Comments: The Winter Flounder has a thicker body and broader caudal peduncle than any other small flounder species in its range. South of New York, it goes into deep water in the summer and reappears in shoal waters during the winter; hence the common name Winter Flounder. It is an important food fish.

SOLES
(Family Soleidae)

These flatfishes have both eyes on the right side of the body, which is rounded or oval. They are usually blackish brown with blotches or bars. The edge of the preopercle is hidden by skin. The mouth is small and oblique. The lips are fleshy and usually fringed with dermal flaps, and the small eyes are closely set. There are no spines in the fins. The lateral line is almost straight and often crossed with accessory branches or minute fleshy flaps. Soles occur in shallow coastal waters to depths of about 100 fathoms. There are 5 species in North America.

291 Naked Sole
(*Gymnachirus melas*)

Description: To 6¼″ (16 cm). Oval, depth half to three-fifths length, eyes on right side; eyed side, including caudal fin, dark brown or black with beige or brown *zebralike stripes* extending onto median fins; blind side whitish, with dusky edges on median fins. Head very small; mouth small, twisted; preopercular margin hidden. Pectoral fin small on eyed side only, sometimes hidden under skin; pelvic fins small, concealed by skin, continuous with anal fin; dorsal and anal fins enclosed in loose skin. *Skin unscaled,* soft and fleshy. Lateral line has branches at right angles.

Habitat: Over sand on continental shelf to 100 fathoms.

Range: From Massachusetts south along coast to Pensacola, Florida.

Similar Species: Fringed Sole (*G. texae*) has long dermal cirri on right side; occurs over mud, usually at 30–50 fathoms, from E. Gulf of Mexico west to Yucatán, Mexico.

Comments: These similar species overlap in a very narrow zone east and west of Mobile Bay, Alabama. This is probably because of the difference in the bottom, which is sandier east of the zone of overlap and muddier west of it.

70, 290 Hogchoker
(*Trinectes maculatus*)

Description: To 6″ (15 cm). Depth more than half length, *eyes on right side; dusky usually with 7–8 narrow, black bars;* fins have dark streaks or spots, particularly in juveniles; blind side white, often partly pigmented. Head blunt; mouth and eyes very small; preopercular margin hidden. No pectoral fins; right pelvic fin connected to anal fin; dorsal fin origin over snout, first ray shortest. Lateral line visible as nearly straight, narrow, dark stripe; no dermal flaps; *scales small,* strongly ctenoid.

Habitat: Shallow coastal waters over mud, silt, or sand in bays and estuaries; occasionally in fresh water.

Range: Along coast from Maine to Yucatán, including Gulf of Mexico.

Comments: Young Hogchokers ascend streams for distances of 150 miles (240 km) or more. However, spawning takes place in the estuaries.

TONGUEFISHES
(Family Cynoglossidae)

These tongue-shaped flatfishes taper to
a narrow point posteriorly. The eyes are
on the left side of the body, which is
brownish with darker bars or blotches.
The edge of the preopercle is hidden by
skin and scales. The mouth is quite
small. The fins have no spines, and the
dorsal and anal fins are continuous with
the caudal fin. Tonguefishes have no
pectoral fins; a single pelvic fin is
attached by a membrane to the anal fin.
The scales are ctenoid. There are 12
species in North America.

Largescale Tonguefish
(*Symphurus minor*)

Description: To 3″ (7.5 cm). Elongate, rounded
anteriorly, pointed at tail, eyes on left
side. Eyed side brownish, no distinct
color markings, irregularly blotched or
spotted, *no large, black spot on opercle,* no
distinct spots on fins; blind side white.
Preopercular margin hidden; eyes and
mouth small. Pelvic fin single; no
pectoral fins; dorsal fin, with origin
over eyes, and anal fin continuous with
caudal fin rays. *Scales ctenoid, rather
large, about 55 in lateral series;* no lateral
line on either side.

Habitat: Continental shelf to about 100
fathoms.

Range: From Nova Scotia to E. Florida and E.
Gulf of Mexico.

Comments: The California Tonguefish (*S. atricauda*)
is the only species in this family to
occur on the Pacific Coast of the United
States. The other North American
species occur in the Atlantic and the
Gulf of Mexico. All tonguefishes have a
similar body shape, but they differ in
coloring, in the number of fin rays, and
in scalation. These bottom-dwelling
fishes are found in bays and estuaries

over mud, or in deeper water over sand. They feed on small invertebrates such as crustaceans and polychaete worms.

Order Tetraodontiformes

These fishes exhibit greater diversity in size, body form, scalation, color, and habitat than virtually any other order of fishes in the world. Some have scaleless bodies, whereas others are covered with spikelike processes or even encased in immovable bony plates. The pelvic fins, if present, are reduced to nothing more than a ventral spine. There are 6 families in North America.

LEATHERJACKETS
(Family Balistidae)

Some leatherjackets are brightly colored fishes that live around rocky or coral reefs and surrounding grass beds; others live among sargassum on the open seas. In all of them the pelvic fins, if present, are reduced to a spiny projection of the pelvic bone. There are 18 North American species in the family, which consists of 2 distinct groups: filefishes and triggerfishes. The 10 species of filefishes have a deep, highly compressed body covered with velvetlike skin consisting of innumerable minute scales. There are usually 2 dorsal spines, the first much larger than the second, which may lock into an erect position. There are 6 outer teeth in each jaw. The 8 species of triggerfishes have an oval, compressed body covered with large, thick, diamond-shaped scales resembling a coat of mail. The scales just above the pectoral fin base are usually enlarged and slightly separated to form a flexible "tympanum." There are 3 dorsal spines; the first can be locked into an upright position by the second. There are 8 strong outer teeth in each jaw.

⚠ Some triggerfishes are good to eat; others, however, are toxic.

318 Orange Filefish
(*Aluterus schoepfi*)

Description: To 24" (61 cm). Oblong, deep, strongly compressed; grayish to brownish with large, irregular, pale blotches; *head and body covered with numerous, small, orange to yellowish spots.* Snout pointed; mouth terminal; 6 outer teeth in each jaw. Gill slits oblique. *No pelvic fins;* first dorsal fin spine prominent, long, but weak, second hardly visible; first dorsal fin well separated from soft dorsal, which has 32–41 rays. Scales numerous, minute.

Habitat: In shallow water over sand or mud with sea grasses; also to 25 fathoms.

Range: From Nova Scotia south to Brazil, including Bermuda, Gulf of Mexico, and Caribbean.

Comments: This is one of the largest of the filefishes. It feeds on a variety of plants, including algae and sea grasses. Juveniles may be found on the surface of open seas in rafts of sargassum. The large keel-like pelvic bone of an adult specimen makes an unusual letter opener.

316 Scrawled Filefish
(*Aluterus scriptus*)

Description: To 3' (91 cm). Elongate, very compressed; *light bluish-gray to olive or brown, body and head have blue or blue-green spots, irregular lines, and scattered small, black spots. Snout very long;* lower jaw projects well beyond upper; 6 outer teeth in each jaw. Gill slits oblique.

Pelvic bone lacks external spine; first
dorsal fin spine long, slender, often
broken; 43–49 dorsal fin rays; caudal
peduncle deeper than long; caudal fin
long, rear profile rounded. Scales
numerous, minute.

Habitat: Seagrass beds in tropical and
subtropical seas.

Range: From New England south to Brazil,
including Bermuda, Gulf of Mexico,
and Caribbean.

Related Species: Dotterel Filefish (*A. heudeloti*) has
deeper body; 36–41 dorsal fin soft rays;
occurs in similar habitat south from
Massachusetts to Brazil.

Comments: This fish will often assume a vertical
head-down position, to mimic blades of
grass or to survey the bottom for food.

330 Queen Triggerfish
(*Balistes vetula*)

Description: To 20″ (51 cm). Oval, compressed;
greenish- or bluish-gray above, yellow-
orange below; *blue lines, outlined in
yellow, radiating from eye; 2 oblique,
bright blue stripes from mouth to pectoral fin
base;* blue submarginal band on median
fins; wide bluish band around caudal
peduncle. 8 outer teeth in each jaw. 3
dorsal spines easily visible; soft dorsal
and anal fins notably elongated
anteriorly; caudal fin emarginate in
young, *lunate in adults.* Scales thick,
diamond-shaped; no keels on posterior
part of body.

Habitat: Rocky and coral reefs, pilings, stone
jetties, and adjacent sandy and grassy
areas.

Range: From Massachusetts south to Brazil,
including Gulf of Mexico and
Caribbean. Occasional summer
stragglers north of Cape Hatteras,
North Carolina.

Comments: The Queen Triggerfish can change
color in response to changes in its
background and in light intensity;

however, the bright blue stripes on the head persist. It is common and used as food throughout much of its range.

325 Black Durgon
(*Melichthys niger*)

Description: To 20" (51 cm). Oval, compressed; *black, sometimes with dark greenish cast; pale blue band at bases of soft dorsal and anal fins;* scale edges on front of head sometimes orange. 8 outer teeth in each jaw. Third dorsal fin spine small, not readily visible; soft dorsal and anal fins not notably elongated anteriorly, edges more or less straight; upper and lower caudal fin rays slightly longer than rest of fin. Scales thick, diamond-shaped, *on posterior part of body with prominent keels forming lengthwise ridges.*

Habitat: Clear water of outer reefs to about 60' (18.3 m); occasionally on surface.

Range: In Atlantic from Gulf of Mexico and SE. Florida to Brazil, including Caribbean and West Indies; in Pacific from San Diego, California, to Isla de Malpelo, Colombia.

Comments: The Black Durgon is omnivorous, but probably feeds more on plants than animals. It grazes on algae attached to rocks or coral; it will rise to the surface to feed on floating plants or planktonic invertebrates.

317 Planehead Filefish
(*Monacanthus hispidus*)

Description: To 9" (23 cm). Very deep, greatly compressed; *gray, tan, and brown, sometimes greenish, with irregular, darker blotches or spots; color varies with background;* caudal fin dusky yellow, other fins yellow. 6 outer teeth in each jaw. Gill slits almost vertical. Pelvic bone has prominent external spine, disappearing in large specimens; first dorsal fin spine strong, second dorsal soft ray forms 1 long filament in adult males; caudal fin roughly rounded. Scales on side of caudal peduncle prolonged to form bristles; skin velvetlike.

Habitat: Open seas or near shore around vegetation.

Range: From Nova Scotia to Brazil, including Bermuda and Gulf of Mexico.

Related Species: Fringed Filefish (*M. ciliatus*) has large ventral flap; ranges from Newfoundland to Brazil, including Bermuda, Gulf of Mexico, and Caribbean. Pygmy Filefish (*M. setifer*) has rows of dark streaks on sides; ranges from North Carolina and Bermuda to Bahamas and Gulf of Mexico. Both in similar habitat.

Comments: These fishes, especially the young, are found in the open ocean among floating sargassum or inshore around seagrass beds. Adults move seaward in winter.

BOXFISHES
(Family Ostraciidae)

scales

This family takes its name from the protective carapace, or shell formed of modified scales, that almost completely encloses these fishes. This shell has openings for the mouth, eyes, gill slits, and fins; the only part of the body left unprotected is the caudal peduncle. These small, slow-swimming fishes depend on the shell to discourage predators. Some species have hornlike spines on the head and rear underside of body. Boxfishes lack pelvic fins. They frequent coral or rocky reefs or sandy and grassy areas to depths of about 45 fathoms. They are highly prized as food in the Caribbean, but some species are toxic. The family has 6 North American species.

314 Spotted Trunkfish
(*Lactophrys bicaudalis*)

Description: To 21″ (53 cm). Deep, wide ventrally, almost completely encased in immovable carapace, complete behind dorsal fin; *spine projects posteriorly from rear of ridge on each lower side of body. Pale gray or whitish with numerous brown or blackish spots;* large individuals have 3 large, white spots behind eye. *No hornlike spines on head;* head profile steep, concave, eyes on upper sides; snout blunt; mouth small, ventral, terminal; teeth conical; lips whitish. No pelvic fins; pectoral, dorsal, and anal fins small, rounded; caudal fin larger.

Habitat: Seagrass beds in shallow water; coral reefs.

Range: From Florida to Brazil, including Bermuda, parts of Gulf of Mexico, Caribbean, and West Indies.

Comments: Spotted Trunkfishes are suspected of secreting a poison that kills other fishes.

---

315 Scrawled Cowfish
(*Lactophrys quadricornis*)

Description: To 19″ (48 cm). Deep, wide ventrally, almost completely encased in immovable carapace, complete behind dorsal fin; *spine projects posteriorly from rear of ridge on each lower side of body.* Grayish brown or grayish green with numerous bright blue or blackish-blue irregular spots, bars, and short lines on back and sides; *3–4 distinct, blue, horizontal stripes on cheeks. Forward-pointed, hornlike spine over each eye;* head profile steep, eyes on upper sides; mouth small, ventral, terminal; lips fleshy; teeth conical. No pelvic fins; pectoral, dorsal, and anal fins small, rounded; caudal fin larger.

Habitat: In shallow water, mostly in grassy

areas, sometimes to 40 fathoms.

Range: From Massachusetts to Brazil, including Bermuda, Gulf of Mexico, and Caribbean.

Related Species: Honeycomb Cowfish (*L. polygonia*) has dark, netlike pattern on head, body olive; occurs primarily on reefs in shallow water from New Jersey to Brazil, but not Gulf of Mexico.

Comments: Reported to be an excellent food fish, the Scrawled Cowfish feeds primarily on tunicates, gorgonians, sea anemones, and crustaceans.

313 Trunkfish
(*Lactophrys trigonus*)

Description: To 21″ (53 cm). Deep, wide ventrally, encased in immovable carapace, incomplete behind dorsal fin; *spine projects posteriorly from rear of ridge on each lower side of body; greenish, tannish, or olive, with small, white spots and 2 dark, blackish, diffuse chainlike markings on sides of shell. No hornlike spines on head.* Head profile steep, concave, eyes on upper sides; snout blunt; mouth small, ventral, terminal; teeth conical. No pelvic fins; Pectoral, dorsal, and anal fins small, rounded; caudal fin larger.

Habitat: Seagrass beds in shallow water; coral reefs.

Range: From Massachusetts south to Brazil, including Bermuda, Gulf of Mexico, and Caribbean.

Comments: Highly esteemed as food in the Caribbean area, the Trunkfish may cause ciguatera poisoning if not properly prepared.

312 Smooth Trunkfish
(*Lactophrys triqueter*)

Description: To 11″ (28 cm). Deep, wide ventrally, body almost completely encased in immovable carapace; *carapace without spines, complete behind dorsal fin. Blackish brown with numerous white to golden yellow spots, lips and bases of fins blackish.* Head profile steep, eyes on upper sides; snout projects somewhat; mouth small, ventral, terminal; lips fleshy; teeth conical. No pelvic fins; pectoral fin larger; dorsal, anal, and caudal fins small, rounded.

Habitat: Over sand near rocks and coral reefs.

Range: From Massachusetts to Rio de Janeiro, Brazil, including Bahamas, Gulf of Mexico, and Caribbean.

Comments: This is one of the smallest trunkfishes and the only one without spines on the carapace. It may secrete poison when excited and therefore should not be kept with other fishes. It shoots water from its mouth into the sand to uncover the small invertebrates on which it feeds.

PUFFERS
(Family Tetraodontidae)

As their common name implies, these fishes are capable of rapidly inflating their bodies with either water or air. Most species are drably colored on the back, with various markings, and are silvery or white on the sides and belly. The head is bluntly rounded, with the eyes high on the sides, and the mouth is terminal. There are 2 teeth in each jaw. There are no pelvic fins, and the broad pectoral fins are well developed. The dorsal and anal fins are short-based and posteriorly placed. The skin is unscaled, although spiny prickles may be present, and some species have small, fleshy flaps called lappets on each side of the body. Some puffers are toxic. There are 12 species that occur in North America.

teeth

301   Sharpnose Puffer
(*Canthigaster rostrata*)

Description: To 3¾" (9.5 cm). Elongate, round in
cross section; orange-brown to purple-
brown on upper third, lower two-thirds
abruptly white to orange; blue lines
radiate from eye onto caudal peduncle;
lower part of caudal peduncle slightly
darker, with narrow, blue, parallel
bars; upper and lower caudal rays dark,
middle rays and all other fins pale
orange. Each jaw with 2 teeth. No
pelvic fins; 10 dorsal fin soft rays; 9
anal fin soft rays; dorsal fin opposite
anal fin; caudal fin emarginate. *Ridge or
keel on back in front of dorsal fin.* Prickles
absent or greatly reduced; no fleshy
flaps.

Habitat: Coral reefs and grass beds to depths of
85' (26 m); always in clear water.

Range: From North Carolina, Bermuda,
Bahamas, and Florida south to N. coast
of South America, including Gulf of
Mexico and West Indies.

Comments: In the United States the Sharpnose
Puffer is most abundant in southern
Florida. It is frequently found around
sea fans and stinging coral. This
species, like other puffers, feeds
primarily on shellfishes.

307, 308   Smooth Puffer
(*Lagocephalus laevigatus*)

Description: To 3'3" (99 cm). Elongate, round in
cross section, globular when inflated;
back gray, greenish, blue-green, or
blue-gray, sides silvery, belly white;
dark saddlelike bars may cross sides and
back. Head bluntly rounded; mouth
terminal; eyes high on head; 2 teeth in
each jaw. No pelvic fins; dorsal and
anal fins moderately acute, *each with 12
or more rays,* anterior rays longest,
caudal fin concave, lower lobe slightly
longer than upper. *Skin smooth, belly*

with prickles, no fleshy flaps.

Habitat: At and near shore to depths of about 60′ (18 m) over sand or mud.

Range: From New England to Argentina, including Bermuda, Gulf of Mexico, and West Indies.

Comments: This is the largest puffer in North America. Its flesh is considered good quality. Unlike the flesh of some other puffers, it is apparently not toxic. Puffers may scare away some predators by rapidly increasing their size as they inflate their bodies.

---

310 Northern Puffer
(*Sphoeroides maculatus*)

Description: To 10″ (25 cm). Elongate, round in cross section, globular when inflated; gray to brown above with vague black spots or saddlelike blotches, belly yellow to white; *back, sides, and cheeks with tiny, black spots; lower sides with series of barlike markings.* 2 teeth in each jaw. No pelvic fins; 8 dorsal fin soft rays; 7 anal fin soft rays; caudal fin slightly rounded. Covered with prickles; no fleshy flaps.

Habitat: Bays and estuaries over sand, silt, or mud to about 30 fathoms. Inshore in summer, offshore in winter.

Range: From Newfoundland to NE. Florida.

Related Species: Southern Puffer (*S. nephelus*) lacks tiny, jet-black spots; flesh mildly toxic; occurs in similar habitat from North Carolina to Central America, including E. Gulf of Mexico to Louisiana.

Similar Species: Bandtail Puffer (*S. spengleri*) has row of distinct, round or oval spots on lower sides; black bar at caudal fin base and on outer third; fleshy flaps present.

Comments: The Northern Puffer is used as food and marketed as "sea squab." Care should be taken not to confuse it with the Bandtail Puffer, which is definitely toxic, and the Southern Puffer, which is reported to be mildly toxic.

305 Bandtail Puffer
(*Sphoeroides spengleri*)

Description: To 6½" (17 cm). Elongate, round in
cross section, globular when inflated;
olive-green to yellowish-brown above,
with black blotches or spotting;
*lengthwise row of distinct spots on lower
sides; dark bar on base and outer third of
caudal fin,* other fins very pale; belly
white. 2 teeth in each jaw. No pelvic
fins; dorsal and anal fins similar size
and shape; 8 dorsal fin soft rays; 7 anal
fin soft rays; caudal fin slightly rounded
or truncate. Prickles on belly; fleshy
flaps on back and sides.

Habitat: Usually in clear, shallow water, but
occasionally to depths of 40 fathoms.

Range: From Massachusetts to Sao Paulo,
Brazil; most common in Bermuda,
S. Florida, Bahamas, and Caribbean.

Comments: The Bandtail Puffer is often associated
with turtle grass in tropical areas of its
range. It feeds, as do most puffers, on
small crabs, echinoderms, and
mollusks. It is definitely toxic and
should not be eaten.

311 Checkered Puffer
(*Sphoeroides testudineus*)

Description: To 15" (38 cm). Elongate, round in
cross-section, globular when inflated;
dark above with *1 or 2 distinct,
transverse bars between eyes, diverse white
lines and weblike patterns;* sides have
distinct spots; belly white. 2 teeth in
each jaw. Pelvic fins absent; 8 dorsal fin
soft rays, directly opposite anus; 7 anal
fin soft rays; caudal fin straight to
slightly rounded. Prickles on back and
belly; no fleshy flaps.

Habitat: Over mud and sand to 11 fathoms.

Range: From New Jersey to Santos, Brazil,
including Central America and
Caribbean; not known in Gulf of
Mexico.

Comments: This puffer sometimes occurs in nearly
fresh water and often around
mangroves. In the United States, its
center of abundance is southern
Florida. Like all puffers, it is a poor
swimmer and propels itself by flapping
the little dorsal and anal fins.

PORCUPINEFISHES
(Family Diodontidae)

These small to medium-sized puffers
are quite robust and covered with
spines. The spines are either like
erectile quills with 2-rooted bases
(genus *Diodon*), or they are stout and
fixed with 3-rooted bases (genus
Chilomycterus). The bases are visible
when the skin is removed. Members of
this family have a single tooth in each
jaw; the teeth are fused at the midline

teeth   to form a parrotlike beak. The pelvic
fins are absent, the dorsal and anal fins
are short-based, and the pectoral and
caudal fins are well developed. This
family has 7 species in North America.

306 Striped Burrfish
(*Chilomycterus schoepfi*)

Description: To 10″ (25 cm). Oval, broad, slightly
depressed; *covered with stout, 3-rooted,
immovable spines;* green to olive-green or
brownish above, *upper sides with
irregular, oblique, black or brown lines,*
lower sides whitish, belly whitish or
golden yellow; dark blotch at dorsal
and anal fin bases, and above and
behind pectoral fin base. Single tooth
in each jaw, fused to form parrotlike
beak. No pelvic fins; dorsal and anal
fins short-based; pectoral and caudal
fins well developed.

Habitat: Shallow grass beds in summer, deeper
waters in winter.

Range: From Cape Hatteras, North Carolina, south to Brazil, including Bahamas and Gulf of Mexico; to Nova Scotia and Maine as stragglers.

Comments: Striped Burrfishes are quite common, especially south of the Carolinas during the summer months. Those under 3″ (7.5 cm) make good aquarium pets and will readily inflate when gently rubbed on the belly. In an aquarium, they will feed on pieces of fishes, shrimps, or virtually any fleshy food offered.

304 Balloonfish
(*Diodon holocanthus*)

Description: To 18″ (46 cm). Elongate, robust, slightly depressed; covered with *long, erectile spines, longest on forehead. Light brown with scattered, moderate-sized, dark brown spots,* belly light yellow, 4 dark bars on back, 1 on forehead extending down through eyes, no spots on fins. Snout blunt; mouth small; single tooth in each jaw, fused to form parrotlike beak. No pelvic fins; single dorsal and anal fins composed of soft rays only; rear profile of caudal fin rounded.

Habitat: Over shallow reefs and soft bottoms.

Range: In Atlantic from Florida to Brazil. In Pacific from Gulf of California to Peru.

Similar Species: Porcupinefish (*D. hystrix*) lacks dark bars, covered with small, dark spots; longest spines posterior to pectoral fin.

Comments: Balloonfishes inflate themselves with water or air when molested. Their skin secretes a mild toxin which is probably distasteful to potential predators. These slow-moving fishes are easy to approach and make good photographic subjects for divers. In some areas they are harvested and dried in their inflated state to be sold to tourists.

302, 303 Porcupinefish
(*Diodon hystrix*)

Description: To 3′ (91 cm). Wide, slightly
depressed, cylindrical in cross section,
covered with *erectile, 2-rooted, spike-like
spines;* tannish with greenish hue above,
sides lighter; *covered with small, evenly
distributed dark brown or blackish spots
same diameter as spines;* belly white;
dusky bar below each eye, another in
front of each gill slit. Single tooth in
each jaw, fused at midline to form
parrotlike beak. No pelvic fins; dorsal
and anal fins short-based; pectoral and
caudal fins well developed.

Habitat: Shallow coastal waters to depths of
about 50′ (15 m).

Range: In Atlantic from Massachusetts to
Brazil, including Gulf of Mexico and
Caribbean. In Pacific from San Diego,
California, to Chile.

Similar Species: Pacific Burrfish (*Chilomycterus affinis*)
has short spines with 3-part base;
occurs in same habitat from San Pedro,
California, to Galápagos Islands.
Balloonfish (*D. holocanthus*) has longer
spines on forehead; spots larger than
diameter of quills.

Comments: Most porcupinefishes collected are 10″
(25 cm) or less in length (or diameter
when inflated). Gastropods, sea
urchins, crabs, and other crustaceans
constitute most of their diet. They use
their strong beaks to crush mollusks
and other hard-shelled invertebrates.
Porcupinefishes are not ordinarily used
for food.

MOLAS
(Family Molidae)

These distinctive and unusual oceanic
fishes have very deep and compressed
bodies. The posterior portion of the
body looks as though it has been cut
off. The mouth is very small, and the

snout is short and blunt. The gill opening is reduced in size to a small, round-to-oblong pore. Molas lack pelvic fins and scales. They have very short-based dorsal and anal fins, usually with extremely long rays. The caudal fin is reduced to a leathery flap except for the Sharptail Mola. There are 3 species, all found in North American waters.

309   Ocean Sunfish
(*Mola mola*)

Description: To 13′ (4 m); 3,300 lbs (1,497 kg). Deep, almost round, highly compressed; back gray-blue, sides and belly metallic silver. Snout short, rounded; mouth small; gill openings small. *No pelvic fins; dorsal and anal fins very long,* consist of soft rays only, placed far back; *caudal fin greatly reduced, rounded, flaplike.* Covered with thick mucus; scaleless.

Habitat: Surface of open seas, occasionally near shore.

Range: In Atlantic from Gulf of St. Lawrence to Argentina. In Pacific from British Columbia to South America.

Related Species: Sharptail Mola (*M. lanceolata*) has lobelike blunt-tipped projection just above middle of body; caudal fin evident, 18–20 soft rays; found in Atlantic from North Carolina to Cuba. Slender Mola (*Ranzania laevis*) has long, slender body; no caudal fin; occurs in Pacific from Oceano, San Luis Obispo County, California, to Chile. Both in similar habitat.

Comments: These fishes feed on jellyfishes, ctenophores, and salps. They are not sought by anglers or commercial fishers, but they are a familiar sight drifting lazily on the surface of the water during the late summer.

MAMMALS
(Class Mammalia)

This class consists of animals in which the young are usually born alive and are suckled on milk provided by the mother. Their internal body temperature is high and relatively constant, except in certain groups (other than the cetaceans) during hibernation, estivation, dormancy, or when young. Hair is present at some stage during the lives of all mammals, in cetaceans usually in the form of a few bristles or hairs on the snout of the newborn.

As with all mammals, cetaceans breathe air, and their nostrils, called blowholes, are located on top of the head to facilitate breathing while swimming. The brain is relatively large in comparison with that of other vertebrates, including fishes.

There are about 4,060 living species of mammals worldwide, and about 85 of these are cetaceans.

Watching Whales, Dolphins, and Porpoises

Sighting a whale or a group of cavorting dolphins is one of the most exciting experiences, whether walking along a beach or cruising on the ocean. You are most likely to spot large whales in the open sea, although Gray, Right, and Humpback whales sometimes swim near shore, especially during their migrations. Bottlenosed Dolphins have been known to enter estuaries, the lower reaches of large rivers, and even harbors. As their name implies, Harbor Porpoises may be found in ports and other places close to shore.

What to Look For: Observing whales, dolphins, and porpoises at sea is not always easy—it depends on both careful searching and chance. If you should see a whale, dolphin, or porpoise, make careful notes on its characteristics: its coloring, the shape of the front portion of the snout, whether it has a dorsal fin, and its general behavior. Notice how a whale dives—whether or not it throws its flukes out of the water, and if the entire top of the head appears—and for large whales, note the shape and height of the spout. Make a rough sketch of what you see or take a photograph. These records will be helpful when you try to identify the species using this guide. Furthermore, since many cetaceans are barely known, such details as the time of day, location and date of sighting, and the number, age, behavior, and direction of travel may be of scientific value.

Stranded Animals: Not all whales, dolphins, and porpoises are seen at sea. Some, unfortunately, can be found stranded on beaches. If you encounter a stranded animal, immediately contact the nearest coastal marine laboratory, oceanarium, aquarium, or the National Marine Fisheries Service.

While waiting for help to arrive, keep the animal wet and place a wet cloth, such as a handkerchief or a wet paper towel, over its eyes. Cetaceans die very quickly in the sun from overheating because they lack sweat glands. If the animal is in a puddle, try to keep it upright so that its blowhole is clear for breathing. Do not try to push the animal back into the water; for unknown reasons, it usually comes right back to the beach. Although no one is quite sure why whales, dolphins, and porpoises become stranded, the causes are probably varied, resulting from a combination of health and social factors.

Despite the tragedy of the situation, a stranded animal offers an opportunity for detailed study. While alive, the color and shape remain normal. However, color changes rapidly on a dead animal—the color patterns fade, the skin may turn black, and the body may bloat. Never try to remove any parts of a carcass, even teeth; this is illegal without permission from the federal, state, or provincial marine authority.

Where to Go: Sighting dolphins and porpoises is usually a matter of luck and hardly ever planned. Whale-watching, however, has become a small tourist industry in various coastal areas, with enthusiasts setting out on scheduled boat trips throughout the year. Although few places can guarantee whales on any given day, you should check with your local oceanarium or marine authority to find the most likely places in your area. Remember that while patience is always important when looking for whales, dolphins, and porpoises, it is often well rewarded.

Order Cetacea

This order includes whales, dolphins, and porpoises. These carnivorous, aquatic mammals never leave the water at any stage of their lives. They have a fusiform body with paddle-shaped anterior flippers that evolved from mammalian forelegs, but normally have no hind limbs, external digits, or claws. The posterior portion of the tail is flattened laterally to end in horizontally flattened (depressed) flukes. Most cetaceans have a dorsal fin on the midline of the back. Cetaceans occur in all seas and in certain fresh waters. There are 8 families in North America.

Cetaceans are divided into 2 suborders, Mysticeti and Odontoceti. Mysticetes, called baleen whales, lack teeth but have plates, or horny baleen, hanging down from the upper jaw, through which the animal's food is strained from a large mouthful of water. Mysticetes have paired blowholes (nostrils) on top of the head and produce a visible spout or blow. This suborder includes the Rorquals (Family Balaenopteridae), Right Whales (Family Balaenidae), and Gray Whales (Family Eschrichtidae).

All Odontocetes have teeth, although the number varies greatly among species. There may be only a single tooth in each side of the lower jaw and none in the upper, or as many as 65 or more in each side of both jaws. Odontocetes have a single blowhole (nostril) on top of the head; its placement varies with the species. The Sperm Whale is the only member of this group to produce a visible blow or spout; other animals may occasionally emit a light puff, depending on the weather conditions and humidity. This suborder includes the Beaked Whales (Family Ziphiidae), Sperm Whales (Family Physeteridae), Narwhal and

White Whales (Family Monodontidae),
Ocean Dolphins (Family Delphinidae),
Porpoises (Family Phocoenidae), and
River Dolphins (Family Platanispidae);
the last do not occur in North America.

RORQUALS
(Family Balaenopteridae)

These long, slender whales are much
more streamlined than other large
whales. They have a pointed snout,
paired blowholes, and a broad, flat
rostrum. The baleen plates are broad
and short, and the left and right rows
are continuous anteriorly. The dorsal
fin is falcate. Rorquals have grooves of
varying lengths covering the region of
the throat and chest. All have been
hunted and some still are, although
they are now protected by all nations
subscribing to the International
Whaling Commission. There are 6
species in North America.

625, 683	**Minke Whale**
	(*Balaenoptera acutorostrata*)

Description: To 33' (10.1 m). Fusiform, tapering
posteriorly; dark gray to black above,
belly and underside of flippers white,
crescent-shaped marks sometimes
present on upper side in front of
flippers, *diagonal white band on flippers.*
Baleen plates yellowish white
anteriorly, sometimes dark posteriorly.
Rostrum flat, narrow, pointed, triangular,
with single median dorsal ridge; paired
blowholes on top of head. *Dorsal fin
tall, falcate.* Ventral grooves end
slightly anterior to navel.

Habitat: Open seas, but mainly over continental
shelf; sometimes in bays, inlets, and
estuaries.

Range: In Atlantic from pack ice to Lesser

Antilles, including E. and NW. Gulf of Mexico. In Pacific from Bering and Chukchi seas to equator. Seasonal variations in both oceans.

Similar Species: Sei Whale (*B. borealis*) appears similar when floating, but dorsal fin relatively shorter. Fin Whale (*B. physalus*) has no white band on flippers; rostrum less pointed. Baird's Beaked Whale (*Berardius bairdii*) has bulging forehead; beak long, cylindrical. Northern Bottlenosed Whale (*Hyperoodon ampullatus*) has bulbous forehead; single blowhole.

Comments: The Minke Whale is the smallest baleen whale in North American waters. Its seasonal distribution is contingent upon food availability. Individuals often approach vessels and may be seen breaching, that is, leaping up through the water's surface. The Minke Whale is also called Little Piked Whale, Sharp-headed Finner, Little Finner, and Lesser Rorqual.

681   Sei Whale
(*Balaenoptera borealis*)

Description: To 62' (18.9 m). Fusiform, tapering posteriorly; dark steel-gray, *often appears galvanized,* belly grayish white near ventral grooves; right lower lip uniformly gray; baleen plates mostly grayish black; leading edges of flukes sometimes white. Snout slightly arched; rostrum not very pointed, *with single median dorsal ridge;* paired blowholes on top of head. *Dorsal fin tall, strongly falcate,* placed two-thirds of body length back from head. *Ventral grooves extend only midway between base of flippers and navel.*

Habitat: Near shore and offshore, primarily in temperate open seas.

Range: In Atlantic from S. Arctic Circle to NE. Venezuela, including NW. and S. Gulf of Mexico. In Pacific from Gulf of

Alaska to vicinity of Islas
Revillagigedo, off Baja California.
Seasonal distribution varies.

Similar Species: Minke Whale (*B. acutorostrata*) appears
similar when floating, but dorsal fin
taller. Bryde's Whale (*B. edeni*) has 3
rostral ridges; ventral grooves extend at
least to navel. Blue Whale (*B. musculus*)
has dorsal fin further back. Fin Whale
(*B. physalus*) has snout more acutely
pointed; dorsal fin further back; ventral
grooves extend to navel.

Comments: The Sei Whale derives its name from
its association with the Sei fish, the
Norwegian name for the Pollock
(*Pollachius virens*). In Great Britain, this
fish is called the Coalfish, which is
another popular name for the Sei
Whale. Other common names are the
Pollack Whale, Rudolph's Rorqual,
and Sardine Whale. The Sei Whale
feeds on surface plankton, krill, small
schooling fishes, and squids. Like all of
the baleen whales, it does not feed
everywhere in its distribution—such as
in the southern portions of its range—
but only where food is abundant.

614, 684 Bryde's Whale
(*Balaenoptera edeni*)

Description: To 46′ (14 m). Fusiform, tapering
posteriorly; dark smoky gray, baleen
plates slate-gray with lighter gray
bristles, underside and front edges of
flippers grayish white. Snout slightly
arched when viewed from side, not
acutely pointed; *rostrum with 3 median
dorsal ridges* (median ridge flanked by
secondary ridges); paired blowholes on
top of head. Dorsal fin extremely
falcate, often irregularly notched.
Ventral grooves extend at least to
navel.

Habitat: Near shore and offshore.

Range: In Atlantic from Virginia to SE.
Caribbean, including N. and E. Gulf

of Mexico. In Pacific from extreme S. California to Gulf of Panama, possibly to equator.

Similar Species: Sei Whale (*B. borealis*) has single median dorsal ridge on rostrum; ventral grooves reach only to midway between base of flippers and navel. Fin Whale (*B. physalus*) has single median dorsal ridge on rostrum.

Comments: Bryde's Whales are believed to be deep divers. They feed on small schooling fishes and surface-dwelling crustaceans. They often approach vessels.

611, 622, 680 Blue Whale
(Balaenoptera musculus)

Description: To 98' (29.9 m). Fusiform, tapering posteriorly; light bluish-gray above *mottled with gray or grayish-white,* belly sometimes yellowish, baleen plates black. *Rostrum broad, flat, nearly U-shaped,* with single median dorsal ridge; paired blowholes on top of head. *Dorsal fin extremely small,* nearly triangular to falcate, far back on tail stock. Ventral grooves extend to or slightly past navel. Blow high, oval.

diving sequence

Habitat: Usually open seas, but sometimes in shallow inshore waters.

Range: In Atlantic from Arctic Circle to Panama, including NW. Gulf of Mexico. In Pacific from S. Chukchi Sea to Panama.

Similar Species: Sei Whale (*B. borealis*) has dorsal fin placed two-thirds of body length back from head. Fin Whale (*B. physalus*) has more V-shaped rostrum.

Comments: The yellowish coloring on the belly of this species is due to diatoms accumulated in colder water, inspiring the alternate name Sulphur Bottom Whale. It is a relatively shallow feeder, and its diet consists mainly of krill. The Blue Whale is probably the largest animal known, even larger than the dinosaurs. It has been estimated to reach a weight of about 196 tons (178,000 kg). At one time this animal was near extinction, but recent protection has enabled its numbers to increase.

613, 626, 682 Fin Whale
(*Balaenoptera physalus*)

Description: To 79' (24.1 m). Fusiform, tapering posteriorly; blue-black above, undersides white. *Grayish-white chevron behind head,* apex on dorsal midline, arms extending backward. *Right lower lip, including mouth cavity, yellowish white,* right upper lip occasionally also white, *left lips dark.* Right front baleen plates white, remainder striped with alternate yellowish-white and bluish-gray to grayish-white. Snout V-shaped with *single median dorsal ridge;* top of head flat, with paired blowholes. Dorsal fin steeply angled, placed far back. *Back distinctly ridged posterior to dorsal fin.* Ventral grooves extend at least to navel.

Habitat: Inshore and offshore.

Range: In Atlantic from Arctic Circle to Greater Antilles, including Gulf of Mexico. In Pacific from Bering Sea to Cabo San Lucas, Baja California.

Similar Species: Minke Whale (*B. acutorostrata*) has white band on flippers; snout more pointed. Sei Whale (*B. borealis*) has ventral grooves reaching only midway between base of flippers and navel; dorsal fin origin two-thirds of way back from head. Bryde's Whale (*B. edeni*) has 3 median dorsal ridges on rostrum. Blue Whale (*B. musculus*) has U-shaped rostrum.

Comments: The Fin Whale is also known as the Finback Whale, Finner Whale, and Common Rorqual. In addition, it is called the Razorback Whale because of the ridges between the dorsal fin and the tail. The falcate dorsal fin, an obvious characteristic, is easily seen at sea. The Fin Whale feeds on small fishes, pelagic crustaceans, and squids. It sometimes leaps clear of the surface, yet is also a deeper diver than some of the other baleen whales.

616, 618, 623, 679 Humpback Whale
(*Megaptera novaeangliae*)

Description: To 53′ (16.2 m). *Robust, narrowing rapidly to tail;* mostly black, belly sometimes white, flippers and underside of flukes nearly all white, baleen plates black with black or olive-black bristles. Top of head and lower jaw with string of *fleshy knobs or protuberances* randomly distributed; paired blowholes on top of head; *distinctive, rounded projection on tip of lower jaw. Flippers very long,* front edges scalloped. *Dorsal fin small,* variably shaped, *placed on small hump* slightly more than two-thirds of way back from head. Flukes deeply notched, concave, rear edges scalloped. Blow wide, balloon-shaped.

diving sequence

Habitat: Along coast; usually on continental shelf or island banks; sometimes in open seas.

Range: Migratory. In Atlantic from N. Iceland and W. Greenland south to West Indies, including N. and E. Gulf of Mexico. In Pacific from Bering Sea to S. Mexico.

Comments: The median rostral ridges are not as obvious in the Humpback Whale as in other members of the family. Humpback Whales migrate seasonally and feed on krill and small schooling fishes. They are known to concentrate the food by forming a bubble curtain, created by releasing air bubbles while swimming in a circle beneath the water surface. Humpback Whales often "sing," vocalizing a long series of repeated phrases; the vocal patterns are apparently specific to separate populations of whales but may vary from year to year. It is possible that individual animals can be recognized by some of their sounds. Humpbacks sometimes leap clear of the water and may be seen slapping their flukes or a flipper on the surface.

RIGHT WHALES
(Family Balaenidae)

In North American waters these robust whales lack a dorsal fin and ventral grooves. The body is black with various white markings, especially ventrally. The head is large, comprising 28–33% of the body. The rostrum is narrow and highly arched, giving a distinct curvature to the top of the head. There are paired blowholes on top of the head. The baleen plates are long and narrow, with an anterior separation of the left and right rows. There are 2 species in North America, both highly endangered.

676 Bowhead Whale
(*Balaena mysticetus*)

Description: To 65′ (19.8 m). Robust, top of head and entire back form 2 curves in swimming adults; black overall, *chin unevenly white,* sometimes with series of grayish to black spots, baleen plates dark gray or black, sometimes with whitish front edges. *Jaws highly arched; head smooth;* paired blowholes widely separated, resulting in 2 distinct spouts. *No dorsal fin;* flukes broad, tips pointed, greatly concave toward deep notch, dark below.

Habitat: Around pack ice, often in shallow water.

Range: In Atlantic off E. Greenland, Davis

Straits, Baffin Bay, James Bay, and adjacent waters. In Pacific in Bering, Chukchi, and Beaufort seas. Distribution follows edge of Arctic ice.

Similar Species: Right Whale (*Eubalaena glacialis*) has yellowish callosities, or bumps, on head. Gray Whale (*E. robustus*) has obvious mottling.

Comments: The Bowhead Whale derives its name from the high arch of its jaws. It is also known as the Greenland Whale, Greenland Right Whale, Arctic Right

diving sequence

Whale, and Great Polar Whale. Bowhead Whales sometimes breach, with most of the body leaving the water and returning with a loud splash. The reason for this behavior is uncertain; it may be to remove parasites, to communicate with other whales, or to have fun. They feed primarily on small crustaceans, which they skim from near the surface, but they may also feed at or near the bottom in shallow waters. These whales are highly endangered, but native Alaskans are permitted limited fishing privileges.

619, 621, 677 Right Whale
(*Eubalaena glacialis*)

Description: To 53′ (16.2 m). Large, rotund; brown to almost black, mottled overall, with some white on chin and belly, baleen plates dark brownish to dark gray or

diving sequence

black, may appear pale yellowish gray further offshore. *Jaw highly arched, curves upward along side of head; callosities, or bumps, on head light yellowish,* largest, or "bonnet," in front of large, paired blowholes. *No dorsal fin or ridge.* Flukes broad, tips pointed, greatly concave toward deep notch, dark below. *Blow characteristic, V-shaped.*

Habitat: Often near shore in shallow water; sometimes in large bays.

Range: In Atlantic from Iceland to E. Florida, occasionally into SE. and SW. Gulf of Mexico, rarely to West Indies. In Pacific from Gulf of Alaska and SE. Bering Sea to central Baja California.

Similar Species: Bowhead Whale (*Balaena mysticetus*) lacks light-colored callosities on head. Gray Whale (*Eschrichtius robustus*) has obvious mottling.

Comments: Also called the Black Right Whale, this species was named the Right Whale by early whalers who believed it to be the "right" or "correct" whale to take, since it swims slowly, is easy to approach and kill, and does not sink when dead. One animal measuring 51′ (15.4 m) weighed 46.2 tons (42,000 kg). Once killed, the Right Whale yielded an abundance of valuable oil and baleen to be used for corset stays and other decorative or utilitarian objects. As an endangered species, these whales are fully protected and more are being seen. There is growing evidence that calves are born when the whales are at the southern end of their migration—in the Atlantic off northeastern Florida, Georgia, and possibly the Carolinas. They may come very close to shore in northeastern Florida. Only newborn whales lack the callosities, which may be useful in identifying individual whales.

GRAY WHALES
(Family Eschrichtidae)

This family has a single living species, the well-known Gray Whale that migrates past California to the lagoons of Baja California in Mexico to bear its calves. Observation of these whales has developed into a thriving seasonal tourist industry. Gray Whales are still considered to be endangered, but strong protection has enabled their numbers to increase dramatically.

620, 624, 678   **Gray Whale**
(*Eschrichtius robustus*)

Description: To 46' (14 m). *Viewed from above, body tapered at both ends; mottled gray,* may appear uniformly slate-blue or white from surface. Baleen plates short, yellowish to white with yellowish-white bristles. Head narrowly triangular, *sloping steeply downward from paired blowholes; long mouth line curving upward slightly;* 2–5 deep lengthwise throat grooves. *Back has low hump* two-thirds of way from snout tip to flukes, followed by serrated ridge. No ventral grooves.

Habitat: Generally coastal waters. Migrate close to shore, calve in shallow southern lagoons. Some move further offshore in summer.

Range: From Bering and Chukchi seas to Baja California.

Similar Species: Bowhead Whale (*Balaena mysticetus*), Right Whale (*Eubalaena glacialis*), and Sperm Whale (*Physeter catodon*) lack obvious mottling, color relatively uniform.

Comments: Most Gray Whales calve in Mexican waters. As with all cetaceans, the young are born underwater and are immediately able to swim on their own. However, the calves depend on a diet of rich milk for at least 6 months. Early whalers called the Gray Whale the Devilfish because females strongly defend their calves against enemies, including Killer Whales (*Orcinus orca*), sharks, and people. Gray Whales grub along the bottom for gammarid amphipods, the staple of their diet, and leave a cloud behind them as they move. Their spout is not distinctive. These whales were believed near extinction early in the 20th century, but full protection since 1946 has allowed them to increase their numbers significantly although they are still considered to be endangered.

BEAKED WHALES
(Family Ziphiidae)

These medium-sized to moderately large whales have a single pair of grooves on the throat. There is a distinct snout, and often the few teeth present are visible only in adult males. They have a single nostril or blowhole. Beaked whales are generally slender with a small dorsal fin placed towards the rear on the back. The rear edge of the flukes usually lacks a well-defined notch. These whales are deep divers and rarely seen. Many species are known only from a few specimens, and little is known about the life history and biology of the group. All members of this family, except Blainville's Beaked Whale, are difficult to distinguish from each other, and study by museum experts is usually necessary for identification. There are 11 species in North America.

---

662 Baird's Beaked Whale
(Berardius bairdii)

Description: To 42' (12.8 m). *Long, rotund;* slate gray, may appear brown; white blotches on undersides. *Forehead prominent, bulging, sloping to long, cylindrical beak;* lower jaw extends slightly beyond upper, paired teeth at tip exposed in adults; single blowhole on top of head. *Dorsal fin prominent,* nearly triangular, more than two-thirds of way back from head. Flukes with nearly straight edges, slight central prominence or depression, usually no distinct notch.

Habitat: Offshore waters.

Range: From Bering Sea south to Baja California.

Similar Species: Minke Whale (*Balaenoptera acutorostrata*) has head flat in front of paired blowholes.

Comments: Baird's Beaked Whale is also known as
the Giant Bottlenosed Whale and the
North Pacific Great Bottlenosed
Whale. It is the largest of the beaked
whales and is known to feed on squids
and octopuses as well as crustaceans, sea
cucumbers, and a variety of deep-sea
and other fishes. Its bulging forehead
and long, cylindrical beak may appear
out of the water when the animal rises
to breathe.

671 Northern Bottlenosed Whale
(*Hyperoodon ampullatus*)

Description: To 32′ (9.8 m). Robust; brownish,
often lighter below; light blotches on
back and sides with increasing age;
juveniles uniformly chocolate brown; in
very large individuals, presumably
older males, head often white. *Forehead
bulbous,* more pronounced on larger
individuals, most distinctive on adult
males; *blowhole in indented area behind
forehead;* beak narrow and cylindrical.
*Dorsal fin distinctly falcate, placed two-
thirds of way back from head.* Flukes
often lack distinct notch.

Habitat: In deep Arctic and cold temperate
offshore waters at 100 fathoms or more.

Range: From Davis Straits and entrance to
Hudson Straits to Rhode Island.

Similar Species: Minke Whale (*Balaenoptera acutorostrata*)
has head flat in front of paired
blowholes. North Sea Beaked Whale
(*Mesoplodon bidens*) lacks pronounced
bulbous forehead.

Comments: Northern Bottlenosed Whales are said
to hold the record for the longest dives,
lasting more than 2 hours. They are
probably deep divers as well, feeding
primarily on squids and possibly on
fishes. These whales may approach
ships from far away. After stocks of
Bowhead Whales (*Balaena mysticetus*)
were depleted in the late 19th century,
arctic whalers began to capture

Northern Bottlenosed Whales, since whale oil can be extracted from their blubber, and like Sperm Whales, they have foreheads that yield significant quantities of spermaceti.

663 North Sea Beaked Whale
(*Mesoplodon bidens*)

Description: To 16′6″ (5· m). *Distinctly fusiform;* dark gray above, lighter below, light spots overall. Beak moderate to long; *pronounced bulge in front of single blowhole,* forehead slightly concave; *teeth, in lower jaw only, about midway between snout tip and corner of mouth.* Dorsal fin tall, varies from triangular to falcate, located just behind midpoint of back. Flukes not notched, rear edges sometimes very concave.

Habitat: Offshore waters, sometimes near shore when feeding.

Range: From pack ice south to latitude of New England.

Similar Species: Northern Bottlenosed Whale (*Hyperoodon ampullatus*) has pronounced bulbous forehead.

Comments: This species is also known as Sowerby's Beaked Whale. Although 16′ 6″ (5 m) is the greatest verifiable length, they are estimated to reach as much as 18′ (5.5 m) long. The North Sea Beaked Whale feeds on squids. The function of the beak in the family Ziphiidae is unknown. It may be used to gather and hold onto food, or its function may be related to echolocation. Many cetaceans can recognize and locate objects by beaming a train of sound pulses onto a target and then processing the return echoes. The echolocation organs are located in the soft tissue above the skull.

668 Hubb's Beaked Whale
(*Mesoplodon carlhubbsi*)

Description: To 17'6" (5.3 m). Fusiform; head small, tail narrow; *adult males black,* sometimes considerably scarred; *distinctive white bump* ("cap" or "beanie") *on top of head* just anterior to blowhole; *front half of lower jaw white;* females markedly lighter below. Forehead slopes into prominent beak, no crease between beak and head. *Adult males have single, substantial, compressed tooth* on each side of lower jaw at midpoint of mouth; in females and juveniles teeth buried in gum, mouth line forms S-shaped curve. Dorsal fin falcate, well behind middle of back. Flukes not notched.

Habitat: Probably upper layers of open seas.

Range: From British Columbia opposite N. tip of Vancouver Island to San Diego, California.

Similar Species: All other whales of genus *Mesoplodon* lack white bump; anterior lower jaw not white.

Comments: Hubb's Beaked Whale was first recognized in 1963 and little is known of its biology. It is believed to be a deep diver that feeds on squids and fishes in mid-water. Like some whales that are deep divers, after resurfacing it may stay on the surface to fully ventilate its lungs and restore oxygen to the blood before diving again.

627, 666 Blainville's Beaked Whale
(*Mesoplodon densirostris*)

Description: To 17' (5.2 m). Fusiform; black to dark gray above, lighter below, sometimes blotched with grayish white. Beak distinct, *head marked by prominent rise of lower jaw near corner of mouth;* mouth with high arching contour, especially in adult males; teeth on rise of lower jaw only;

flattened area in front of blowhole.
Dorsal fin small, triangular to nearly
falcate, behind midpoint of back.
Flukes rarely notched, occasionally
bulging slightly backward near center
of posterior edges.

Habitat: Probably in tropical and warm
temperate offshore waters.

Range: In Atlantic from Nova Scotia to Florida
and Bahamas; N. Gulf of Mexico. In
Pacific recorded only off N. California.

Comments: The stomachs of stranded individuals
have contained the remains of squids.
This species is also known as the
Dense-beaked Whale and Tropical
Beaked Whale. Adult males are the
only easily identifiable members of the
beaked whale family. They are easily
distinguished from others in the genus
Mesoplodon by the high arching contour
of the corner of the mouth. Females
and juveniles are difficult to distinguish
from other species.

667 Antillean Beaked Whale
(*Mesoplodon europaeus*)

Description: To 15′5″ (4.7 m). Moderately large,
slender, somewhat compressed; dark
grayish-black above, somewhat lighter
below. *Head very small,* tapering rapidly
to distinct narrow beak. In adult males,
*single tooth visible about one-third of way
between snout tip and corner of mouth,* in
large males at anterior connection of
lower jaw. Dorsal fin small, on rear
third of back, triangular to falcate.
Flukes not notched.

Habitat: Probably open sea.

Range: From latitude of Long Island, New
York, to Trinidad, including Gulf of
Mexico.

Comments: The Antillean Beaked Whale is also
known as the Gulfstream Beaked
Whale and Gervais' Beaked Whale,
and the scientific name *Mesoplodon
gervaisi* has been applied to this species.

These whales feed on squids. Females, with or without calves, are frequently found stranded, suggesting they approach shore while calving.

669 Ginkgo-toothed Beaked Whale
(*Mesoplodon ginkgodens*)

Description: To 16′ (4.9 m). Fusiform; stranded animals black, lighter below, belly and sides usually with oval, white scars; females believed to have light-colored heads. *Forehead smoothly sloping, beak prominent;* no crease between beak and head. *Mouth line curves abruptly upward about midway between snout tip and eye, forming raised area on both sides of lower jaw* with single, flattened tooth on top in front in males. Dorsal fin falcate or triangular, nearer tail than head. Flukes usually lack median notch on rear edges.

Habitat: Unknown, but probably in upper layers of open seas.

Range: Near San Diego, California; near mouth of Laguna Ojo de Liebre (Scammon's Lagoon), Baja California.

Comments: The Ginkgo-toothed Beaked Whale, also known as the Japanese Beaked Whale, derives its primary common name from the resemblance of the adult male's tooth to the leaf of the ginkgo tree. This whale has only been described recently, and its coloration is known from stranded specimens that may have been darkened by the sun, distorting their true coloring. Scientific opinion is divided over coloration and other body features.

664 Hector's Beaked Whale
(*Mesoplodon hectori*)

Description: To 14′6″ (4.4 m). Fusiform; dark gray-brown above, lighter below; adult males with white on undersides of flukes, possibly with white area around navel. Head small; beak relatively short; *paired teeth at tip of lower jaw, erupt only in adult males.* Dorsal fin small, falcate, nearer tail than head. Flukes sometimes slightly notched.

Habitat: Upper layers of open seas; around islands.

Range: S. California and near Catalina Island.

Similar Species: Cuvier's Beaked Whale (*Ziphius cavirostris*) grows to 24'9" (7.5 m); head pale, white in old males.

Comments: Hector's Beaked Whale was first seen in the northern Pacific in 1980, and little is known about it. Individuals are believed to have approached vessels. Adult males of both these species can be readily distinguished from other beaked whales by the teeth at the tip of the lower jaw.

661 True's Beaked Whale
(*Mesoplodon mirus*)

Description: To 17' (5.2 m). *Chunky at midbody, rapidly narrowing towards tail;* dull black to dark gray above, sides lighter slate gray, often covered with light spots or splotches; belly white. Head small, slight indentation near blowhole, slight bulge on forehead; beak pronounced; *teeth of adult male sometimes visible near tip of lower jaw. Dorsal fin small,* slightly falcate, on rear third of back; tail stock has pronounced ridge. Flukes sometimes very slightly notched.

Habitat: In offshore waters and upper layers of open seas.

Range: From Nova Scotia to NE. Florida.

Comments: The diet of True's Beaked Whale, though unrecorded, is probably similar to that of other beaked whales, and therefore may well consist mostly of squids. Most Odontocetes do not chew their food but swallow it whole.

665   Stejneger's Beaked Whale
(*Mesoplodon stejnegeri*)

Description: To 17′6″ (5.3 m). Fusiform; grayish-brown above, lighter below, light brush marks may extend up sides behind head, at neck, and around mouth. *Oval, white scars usually on flanks of adults,* sometimes extend up back and sides. *Head has well-defined beak; paired teeth in lower jaw of males erupt well outside gum, emerging from prominent arches in lower jaw far behind tip of beak and appearing to constrict upper jaw.* Dorsal fin falcate, placed well beyond middle of back. Rear edges of flukes usually without median notch.

Habitat: In upper layers of open subarctic and cold temperate seas, but often near islands over deep water.

Range: From S. Bering Sea to Cardiff, California.

Comments: Stejneger's Beaked Whale is also known as the Bering Sea Beaked Whale and the Saber-toothed Whale. The males may be covered with scars that other males have inflicted with their teeth. Such scars are found on adults of several species of adult beaked whales. The coloration of Stejneger's Beaked Whale is only known from freshly stranded animals. Cetaceans darken quickly in the sun, so that allowances should be made for possible color variations.

670   Cuvier's Beaked Whale
(*Ziphius cavirostris*)

Description: To 24′9″ (7.5 m). *Robust;* dark rust-brown, slate-gray, or fawn-colored, belly lighter, frequently covered with light blotches; juveniles and some females lighter; head frequently pale, *distinctly white on old males. Head small,* upper profile slightly concave; *mouth opening small; beak indistinct in larger individuals; paired teeth at tip of lower*

jaw, *erupt only in adult males.*
Pronounced indentation on back
behind head. Dorsal fin tall, distinct,
nearer tail than head.

Habitat: Upper layers of open seas; often near
shore.

Range: In Atlantic from Massachusetts to West
Indies, including Gulf of Mexico. In
Pacific from S. Bering Sea to equator.
Widely distributed in nonpolar seas.

Similar Species: Hector's Beaked Whale (*Mesoplodon
hectori*) has smaller body; male lacks
white head.

Comments: Cuvier's Beaked Whale is also known as
the Goosebeaked Whale and Ziphius.
This species feeds on squids and
deepwater fishes. These whales,
reputedly vigorous swimmers, may
appear and disappear suddenly as they
rise from deep water and dive again
after a short rest at the surface.

SPERM WHALES
(Family Physeteridae)

Both genera of sperm whales have a
lower jaw that is conspicuously
receding and is located under the center
of the head. They have a single
blowhole and no ventral grooves. There
are obvious teeth in the lower jaw, and
teeth may also be present in the upper
jaw. In the genus *Physeter,* the head is
so huge that the animal appears to be
"all head," although the rest of the
body, while smaller in circumference,
comprises some 65% of the animal's
total length. *Kogia,* the other genus in
this family, consists of animals that
lack the comparatively huge head and
are much smaller overall; they can be
distinguished from other cetaceans by
their exceptionally short rostrum. This
family has 3 species in North America.

660 Pygmy Sperm Whale
(*Kogia breviceps*)

Description: To 12′ (3.7 m). *Extremely robust,
              tapering rapidly to tail;* back dark steel-
              gray, sides lighter gray, belly dull
              white; light gray crescent-shaped mark
              ("bracket mark") resembling opercle
              usually on each side of head. Head
              squarish, often looks bluntly rounded
              from above; single blowhole on top of
              head well back from snout tip. *Lower
              jaw well behind snout tip,* 10–16 large,
              pointed teeth on each side; no teeth in
              upper jaw. *Dorsal fin small, falcate, on
              posterior half of back.*

Habitat: In deep offshore waters; close to shore
           during calving season.

Range: In Atlantic from Nova Scotia to Greater
         Antilles, including N., E., and W.
         Gulf of Mexico. In Pacific from Gray's
         Harbor, Washington, to Baja
         California.

Similar Species: Dwarf Sperm Whale (*K. simus*) grows to
                   9′ (2.7 m); dorsal fin tall, about
                   halfway back, 8–13 teeth in each side
                   of lower jaw, sometimes up to 3 in each
                   side of upper jaw.

Comments: The Pygmy Sperm Whale is one of the
            species most commonly found stranded
            along the southeastern coast of the
            United States. This whale feeds on
            squids, crabs, shrimps, and some
            fishes. When startled at sea it may eject
            a large amount of dark reddish-brown
            fluid into the water, leaving a cloud
            that is apparently intended to confuse a
            predator while the whale escapes. This
            behavior is reminiscent of that of
            squids and octopuses, which escape by
            producing an ink cloud.

659 Dwarf Sperm Whale
(*Kogia simus*)

Description: To 9′ (2.7 m). *Extremely robust, tapering
              rapidly near tail stock;* dark steel-gray

above, sides lighter gray, belly dull white; light gray crescent-shaped mark ("bracket mark") resembling opercle usually on sides of head. *Head squarish, often looks bluntly rounded from above;* single blowhole on top of head well back from snout tip. *Lower jaw well behind snout tip,* 8–13 small, very sharp teeth in each side; sometimes up to 3 in each side of upper jaw. *Dorsal fin tall, falcate, near middle of back.*

Habitat: In deep offshore waters; close to shore during calving season.

Range: In Atlantic from New Jersey to Lesser Antilles, including N., E., and W. Gulf of Mexico. In Pacific from central California to tip of Baja California.

Similar Species: Pygmy Sperm Whale (*K. breviceps*) grows to 12′ (3.7 m); has small dorsal fin posteriorly placed; 10–16 teeth in each side of lower jaw, none in upper.

Comments: Dwarf Sperm Whales were clearly recognized as a species distinct from Pygmy Sperm Whales (*K. breviceps*) only a few years ago. They are known to feed on squids, crustaceans, and fishes. At sea they may be confused with most dolphins because of their tall dorsal fin.

615, 675 **Sperm Whale**
(*Physeter catodon*)

Description: To 69′ (21 m). *Head huge, one-quarter to one-third length;* dark brownish gray, skin appears corrugated or shriveled; sometimes belly and front of head grayish and mouth area white. Snout blunt, squarish, *projects far beyond lower jaw tip. Single blowhole well to left of midline and far forward on head; small bushy "spout" emerges forward at sharp angle.* Row of large teeth on each side of lower jaw, small teeth buried in upper jaw. Distinct dorsal hump two-thirds of way back from snout tip, followed by series of crenulations or bumps. Ventral keel present. Flukes

diving sequence

broad, triangular, not concave, deeply notched on rear edges.

Habitat: Mostly in temperate and tropical oceans; rarely at depths less than 100 fathoms and along edge of continental shelf.

Range: In Atlantic from Davis Straits to Venezuela, including Gulf of Mexico. In Pacific from Bering Sea to equator.

Similar Species: Gray Whale (*Eschrichtius robustus*) has obvious mottling.

Comments: This species can be identified by its distinctive spout. It feeds primarily on squids (including giant species), but may also eat a variety of fishes. The scientific name *P. catodon* has often been changed to *P. macrocephalus* in recent literature. These whales, also called Cachalot, were hunted extensively; the forehead contains spermaceti and a fine grade of oil, and the teeth were favored material for scrimshaw, the ivory objects carved by sailors and artisans. It was the search for an albino Sperm Whale that inspired the novel *Moby Dick,* but today individuals of over 50' (15.2 m) are rare. These whales produce offspring about every 4 years, after a gestation period of about 16 months. Like all other cetaceans, they are usually born tail first; this prevents the calf from drowning during birth.

NARWHAL AND WHITE WHALES
(Family Monodontidae)

Members of this family are medium-sized whales that live primarily in the Arctic pack ice, where they are still pursued by Eskimo fishermen. They are gregarious, sometimes occurring in huge herds. Both genera have rounded heads and lack dorsal fins. There are 2 species in North America.

612, 617, 672 White Whale
(*Delphinapterus leucas*)

Description: To 16' (4.9 m). Extremely *robust, tapering to distinct "neck"; adults white;* newborns brown, gradually lightening with age. *Head very small, beak short.* No dorsal fin; narrow ridge of small bumps behind middle of back.

Habitat: Primarily in shallow bays and mouths of rivers; occasionally ascending rivers and open oceans.

Range: In Atlantic from Arctic Circle to New Jersey; most abundant to N. shore of St. Lawrence River. In Pacific in N. Gulf of Alaska and throughout Bering, Chukchi, and Beaufort seas.

Comments: The White Whale is also known as Beluga, Belukha, White Porpoise, and Sea Canary; this last name comes from the frequent whistling noises that these whales can often be heard to make. White Whales may occur in herds of hundreds or even thousands. They feed on fishes (including cods and capelins), squids, and bottom-dwelling crustaceans. They are preyed upon by Killer Whales and also by polar bears, which have been seen to capture a full-grown White Whale through a hole in the ice.

610, 674 Narwhal
(*Monodon monoceros*)

Description: To 16' (4.9 m). Medium-sized; *dark bluish gray or brownish, adults with leopardlike spots* on back and sides. *Head rounded;* 2 teeth, in large adult males 1, sometimes both, *emerge from upper jaw as long tusk;* tusks usually absent or only slightly exposed in females; rarely, both tusks fully exposed. No dorsal fin; series of bumps about 2" (5 cm) high usually visible along dorsal midline from middle of back to tail.

Habitat: Near shore in bays, around pack ice in

warmer months.

Range: High Arctic of W. North America,
primarily Lancaster Sound and fringes.
More abundant in central Arctic;
uncommon in W. Arctic. Tends to be
found in pockets within its range rather
than widely spread over region.

Comments: The male Narwhal's long tusk, seen
detached from the animal, may have
given rise to the myth of the unicorn,
and in fact the Narwhal was once called
the Unicorn Whale. For centuries the
tusk has been prized material for
artisans; these whales are also hunted
for their blubber. The Narwhal may
use the tusk to dig clams from the sea
floor. But it is more likely that the tusk
is a weapon for territorial or sexual
battles, as broken tusks are often found.
There are even records of a Narwhal's
tusk being found jammed into the end
of a broken tusk from another Narwhal.
These animals feed mainly on squids,
but also eat fishes and crabs.

OCEAN DOLPHINS
(Family Delphinidae)

These small to medium-sized animals
are fusiform and cylindrical. They
usually have either a prominent beak
or, as in the genera *Grampus* and
Globicephala, a short beak and a
bulbous head. The teeth are conical and
are usually present in both jaws; in
some species they are extremely large
and strong. The dorsal fin is prominent
in all but the genus *Lissodelphis,*
has none. Ocean dolphins are primarily
distinguished from beaked whales on
the basis of size. However, because of
their comparatively large size, some
members of this family are commonly
called whales. This is the most varied
group of cetaceans, and the most
abundant in the order, although some
are considered rare but not endangered.

Most species are not sought by commercial fishers, although in the Pacific they may be caught in nets meant for tunas and other kinds of fishes. This family has 18 species in North America.

633, 648 Common Dolphin
(*Delphinus delphis*)

Description: To 8′6″ (2.6 m). Fusiform, slender, not robust; back black or brownish black, coloration and markings variable; chest and belly cream to white. *Sides distinctly marked with hourglass or crisscross pattern of tan or yellowish tan. Beak well-defined,* moderately long, often dark with white tip. *1 or more dark stripes from center of lower jaw to flipper.* Dorsal fin nearly triangular to distinctly falcate, usually black with lighter grayish region of varying size near middle, tip pointed.

Habitat: Offshore over outer continental shelf, often near ridges. Rarely inshore.

Range: In Atlantic from Newfoundland and Nova Scotia to N. South America. In Pacific from Victoria, British Columbia, to equator.

Similar Species: Pacific White-sided Dolphin (*Lagenorhynchus obliquidens*) has gray flippers. Clymene Dolphin (*Stenella clymene*) has stripe from eye to flipper. Striped Dolphin (*S. coeruleoalba*) lacks crisscross pattern on sides. Spinner Dolphin (*S. longirostris*) has black circle around eye.

Comments: The Common Dolphin is also known as the Saddleback Dolphin, Saddleback Porpoise, Crisscross Dolphin, White-bellied Porpoise, Hourglass Dolphin, and Saddleback. These animals often travel in huge herds of more than a thousand. They frequently leap clear of the water and ride bow waves of vessels for a long time.

656   Pygmy Killer Whale
(*Feresa attenuata*)

Description: To 9′ (2.7 m). *Relatively slender;* dark gray or black above, light color often on sides, extending higher in front of dorsal fin; small patch of white on underside; *distinctive white regions around lips, chin sometimes completely white.* Head rounded; lower jaw broad, receding; no beak; teeth obvious in both jaws. Dorsal fin falcate, at about middle of back.

Habitat: Warmer waters offshore.

Range: In Atlantic from N. Carolina to N., E., and W. Gulf of Mexico and Lesser Antilles. In Pacific limited to tropical waters south of Mexico.

Similar Species: False Killer Whale (*Pseudorca crassidens*) grows to 19′6″ (5.9 m), has distinct, characteristic hump on front edge of flippers.

Comments: The Pygmy Killer Whale is also known as the Slender Blackfish and the Slender Pilot Whale. It feeds on fishes and squids and there is reason to suspect it may attack other marine mammals. Captives are sometimes extremely aggressive towards their handlers.

635, 658   Short-finned Pilot Whale
(*Globicephala macrorhynchus*)

Description: To 23′ (7 m). Robust; black overall, anchor-shaped gray patch on chin, gray area on belly, sometimes light chevrons extend posteriorly from each side of blowhole, gray saddle sometimes behind dorsal fin. *Head thick, bulbous,* sometimes flattened or squarish in front, especially in older males. *Flippers relatively short, one-sixth body length. Dorsal fin falcate, low, with long base, far forward on back.*

Habitat: Tropical and temperate waters from outer edges of continental shelves seaward, sometimes close to shore.

Range: In Atlantic from New Jersey to Venezuela, including Gulf of Mexico; known from Delaware Bay. In Pacific from Gulf of Alaska to Guatemala.

Similar Species: Long-finned Pilot Whale, (*G. melaena*) has flippers one-fifth body length. False Killer Whale (*Pseudorca crassidens*) has less robust body; less bulbous head.

Comments: The Short-finned Pilot Whale is also called the Blackfish, Pothead, Pilot Whale, and Shortfin Pilot Whale. Off California, the scientific name *G. scammoni* is sometimes applied. These whales often occur in very large herds and are frequently stranded in masses. In the Lesser Antilles they are killed for both oil and meat, and hunted with harpoons from open boats. They feed on squids and fishes. Short-finned Pilot Whales have been reported to "spy-hop," or "pitchpole" (hang vertically in the water with their head out), but they rarely breach. They do not ride bow waves of boats. When resting on the surface, individuals often position themselves side by side in long lines. Their habit of slapping their flukes on the surface is called lobtailing.

635, 657 Long-finned Pilot Whale
(*Globicephala melaena*)

Description: To 20′ (6.1 m). Robust; black with anchor-shaped patch of grayish white on chin, gray area on belly, both variable in intensity and shape; gray saddle behind dorsal fin in some large individuals. *Head thick, bulbous,* sometimes flattened, squarish in front, especially in adult males. *Flippers long, to one-fifth body length; dorsal fin falcate, low, with long base, set far forward on back.*

Habitat: Generally offshore waters; inshore waters and bays in summer.

Range: From Iceland and Greenland to North Carolina; possibly to Georgia.

Similar Species: Short-finned Pilot Whale (*G. macrorhynchus*) has flippers one-sixth body length. False Killer Whale (*Pseudorca crassidens*) has less robust body; head less bulbous.

Comments: The Long-finned Whale is known by many other names: the Northern Pilot Whale, Atlantic Pilot Whale, Calling Whale, Caa'ing Whale, and Blackfish. Because its large bulbous melon, or bump on the forehead, looks much like an inverted cook pot, it is also known as the Pothead. These whales may be stranded in large numbers; in the past, they were also driven ashore by coastal fisheries and slaughtered primarily for their oil. Long-finned Pilot Whales sometimes "spy-hop" or "pitchpole," that is, hang vertically in the water with the head and part of the back out of water. They also slap their flukes on the surface, or "lobtail," but do not ride bow waves of ships and do not often breach. Males are usually larger than females.

636, 654   Risso's Dolphin
(*Grampus griseus*)

Description: To 13′ (4 m). Robust anteriorly, tapers rapidly to narrow tail; dark gray at birth, darkening to almost black when young, with distinctive grayish-white regions on belly; *numerous scars;* color lightens overall, particularly on head, with increasing age; dorsal fin, flippers, and flukes usually remain dark. *Head bulbous, V-shaped crease on front pointing downwards, dividing melon, or bump, into 2 parts;* no distinct beak. Dorsal fin tall, distinctly falcate, at middle of back.

Habitat: Near surface of open temperate and tropical seas, most often seaward from outer edge of continental shelf; possibly coastal waters where shelf edge is close to shore.

Range: In Atlantic from E. Newfoundland to Lesser Antilles, including N. and E. Gulf of Mexico. In Pacific from off N. Washington to tropics.

Similar Species: Bottlenosed Dolphin (*Tursiops truncatus*) lacks bulbous head with crease in front; beak distinct, short.

Comments: The Risso's Dolphin is also known as Grampus, Gray Grampus, White-headed Grampus, Mottled Grampus, White Blackfish, and Risso's Porpoise. These animals sometimes occur in herds of several hundred, but are more common in groups of a dozen or less. They sometimes ride bow waves and stern wakes, and may leap clear of the surface. They feed chiefly on squids but also eat some fishes.

631, 649 Atlantic White-sided Dolphin
(*Lagenorhynchus acutus*)

Description: To 9′ (2.7 m). Robust; black above, color on sides variable with zones of gray, tan, and white, belly white; *sides have elongate zone of white and yellowish white from just below dorsal fin to above anus. Beak black, small but distinct.* Dorsal fin tall, often partly gray, distinctly falcate, tip pointed. *Tail stock extremely thick, narrowing laterally just in front of flukes.*

Habitat: Primarily cool offshore waters.

Range: From S. Greenland to N. Virginia.

Similar Species: White-beaked Dolphin (*L. albirostris*) has 2 grayish areas, 1 in front of and other below and behind uniformly dark dorsal fin; beak sometimes white or light gray.

Comments: Atlantic White-sided Dolphins are also known as Atlantic White-sided Porpoises and Jumpers. They are very visible at sea and are sometimes found in extremely large herds. These animals seem to be wary of ships and do not ride bow waves. This species feeds on squids and fishes. It is believed that dolphins communicate with each other; the sounds they make have been variously described as barks, groans, chirps, and whistles. They may also communicate by means of body posture and by slapping the flukes on the water's surface.

650 White-beaked Dolphin
(*Lagenorhynchus albirostris*)

Description: To 10' (3 m). Robust; tail gently tapering, moderately compressed; dark gray to black above, belly white to light gray; sides with 2 grayish areas in front of and behind and below dorsal fin. *Beak short but distinct, light gray, sometimes white, above and below. Dorsal fin tall, uniformly dark gray.*

Habitat: Offshore waters.

Range: From Davis Straits and S. Greenland to Cape Cod.

Similar Species: Atlantic White-sided Dolphin (*L. acutus*) has elongated band of white and yellowish white on sides behind and below dorsal fin; beak black; dorsal fin with areas of black and lighter gray.

Comments: The White-beaked Dolphin is also known as the White-beaked Porpoise and Squidhound. Like all Odontocetes, it has a gestation period of about 1 year; it may give birth to 2 or more calves, but only 1 usually survives.

632, 647 Pacific White-sided Dolphin
(*Lagenorhynchus obliquidens*)

Description: To 7'6" (2.3 m). Fusiform, cylindrical; head tapers continuously and smoothly to *abbreviated dark beak.* Back black, belly white or light gray stripe on both sides begins at forehead, curves over head, continues past dorsal fin, widening and curving toward anus, forming prominent light gray patch on flank. Narrow, dark stripe between corner of mouth and flipper, continuous with dark lips. Light gray zone on both sides from forehead to dorsal fin. *Flippers gray with dark line from axil extending to dark area on flank.* Dorsal fin tall, strongly falcate, base near middle of back, dark on forward third, remainder light gray. Flukes dark.

Habitat: Offshore waters, also inside outer edge of continental shelf; often close to shore near deep canyons.

Range: From Amchitka Island in Aleutians, throughout Gulf of Alaska to tip of Baja California.

Similar Species: Common Dolphin (*Delphinus delphis*) has crisscross pattern on sides; dark saddle on back; saddle pattern and coloration variable; beak long; dorsal fin usually only slightly falcate. Dall's Porpoise (*Phocoenoides dalli*) has short, poorly defined beak; head small; dorsal fin relatively low.

Comments: The Pacific White-sided Dolphin is also known as the Lag, White-striped Dolphin, and Hookfin Porpoise. These animals may occur in herds of up to several thousand. They eat a wide variety of fishes and squids. As with all cetaceans, the maximum age is difficult to determine. Many cetaceans are known to have long lifespans, and some have lived for 30 years. Captive Pacific White-sided Dolphins have lived for just over 10 years.

673 Northern Right Whale Dolphin
(*Lissodelphis borealis*)

Description: To 10' (3 m). *Long and slender, tapering to extremely narrow tail stock;* black with distinct, variable white pattern on belly from chest to far back on tail, narrowing abruptly just behind flippers; tip of lower jaw usually with small, white mark. Calves much lighter than adults. *Virtually no forehead or chin;*

beak indistinctly set off by faint crease above long, straight mouth. No dorsal fin or ridge.

Habitat: Temperate waters off outer edge of continental shelf, also over shelf waters.

Range: From S. British Columbia to N. Baja California.

Comments: This species is often found in large herds of more than 100 animals. Northern Right Whale Dolphins are fast swimmers. Although they often run from approaching vessels, they sometimes ride bow waves, leap clear of the water on an even keel, belly flop, side slap, or lobtail as they run. This species feeds on squids and mid-water fishes.

628, 629, 651   Killer Whale
(Orcinus orca)

Description: To 31' (9.4 m). Males more robust than females; black with white, tan, or yellow region on undersides from lower jaw to anus extending onto sides behind dorsal fin; oval, white patch just above and behind eye; usually light-gray saddle behind dorsal fin; undersides of flukes usually white. Head broad, rounded; mouth large; teeth large, pointed; no pronounced beak. *Flippers large, paddle-shaped, rounded. Dorsal fin tall,* distinctly falcate in females and juveniles, taller and erect in adult males, sometimes appears to bend forward.

Habitat: Upper layers of cooler coastal seas; occasionally large rivers and tropical seas.

Range: In Atlantic from pack ice to Lesser Antilles, including N., E., and W. Gulf of Mexico. In Pacific from Chukchi Sea to equator.

Similar Species: False Killer Whale (*Pseudorca crassidens*) has faint gray blaze; body dark overall.

Comments: The Killer Whale is also known as the Blackfish, Grampus, Orca, and, because large males have a tall dorsal fin, the Sword Fish. The scientific names *Grampus orca* and *Orca gladiator* have been applied until fairly recently; the latter seems especially appropriate, since Killer Whales are often ferocious in their feeding habits. On occasion groups of these animals attack baleen whales, pinnipeds such as seals, and small Odontocetes. They are also known to feed on fishes, squids, sea turtles, and sea birds. They have been known to attack and mortally wound baleen whales, and then leave without eating them. While there are no reliable records of unprovoked attacks on humans, people should be extremely cautious of these animals.

637, 655 False Killer Whale
(*Pseudorca crassidens*)

Description: To 19'6" (5.9 m). Long, slender; black, often with faint gray blaze on belly between flippers; scars sometimes present. *Head narrow, gently tapered from blowhole forward;* rounded bump on forehead, or melon, somewhat overhangs long lower jaw; teeth large, strong. Dorsal fin tall, falcate, just behind middle of back. Flippers very long, with *broad hump near middle of front edge.*

Habitat: Tropical and warm temperate seas; strandings in sandy bays and estuaries.

Range: In Atlantic from Maryland to Venezuela, including E. and NW. Gulf of Mexico. In Pacific from Aleutian Islands and Prince William Sound, Alaska, to Central America and N. South America.

Similar Species: Pygmy Killer Whale (*Feresa attenuata*) has white around chin. Short-finned Pilot Whale (*Globiocephala macrorhynchus*) has thick, bulbous head. Long-finned Pilot Whale (*G. melaena*) has more bulbous head. Killer Whale

Comments: (*Orcinus orca*) has taller dorsal fin.
False Killer Whales have been known
to steal fishes from both commercial
and sport fishing lines. They often
approach ships and frequently jump
clear of the water despite their
relatively large size.

645 Clymene Dolphin
(*Stenella clymene*)

Description: To 6'6" (2 m). Moderately slender;
back dark gray to black, sides lighter,
belly white. *Bottom edge of dark cape
below dorsal fin dips toward belly. Black
stripe narrows from flipper to eye.* Beak
moderately long, with pale gray to
white lateral area on top adjacent to
distinctly black tip and lips. Dorsal fin
erect, falcate.

Habitat: Open seas and deep coastal waters near
islands.

Range: From New Jersey to Lesser Antilles.

Similar Species: Common Dolphin (*Delphinus delphis*)
has crisscross pattern on sides; black
stripe between middle of lower jaw and
flipper; no black stripe from eye to
flipper. Spinner Dolphin (*S. longirostris*)
has longer beak, dark on top, pale to
dark gray on sides near black tip.
Bottom border of dark cape below
dorsal fin parallel to lower edge of
lighter gray sides; edges of stripe
between eye and flipper parallel.

Comments: Only recently recognized as a distinct
species, the Clymene Dolphin was for a
brief time called the Short-snouted
Spinner Dolphin. This species rides
bow waves. It also spins, although not
as high above the surface or in as
complex a manner as the Spinner
Dolphin (*S. longirostris*). Very few
dolphins spin, and the reason for this
behavior is unknown. It may be to
dislodge parasites, or purely for
pleasure. The Clymene Dolphin feeds
on squids and small fishes.

646 Striped Dolphin
(*Stenella coeruleoalba*)

Description: To 9′ (2.7 m). Moderately robust; top
of head and back dark gray to bluish
gray, sides lighter gray, throat and
belly white. *Black stripes on lower half of
each side, single or double stripe from eye to
flipper,* another from eye to anus,
usually with short, ventral branch
ending above and somewhat behind
flipper. Beak black, long, sharply
defined; black patch around each eye
connected to beak. Dark cape on back.
*Distinctive light blaze usually extends up
and back from light side into cape toward
dorsal fin.* Dorsal fin dark, falcate.

Habitat: Warmer temperate and tropical waters
off edge of continental shelf; warm
fingers of water in northern areas.

Range: In Atlantic from Halifax, Nova Scotia,
to Lesser Antilles, including Gulf of
Mexico. In Pacific from Bering Sea to
NW. South America.

Similar Species: Common Dolphin (*Delphinus delphis*)
has crisscross pattern on sides; darker
back; distinct, black stripe from
middle of lower jaw to flippers.

Comments: Other common names for the Striped
Dolphin are Meyen's Dolphin, Blue-
white Dolphin, Gray's Dolphin,
Striped Porpoise, Streaker Porpoise,
Euphrosyne Dolphin, and Whitebelly.
These animals, which often occur in
large herds of several hundred
individuals, may ride bow waves and
jump clear of the water. They feed at
mid-depths on fishes, squids, and
crustaceans. They often associate with
schools of tunas in the eastern Pacific,
and many Striped Dolphins are killed
by accident when caught with the tunas
in purse seines. Successful efforts are
being made to reduce these losses.

641 Bridled Dolphin
(*Stenella frontalis*)

Description: To 7' (2.1 m). Moderately robust; back
dark gray, fading to lighter gray on
sides and belly; dark areas with light
spots and light areas with dark spots.
Border between back and side colors
blurred except on head where cape clear
and dark. Beak distinct, moderately
long, lips white or pinkish. Side of
head light gray with *black circle around
eye extending to junction of rostrum and
melon. Broad, black stripe from corner of
mouth to insertion of flipper,* becoming less
distinct in older individuals as spotting
increases. Dorsal fin falcate, dark gray.

Habitat: Near coastal areas and islands, also
offshore tropical waters.

Range: From Massachusetts to Lesser Antilles,
including E. and possibly W. Gulf of
Mexico.

Similar Species: Atlantic Spotted Dolphin (*S. plagiodon*)
has distinct, dark cape on head hidden
as spotting increases; no dark stripe
from corner of mouth to flipper; older
animals have light blaze angling
upward and backward from dark upper
portion of side toward center of dorsal
fin base. Rough-toothed Dolphin (*Steno
bredanensis*) has pinkish-white beak.

Comments: This animal is also known as the
Bridled Spotted Dolphin, Cuvier's
Dolphin, and Bridled Porpoise. The
scientific name *S. froenatus* has been
applied to it in recent years. The
Spotted Dolphin (*S. attenuata*) of the
eastern Pacific is considered by some
authorities to be the same species. The
Bridled Dolphin owes its common
name to the black area circling the eye
and extending forward. This species
rides bow waves and feeds on squids,
fishes, and shrimps.

638, 644 Spinner Dolphin
(*Stenella longirostris*)

Description: To 7' (2.1 m). Slender; back dark gray
to black, sides tan to yellowish brown,
belly white. *Dark cape below dorsal fin
with lower border parallel to lower edge of
lighter gray sides. Upper and lower edges of
stripe between eye and flipper roughly
parallel.* Some large individuals almost
black with faint, light speckling. *Beak
usually extremely long and slender,*
occasionally only moderately long,
usually dark on top with pale to dark
gray lateral area adjacent to black tip.
Lips black; transverse groove from
forehead to snout. Dorsal fin erect,
moderately falcate, sometimes nearly
triangular or tilted forward in adult
males, often lighter gray near middle
bordered by black or dark gray.

Habitat: Tropical oceanic and coastal waters.

Range: In Atlantic from North Carolina to S.
Brazil and in N., E., and W. Gulf of
Mexico. In Pacific not known north of
United States—Mexico border.

Similar Species: Common Dolphin (*Delphinus delphis*)
has crisscross pattern on side; stripe
from middle of lower jaw to flipper.
Clymene Dolphin (*S. clymene*) has
shorter beak with pale gray to white
lateral area on top adjacent to black tip;
bottom border of dark cape below
dorsal fin dips toward lower margin of
lighter gray lateral region; margins of
flipper stripe converging toward eye.
Rough-toothed Dolphin (*Steno
bredanensis*) has pinkish-white beak.

Comments: The Spinner Dolphin is also known as
the Long-snouted Dolphin, Long-
beaked Porpoise, Spinner Porpoise, and
Spinner. The term "spinner" comes
from this dolphin's frequent habit of
leaping clear of the surface and rotating
on its long axis. Spinner Dolphins ride
bow waves. They may occur in large
herds; enormous numbers have been
killed in the tropical eastern Pacific
when surrounded by tuna fishermens'

purse seines. The nets have now been modified to reduce dolphin deaths.

640   Atlantic Spotted Dolphin
(*Stenella plagiodon*)

Description:
To 8′ (2.4 m). Robust. Adults dark above, profusely marked with light spots; sides and belly lighter gray to white with progressively darker spots. *As spotting develops, light blaze of spotting angles up and back through dark upper portion of side toward center of dorsal fin base. Light line from eye to flipper.* Distinct dark cape to behind dorsal fin, present in juveniles, becomes less obvious as spotting increases with age. Head slender, beak distinct, moderately long, *tip and lips often white.* Transverse groove between snout and forehead. Dorsal fin distinctly falcate, tip pointed.

Habitat:
Generally offshore waters at over 100 fathoms at least 5 miles (8 km) from coast. Seasonally may approach very close to shore.

Range:
From latitude of Cape May, New Jersey, along mainland shores to Venezuela, including Gulf of Mexico and Lesser Antilles.

Similar Species:
Bridled Dolphin (*S. frontalis*) has less robust body; lacks spinal blaze; adults have more distinct dark cape on head, dark stripe between corner of mouth and flipper. Rough-toothed Dolphin (*Steno bredanensis*) has pinkish-white beak. Bottlenosed Dolphin (*Tursiops truncatus*) has well-defined beak.

Comments:
This species is also known as the Spotter, Gulf Stream Spotted Dolphin, Spotted Porpoise, and, in older literature, Long-snouted Dolphin. Atlantic Spotted Dolphins may occur in herds of several thousand, but smaller groups are more common. They may jump clear of the water and sometimes ride bow waves.

634, 643 Rough-toothed Dolphin
(*Steno bredanensis*)

Description: To 8′ (2.4 m). Fusiform, cylindrical; dark gray to dark purplish with pinkish-white blotches below, often scarred with white scratches; *usually white to pinkish-white along both sides of beak and on one or both lips and snout tip. Head long, almost conical,* forehead and sides of head slope smoothly into snout; no transverse groove between forehead and snout; surface of teeth rough to touch. Dorsal fin tall, falcate, base long.

Habitat: Offshore waters, usually off edge of continental shelf.

Range: In Atlantic from Virginia to NE. South America, including E. and NW. Gulf of Mexico. In Pacific from central California through tropics.

Similar Species: Bridled Dolphin (*Stenella frontalis*), Spinner Dolphin (*S. longirostris*), Atlantic Spotted Dolphin (*S. plagiodon*), and Bottlenosed Dolphin (*Tursiops truncatus*) have transverse groove between forehead and snout; forehead not long, slender, and sloping.

Comments: This species is also known as the Rough-toothed Porpoise, Black Porpoise, Goggle-eyed Porpoise, and Steno. Rough-toothed Dolphins feed on squids and pelagic octopuses. The rough surfaces of their teeth are often obvious only to the touch.

639, 642 Bottlenosed Dolphin
(*Tursiops truncatus*)

Description: To 12′ (3.7 m). Robust; *back usually dark gray, sides lighter gray, shading to pink or white on belly;* individuals vary from albino to nearly black; distinct dark cape often on head and back; old females may have spots on belly. *Beak well defined but relatively short;* transverse groove between forehead and snout.

Dorsal fin near center of back, prominent, broad-based, falcate, tip pointed.

Habitat: Inshore waters including estuaries, shallow bays, waterways, and freshwater rivers; sometimes to edge of continental shelf.

Range: In Atlantic from Nova Scotia to Venezuela, including Gulf of Mexico. In Pacific from S. California to tropics.

Similar Species: Risso's Dolphin (*Grampus griseus*) has bulbous head with V-shaped crease. Atlantic Spotted Dolphin (*Stenella plagiodon*) has spots on mature individuals; snout longer. Rough-toothed Dolphin (*Steno bredanensis*) has long, sloping snout, not clearly separated from forehead.

Comments: The Bottlenosed Dolphin is also known as the Bottlenosed Porpoise, Gray Porpoise, Common Porpoise, and Black Porpoise. The name may be prefixed by "Atlantic" or "Pacific." These dolphins feed on a wide variety of fishes, squids, shrimps, and crabs, and often follow trawlers and other fishing boats to feed on the unwanted fish that are thrown overboard and on organisms stirred up by the nets. They are particularly adept at locating prey using echolocation, that is, projecting a sound beam and listening to the echo. They ride the bow waves of boats and even surf waves. There are many records of wild Bottlenosed Dolphins voluntarily approaching humans closely enough to be touched. While these dolphins do communicate among themselves (as probably all cetaceans do), there is no good evidence that they talk to people.

PORPOISES
(Family Phocoenidae)

Porpoises are smaller than most other cetaceans and generally swim slowly, although members of the genus

Phocoenoides are among the fastest cetaceans. They have a fusiform body with a rounded and blunt head. Both jaws have flat, compressed, spadelike teeth. A single blowhole is present. The dorsal fin is triangular and not falcate. Many people, including some scientists, refer to all small cetaceans as "porpoises." This family has 2 species off the United States; another species, the Cochito (*Phocoena sinus*) occurs only in the lower Gulf of California.

653 Harbor Porpoise
(*Phocoena phocoena*)

Description: To 6′ (1.8 m). Chunky; back dark brown or gray fading to lighter grayish-brown on sides, often speckled in transition zone; white on belly extends up sides, especially in front of dorsal fin. *Head small, rounded; beak very short, indistinct. Dorsal fin small, dark, triangular, tip blunt.*

Habitat: Subarctic and cold temperate waters, usually inshore within 10-fathom curve, rarely to 100 fathoms offshore. Often in bays, harbors, estuaries, and river mouths.

Range: In Atlantic from Davis Straits and SE. Greenland to North Carolina. In Pacific from Gulf of Alaska and E. Aleutian chain to S. California; uncommonly from Chukchi and Beaufort Seas.

Similar Species: Dall's Porpoise (*Phocoenoides dalli*) has white patch on upper half of dorsal fin and on flank.

Comments: The Harbor Porpoise is also known as the Common Porpoise, Herring Hog, and, because of its loud blow, Puffing Pig. This species tends to be wary of vessels and does not ride bow waves. It often swims quietly at the surface. Harbor Porpoises are known to feed on octopuses, squids, and fishes, including herrings. In turn they may be preyed upon by large sharks and by Killer

Whales. Because they live mostly inshore, they are often adversely affected by human activities. Each female produces a single offspring about once every year.

630, 652 Dall's Porpoise
(*Phocoenoides dalli*)

Description: To 7′ (2.1 m). Extremely robust; head and flukes small. *Shiny black overall, sides with large, conspicuous, oval, white patch, sometimes with faint dark spots beginning well below dorsal fin and meeting at midriff;* some individuals entirely black; dorsal fin usually white above, black below. Wide variation in pigmentation. Forehead slopes steeply to short, poorly defined beak; mouth small, narrow. Dorsal fin triangular, base long. Tail has pronounced keel above and below.

Habitat: Often well offshore and beyond outer edge of continental shelf, but also in deeper inshore waters.

Range: From Pribilof Islands, possibly Bering Strait, to Baja California.

Similar Species: Pacific White-sided Dolphin (*Lagenorhynchus obliquidens*) has abbreviated dark beak. Harbor Porpoise (*Phocoena phocoena*) has coloring mainly in subdued shades of brown and gray.

Comments: Dall's Porpoises, also known as True's Porpoises and Spray Porpoises, are usually seen in small herds of 20 or less. They are extremely fast swimmers, sometimes moving through the water so rapidly that they throw up a plume of water like the "rooster tail" of a racing hydroplane. They may ride bow waves. This species feeds on squids, crustaceans, and deep-sea fishes. Its known predators include the Killer Whale and sharks. Many are harpooned intentionally by Japanese fishermen in the northern Pacific; some are killed by drifting into salmon nets.

Part III
Appendices

GLOSSARY
Page numbers refer to marginal illustrations.

Acute Pointed.

Adipose eyelid A thick, transparent membrane covering part of the eyeball in some fishes.

Adipose fin A fleshy fin, without supporting rays, behind the dorsal fin in some fishes.

Anadromous Migrating from marine waters upstream to breed in fresh water.

Anal Pertaining to the anus or the area around it.

Anal fin The median fin behind the anus.

Anterior Located toward the front.

Axil The inner angle at which a pectoral fin is joined to the body.

Axillary process An enlarged, elongated scale at the insertion of the pectoral or pelvic fins of some fishes (p.8).

Axillary scale See Axillary process.

Baleen In some whales, the fibrous plates in parallel rows on either side of the upper jaw.

Band A pigmented diagonal or oblique line.

Bar A short, broad, pigmented vertical line.

Barbel A fleshy projection of the skin, often threadlike, usually found near the mouth, chin, or nostrils.

Basibranchial teeth Very small teeth just behind the base of the tongue.

Beak In many toothed whales, the elongated forward portion of the head, consisting of the rostrum and the lower jaw.

Benthic   Living on or asssociated with the ocean bottom.

Bicuspid   Having 2 cusps, as in the incisor teeth of some fishes *(p. 505)*.

Blaze   In cetaceans, a streak or "smear" of light pigmentation on the upper side of the front portion of the body.

Blow   In cetaceans, the expulsion of air at the surface through the blowhole(s), or nostril(s), during exhalation; also called the spout.

Blowhole   In cetaceans, the single or paired respiratory opening.

Brackish water   Slightly less salty than sea water.

Branchial   Pertaining to the gills or gill chamber.

Branchiostegal ray   One of the long, slightly curved raylike bones that support a gill membrane.

Breach   To leap through the water surface.

Canine teeth   Long, pointed, conical or lance-shaped teeth *(p.5)*.

Cape   In some cetaceans, a dark area usually on top of the head or on the back in front of the dorsal fin.

Cardiform teeth   Sharp teeth that are closely set in rows and look like the bristles of a brush *(p.5)*.

Catadromous   Migrating from fresh water downstream to breed in salt water.

Caudal   Pertaining to the tail.

Caudal fin   The fin on the hindmost part of the body.

Caudal peduncle   The part of the body of a fish between the posterior end of the anal fin base and the caudal fin base.

Cephalic   Pertaining to the head.

Ciguatera poisoning   An illness in humans caused by eating fish with toxic flesh.

Cirrus (pl. cirri)   A fingerlike protuberance, sometimes occurring in a fringelike series.

Claspers   Modified parts of the pelvic fins of male sharks, rays, and skates; used in copulation.

Compressed   Flattened from side to side so that the fish is higher than wide.

Continental shelf   The submerged, relatively flat and gently sloping part of a continent extending from shore to about 100 fathoms.

Corselet A girdle of small scales on the anterior part of the body in mackerel-like fishes.

Ctenoid scale A scale with spines along the rear edge or exposed surface *(p.8)*.

Cusp A pointed projection on a tooth.

Cycloid scale A smooth scale without spines *(p.8)*.

Deciduous scale A loosely attached scale, easily shed.

Decurved Curved downward.

Denticle One of the small teeth or prickles on the skin of sharks and rays.

Depressed Flattened from top to bottom so that the fish is wider than high.

Dermal ridge A ridge of skin.

Dorsal Pertaining to the back or upper surface of the body.

Dorsal fin The fin along the midline of the back, supported by rays; often notched or divided into separate fins.

Dorsal spine One of the hard rays supporting the membrane of the dorsal fin.

Drainage An area drained by a system of streams that join and flow into a major river.

Emarginate Notched, but not deeply forked.

Falcate Strongly curved or lunate.

Fathom A unit of measurement used to indicate water depth, and equal to 6′ (1.8 m).

Filament A long, threadlike structure.

Finlet One of several small, isolated fin rays behind the dorsal or anal fins.

Flippers In cetaceans, the forelimbs.

Flukes In cetaceans, the horizontally positioned tail fin, resembling the tail of a fish, but not vertical.

Frenum A fleshy bridge connecting the upper lip to the tip of the snout *(p. 565)*.

Fusiform Spindle-shaped; tapering toward ends.

Ganoid scale A thick, hard, diamond-shaped scale occurring on certain primitive bony fishes *(p.8)*.

Gill arch A bony or cartilaginous structure bearing gill filaments and gill rakers, located in the side of the gill chamber.

Gill membrane An external tissue that serves as a valve in respiration.

Gill rakers Slender, bony or hardened extensions of the inner side of a gill arch *(p. 702)*.

Gills The filamentous respiratory organs of fishes.

Gular plate A bony plate between the lower jaw bones of certain fishes *(p. 373)*.

Heterocercal fin A caudal fin in which the upper lobe is considerably larger than the lower; it contains the vertebral column.

Homocercal fin A caudal fin with lobes of about the same size, neither penetrated by the vertebral column.

Humeral Pertaining to the area just behind the opercle and above the pectoral fin base.

Incisor teeth Flattened teeth at the front of the mouth, forming a cutting edge *(p.5)*.

Insertion The point at which each paired fin is joined to the body.

Isthmus The narrow extension of the breast between the gill openings.

Keel A sharp ridge located, in certain fishes, on the back, belly, or caudal peduncle, and in some cetaceans, usually just in front of the flukes.

Krill Shrimplike crustaceans occurring in huge numbers in the open seas, and eaten by baleen whales.

Lamella (pl. lamellae) On a gill filament, one of a series of thin, platelike subdivisions that increase the surface area for respiration.

Lateral line A series of tubes or pored scales associated with the sensory system; usually extending from just behind the opercle to the base of the caudal fin.

Lobe A rounded projection.

Lobtail In cetaceans, to slap the flukes on the water's surface, making a loud splash.

Lunate Crescent-shaped.

Margin The edge farthest from the point of attachment.

Maxilla The rear and usually larger of 2 bones forming the upper jaw.

Median fins The unpaired fins—dorsal, anal, and caudal.

Melon In many toothed whales, the bulging forehead, often containing oil.

Mesopelagic Living in the midwaters of the open ocean.

Molar One of the broad, flat teeth used for grinding or crushing food *(p.5)*.

Nape The area along the back between the head and the dorsal fin.

Nasal Pertaining to the nostrils and the surrounding area.

Occiput The hindmost edge of the top of the head, where the head joins the nape.

Ocellated Having one or more eyespots, or ocelli.

Ocellus (pl. ocelli) A pigmented eyelike spot, usually dark with a lighter border.

Opercle A large, flat bone covering most of the gill chamber. *Adj.* opercular.

Origin The point at which the front of the dorsal or anal fin is attached to the body.

Oviparous reproduction Laying eggs, as opposed to giving birth to live young.

Ovoviviparous reproduction Giving birth to live young that have hatched from eggs; held inside the body without receiving nutrients from the mother.

Paired fins The fins that occur in pairs—the pectorals and the pelvics.

Palatine teeth The teeth on the palatine bone, located to the rear of the roof of the mouth.

Papilla (pl. papillae) A small, nipplelike projection, often occurring in groups.

Pectoral fins The paired fins attached to the shoulder girdle.

Pelagic Pertaining to or living in the open waters of seas or large lakes.

Pelvic fins The paired fins on the lower part of the body, usually just below or behind the pectoral fins.

Peritoneum The membrane lining the abdominal cavity.

Persistent Remaining visible as the fish matures; not shed.

Pharyngeal teeth Teeth, sometimes molarlike, located on the bones of the pharynx, the passage between the mouth and the esophagus.

Photophore A light-emitting organ or spot on certain marine fishes.

Plankton   Microscopic plants and animals that drift near the surface of open waters.

Plicate   Folded, grooved, or wrinkled.

Pored scale   One of a series of scales with a small opening into a sensory system; usually found along the lateral line.

Posterior   Located toward the rear.

Predorsal   Pertaining to the area on the back between the snout and the dorsal fin origin.

Preopercle   The foremost bone of the gill cover below and behind the eye.

Protractile   Capable of forward extension; usually pertaining to a mouth.

Ray   One of the supporting structures in the fin membranes, either flexible (soft ray) or stiff (spine).

Reabsorbed   Becoming hidden in the flesh as a fish matures; assimilated.

Recurved   Curved or bent backward.

Reticulate   Marked with a network or chainlike pattern of lines.

Riffle   Shallow rapids or shoals in a stream where water breaks into waves.

Rostrum   In fishes, a forward projection of the snout; in cetaceans, a forward extension of the upper jaw. *Adj.* rostral.

Saddle   A blotch or patch of pigment that extends across the midline of the back and onto the sides.

Sargassum   A free-floating brown seaweed that occurs in warm marine environments.

Scale   One of many hard or bony plates that cover the skin of fishes.

Scute   A modified scale, often large and shield-like, with 1 or more ridges *(p. 383)*.

Serrated   Saw-toothed or jagged.

Snout   The part of the head extending from the front margin of the eye to the anterior tip of the head.

Spawn   To release eggs and sperm into the water.

Spine   A usually rigid, unsegmented, unbranched structure that supports the thin membrane of a fin; a sharp, bony projection, usually on the head.

Spiracle	In certain fishes, a respiratory opening, varying in size, on the back part of the head above and behind the eye; in whales, the blowhole.
Spout	A visible cloud expelled by a cetacean during exhalation at the water surface; also called the blow.
Striations	Narrow, parallel grooves or lines.
Stripe	A thin horizontal line or area of pigment.
Subopercle	A bone below the opercle, and a part of the gill cover.
Substrate	The bottom of a body of water.
Subterminal	Located just to the rear of the tip of the snout; describing the position of the mouth of a fish.
Sucking disc	An adhesive structure; a disc formed by a jawless mouth, the union of paired fins, or a modification of the dorsal spines.
Tail stock	In cetaceans, the tapered rear part of the body, just in front of the flukes.
Terete	Slightly tapering at both ends.
Terminal	Located at the tip of the snout; describing the position of the mouth of a fish.
Tricuspid	Having 3 cusps, as in the incisor teeth of some fishes *(p. 506)*.
Truncate	Having the edge vertical and straight.
Tubercle	One of a group of conical projections that develop on the body of a fish.
Ventral	Pertaining to the underside or lower part of the body.
Ventral grooves	In some baleen whales, the furrows extending backwards from the chin.
Vermiculations	Fine, wavy lines.
Vertical fins	See Median fins.
Villiform teeth	Minute, slender teeth in compact patches or bands *(p.5)*.
Viviparous reproduction	Bearing live young that have received nutrients from the mother during development.
Vomer teeth	The teeth on the vomer bone, located in the front part of the roof of the mouth behind the upper jaw.

PICTURE CREDITS

The numbers in parentheses are plate numbers. Some photographers have pictures under agency names as well as their own. Agency names appear in boldface. Photographers hold copyrights to their works.

Charles Arneson (258, 268, 269, 273, 281, 282, 284, 325, 331, 340, 342, 343, 355, 356, 359, 360, 363, 364, 366, 373, 374, 375, 385, 398, 406, 417, 424, 436, 464, 477, 480, 504, 505, 534, 535, 542, 544, 570, 594)

Peter Arnold, Inc.
Bob Evans (270)
John Zoiner (2)

David Ballantine (296, 537)
Roger W. Barbour (37, 48, 49, 50, 53, 74, 114, 148, 150, 178, 188, 224, 225, 226, 237, 238, 241, 247, 250, 251, 252, 253, 254, 255)
Bruce H. Bauer (87, 165)
Thomas M. Baugh (187, 202, 211)
David W. Behrens (434, 465, 567)
Charles Biggar (119, 163)
Stephen A. Bortone (286, 287, 291, 448)

Edward B. Brothers (123, 519, 573, 577)
Fred Bruemmer (610, 612, 617)
Richard T. Bryant (29, 32, 40, 47, 51, 52, 73, 80, 107, 109, 110, 113, 115, 116, 145, 149, 153, 154, 158, 159, 162, 168, 177, 185, 192, 196, 197, 198, 217, 221, 232, 245, 248, 349, 350, 352, 566)
George H. Burgess (70, 263, 288, 290, 387, 422, 452, 521)
David K. Caldwell (616, 634)
David K. Caldwell/ Marineland of Florida (627)
Craig Cary (309)
Patricia Caulfield (1)
Patrice Ceisel (95, 96, 122, 381, 500, 575)
Tony Chess (312, 329, 380, 390, 393, 394, 396, 401, 527, 530)

Bruce Coleman, Inc.
E. R. Degginger

(82) Phil Degginger (267) D. Lyons (71, 285) M. Timothy O'Keefe (77, 578) Leonard Lee Rue III (118) Ron and Valerie Taylor (593, 597) Norman Owen Tomalin (515, 550)

F. B. Cross (170)
E. R. Degginger (7, 24, 61, 62, 139, 303, 351, 501, 545)
Jack Dermid (423)

Design Photographers International
Andrew Gifford (601) Dr. Charles Steinmetz, Jr. (426)

DRK Photo
Stephen J. Krasemann (6)
Wayne Lankinen (21)

Earth Images
Terry Domico (531)
Doug Maier/Al Salonsky (428) Al Salonsky (599)

John Eastcott and Yva Momatiuk (20)

Douglas Faulkner (295)

Jeff Foott (439, 569)

Franklin Photo Agency
Nelson Groffman (549)

Laurel Giannino (260, 275, 289, 292, 299, 338, 339, 341, 357, 384, 438, 454, 457, 473, 485, 489, 502, 533, 551, 589)
Brian Gibeson (556)
Daniel W. Gotshall (63, 76, 92, 274, 276, 277, 320, 326, 327, 358, 371, 377, 383, 388, 389, 391, 397, 399, 403, 404, 407, 408, 411, 412, 414, 416, 419, 427, 432, 437, 450, 451, 467, 472, 487, 497, 520, 525, 528, 529, 543, 553, 560, 602, 606)
Annie Griffiths (18)
A. Grotell (301, 516)
John L. Harris (143, 164, 173, 179, 195, 212)
Phil and Loretta Hermann (54, 306, 319)

Hubbs Sea World Research Institute
Stephen Leatherwood (637) Bob Pitman (639) Scott Sinclair (630) Randall S. Wells (633)

Paul Humann (256, 259, 271, 304, 305, 313, 314, 316, 321, 336, 337, 344, 361, 362, 370, 372, 376, 378, 382, 413, 418, 421, 429, 453, 471, 506, 508, 512, 526, 536, 538, 547, 548, 552, 555, 558, 583, 584, 587)

Jacana
Laboute (598)
Noailles (297)

Stan Keiser (334, 365, 379)
Richard Lang (415, 541, 581)
G. W. Link (88, 262, 294, 345, 425, 431, 446, 449, 461, 462, 481, 514)
Allen Loe (135)
Ken Lucas (35, 65, 72, 94, 272, 278, 279, 330, 392, 402, 409, 410, 455, 456, 463, 468, 496, 498, 507, 557, 605)
Richard L. Mayden (104, 108, 183, 200, 206, 214, 348, 353)
Miami Seaquarium (264, 311, 395, 430, 475, 476, 478, 479, 503, 509, 513, 522, 523, 546, 580, 586)
C. Allan Morgan (105, 620)
Peter Moyle (125)
David Muench (3, 4, 5, 8, 9, 10, 11, 12, 13, 14, 16, 17, 19, 22, 23)
Tom Myers (33, 66, 193, 194, 208, 302, 441, 499, 588, 604)

National Audubon Society Collection/ Photo Researchers, Inc.
Roy Attaway (585)
Joseph T. Collins (55, 86, 169)
William Curtsinger (619) Treat Davidson (31) John

Deitz (386)
Townsend P. Dickinson (636)
Richard Ellis (640, 641, 642, 643, 644, 645, 646, 647, 648, 649, 650, 651, 652, 653, 654, 655, 656, 657, 658, 659, 660, 661, 662, 663, 664, 665, 666, 667, 668, 669, 670, 671, 672, 673, 674, 675, 676, 677, 678, 679, 680, 681, 682, 683, 684)
Robert J. Erwin (181, 246) Gary Gibson (42, 442)
Francois Gohier (628, 629) William J. Jahoda (539) Russ Kinne (25, 39, 121, 140, 445, 486, 490, 576, 611) Russ Kinne/Bergen Aquarium (491)
George Lower (565)
Tom McHugh (117)
Tom McHugh/ Dallas Aquarium (79) Tom McHugh/ Marineland of the Pacific (90, 510)
Tom McHugh/ Pt. Defiance Aquarium (64, 447, 492, 495, 574) Tom McHugh/Sea World (608) Tom McHugh/ Shedd Aquarium (44, 93) Tom McHugh/Steinhart Aquarium (45, 132, 133, 134, 209, 218, 354, 405, 444, 460, 469, 571, 590, 591, 592) Allan Power (484) C. Ray (458, 517)

Nebraska Game and Parks Commission (84, 97, 98, 99, 106, 126, 190, 227, 249)

INDEX
Numbers in boldface type refer to color plates.
Numbers in italics refer to pages. Alternate
common names appear in quotation marks.

THE AUDUBON SOCIETY

The National Audubon Society is among the oldest and largest private conservation organizations in the world. With over 500,000 members and more than 480 local chapters across the country, the Society works in behalf of our natural heritage through environmental education and conservation action. It protects wildlife in more than seventy sanctuaries from coast to coast. It also operates outdoor education centers and ecology workshops and publishes the prizewinning AUDUBON magazine, AMERICAN BIRDS magazine, newsletters, films, and other educational materials. For further information regarding membership in the Society, write to the National Audubon Society, 950 Third Avenue, New York, New York 10022.

THE AUTHORS

Dr. Herbert T. Boschung, Jr., (Atlantic and Gulf Coast Fishes) is Professor of Zoology at the University of Alabama. He has been Curator of Zoology at the Alabama Museum of Natural History since 1978, and Curator of Fishes for the University of Alabama Ichthyological Collection since 1966. Dr. Boschung has written many technical and popular papers and identification manuals about marine fishes of the Gulf of Mexico and the Atlantic Coast. He is also Ichthyological Editor of the journal *Northeast Gulf Science.*

Dr. James D. Williams (Freshwater Fishes) is Research Associate with the National Museum of Natural History, Smithsonian Institution, and Ichthyology Editor of the journal *American Midland Naturalist.* He is author of numerous technical and popular papers on freshwater fishes, especially endangered and threatened species, and is co-author of *Vanishing Fishes of North America.*

Mr. Daniel W. Gotshall (Pacific Coast Fishes) is Senior Marine Biologist-Supervisor at the California Department of Fish and Game; he is also Research Associate in Ichthyology for the Los Angeles County Museum of Natural History, Vice-chairman of the California Advisory Board on Underwater Parks and Reserves, and Associate in Invertebrate Zoology at the California Academy of Sciences. He has written numerous publications, including *Pacific Coast Inshore Fishes,* and most recently, *Marine Animals of Baja California.* In addition, Mr. Gotshall is a professional underwater photographer.

Dr. David K. Caldwell (Whales and Dolphins) is Research Scientist at the Institute for Advanced Study of the Communication Processes, State University of Florida, as well as Field Associate in Mammalogy and Bioacoustics at the Florida State Museum. He is author of numerous papers on the behavior of whales, porpoises, and dolphins, and co-founder with Mrs. Caldwell of the cetacean journal *Cetology.* Together, Dr. and Mrs. Caldwell have studied cetaceans at sea throughout the Gulf of Mexico, along the Atlantic Coast of the United States and off Newfoundland, and, on the Pacific Coast, in California and along the western coast of Mexico.

Mrs. Melba C. Caldwell (Whales and Dolphins) is Associate Research Scientist at the Institute for Advanced Study of the Communication Processes, State University of Florida. She is also Field Associate in Bioacoustics at the Florida State Museum. Co-founder with Dr. Caldwell of *Cetology,* she has written numerous scientific and popular papers in the field.

STAFF

Prepared and produced by Chanticleer Press, Inc.

Publisher: Paul Steiner
Editor-in-Chief: Gudrun Buettner
Managing Editor: Susan Costello
Project Editor: Jordan Verner
Senior Editor: Jane Opper
Natural Sciences Editor: John Farrand, Jr.
Assistant Editors: Jill Hamilton, Constance V. Mersel
Production: Helga Lose, Amy Roche
Art Director: Carol Nehring
Art Assistants: Ayn Svoboda, Karen Wollman
Picture Library: Edward Douglas, Dana Pomfret
Symbols and Range Maps: Paul Singer, Alan Singer
Drawings: Dolores R. Santoliquido
Design: Massimo Vignelli

THE AUDUBON SOCIETY FIELD GUIDE SERIES